HOLLYWOOD GOES TO WAR

How Politics, Profits, and Propaganda Shaped World War II Movies

Clayton R. Koppes
Gregory D. Black

UNIVERSITY OF CALIFORNIA PRESS
Berkeley · Los Angeles

University of California Press
Berkeley and Los Angeles, California
First Paperback Printing 1990

Copyright © 1987 by The Free Press
                    A Division of Macmillan, Inc.

This edition is reprinted by arrangement with The Free Press,
A Division of Macmillan, Inc.

Printed in the United States of America

Library of Congress Cataloging-in-Publication Data

Koppes, Clayton R., 1945–
    Hollywood goes to war : how politics, profits, and propaganda
shaped World War II movies / Clayton R. Koppes, Gregory D. Black.
        p.   cm.
    Includes bibliographical references.
    ISBN 978-0-520-07161-2
    1. World War, 1939–1945—Motion pictures and the
war.   2. Motion pictures in propaganda—United States—
History.   3. Motion pictures—Censorship—United
States.   I. Black, Gregory D.   II. Title.
[D743.23.K66   1990]   90-34552
303.3'75—dc20   CIP

Excerpt from lyrics of "What the Well Dressed Man in Harlem Will Wear" by Irving Berlin
at page 182.

© Copyright 1942 Irving Berlin

© Copyright renewed 1970 Irving Berlin

© Copyright Assigned to Trustees of the God Bless America Fund.

Reprinted by permission of Irving Berlin Music Corporation.

12 11
12 11 10

The paper used in this publication meets the minimum requirements of
ANSI/ NISO Z39.48-1992 (R 1997) (*Permanence of Paper*). ∞

To our parents,
Dale *and* Marcella Black
and
Clinton *and* Effie Koppes,
and to
Carol, Jason, *and* Bill

Contents

Preface

Hollywood went to war with gusto. Blatant morale-building propaganda was a staple of its plots, speeches, and visual images. A marine, having just dispatched a horde of treacherous Japanese attackers, pauses to utter a paean to democracy. A young mother, newly widowed when her husband was killed in combat, chokes back the tears and tells her infant son that daddy died so he could have a better future. A Norwegian town rises up as one against Nazi terror. From today's perspective these propaganda touches may seem quaint, intrusive, or manipulative. They may also provoke the question of how they came to be so common in wartime films. At one level the answer is simple: Hollywood was trying to boost the war effort. Yet, as this book tries to show, considerably more was involved than the movie makers' patriotism.

During the war the government, convinced that movies had extraordinary power to mobilize public opinion for war, carried out an intensive, unprecedented effort to mold the content of Hollywood feature films. Officials of the Office of War Information, the government's propaganda agency, issued a constantly updated manual instructing the studios in how to assist the war effort, sat in on story conferences with Hollywood's top brass, reviewed the screenplays of every major studio (except the recalcitrant Paramount), pressured the movie makers to change scripts and even scrap pictures when they found objectionable material, and sometimes wrote dialogue for key speeches. OWI attained considerable influence with the Office of Censorship, which issued export licenses for movies, and it controlled the exhibition of American films in liberated areas. Since foreign exhibition often made the difference between profit and loss for a picture, studio executives found it quite expedient to follow OWI's advice. With this wide range of options, the government was able to exercise considerable influence over the content of wartime Hollywood movies. This book deals, then, with the enduring question of the appropriateness of governmental coercion and censorship of private media, the ways in which American society was mobilized for war, and the consequences of these methods for the peace.

It would be misleading, however, to focus solely on government influence. For although the wartime intrusion of the government was new, censorship and coercion of the movie makers was as old as Hollywood itself. The most significant form of censorship was that exercised by the Production Code Administration, a branch of the Motion Picture Producer and Distributors of America, better known as the Hays Office, after its longtime head, Will Hays. The wartime experience can only be understood in that larger context of censorship, which had been imposed by the industry itself. It is often said that the movies reflect American society. But this contention needs to be balanced with an awareness that, through censorship and other external forces, those reflections are refracted through multiple mirrors, each of which distorts and sometimes obliterates certain images. One of the paradoxes of American film history is that when Hollywood was most popular, the medium was controlled by a tight corporate oligarchy and a rigid code of censorship. Most film history has focused, understandably, on the creative process in isolation. But once we take fully into account the reality of censorship and other external forces, we see movies in a new light.

This book is not a comprehensive history of the movies of World War II. From 1939 to 1945 some 2500 pictures were released. We deal with those movies that had some bearing on the evolution of the relationship between the government propagandists and Hollywood and on pictures that were in some way representative of key issues of censorship and propaganda. Inevitably, some favorite movies of the authors' and readers' alike are omitted.

We are indebted to many people who helped us in various stages of research and writing. At the Washington National Records Center in Suitland, Maryland, where the massive OWI records are kept, we are indebted to William Lewis, James Miller, and David Pfeiffer. Sam Gill and his staff at the Margaret Herrick Library of the Academy of Motion Picture Arts and Sciences in Beverly Hills, California, were of much help with the files of the Production Code Administration. Robert Knutson and his staff at the Doheny Library of the University of Southern California in Los Angeles helped us with the Warner Brothers Production Files. At the Franklin D. Roosevelt Library in Hyde Park, New York, William Stewart and William Emerson offered knowledgable assistance. Jerry Gibson and his staff at the Library of Congress Motion Picture Division efficiently and cheerfully made available many films for screening. We also appreciate the assistance provided by the staffs at the following libraries and archives: Harry S. Truman Library, Library of Congress Manuscript Division, Herbert Hoover Library, Nelson Poynter Memorial Library, Jesuit Missouri Province Archives, Indiana State Library, Special Collections Department and Theater Arts Library of the University Research Library at the University of California at Los Angeles, Wisconsin State Historical Society, and Archives of the Archdiocese of Los Angeles. At Oberlin College Barbara Turek and Thelma Kime were invaluable in helping to prepare the final manuscript. For financial support we are indebted to the Weldon Springs Fund at the University of Missouri, the National Endowment for the Humanities summer stipend program, and the Oberlin College Research and Development Committee and Dean's Office. Colleagues at our home institutions and others have helped us think about the project in various ways. We thank particularly Richard McKinzie, Gaylord Marr, Thomas Cripps, David Culbert, Daniel Leab, Allan Winkler, Nicholas O. Warner, Geoffrey T. Blodgett, Garth Jowett, Robert A. Rosenstone, Lary May, Theodore A. Wilson, and Robert Sklar. At the Free Press Joyce

Seltzer deftly provided a combination of percipient criticism and thoughtful support, and Victor Rangel-Riberio copyedited the manuscript with sensitivity. Finally, Carol and Jason Black and William P. Norris afforded that mixture of encouragement and forbearance without which work is impossible.

Santa Cruz, California   C.R.K.
                                                          G.D.B.

I.

Hollywood, 1939

In the movie colony, as in the content of the movies themselves, romantic individualism, the most compelling idea in American history, has reached the apogee of its glory.

—Leo Rosten, *Hollywood:
The Movie Colony,
The Movie Makers,* 1941

Hollywood, 1939: This was the mythic Hollywood of the golden age of American film. It was the legendary world of stars like Clark Gable and Vivien Leigh alighting from silvery limousines, bathed in the luminescence of sky-sweeping searchlights and a thousand flashbulbs, to attend the première of Selznick's *Gone With the Wind,* the movie probably seen by more people than any other in American history. It was an age when movie stars were a kind of American royalty; when the movie capital lured the best talent in all fields; when moguls like Mayer, Zanuck, Harry Cohn, the Schencks, and the Warners ruled their domains like private fiefdoms, when Hollywood was the end of the rainbow for legions of star-struck fans. Each week eighty million Americans—two-thirds of the country's population—lived the Hollywood experience vicariously as they trooped to their neighborhood movie houses for the combination of a newsreel, a short, perhaps a cartoon, and then the feature, which more often than not unveiled a fantasy world of adventure, romance, luxury, and success that relieved some of the depression-era grimness of Flatbush Avenue and Grovers Corners. But Hollywood was more than an American craze—it was an international obsession. The movie capital's pictures occupied 80 percent of the world's screen time in the 1930s, and tabloids and photomagazines from Paris to Peking, from Rome to Rio, lavished attention on tinsel town.

Hollywood—the very name was a symbol, a term of art. Ironically the movie industry became known by that shorthand term just as Hollywood proper itself ceased to exist. The crossroads of the movie colony was formed in a sense by the intersection of Hollywood Boulevard and Vine Street, on the escarpment rising from the flat expanse of downtown Los Angeles to the Hollywood Hills. Grauman's Chinese Theater, one of the classic movie palaces which in the 1920s created a foreign fantasy-setting for its patrons, stood just to the west. Around the corner were the famous film trade restaurants—the Brown Derby and Musso and Frank's. Several companies made pictures in the Hollywood district. But the movie colony was more amorphous than this crossroads would suggest. The dominant studio, Metro-Goldwyn-Mayer, was located ten miles or so to the southwest in the nondescript suburb of Culver City; Universal clung to the flank of Cahuenga Pass, on the opposite side of the Hollywood Hills; Warner Brothers' facilities rambled across the declassé San Fernando Valley, long before Laugh-In made "beautiful downtown Burbank" a national joke or Moon Zappa's "Valley Girls" immortalized that expanse of suburban sprawl. The stars and moguls hid their homes in the canyons of Bel Air and Beverly Hills or sought sea solace in Santa Monica and Malibu. Hollywood, scarcely even a geographical expression, was, as countless observers put it, a state of mind.

The movie colony lent itself to hyperbole, but still more to the language of paradox. The central paradox, said the leading film critic Manny Farber, was that the American movie industry represented a unique combination of art and business. At its best the American movie industry produced masterpieces of popular culture as well as some unqualified artistic triumphs. But among the 500 or so pictures released annually in the 1930s and 40s there were many "dogs"—unbearable B features that paid the overhead and little more. Movies reflected American society in a way, but the mirror that the movies held up to America displayed an image that was distorted and refracted by myriad forces, not least of them the profit motive. "You're only as good as your last picture" went the old Hollywood axiom—and "good" meant how well your picture did at the box office.

This tension stemmed from the very origins of the industry in America. Many of the other art forms developed among the aristocracy or the bourgeoisie and then either remained the province of an elite or were also adopted by the masses. By contrast, movies are "the democratic art," said film historian Garth Jowett. They were born among the working class, especially the waves of immigrants who flooded America in the late 1800s and early 1900s. Appealing to a wide spectrum of non-affluent patrons, the early films borrowed heavily from the techniques of the music hall and vaudeville—they had simple, stereotyped, often melodramatic plots, slapstick, and broad humor. They were adept at the "visceral cliché." They relied on the medium's inherent propensity to show action: speeding trains, automobile chases, and feats of derring-do were the stock in trade of the early movies. It was movement that excited poet Vachel Lindsay in his pioneering analysis of the motion picture.[1]

European film makers retained some of the distinctions between high and low culture. Hollywood admired the art films of European directors, for they advanced the medium. German director Fritz Lang's *M* (1931) earned accolades in the movie capital, and he was lured to Hollywood. But Irving Thalberg, MGM's boy genius, said the studio would not have allowed Lang to make *M*. Although studios for reasons of prestige sometimes made films they did not expect to turn a profit, there was a persistent tension between the demands of art and the bottom line. American film makers kept at least three audiences in mind as they made their pictures: a fickle mass audience, the box office, and their own peers, whose approbation they sought. Government propaganda officials represented yet another audience, whose goals potentially were at odds with those of the other audiences.

Even as American producers broadened their appeal to tap a middle-class clientele, they kept a mass audience in mind. Indeed, the fantasyland movie palaces of the 1920s and 30s assembled audiences that were perhaps as diverse in class and status as any type of gathering. The very diversity of the movies'

HOLLYWOOD GOES TO WAR

audience reinforced the studios' tendency to produce homo-
geneous products; they strove to avoid giving offense to any
powerful group.

Most of the early film makers were American Protestants,
and their production facilities were located in the East and Midwest. From the early 1910s to early 1920s a geographic, economic, and ethnic shift was underway that created the Hollywood of the golden age. Within a few years the industry
expanded and reorganized, and the "Big Eight" companies
came to dominate the industry, these dominant corporations
created a vertically-integrated industry—in this case, they controlled the entire process from casting and production through
distribution (wholesaling) and exhibition (retailing). The Big
Eight reaped 95 percent of all motion picture rentals in the U.S.
in the late 1930s. Their control over theater chains, particularly
the all-important first-run urban houses which determined a picture's future, was critical. Although the Big Eight owned only
2,800 of the 17,000 theaters in the country, that figure included
80 percent of the metropolitan first-run houses, and all exhibition in cities of more than 1,000,000 population. The eight
firms' investment in theater real estate far exceeded their investment in film production. Indeed, what drove the industry was
the need to turn out a large number of pictures to meet the
nearly insatiable demands of their theaters. Independent ex-
hibitors had to book the majors' pictures on a virtual take-it-or-
leave-it basis, and independent producers could be frozen out
if they did not cooperate with the majors. The movies, once a
marginal activity, had become big business. The "democratic
art" issued from a corporate structure.[2]

The men who guided the industry in its transition to big
business were mostly Jewish theater owners, who were uniquely
suited to the task. The playwright and screenwriter Ben Hecht
once observed that Hollywood constituted "a Semitic renais-
sance sans rabbis and Talmud." As landless tradesmen in eastern and central Europe, Jews developed extraordinary skill at
satisfying the dominant society's consumer tastes. In immigrant
America they perfected these talents in such activities as ready-
to-wear and entertainment. The young Adolph Zukor, who built
Paramount, sold furs. Samuel Goldwyn, of MGM and later an
independent producer, made gloves. Carl Laemmle, the man

behind Universal, got the stake for his first nickelodeon by selling clothing in Oshkosh. Louis B. Mayer, who reigned as the
most powerful man in the movies in the 1930s and 40s, ran a
burlesque house. "Critically important in all these skills," historian Lary May has pointed out, "was the ability to suspend
one's own tastes and calculate the desires of others." Laemmle
compared merchandising pictures to his experience as a hab-
erdasher. "The public is never wrong," said Goldwyn in an oft-
quoted statement. To hone his sense of what the public wanted,
he would sit with his back to the screen, watching the audience's
reaction to the show.[3]

As the industry was reorganized, its new captains shifted
most of its production from the East and Midwest to greater
Los Angeles. The region's juxtaposition of sea, mountains, and
deserts, bathed in perpetual sunshine, afforded an ideal location for movie making. A less savory reason for the transcon-
tinental trek was the city's strongly anti-union posture. Wage
costs were perhaps only half those of New York, and the absence
of unions gave the moguls a free hand until some bitter disputes
in the 1930s culminated in union recognition in Hollywood.

Moreover, Los Angeles embodied the very symbolic life that
the movies came to project. The area combined two powerful
romantic elements—the frontier West and the Spanish border-
lands. Whatever the facts of the matter, the frontier had long
symbolized freedom, a chance to escape the grip of society and
hierarchy and to create a new individualistic future. Is it any
wonder that outsiders such as the movie moguls saw Southern
California as a land of promise for them and their new industry? Numerous studio executives testified that in making the
journey across the country they felt as if they were reliving the
national epic. In Southern California they appropriated the
Spanish hacienda tradition, which gave these nouveaux riche a
patina of Old World culture and graciousness. Spanish motifs
became a signature for Hollywood. Universal created its studio
in the Spanish revival style; one entered Paramount's lot
through a gigantic Spanish gate; and the movies themselves frequently invoked Iberian-cum-California motifs. The liberation
from the drab, factory-like studios of Biograph in the Bronx or
Vitagraph in Brooklyn was complete.[4]

Los Angeles was itself a colossal improvisation—the most

improbable metropolis in the United States, according to its early historian Carey McWilliams.[5] Much as one created an artificial environment for a movie, Los Angeles boosters fashioned a new form of urban space through the technological manipulation of nature. The parched city lacked the very basis of life: water. Its lifeline was a 233-mile aqueduct that poured water that had been almost literally stolen from a ranching community behind the Sierras. (That water heist figured, appropriately enough, in a Hollywood picture: Roman Polanski's *Chinatown* [1974]). With imported water and alien shrubbery Los Angeles created an artificial humid environment in the desert, much as the movies conjured up their own worlds of illusion. As in most boom towns, life was fluid. Los Angeles was a city of infinite beginnings. The area thrived on the promise of the future, whether it was new technologies, such as aircraft, new patterns of consumption, or the ubiquitous speculation in real estate. As harbingers of the mass leisure industry of the twentieth century, the movies fit in Los Angeles, both creating and legitimating a blend of conspicuous consumption, new morals, and personal gratification that helped undermine the Eastern-dominated, WASP Victorian culture.

Yet the movie makers paid a price for being ensconced in lotus land. Los Angeles was the most isolated of America's major metropolises. America was not yet a bicoastal country. In 1939 New York was a costly, two-and-a-half days away on the crack streamliners of the stars, the *Super Chief* and *Twentieth Century Limited.* The fastest letter—air mail special delivery—took two days from coast to coast. The intellectual and political life of the country was still disproportionately centered in the East and Midwest; Hollywood's ties to that life were accordingly attenuated. Geographical isolation compounded the movie industry's self-absorption. In the relative absence of the cultural attractions of other major cities, movies became the focus of aesthetic life. After a day on the set, an evening's entertainment at home or on the town would probably be a movie. The allure of Southern California for European émigrés—they numbered such eminences as Thomas Mann, Igor Stravinsky, and Arnold Schoenberg—increased the area's cosmopolitan flavor in the late 1930s. Nonetheless contemporary observers often remarked on the insularity of movie personnel. When the world tensely watched the Ethiopian crisis of 1935, a studio mogul was asked if he had heard any late news. He responded with agitation: "Italy just banned *Marie Antoinette!*"[6]

As local geography was transformed, so too did Hollywood effect magical personal transfigurations. Movie stars were demigods, but they were at the same time just like you and me, only luckier. Clark Gable had knocked about as an oil field worker; Ronald Reagan had been "Dutch" Reagan, Iowa sportscaster and lifeguard; Walt Disney had been just another Kansas City kid who liked to draw. All anyone needed to be discovered was a little luck. Hadn't unknowns been plucked from a fountain stool at Schwab's, the Hollywood drug store, and turned into stars? Personal deficiencies were no obstacle. Too short? You could be shot standing on a box, like Alan Ladd. Too tall? You could stand in a trench. Teeth crooked? They could be straightened and capped. No acting experience? You could be trained, even if, like postwar star Rock Hudson, a former truck driver, you needed thirty-eight takes to get through your first line. Even your name could be changed to fit your new identity. Not Constance Frances Marie Ockelman of Brooklyn but Veronica Lake ... ah!

Yet for the vast majority of those who acted on their urges to be in pictures, Hollywood was not the end of the rainbow but the end of the road. The town was littered with disappointed actors and actresses who lived hand-to-mouth existences as extras, grips, or fry cooks. Despite this the myth died hard, particularly in Depression America, when ability and hard work—the traditional Protestant virtues—seemed to count for so little.

Youth was at a premium, not only among the stars but in all sectors of the industry. The executives came to power at an early age. Irving Thalberg was recognized as one of the most creative figures in Hollywood before he was 30, and when he died at age 37 in 1936 the streamlined sleek office building at MGM was named in his honor. Fresh from Wahoo, Nebraska, Darryl F. Zanuck at 22 was writing scenarios for Rin Tin Tin (sometimes known as the dog who saved Warner Brothers); at 26 he was Warners' head producer; and at 30 he was running production at Twentieth Century-Fox. David O. Selznick was vice president in charge of production at RKO at 29; two years later he became an MGM vice president and producer, and soon formed his own independent company. Hal B. Wallis became chief executive producer at Warners at 32. Hollywood began to age a bit in the 1930s as the heady growth years gave way to a depression-induced cautiousness. Men like Selznick, Wallis, and Zanuck remained towering figures in 1939. Though they were only in their 40s, they were veterans. When in 1941 Leo Rosten compiled his important sociological profile, *Hollywood: The Movie Colony, the Movie Makers,* youth still dominated. Half the producers were under 45, as were two-thirds of the directors; 70 percent of the writers had yet to celebrate that birthday, and nearly a third were under 35. "The movie people—famous, pampered, rich—are very young to be so famous, so pampered, and so rich," Rosten concluded.[7]

The youthfulness of the industry and its people reinforced anxieties about their acceptability in American society. In part this was the perennial fear of the nouveaux riche. But in the case of Hollywood it was exacerbated by the knowledge that anti-Semitism still thrived, and by the recurrent dread that the movies, for all their popularity, were somehow not quite respectable. In casting a Jewish officer in the World War II picture *Objective Burma,* Jack Warner demanded: "See that you get a good clean-cut American type for Jacobs." The exaggerated salesmanship, the celebration of America, the insatiable need for ego reinforcement all betrayed a continuing quest for acceptance. As the industry aged, its titans sought reassurance in the trappings of aristocracy and old money that belied their real metier: American market culture. F. Scott Fitzgerald wrote of Monroe Stahr, the main character based on Thalberg in *The Last Tycoon,* "he cherished the parvenu's passionate loyalty to an imaginary past." In Selznick's *A Star Is Born* (1937) the producer is a suave, aristocratic gentleman, played by Adolphe Menjou, clad in a dark three-piece suit with a gold watch chain draped across his vest. Always hearing footsteps behind them and worrying about adverse publicity, the industry executives of the 1930s tried to make their products as noncontroversial as possible.[8]

But whatever the lingering doubts about their position in American society, the movie makers had completed one of the classic transitions of the American dream. They embodied in a particular temporal form the triumph of the Horatio Alger myth. As Leo Rosten put it: "In the movie colony, as in the content of the movies themselves, romantic individualism, the most compelling idea in American history, has reached the apogee of its glory." The movie makers celebrated their success in their pictures. The dominant theme of American movies in the golden age, said the critic Parker Tyler, was the "success story." The movie makers projected their success on the screen to a public that wanted to believe.[9]

Though Hollywood was still relatively young in 1939, it increasingly bore the marks of a mature industry. The studios were already heavily bureaucratized. The earlier free-wheeling, less structured organizations had disappeared. This phenomenon could be traced in part to the sheer growth of the industry. Most of the major firms were locked into a complex corporate structure of multiple subsidiaries that almost defied analysis. The king of the hill, Loew's Incorporated, controlled approximately 123 subsidiaries, among them its chief producing company, Metro-Goldwyn-Mayer. The depression had hastened the trend to bureaucracy. Strapped for cash as box office receipts plummeted in the early 1930s—several firms went bankrupt or were reorganized—the motion picture companies became critically dependent on big banks for financing. That dependence reinforced bureaucratic caution.

Though its products were infinitely more glamorous, the movie industry was as tightly controlled and as rigidly hierarchical as coal, steel, or widget manufacturing. At the top were the all-powerful studio heads; and the arbitrary, almost despotic control they and their circles of sycophants exercised became a central theme of Hollywood memoirs and fiction. In her landmark study, *Hollywood: The Dream Factory*, the prominent anthropologist Hortense Powdermaker in 1950 compared the studios to plantation fiefdoms or feudal baronies, but with more waste and inefficiency. The moguls' personal tastes exerted a strong influence on the style of each studio. Zanuck liked blonde ingenues opposite dark-haired leading men. The brothers Warner favored sassy underdogs in slightly suspect settings. Most of the bosses had a good sense of what would play at the box office. Columbia's Harry Cohn judged a picture by whether he could sit comfortably or began to shift in his seat. "Just imagine," said screenwriter Herman Mankiewicz, "the whole world wired to Harry Cohn's ass!" That very intuition about what the public would and would not sit through tended to ensure the repetition of proven formulas and to discourage innovation. Like chief executive officers in coal, steel, and widgets, movie moguls liked a business that was predictable.[10]

Movie executives were lavishly paid for their hunches. In 1940 five of the fifteen highest salaries in the country went to movie people. Atop the greasy pole was the quintessential mogul, Louis B. Mayer, whose princely $1.3 million in salary and bonuses in 1937 probably surpassed the compensation paid to any other American executive. Hollywood paid out more in salaries than any other major industry, and the number of executives swelled through the 1930s, even though there was no increase in production.[11]

This bloated hierarchy presided over a rigid production system. Movies were produced on exacting schedules, and woe betide the director who fell behind or came in over budget. When a movie was being shot the work day often stretched to ten or twelve hours. "Hollywood is the world's first squirrel cage," said Otis Ferguson, film critic for *The New Republic* in the 1930s. "To keep your nose above water, i.e., in the leisure class, you work like hell." Producers viewed the daily "rushes"—the day's finished footage—and peppered the director with suggestions for changes and with reprimands for lagging production. In this closely monitored system only approved ideas were disseminated.[12]

The studio system commanded an awesome array of talent. Even a partial listing of the stars would take pages, but consider the Oscar winners for best actor and best actress, 1930–40: Lionel Barrymore, Wallace Beery, Frederic March, Charles Laughton, Clark Gable, Victor McLaglen, Paul Muni, Spencer Tracy (twice), Robert Donat, and James Stewart; Marie Dressler, Helen Hayes, Katharine Hepburn, Claudette Colbert, Bette Davis (twice), Luise Rainer (twice), Vivien Leigh, and Ginger Rogers. Directors like Frank Capra, John Ford, Orson Welles, William Wyler, Leo McCarey, Lewis Milestone, Alfred Hitchcock, Michael Curtiz, and Preston Sturges merely suggest the extent of talent. Master screenwriters such as Ben Hecht, Robert Riskin, Dudley Nichols, Dalton Trumbo, and Anita Loos were augmented—not always with happy results—by such luminaries of serious literature as William Faulkner, F. Scott Fitzgerald, Robert Sherwood, and Clifford Odets.

The writers, and to a perhaps lesser extent the directors, found themselves trapped in the conflicting demands of art and business. "A writer out here is a factory worker," lamented John Balderston, one of the highest paid writers in Hollywood.[13] The writer's ideal of unfettered self-expression had to be laid aside in the movie colony. Writers had little control over their assignments or over what happened to their products. Screenplays were often the product of several writers; changes were often made by other writers or by higher-ups for commercial rather than artistic reasons; directors might shoot or cut a picture in ways that, from the author's point of view, ruined it. Though the writers played a key role in the genesis of films, they had to rely on others to breathe life into their creations.

Screenwriters often chafed under these constraints. They sometimes felt that they had sold out their art, but found the sunshine, swimming pools, and high salaries irresistible (seventeen writers made more than $75,000 each in 1938). The writers' discomfiture was sometimes heightened by their politics. They were the most political, and most leftist, group in the movie capital. A small number of Hollywood figures were members of the Communist Party, and they were chiefly writers. Only a few of them were genuinely prominent craftsmen, however, and none fell into the charmed circle of those earning $75,000 per year. Their politics remained a subject mostly for small study groups. During the war, however, the Office of War Information found these screenwriters receptive to its propaganda impulse, which helped nurture the controversy between OWI and the studio executives.[14]

These vast resources gave Hollywood a legendary power. Movie stars, in a consumerist democracy, had their comings-and-goings, manners, and mores charted like those of the French court pre-1789. The marriage in 1920 of "America's sweetheart," Mary Pickford, to the handsome, dashing Douglas Fairbanks, and their ensconcement in their fabled mansion Pickfair, seemed to star-struck millions a modern fulfillment of the Cinderella legend. Some 400 correspondents, including one for the Vatican, were posted in Hollywood in the late 1930s; only

New York and Washington, D.C., had more. A wink, a smile, a gesture from a Hollywood legend could be big news. When Clark Gable stripped off his shirt in *It Happened One Night* (1934) and revealed that he didn't wear an undershirt, sales of that intimate garment for men plummeted. Even in the midst of war, fans thirsted for news of their favorites; during the bombing of London the *London Mirror* wired its movie correspondent for two hundred words on Ann Sheridan's contract dispute with Warner Brothers. Veronica Lake's peek-a-boo hairdo had so many imitators among American women during the war that the government prevailed on her to change it because too many "riveting Rosies" were getting their dangling tresses caught in machinery.

Worry about the effect movies might have on public morals, particularly those of children, began even earlier, and was a recurrent concern. Social scientists made repeated attempts to measure the movies' influence. The extent of the concern triggered a multi-volume study underwritten by the Payne Fund in the early 1930s; its judicious findings were promptly used in an irresponsible potboiler as *Our Movie Made Children*. Later, historian Robert Sklar posited a *Movie-Made America* for the era of the 1920s to the 1950s. In 1965 the critic John Clellon Holmes argued that "the movies of the 1930s constitute, for my generation, nothing less than a kind of Jungian collective unconsciousness, a decade of coming attractions out of which some of the truths of our maturity have been formed."[15]

But however potent an influence Gable's bare chest or Lake's tresses might have on an imitative public, the more general effect of Hollywood on morals—or, in a still more problematic area, on the formation of political attitudes—was extremely difficult to gauge. A host of other influences, including home environment, the schools, and other media, needed to be weighed as well. As Robert Coles has demonstrated more recently, people of varying backgrounds find diverse messages in films, sometimes even reading them in ways quite contrary to the film makers' clear intentions.[16] The safest conclusion seems to be that movies during Hollywood's golden age had a profound but hard to measure effect on assumptions about personal life and expectations from society; in specific areas such as political attitudes and the like, however, the effects were murky indeed.

Nonetheless the presumed power of the movies made their content a hot issue from the earliest days of the nickelodeon. In an effort to control this medium, scores of cities and many states set up censorship boards early in this century to snip and chop scenes that might offend conservative ideas of morality, or that might threaten public order. The United States Supreme Court unanimously upheld state and municipal censorship of movies in 1915. The justices justified their opinion by citing films' possible danger to morals. The movies were declared to be a business "pure and simple" and hence not included under the First Amendment's guarantee of freedom of expression.[17]

By all odds the most important censorship, however, was that which Hollywood itself undertook in 1934. Hard pressed by the depression, the studios released increasingly daring pictures. Claudette Colbert took a suggestive milk bath in *Cleopatra;* Hedy Lamar swam nude in a European import, *Ecstacy;* starlets in *Murder at the Vanities* extolled the virtues of "sweet marijuana." Equally disturbing to some people was the industry's perceived preference for themes dealing with social problems. In *I Am a Fugitive from a Chain Gang* (1932) Paul Muni graphically portrayed the evils of forced labor in Southern prisons. *Gabriel over the White House* (1933) flirted with a quasi-fascist dictatorship as a way of solving the depression. Gangster pictures brought the depiction of a breakdown of law and order to every neighborhood theater. From a later perspective, the exploits of Hedy Lamar and Paul Muni seem tepid to a genneration reared on batteries of R and X-rated movies and accustomed to movies such as *The Killing Fields* which invade political territory. The violence that shocked viewers in the original version of *Scarface* pales before the self-indulgent violence of Al Pacino's remake of the movie. Nonetheless these trends in the movies generated increasingly vociferous protests.

These trends also alarmed some industry insiders, notably William Harrison (Will) Hays, who headed the key industry trade group, the Motion Picture Producers and Distributors of America, better known as the Hays Office. As a cautious Hoosier Republican politician who had engineered Warren Harding's "back to normalcy" campaign, Hays preached that Hollywood purveyed only "pure entertainment." In other words, films were wholesome and avoided social and political issues. Hays and some alarmed movie executives feared that, unless the trend in pictures was curbed, the federal government would step in to censor the movies or break up the industry. In short, Hollywood had to clean up its own act or risk having the politicians do it, with perhaps disastrous consequences.[18]

Matters came to a head in 1934. An aroused Roman Catholic hierarchy launched a national movement to purify the polluted springs of Hollywood. The apostolic delegate to the United States, Cardinal Amletto Cicognani, charged the movies with conducting a daily "massacre of innocents." American bishops threatened a nationwide boycott by the faithful. Will Hays realized this was the most serious threat Hollywood had yet seen. It also presented him with an opportunity to curb the excesses that offended him personally and undermined the foundations of the industry.[19]

The solution was simple but far-reaching. In 1930 Hollywood had agreed to abide by a production code written by Daniel Lord, S.J., in consultation with Martin Quigley, a prominent Catholic layman who ran the trade paper *Motion Picture Herald*. But the studios had ignored the code. In mid-1934 the Catholic bishops made Hollywood a simple proposition: live up to the code and we will call off the boycott. Hays agreed and sold the idea to the industry executives. He upgraded the enforcement mechanism, the Production Code Administration (PCA), and at its head he placed a conservative Catholic journalist, Joseph Ignatius Breen. Films had to conform to his interpretation of the code to receive the PCA seal. Without that seal none of the Big Eight companies would handle a picture, effectively killing its market. From mid-1934 into the 1950s Breen's tough, narrow administration of the code sharply limited the subject matter Hollywood might undertake. After an early encounter with Breen, Warner's anguished Hal Wallis cried: "Hollywood might as well go into the milk business!"[20]

Once the movies had gone through Breen's purification process, much of the froth and some of the cream had been removed. Despite Wallis's outburst, protests from inside Hollywood were rare. Breen's PCA brought order to the threatened

chaos of subject matter, much as trade associations in other industries made operations rational and predictable. The producers understood they needed an organization to keep them
in line. As one put it in 1938: "Mr. Hays and Mr. Breen are
efficient zoo attendants, in charge of the monkey house, and
fully realize that upon the slightest provocation their charges
are ready to make indecent gestures for any who offer more
abundant peanuts."[21]

The code, a blend of conservative Roman Catholic morality
and bourgeois propriety, imposed sharp restrictions on the
movies' treatment of a wide range of subjects. Central to the
code was its insistence that wrongdoing—admittedly a dramatic
necessity—was to be shown as always being punished in the end,
and that the sympathy of the audience should never lie with the
wrongdoer. Exposure of flesh was sharply curtailed, as was the
discussion of sexual matters. Men and women could not be
shown in bed together, even if married. Abortion, homosex-
uality, and even birth control (which Breen considered "a pa-
ganistic-Protestant viewpoint") could not be mentioned. Pro-
fanity was forbidden, as was a long list of popular slang terms.
Religion always was to be treated respectfully. The code also
had a conservative political effect, though this fact is less well
known: it admonished movie makers to uphold established political and judicial institutions. Crime or corruption were shown
as individual aberrations, not systemic problems. From time to
time pictures were proposed that did not violate specific pro-
visions of the code but which Breen and Hays considered risky
for the industry. In such cases they invoked "industry policy"
and pressured the studios to drop these projects. "Industry policy" was especially sensitive about films dealing with foreign
countries, and proved to be a major hurdle as Hollywood was
tempted to make pictures about the European crisis in the late
1930s.[22]

The code in fact cut the industry off from a wide range of
social and political issues that were freely debated nationally in
all other media. Films dealing with social issues, though never
eliminated entirely, dropped sharply after the PCA was given
new teeth in mid-1934. Indeed, Breen locked up many of the
films made in the early 1930s, and they were not seen again
publicly until the 1960s. The studios tried now and then to cir-

cumvent the code, and Breen countenanced certain compromises and evasions. Despite the crackdown, there was no mistaking the continuing sexual allure in the movies. The code had its defenders, not only from among conservative moralists, but also from such liberals as writer-director Philip Dunne, who contended that the code encouraged subtlety instead of today's coarseness. In most literary and intellectual circles, however, the code was regularly denounced as the worst kind of censorship—that of "private bigots." They especially condemned the Hays Office's restrictions concerning social and political subjects.[23]

Always controversial, the messages in American movies took on new urgency as the world careened into war in 1939. The war was an irresistible subject for Hollywood, but it also threatened the comfortable and profitable assumptions of the code and the doctrine of "pure entertainment." This was "total war," as politicians and pundits endlessly intoned. As the nation geared for battle down to the most intimate details of daily life— how much cloth you could wear in your pants, how much gasoline you could burn on your Sunday drive, and how much bacon you could eat for breakfast—the movies became a prime instrument for public persuasion. The war brought the most sustained and intimate involvement yet seen in America between the government and a medium of mass culture as the Roosevelt administration applied pressure on Hollywood to make feature films that were propaganda vehicles. The conflict between the studios and the government, and the eventual cooperation between them, helped shape public opinion during and after the war. The relationship between government propagandists and a medium of mass culture brought into sharp focus crucial questions about how the public is mobilized for war and the control of a popular but corporate entertainment medium. Hollywood, 1939: the stage was set for a struggle in the world's dominant medium of popular culture over the conflicting demands of politics, profits, and propaganda.

II.

Hollywood Turns Interventionist

Are we ready to depart from the pleasant and profitable course of entertainment, to engage in propaganda?

—Production Code
Administration, internal
memo, December 1938

The spectacle that began on September 9, 1941, required the best talents of Hollywood and the United States Senate—two American institutions that, whatever their serious purposes, were no strangers to illusion or melodrama. The setting was the Caucus Room of the Senate Office Building, whose ostentatious grandeur even a movieland set designer would have found hard to surpass. The occasion was serious. A specially empaneled subcommittee of the Committee on Interstate Commerce began an investigation of "war propaganda disseminated by the motion picture industry and of any monopoly in the production, distribution, or exhibition of motion pictures."[1]

If not quite a cast of thousands, the proceedings nonetheless attracted a diverse crowd of principals and hangers-on: senators, lawyers, America-Firsters, journalists, publicists, movie moguls and their retinues. Much of the attention focused on Senator Gerald P. Nye, the isolationist firebrand from North Dakota, whose charges against Hollywood had triggered the hearing. Jostling with Nye for the spotlight was the industry's counsel,

Wendell Willkie, the 1940 Republican presidential nominee who had become a staunch supporter of President Roosevelt's international policies. Playing unfamiliar supporting roles were the studio heads.

They faced serious charges. Isolationists, frustrated with their losing battle to get their case into national media, contended that Hollywood had embarked on a devious campaign to inject its entertainment pictures with propaganda and drag America into the war. That charge was closely related to another—that through monopoly control the industry dictated what could and could not be shown in the movies. The ostensible purpose of the hearings was to determine whether Congress should enact legislation to deal with the age-old problem of motion-picture content; Willkie and the industry, however, charged that the hearings' real purpose was to gain publicity for the isolationist cause. Since Hollywood and the Senate both thrived on publicity, in combination they were sensational.[2]

The 1941 hearings were but one of a series of encounters between Hollywood and Congress during the turbulent 1940s. Although the Hays Office tried to steer the studios away from political subjects, the movie producers, whether for reasons of conscience, profit, or sheer human interest, could not avoid politics and war. The industry fared much better in the 1941 hearings than in postwar inquests into communism in Hollywood, thanks both to the ineptitude of the isolationists and to the forthright defense orchestrated by Willkie. The occasion turned into something of a political coming-out party for an industry that had officially kept its politics closeted.

The international situation was tense indeed in the fall of 1941, and Americans carried on an increasingly acrimonious debate about how to respond to it. Hitler's army straddled Europe, from the English Channel to the Ukraine, from Norway to North Africa. The Red Army, reeling in the face of the lightning thrusts of the panzer divisions of the Soviet Union's erstwhile ally, would eventually make a heroic winter stand at Stalingrad that would turn the tide of the war. But in September 1941 a Russian defeat seemed possible, which would leave Hitler master of all Europe. The Japanese, having occupied a sizable portion of China and all of Indochina, were moving on the Dutch East Indies in search of the oil that was essential to their war machine. A demoralized France had fallen in six weeks in the spring of 1940. Great Britain, indomitable in the face of the Luftwaffe's blitz, held the torch for the democracies. But it was short of everything—men, money, matériel—and clung to the hope that "in God's good time" the New World would come to the rescue of the old.

The United States, convoying British ships laden with Lend-Lease goods across the Atlantic, was increasingly drawn into an undeclared naval war with Germany. As the skirmishes escalated, President Roosevelt issued a "sink-on-sight" order against the German U-boats—"the rattlesnakes of the Atlantic," in his potent phrase—and the non-existent war would claim the lives of 110 American seamen by Thanksgiving. As inconclusive peace negotiations with Japanese envoys ground on in a Washington hotel room, no one could anticipate that the great debate would end on the first Sunday morning in December when sudden death rained from a clear sky at Pearl Harbor.

Instead, the isolationists girded for a last-ditch struggle against America's inexorable drift towards intervention. They knew that three-fourths of the public supported Roosevelt's policy of "all aid short of war" to the nations fighting the Axis. The non-interventionists rejoined, however, that "all aid short of war" led ineluctably to war. Fearing a bloodbath, and believing that the United States could do business with Hitler, they mounted an increasingly shrill campaign against the president and his policies. One of their leaders, Senator Burton K. Wheeler, Democrat of Montana, attacked Roosevelt's internationalism as a foreign policy AAA—"it will plough under every fourth American boy." The president responded that this was "the rottenest thing" he'd ever heard in American public life. "I hate war," Roosevelt declared in his 1940 campaign for a third term. "Your boys are not going to be sent into any foreign war." But after FDR's re-election, Congress—following an impassioned radio appeal by the president—passed Lend-Lease. And, in an extraordinary departure for the head of a nonbelligerent nation, Roosevelt met secretly with Churchill off the coast of Newfoundland in August 1941. From this "first summit" they jointly issued the "Atlantic Charter," a declaration of Anglo-American war aims even though the United States was not at war.[3]

Roosevelt well knew that the modern president, embodiment of what is sometimes styled an "imperial presidency," commands policy, and commands news. Members of Congress were no match for him on radio which, unlike print, tends to focus on one individual at a time. The isolationists knew they were being outflanked by the media-wise Roosevelt and resented it deeply. Unable to rein him in, they turned their anger on the media.

In late December 1940, on the eve of the Senate's debate on Lend-Lease, Roosevelt delivered one of his most famous "fireside chats," his "arsenal of democracy" speech. Senator Wheeler countered with a fiery rebuttal. The national radio networks, bound by the "equal time" doctrine that governed the public air waves, carried Wheeler's rejoinder. But in the private media—the newspapers and the film companies' newsreels—coverage of the isolationists was sparse to nonexistent. Wheeler was furious. "Will you kindly inform me when, if at all, you intend to carry my answer?" he demanded of Paramount News. "And what, if anything, you are going to do about carrying both sides of the controversy on pending legislation which directly involves the question of war or peace?" He added ominously that the motion picture industry's "propaganda for war" had reached the point where legislation might be needed to ensure "a more impartial attitude" on Hollywood's part. Since Wheeler was the powerful chairman of the Committee on Interstate Commerce, his was no idle threat. Even worse he and Nye objected to a series of feature films produced in Hollywood between 1938 and 1941 that in their opinion supported FDR's interventionist policies.[4]

Will Hays responded by denying that the industry was taking a stand on controversial issues. Newsreels in 1940 contained "factual reports" on national defense subjects in only 16 percent of the cases, he said. Political subjects figured in only 2.4 percent of the one and two-reel short subjects, and European political subjects in less than .5 percent. Only 27 of the 530 feature films, or 5 percent, pertained "in any way" to political events. Read from another perspective, Hays' statistics suggested that Hollywood was not paying much attention at all to the rest of the world. Hays did not mind. When war broke out in Europe in 1939 he had issued a widely quoted statement:

"There will be no cycle of 'hate' pictures. The primary purpose of the essential service of motion pictures is entertainment—entertainment which will be effective as such, and entertainment which is, at its best, inspirational." This was pure Hoosier boilerplate. The doctrine had outlived its usefulness as Hollywood confronted a world at war.[5]

Until the late 1930s the American movie industry was economically dependent on a world market for the success of its products. In Latin America, for example, some 5,000 theaters played American films; in Asia, more than 6,000; but Europe had by far the greatest number of all—more than 35,000 theaters where American movies were regularly shown. The rise of fascism offered the American film industry endless opportunities for dramatic movie scripts—but that in itself presented the movie makers with a grave dilemma. Any movies that dealt realistically with Mussolini and his new Roman Empire, Adolf Hitler and Nazi Germany, or the Spanish Civil War, were likely to be banned from thousands of screens in Europe while at the same time being opposed at home by American isolationists. It was a cruel economic choice the movie makers faced, since 40 percent of industry revenues were generated overseas, representing the profit margin for many films; with some companies, the box office take outside the United States went even higher, up to 50 percent of their total.[6]

To compound the problem, the world market was an outlet not only for current productions, but also for the re-release of older films that were no longer being exhibited in the United States. The Hays Office therefore maintained an active foreign relations division under the direction of Frederick Herron to keep foreign markets open for American films, and Herron's people went to great lengths to satisfy foreign governments. When the Nazis demanded that all "non-Aryan" employees in Germany be terminated, the major studios complied "insofar as their business staffs and offices in Germany" were concerned. This was only the first step. The Nuremberg Laws banned films with Jewish actors and actresses, cut the number of American pictures that could be shown in Germany to just twenty per year, and imposed severe restrictions on the repatriation of profits. *Variety* claimed that the companies were up in arms but that the Hays Office wanted "to soft-pedal the fil-

mers for political and diplomatic reasons." As the stain of Nazi
influence seeped across Europe after 1937, Hollywood's markets progressively dried up. By 1940 they were insignificant.
Conversely, the relative importance of the British Commonwealth box office grew. One could graph the inverse relationship between the German-dominated and British-controlled
markets—and observe, in turn, a significant shift in Hollywood's subjects.[7]

Market forces were buttressed by the vigilance of Joseph
Breen. The conservative head of the Production Code Administration was deeply suspicious that Jews in Hollywood, chiefly
writers, were trying to use the Nazis' treatment of Jews to make
propaganda pictures. He felt the center of this conspiracy was
the Hollywood Anti-Nazi League, which was, he said, "conducted and financed almost entirely by Jews." Their response
to the Spanish Civil War was to vilify "the communistic loyalists." Indeed, Breen feared an attempt to *capture the screen of the
United States for Communistic propaganda purposes.*" The censor said
he had been able to eliminate all attempts at propaganda thus
far, but it was increasing at an alarming rate.[8]

Any attempt to portray international politics thus had to
escape Breen's scissors, whose anti-Semitic and anticommunist
posture made him sympathetic to the far right. In 1935 Hays
successfully pressured MGM to drop its plan to make a film
based on Sinclair Lewis's *It Can't Happen Here,* even though the
studio had paid the novelist $50,000 for the rights and invested
a good deal more in the production. The tortuous process of
making Robert Sherwood's Pulitzer Prize-winning antiwar, antifascist play *Idiot's Delight* into an innocuous movie exemplified
the problems the studios faced in making pictures on political
themes. A Broadway hit in 1936, *Idiot's Delight* was set in a small
Italian hotel on the Swiss frontier, where a group of international travelers are stranded when Italy launches a surprise air
attack on Paris. The play stresses that war is folly and condemns
fascism. But the Hays Office would not let the industry make a
movie criticizing Mussolini—this in the late 1930s, after Il
Duce's aggression against helpless Ethiopia, crucial support for
Franco, and adoption of anti-Semitic laws based on those of
Nazi Germany. Instead Joseph Breen went to extraordinary
lengths to pacify the Italian government.[9]

Any Broadway hit interested Hollywood, and several studios considered buying the movie rights. Breen warned them off, pointing out that it would be banned in many countries and subject the industry to reprisals. In late 1936, however, MGM decided to take the plunge and paid Sherwood a handsome $125,000 for the rights. Hays's inner circle warned Breen to watch the production closely because "it is full of dynamite." The PCA chief engaged in protracted negotiations with the Italian consul in Los Angeles in an effort to satisfy Mussolini's government and make sure *Idiot's Delight* could play in Italy. The Italians insisted on drastic changes, including a new title. MGM agreed to alter the content markedly, but it clung to the title—that was almost all it had in common with the play! Mayer brought Sherwood to Hollywood for $135,000 more, and he set about the aesthetically and perhaps morally compromising task of bowdlerizing his own play. The playwright employed a clever strategy. On the one hand, although retaining some generalized statements against war, he cut out the Italian connection. The movie was set in an unnamed Central European country and even used Esperanto as its foreign language. On the other, he heightened the love affair between an American entertainer, Harry Van (played by Clark Gable) and Irene (played by Norma Shearer). Even so, the screenplay had problems. Breen actually carried the script with him to Italy in the summer of 1938 for inspection by Mussolini's government, and after a series of bureaucratic misadventures, Rome finally gave its approval.[10]

The picture was finally released in February 1939 to a mixed reception. With the popular appeal of Gable and Shearer, the picture had some drawing power at the box office. But in that year of rising tension, Spain, France, Switzerland, and Estonia banned it, and it did not play in Italy because new commercial restrictions made the exhibition of American movies unprofitable. Critics questioned the tactics that had turned the Italy of the stage set into "an Alpine never-never land in celluloid" and produced an "adventure in obscurantism." A powerful play had been reduced to another trite love story. This latest example of the Hays Office's "hyprocrisy" highlighted the movies' aversion to important topical themes—a policy that was already forcing the censors onto the defensive.[11]

The first producer to attempt a serious film on events in

Europe was an independent, Walter Wanger. He released *Blockade* through United Artists in 1938. UA had already closed its Spanish office and its European revenues had declined drastically since 1935. Neither Wanger nor UA had much to lose by making a film set in contemporary Spain. However, the national uproar that ensued over the film heightened the apprehension about political films in some major studios.

The Spanish Civil War was one of the great divisive international issues of the 1930's. American liberals and the left generally supported the Loyalist government, three thousand of them joining the Abraham Lincoln Brigade to fight for Republican Spain. The right, including elements of the Catholic Church, generally supported Franco and the fascists. Germany and Italy poured huge amounts of arms and men into Franco's cause and were instrumental in his victory. The Soviet Union supported the Loyalists, but its aid could not match that from Berlin and Rome. Like Great Britain and France, the United States, bound by the Neutrality Acts, stood by. To some, the Spanish Civil War seemed a prelude to World War II.

Wanger discussed the idea of a film on Spain with director Lewis Milestone as early as 1936 and hired the erstwhile radical playwright Clifford Odets to do the screenplay. Wanger was unhappy with Odets' work and in October 1937 brought John Howard Lawson into the project. The Odets script, *The River Is Blue*, was, according to Lawson "an inept melodrama . . . having no bearing on events in Europe." He convinced Wanger "to deal honestly with the actual conflict in Spain." Lawson's idea was to center the story of Spain around a Loyalist-controlled seaport under siege—surrounded by Franco on land and blockaded from the sea by Nazi and Italian submarines. The film would illustrate the issues of the conflict as the starving city awaited rescue from a supply ship.[12]

Wanger submitted Lawson's script to Breen in January 1938. The script, though very cautious, worried Breen. Deathly afraid of taking sides, he warned Wanger that great care should be exercised to avoid identification with either side. The sinking of a food ship should not be identified with combatants of either side. Cautioning Wanger not to make the film too explicit, he gave him permission to go forward with the production. *Blockade* was shot with great circumspection to avoid explicit identification with either camp; painstaking attention ensured that no uniforms were accurate. Wanger later described *Blockade* as nothing more than a "melodramatic spy story and romance in a modern setting—colorful Spain."[13]

Blockade opened at the New York Radio City Music Hall in June 1938. Starring Henry Fonda as a young Spanish farmer and Madeleine Carroll as the beautiful spy, *Blockade* was one of the more realistic films produced by the industry despite the limitations of the Production Code. There were scenes of children starving, and the film illustrated, however obliquely, some of the horrors of modern war. Even though the sides were not identified, few politically conscious Americans in 1938 would have been confused over the issues or the sides battling in *Blockade*. In the gripping ending Fonda turns to the audience:

> Where can you find peace? The whole country's a battleground. There is no peace. There is no safety for women and children. Schools and hospitals are targets. And this isn't war, not war between soldiers. It's not war, it's murder. It makes no sense. The world can stop it. Where is the conscience of the world? Where is the conscience of the world?

"The conscience of the world" was sharply divided. Franco supporters considered the film blatant propaganda. *Blockade* was boycotted and picketed by Catholic organizations throughout the United States. The Knights of Columbus, the Catholic laymen's organization, called it "leftist propaganda" and demanded that the Hays office attach a disclaimer warning audiences they were about to watch a propaganda film. The Legion of Decency attacked it, and parish priests warned their flock not to see it.[14]

The controversy over *Blockade* worried Hays, who made "surreptitious efforts ... to bring about its economic failure," according to *The Nation*. He worked behind the scenes to keep it out of American theaters. Despite favorable audience reactions and a fair financial record—$70,000 during its first week's run at Radio City, with *Variety* reporting *Blockade* as "big in San Francisco," "very good" in Cincinnati, and "okay" in Los Angeles and Seattle—Fox-West Coast, the powerful theater chain, "refused to take 'Blockade' as a regular first feature." The best Fox-West Coast would do was show *Blockade* in a few first-run houses and as a second feature in the rest of the chain. It was quickly

cancelled in Milwaukee, in Flint, Michigan, and in Springfield,
Massachusetts. Martin Quigley entered the campaign with a series of heated editorials condemning the film in his *Motion Picture Herald.* As *The Nation* observed: "The attack on 'Blockade'
is fundamentally an attack . . . on the whole idea of making films
on serious social and political themes." John Howard Lawson
agreed. To the screenwriter, *Blockade* simply proved "that the
screen is not at present free, and that even the simplest hu-
manitarian statement is regarded as 'alarming' and 'dangerous'
to those who want to keep the motion picture in swaddling
clothes." The experiences with *Blockade* suggested how difficult
it would be for the industry to portray events in Europe. To
Hays and the PCA, the lesson was clear—politics translates into
controversy and bad box office.[15]

They reiterated the point when Wanger tried to make *Personal History.* A national best-seller, *Personal History* was journalist
Vincent Sheean's rambling account of revolution and war in
China, and of conditions in the Middle East and Europe. Wanger had purchased the movie rights to the book in 1936 and
again hired Lawson to write the script. Wanger submitted Lawson's script to Breen in June 1938, the same month his *Blockade*
opened in New York. Aware of the Catholic opposition to *Blockade* and of Hays's reaction to the film, Breen read Wanger's
script with apprehension.[16]

Personal History was to take up where *Blockade* had stopped.
The script told of a young college student whose socialist ideals
are turned into a patriotic defense of American democracy. The
young hero quits college and sets off for Europe, where he becomes a newspaper reporter and covers the Spanish Civil War.
In Spain he discovers the brutality of the fascists; in Germany
he discovers the anti-Semitic policies of the Nazi regime. He
dramatically rescues several Jews from persecution and marries
a Jewish girl. The film was to be a strong indictment of Franco
and Hitler with the young reporter abandoning his "radical-
ism" in favor of American patriotism. While the proposed script
combined well-known Hollywood formulas of drama, intrigue,
romance, and support of American democracy, Breen was hesitant to approve it. In his view the young hero was nothing more
than a "half-baked . . . radical college boy." In a conference with

Wanger he admitted he found no specific violations of the code, but believed the proposed film presented "grave dangers" and could run afoul of "industry policy."[17]

Breen then immediately informed Hays of the situation. He told his boss that "industry policy" was involved, since "controversial racial and political questions" would be dramatized on the screen." He felt that *Personal History* would arouse "audience feeling against the present German regime, in the matter of its treatment of the Jews." Breen then again conferred with Wanger. He agreed the script was technically within the Code, but stated that in the opinion of the PCA, the script contained "pro-Loyalist propaganda . . . pro-Jewish propaganda, and anti-Nazi propaganda . . . [which] would inevitably cause enormous difficulty, when you come to release the picture." The producer quietly gave up the fight, citing "casting difficulties." Indeed it was true—difficulties arose because it had cast the realities of Spain and Germany all too accurately for the tastes of Breen and Hays. Wanger would eventually recoup his investment, but in a much-altered product.[18]

The turning point in political films came with Warner Brothers' *Confessions of a Nazi Spy.* It was "a portentous departure," as a worried Breen office staff member described it. Originally titled "Storm Over America," *Confessions* was based on a real incident: Nazi spies who came to the United States had been caught and convicted by a federal court in New York City. Warners sent writer Milton Krims to observe the trial with an eye toward making the courtroom drama into a movie. A two-sentence announcement of Krims' visit, buried in the *Hollywood Reporter*, attracted the attention of the eagle-eyed German consul in Los Angeles, who wrote to Breen telling him to be sure this did not result in "difficulties." Breen passed the consul's letter on to Jack Warner, who in the "damn the torpedoes" tradition that studio moguls venerated in their screen characters but rarely observed in real life, ignored it and forged ahead. *Confessions* was directed by Anatole Litvak, written by John Wexley, and starred Paul Lukas and Edward G. Robinson; it reflected the anti-Nazi ideology of the production cast. Litvak and Lucas were German émigrés, and Wexley and Robinson were active in the Hollywood anti-Nazi movement. *Confessions of a Nazi Spy* pulled no punches in identifying Nazi Germany as a threat to American security. Germany aimed for world domination, the film proclaimed.[19]

Warner Brothers' boldness spread apprehension among other studios. The foreign department of Paramount thought Warners was making a grave mistake. Paramount executives recalled that when Charlie Chaplin first proposed his "burlesque of Hitler"—the picture that eventually became *The Great Dictator*—he had been chastized for devoting "his money-making talents to a film which could only have horrible repercussions on the Jews still in Germany." The same charge would be leveled at Warner Brothers. Luigi Luraschi, of Paramount's Censorship Department, wrote that if the film were "in any way uncomplimentary to Germany, as it must be if it is to be sincerely produced, then Warners will have on their hands the blood of a great many Jews in Germany." He wondered whether this was "smart showmanship." Paramount, Luraschi smugly concluded, would not make any film that was "uncomplimentary" to any nation. Here was a classic case not only of blaming the victim but of traducing those who wanted to help. Paramount thought avoiding the whole issue was morally superior as well as the smartest showmanship.[20]

Warner Brothers dispatched the controversial script to Breen in late December 1938 with a request that he keep it under lock and key so that it would not fall into the hands of the German consul or the German-American Bund. The script touched off a hot debate in Breen's office. One faction objected strenuously, arguing that the screenplay depicted Hitler and his government unfairly. There was no proof that German agitators had come to the United States with the intention of seizing control of the country; after all, they said, every country has spies. Nor was it fair to show Hitler only as "a screaming madman." The film should acknowledge "his unchallenged political and social achievements." Such European events as the dismemberment of Czechoslovakia and the abolition of Christian schools in the Third Reich were "extraneous" to the spy story. Even if everything in the script were true, this group said, it would be "one of the most lamentable mistakes ever made by the industry." The inflammatory intent of the movie was dangerous to the industry. And they questioned whether one should forsake "the pleasant and profitable course of entertainment to engage in propaganda?"[21]

Fearing that there would indeed be a "Storm over America" if he approved the film, Breen temporized. He drafted, but did not send, a letter to Jack Warner in which he argued that the script raised the important policy question of whether the studio should make a picture dealing with such a controversial subject. Breen also drafted a letter to Hays but did not send it either. He raised the policy question but also noted that "certain important government officials" gave the studio "indirect aid": for example, the judge who tried the spy case had allowed Warners' cameras into his courtroom.[22]

Instead of taking a direct stand, Breen decided to appeal to Warner Brothers' economic self-interest in the hope that the market would, as usual, eliminate controversial subjects. The script was technically within the code, Breen conceded, but it "risked political censorship at home and abroad. The "national feelings" section of the code specified that "the history, institutions, prominent people and citizenry of other nations, shall be represented fairly." Was that the case? Breen conceded that the film's depiction of Nazi Germany seemed to be borne out by the evidence brought forth at the trial.[23]

But the truth was not sufficient to allay his fears. He hoped that the threat of censorship by foreign governments would frighten Warner Brothers into withdrawing or modifying the picture without his having to take the heat for such a decision. Breen also claimed to fear that some American state censorship boards would forbid its exhibition out of fear of incitation to riot. Although some World War I films had triggered anti-German riots in the United States, this fear seemed more like scare tactics.[24]

Warners decided to go ahead. Using semi-documentary techniques and long periods of narration, the film identified the German-American Bund as an arm of the German government whose purpose was to destroy the American Constitution and Bill of Rights. Robinson, who plays the FBI agent, declares that Germany is at war with the United States: "It's a new kind of war but it's still war." In the final scene the district attorney lectures the jury—substitute American public—about the dangers of isolationism. After summarizing the nature of Nazi aggression, he tells the jury that America must learn from Europe—we must be prepared to defend our Constitution and Bill of Rights. Today the film seems melodramatic and the internal threat overstated. But Wexley termed *Confessions* "the most exciting and exhilarating work I have ever done in Hollywood."[25]

Public response was mixed. Otis Ferguson of *The New Republic* said: "This is no *Beast of Berlin,* but a statement of sober, inevitable facts, so brilliantly realized that no one can hide from it." *The Hollywood Reporter* termed *Confessions* "unique" in the annals of the screen. A "straightforward" attack on Nazism, it pulled its punches only on the question of anti-Semitism. "It may well . . . sound out the efficacy of a new approach to purposeful entertainment." The preview audience applauded with unusual vigor at the close of the show. *Variety,* on the other hand, found the film melodramatic—the only thing missing was a rape scene by German soldiers, its reviewer said sardonically. Although the picture did well in New York City, *Variety* wondered how it would play in Peoria. It enjoyed modest financial success.[26]

Breen's anticipation of foreign censorship was borne out. Predictably Germany, Italy, and Spain refused to exhibit it. Neutral countries, such as Ireland, Switzerland, and several Latin American republics banned it, often at the behest of the German minister. On August 4, 1939, Holland and Norway both forbade its showing—in view of what would happen a month later they might have been better advised to watch it and take it to heart. The London censor demanded the deletion of several derogatory references to Hitler. In 1940, however, *Confessions* played throughout Great Britain with the cut portions restored. The changing fortunes of war also swept away some Latin American censorship. Venezuela farsightedly lifted its ban in May 1940, but Peru waited until December 8, 1941. Several other nations followed suit, belatedly.[27]

With Warner Brothers' experience to learn from, Wanger decided to avoid trouble with his second attempt at filming *Personal History,* now retitled *Foreign Correspondent.* He was determined, he said, "to make as good a picture as I can." The result was a Hitchcock thriller, but it was not the politically charged *Personal History.* In March 1940 Wanger sent the PCA a new script written by the all-star team of Alfred Hitchcock, Charles Bennett, John Harrison, James Hilton, and Robert Benchley. *Foreign Correspondent* bore "little resemblance to the story we were concerned about two years ago," a relieved Breen told Hays. The film had no problem getting a seal of approval. All references to Spain were removed, and German policy toward the Jews was not dealt with. The picture did not directly attack the Germans or imply that all Germans were evil. Joel McCrea starred as a crass, hard-hitting crime reporter sent to Europe to find out "what was going on over there." The film centered attention on the love affair between McCrea and Laraine Day, with a European spy setting tossed in for atmosphere. While Breen and Hays might have preferred that the film not be made, *Foreign Correspondent* was mild enough to cause little concern.[28]

The credit for perhaps the most significant antifascist film, both politically and artistically, must go to Charles Chaplin, independent producer, director, writer, and actor extraordinaire, for his 1940 classic, *The Great Dictator*. Chaplin was pressured to cancel the project. He said officials at United Artists, the releasing company, had told him they "had been advised by the Hays office that 'I would run into censorship trouble.'" Chaplin was not deterred: "I was determined to go ahead, for Hitler must be laughed at."[29]

As early as October 1938, the German consul in Los Angeles wrote to Breen objecting to the proposed picture. In March 1939, Brooke Wilkinson, secretary of the British Board of Film Censors, cautioned Breen that a delicate situation would arise if Chaplin made *The Great Dictator,* because the board enforced a stringent rule that no living personage could be represented on the screen without his or her written consent. The outbreak of war in September 1939 relieved the British censor of the need for the rather mechanical application of this rule.[30]

Chaplin completed *The Great Dictator* over the summer of 1940 and Breen screened it on September 6. He was delighted. "It is superb entertainment," Breen wrote, "and marks Mr. Chaplin, I think, as our greatest artist." There was, nonetheless, a problem: An embarrassed Breen asked Chaplin to excise the forbidden word *lousy,* spoken by Maurice Moscovitch, from the scene in which Miss Goddard tries on hats. The PCA head described the violation as "small and picayune," but he had no choice in enforcing the code. The offending word was elimi-

nated, presumably making the picture a more wholesome spectacle.[31]

Some critics objected to Chaplin's concluding speech on
aesthetic grounds: "Now let us fight to free the world—to do
away with national barriers—to do away with greed, hate, and
intolerance. Let us fight for a world ... of reason—a world
where science and progress will lead to the happiness of all."
Breen did not object, perhaps because the speech expressed a
universal longing for peace rather than a specific political
course of action. Chaplin made his political statement into good
box office—the film grossed $5 million worldwide and earned
him a profit of $1.5 million. For the genius of the silent screen,
his first talking picture was a personal, professional, political,
and financial triumph.[32]

By 1940 Hollywood had crossed an important threshold.
Some studios had begun to make explicitly interventionist films.
These subjects would remain a small fraction of the industry's
output, but the departure from a sole reliance on "the pleasant
and profitable course of entertainment" marked a significant
shift in thinking. As America's peril deepened, and Hollywood's
remaining European markets dried up, the studios took an increasingly interventionist stand.

Unlike *The Great Dictator,* there was nothing satirical, and no
comic relief, in *Pastor Hall.* Samuel Goldwyn wanted to distribute this 1939 British production through United Artists.
Adapted from a play by Ernst Toller, *Pastor Hall* dramatized the
inspiring courage of Martin Niemoller, the World War I U-boat
captain-turned-pacifist-preacher, in the face of the Nazis. The
film was more direct than any Hollywood production; it vividly
illustrated Nazi stormtroopers moving into a German village,
conducting a campaign of terror, and sending Niemoller to a
concentration camp. While *The Great Dictator's* concentration
camps looked like Boy Scout bivouacs, *Pastor Hall* presented a
realistic view of German terror and violence.[33]

The PCA's Geoffrey Shurlock found *Pastor Hall* a "bitter indictment of the present Nazi government;" he felt that distribution of the film would involve questions of "industry policy."
United Artists officials were divided. Walter Wanger, busy making his toothless *Foreign Correspondent,* opposed distribution because it would serve "no good purpose" for either the company

or the industry. Goldwyn, though he liked the film, would not distribute it if Hays opposed. But Goldwyn insisted that Hays prevent the other majors from buying the film. To Breen the issue was clear: "It is avowedly British propaganda, and its distribution by one of our companies would expose us to the charge of going out of our way to propagandize for the allies." This at the moment of the collapse of France and the Blitz against Britain! None of the major studios took the film.[34]

Instead, James Roosevelt, FDR's son and president of Globe Productions, decided to distribute *Pastor Hall*. He added a prologue written by Robert Sherwood and read by Eleanor Roosevelt. It would have been impolitic for Breen or Hays to tell the President's son he could not distribute the film, so Breen had some of the more violent scenes deleted and quitely issued *Pastor Hall* seal number 02913. The film was eventually released through United Artists. Perhaps because of the fear of propaganda, *Pastor Hall* was a mediocre draw at the box office.[35]

"Hollywood producers have not yet gone so strong in presenting the case against Hitlerism, and undoubtedly will not go as far unless future events veer the attitude," said *Variety*. In the summer of 1940 a concatenation of forces contributed to a rapprochement between the industry and the Roosevelt administration. The outcome was an increasing number of rearmament shorts and sharper portrayals of Nazis in feature films. In July the Hays office established the Motion Picture Committee Cooperating for Defense. This group focused on shorts but drew the line at feature pictures. Through this gesture the industry hoped to reap maximum goodwill from interventionists at minimum cost—that is, without arousing too much criticism from non-interventionists. Some studio heads wanted to go further. The brothers Warner, avid Roosevelt backers, offered to make any short on preparedness without cost, an offer which caught even the administration unprepared.[36]

Hollywood and the White House had every incentive to cooperate. In 1938 Thurman Arnold, the trust-busting assistant attorney general, had filed an antitrust suit against the five major production and distribution companies. The majors feared that this suit, which became the basis for the divorce between production and distribution when it was reintroduced after the war, would bring chaos. In August 1940 the White House told the Justice Department to settle with a consent decree; signed in November, it allowed the companies to continue operations pretty much as they had before. Perhaps the wily politicians around the Oval Office were already counting on the boost that favorable movie publicity would give the president's unprecedented bid for a third term.[37]

In August FDR asked Nicholas Schenck, president of Loew's (parent of MGM), to make a film on defense and foreign policy. By mid-October *Eyes of the Navy,* a two-reeler which a studio executive promised would win the president thousands of votes, graced neighborhood movie houses. Schenck's interest may have been personal as well as patriotic. His brother Joseph, head of Twentieth Century-Fox, was convicted of income tax evasion. President Roosevelt asked Attorney General Robert Jackson to let the studio chief off with a fine, and so did Roosevelt's son James, to whom Joseph Schenck had lent $50,000. But the upright Jackson insisted on a jail sentence. Schenck served four months before being paroled to the studio lot.[38]

On August 17, 1940, Germany banned American films from areas under its control, a move that was not unexpected but still shocking. Italy naturally followed suit. Not only did American studios have incentives to cooperate with their president, but now the last major restraint—market pressure—had been removed. Hollywood took its gloves off.

An emboldened Metro released the industry's first essay on the Jewish question in Germany, *The Mortal Storm,* in 1940. Directed by Frank Borzage, the picture starred James Stewart, Margaret Sullivan, and Robert Young. The film depicts a prosperous university biology professor and his family who are persecuted because he refuses to teach that Aryan blood is superior to all other blood types. His family is torn apart by Nazi ideology—one son is a Nazi while his daughter loves an opponent of the regime. In typical Hollywood fashion, the conflict is set between good Germans and evil Nazis against a romantic background. While Germany is clearly shown as a totalitarian state, the film also establishes that not all Germans support Nazi racism.[39]

Through 1941 Hollywood films made a distinction between the Nazis and the German people. *Four Sons* (1940) depicts a family split by its attitude to Nazism. One son is an ardent supporter, a second son is a member of the resistance movement, a third is killed in battle, and the fourth son finds freedom from totalitarianism by escaping to America. *Escape* (1940) and *I Married a Nazi* both contrasted good and evil Germans. A PCA report on *Escape* noted that the film was not in the "hate" category since "many Germans are shown to be decent people." Chaplin's *The Great Dictator* made it clear that not all Germans were Jew-hating Nazis. This approach was both a Hollywood formula and a requirement of the production code. Evil Germans had to be balanced by a few good Germans. The PCA simply took its formula for avoiding controversy—politicians could be corrupt, but not all politicians could be corrupt; lawyers could be shysters, but not all lawyers were—and applied it to Nazi Germany. The PCA demanded that Hollywood continue to enforce a fairness doctrine, no matter how evil the regime.[40]

When Twentieth Century-Fox submitted Dudley Nichols' adaptation of Geoffrey Household's *Rogue Male* in March 1941, the PCA worried that its formula had been broken. *Man Hunt,* directed by Fritz Lang, depicted all Nazis as evil. Breen considered *Man Hunt* a "hate the Hun" film which the industry was committed to avoid. He pointed out that unlike any script submitted recently, this film characterized all Nazis as "brutal and inhuman people" while all Englishmen were "sympathetic characters." If made as submitted, Breen warned, the film would open the industry to considerable criticism for "not only ... propaganda, but inflammatory propaganda as well." Hays concurred. Breen asked Twentieth Century to tone down *Man Hunt.* The studio removed some of the more brutal scenes and assured Breen that *Man Hunt* would not fall into the category of a "hate picture." The PCA chief approved a revised script.[41]

Man Hunt opens in Nazi Germany with Captain Alan Thorndyke (Walter Pidgeon), a famous big-game hunter who has grown bored with killing animals. To add a bit of spice to his life he decides it would be "amusing to sight a rifle at the bridge of Adolf Hitler's nose—purely *pour le sport....* " But his sport quickly turns sour when he is captured by the Gestapo. Beaten and tortured, mostly off-camera, Thorndyke escapes. Now the hunter becomes the hunted. The Gestapo agent/British spy (George Sanders) tells the Englishman: "You are decadent. We do not hesitate to destroy." As Thorndyke is chased across Germany and pursued in London, he discovers the German regime is totally repugnant to his way of life. He comes to understand what freedom means. After being forced to kill to survive, he joins the British armed forces to fight for democracy. In the end Thorndyke secretly parachutes into Germany to begin his quest in deadly seriousness.

Reviewers found *Man Hunt* an "extraordinary study in the psychology of horror. . . . " Otis Ferguson noted that there is a "vividness about it that makes you wish it could somehow come out more penetrating and terrible." But *Man Hunt* was already as penetrating and terrible as Breen and Hays would allow. Anything more graphic or condemnatory would have been cut by the censors.[42]

As the American defense buildup gathered steam, Hollywood increasingly found subjects at home. Each arm of the military enjoyed its moment of silvered glory in such productions as *I Wanted Wings, Dive Bomber, Flight Command, Navy Blues, Buck Private,* and *Tanks a Million.* Many such pictures had no explicit propaganda message, but the application of movie glamour and its repetition probably helped create a favorable impression of the armed forces. These topics were irresistible, too, to comedians, such as Abbott and Costello who were *Caught in the Draft.* These humorous treatments may have helped "humanize and trivialize" the experience and hence perhaps eased the anxiety of potential draftees and their families. Moviegoers were well advised to laugh while they could, since wartime propagandists frowned on humorous treatments of their deathly serious subject.

The White House was pleased. In a message to the annual Academy Awards banquet in February 1941, Roosevelt thanked the industry for its "splendid cooperation with all who are directing the expansion of our defense forces," and appealed for continued support. The administration found Hollywood more cooperative than radio or, particularly, the press. Lowell Mellett, a presidential aide who handled liaison with the media, reported in March 1941: "Practically everything being shown on the screen from newsreel to fiction that touches on our national purpose is of the right sort." Movie colony patriotism was partly responsible, but he also attributed the support to "the

fact that the picture industry is conscious of the Justice Department."[43]

By mid-1941 the movies crossed another threshold. Without
making explicit policy judgments, they made telling interventionist pitches by analogy. In *A Yank in the R.A.F.* and *International Squadron* Americans were so aroused by Britain's peril
that they joined the Royal Air Force to take an active part in
the fight against Nazism. The grandest development of this
analogy was Warner's *Sergeant York*, which premiered at the Astor Theatre in New York on July 1, 1941. This picture purported
to be the story of Alvin York, a former pacifist who became an
instant hero in World War I when he killed some twenty German soldiers and captured 132 others in the Argonne. The production fulfilled the dream of film pioneer Jesse L. Lasky, who
was thrilled by York's massive homecoming parade down Fifth
Avenue in 1919 and tried to sign him to star in a picture on his
exploits. In 1940 Lasky again approached the aging hero, telling
him that a film about his life would be an inspiration to young
men undergoing the same crisis of conscience he had experienced. York agreed when Lasky delivered $50,000 for the Bible
school he wanted to build and gave him script control.[44]

Warner Brothers walked a narrow ridge between capitaliz-
ing on the Appalachian local color and exploiting it as Dog-
patch, U.S.A. The studio agreed to York's suggestion that the
tall, laconic Gary Cooper play his part. (How often do most people get to see themselves transformed from a paunchy, graying
middle-aged has-been by one of the screen's leading stars!) More
difficult was the choice of an actress to play the hero's wife,
"Miss Gracie" Williams York. Howard Hawks, who directed and
also collaborated on the screenplay, envisioned "Miss Gracie"
as Daisy Mae—a voluptuous backwoods tramp—and wanted
Jane Russell for the role. Co-producer Hal Wallis vetoed this
alluring idea and gave the part to the wholesome sixteen-year-
old Joan Leslie.[45]

The screenplay emerged from the collaboration of Robert
Buckner, Howard Koch (who was to do the scripts for the important wartime pictures *Casablanca* and *Mission to Moscow*),
Abem Finkel, Harry Chandlee, and Hawks. Their first challenge
was to show York's transformation from hellion to devout Chris-

tian. This was accomplished with generous doses of poetic license. While on a hunting outing he sees the pretty, religious "Miss Gracie" and it is, predictably, love at first sight. Depressed by his inability to raise money fast enough to buy a section of good bottom land, he lapses into his old hard-drinking ways. He is riding home in a tremendous thunderstorm after an all night session with the bottle when a bolt of lightning rips his rifle from his hand and twists it into a molten mass. York undergoes a conversion, ratified by the local congregation's rousing rendition of "Give Me That Old Time Religion."

The other key transition—from pacifist to super warrior—was more difficult. When the U.S. enters the war, York, taking literally the Bible's injunction "Thou shalt not kill," tries to register as a conscientious objector. His appeals rejected, he vows to take to the hills to fight. Realizing the contradiction of his position, he meekly goes off to boot camp. York's years of squirrel hunting pay off on the rifle range, where he dazzles everyone; but he doubts he could actually kill anybody. His major, deeply impressed with the sincerity of York's beliefs, sends him home on a ten-day furlough to think things over. But the major orders him to read, along with the Bible, a history of the United States, the story of a "whole people's struggle to be free."

On a lonely ridge York spends a day and night debating the conflicting demands of the Bible and a war for democracy. Finally he finds a way to reconcile his dilemma: the verse in which Christ tells his followers to render unto Caesar that which is Caesar's and unto God that which is God's. York returns to the army and soon is off to France and heroism. That resolution seemed neat enough in 1941, but it rang hollow for screenwriter Koch in retrospect. "If you render unto all the Caesars, past and present, what they demand of us, there is little left for God," he pointed out. "They get what they want—power, glory, money, or whatever—and He comes out on the short end." But interventionists in 1941, convinced that civilization was on the line, did not muse on Koch's percipient point. For them the cause of Caesar was the cause of God.[46]

Hollywood and Washington exploited *Sergeant York* for all it was worth. Warners built a huge publicity campaign around the film. The Astor Theatre was adorned with a four-story caricature of Cooper/York in which 15,000 flashing red, white, and blue lights changed from a "hillbilly carrying a squirrel gun to a soldier carrying a rifle." For the premiere York marched down Broadway, escorted by an honor guard of World War I veterans. The premiere audience included such luminaries as Eleanor Roosevelt, General John "Black Jack" Pershing, General Lewis B. Hershey (selective service director), the 1940 Republican president nominee Wendell Willkie, and Time, Inc., publisher Henry Luce. York was whisked to the White House for an audience with Roosevelt. The sergeant and the commander-in-chief both liked the movie, except for the killing. For young men who got the message that they, like York, should go off and fight for democracy, the army was ready with an eight-page pamphlet on the hero and a hard sell of recruitment material.[47]

Sergeant York capped an evolution in American motion pictures, that took them from being fearful of political subjects to being aggressively interventionist. From the viewpoint of Lowell Mellett and his colleagues, interested as they were in building support for their chief's policies, the result could scarcely have been better. If we take a less partisan stance, however, the progress of events is less ideal. On the one hand, Hollywood came to treat these subjects rather late in the day—in 1939, on the eve of the outbreak of World War II. Other media had given these issues serious, sustained attention for years. Breen's long shears pruned untold feet of political commentary and exacted an unknown toll in self-censorship. Hollywood's boldness was inversely proportional to the extent of its German and Italian market. On the other hand, when the industry did tackle these subjects, it presented only one point of view: varying shades of interventionism. This stood in sharp contast to other media, especially print with its diversely owned sources, where non-interventionist views received attention, although not necessarily in proportion to its following. The oligopolistic structure of the movie industry produced a monolithic political product. This distortion of the leading forum of popular culture angered the isolationists. It should have aroused others as well, but when the isolationists tackled the issue in 1941, their partisan bungling sabotaged what might have been an occasion for serious public reflection about the structure of the industry and its role in propaganda.

As audiences flocked to see *Sergeant York,* in the summer of

1941 the isolationists came after Hollywood in earnest. Wheeler charged that the studios were forcing employees to attend pro-war rallies. He was apparently infuriated by an episode in which Col. Darryl Zanuck led a column of "embattled extras" to an interventionist rally at the Hollywood Bowl. On August 1 Senator Nye launched a full-dress attack in a national radio speech broadcast from St. Louis. Movies "have ceased to be an instrument of entertainment," he cried. They had become agents of propaganda designed "to drug the reason of the American people" and "rouse the war fever in America." Films did not show men "crouching in the mud ... English, Greek, and German boys disemboweled, blown to bits. You see them merely marching in their bright uniforms, firing the beautiful guns at distant targets." Nye considered the interventionist message especially insidious in motion pictures because, expecting entertainment and not politics, audiences had their guard down:

> When you go to the movies, you go there to be entertained. . . . And then the picture starts—goes to work on you, all done by trained actors, full of drama, cunningly devised. . . . Before you know where you are you have actually listened to a speech designed to make you believe that Hitler is going to get you.

This was nonsense, said Nye. America's peril actually was lessening. This was a war "to make the world safe for Empire and Communism.[48]

Nye sensed two sinister forces behind the propaganda pictures. One was the Roosevelt administration, which he believed pressured Hollywood to "glorify" war so that the public would readily accept intervention. The other element was monopoly control. He reasoned that the industry was dominated by a handful of men, who allowed only their own views to grace the screen; their attitudes were buttressed, in turn, by the importance of the British commonwealth market. Hollywood swarmed with foreign actors and directors, chiefly British. To them, he felt, only pro-British pictures were acceptable. Nye demanded: "Are you ready to send your boys to bleed and die in Europe to make the world safe for this industry and its financial backers?[49]

Nye had reassembled the cast of conspirators he flayed so effectively in his "merchants of death" hearings of 1934–36.

Those hearings also stressed the role of skillful British propaganda in preparing America for war. Nye's prairie-bred xenophobia now discovered a new cabal. Reflecting the great power attributed to Hollywood both by its press agents and its alarmed critics, Nye elevated motion picture propaganda to top villain. Just as legions of moral crusaders blamed the movie colony for the corruption of American morals, Nye regarded Hollywood even more than Wall Street as the venue for those who would destroy traditional American isolationism. Nye predicted to a fellow America Firster that the investigation of Hollywood would be "just dandy."[50]

But 1941 was not 1934; World War II was not a crusade to disillusion the nation; and many Americans did think Hitler was going to get them. Nye's remake of the isolationist classic "merchants of death" would have a disastrous run.

Never one to shrink from exercising his prerogatives, Chairman Wheeler stacked the subcommittee with isolationists. Its head was D. Worth Clark, an Idaho Democrat, who proved to be somewhat ineffectual. His fellow isolationist Democrat, Homer Bone of Washington, was too ill to attend. The Republicans were C. Wayland Brooks of Illinois, and Charles W. Tobey of New Hampshire, who attracted attention by his nervous manner of "making dainty thrusts with his cigarette . . . as though he were giving the hot foot to invisible pixies." The lone administration loyalist was Ernest McFarland, a freshman Democrat from Arizona.[51]

Nye was the committee's first witness. In an emotional voice he read a florid forty-one page statement which contributed to his undoing. He sharpened his attack on Jewish control of the industry. He claimed to think it was "quite natural" that American Jews would support a foreign policy directed against their oppressors. "Many people seem to assume," he continued, "that our Jewish citizenry would willingly have our country and its sons taken into this foreign war." He felt it was better to have these "whisperings" out in the open, but claimed that he remained fervently opposed to "the injection of anti-Semitism . . . in American thinking and acting.[52]

The industry's first reaction was to revert to its time-worn defense of "pure entertainment." Hays angled for an appointment with Roosevelt to try to "prove that pictures are *not* being used for defense." But Lowell Mellett, the presidential aide who would play a key role in the battles between the Office of War Information and Hollywood, advised the president not to see Hays. Some of the "best men" in the industry were tired of Hays's tactics, Mellett said. They wanted to come out and say unequivocally that they were producing movies "to make America conscious of the national peril." Roosevelt declined to see the aging film spokesman and filed his request under "Boy Scout."[53]

The hearings could not be limited to an analysis of the movies. They were, as the isolationists intended, a forum for the larger question of the advisability of intervention. A leading interventionist group, Fight for Freedom, shrewdly decided to beat the isolationists at their own game of publicity. Ulric Bell, a former journalist who was FFF's executive director, declared that the Wheeler/Nye hearings were "the most barefaced attempt at censorship and racial persecution which has ever been tried in this country." Bell, who like Mellett would figure prominently in OWI's encounter with Hollywood, suggested that the industry hire Willkie as its counsel. Nye retorted that his fellow Republican would soon wish he had "kept his fingers out."[54]

Willkie was an inspired choice, worth his reported fee of $100,000. He had come to national prominence in the mid-1930's as the lawyer for the utility companies that were engaged in a dogged, if losing, fight against the Tennessee Valley Authority, one of the New Deal's proudest achievements. His appearance as counsel for the movie industry symbolized the growing bipartisanship in foreign affairs that doomed the isolationists to a bitter retreat. Unlike his fellow Indianan Will Hays, Willkie counseled the industry to fight. To the 1941 hearings the perpetually rumpled Willkie brought the same verbal dexterity, flair for the dramatic, and disarming directness that had earned him a national following in the fight against TVA. This time he was, with Roosevelt's blessing, defending a powerful industry against an onslaught from the right.[55]

Willkie's strategy suffered an initial setback when the subcommittee's chairman informed him that committee rules prevented him from cross-examining witnesses. Although he had clearly relished the chance to get Nye on the griddle, Willkie, as one wit noted, took his "second major defeat in a year with irrepressible good humor, retiring into a corner with a microphone handy for banter." He also fired off a twenty-six-hundred-word press release in which he denounced Nye's thinking as un-American—the interventionists could give as good as they got—and questioned the legality of the hearings. "If the Committee feels that the racial and geographic background of American citizens is a condition to be investigated, there is no need for the investigation," Willkie thundered. "We frankly state that in the motion-picture industry there are in positions both prominent and inconspicuous, both Nordics and non-Nordics, Jews and gentiles, Protestants and Catholics, native and foreign-born." On the third day of the hearings, after two days of silent but eloquent grimaces, he grabbed a microphone to point up the fact that the committee thus far had not produced any legislation—the ostensible purpose of such hearings—but merely a vague suggestion that Hollywood produce pictures showing "both sides" of international questions. "This, I presume, means that since Chaplin made a laughable caricature of Hitler, the industry should be forced to employ Charles Laughton to do the same on Winston Churchill."[56]

The point was, Willkie continued, "the motion picture industry and its executives are opposed to the Hitler regime . . . we make no pretense of friendliness to Nazi Germany." Hollywood's anti-Nazi pictures were not propaganda but accurate portrayals. He recounted the history of *Escape:* A best-selling novel, it had enjoyed the endorsement of such middle-brow cultural organs as the Book-of-the-Month Club and *Saturday Evening Post.* The film accurately depicted the "incredible cruelties of the Nazis." He "emphatically and indignantly" denied that such films were made at the behest of the Roosevelt administration. "Frankly," he said, "the motion-picture industry would be ashamed if it were not doing voluntarily what it is now doing in this patriotic cause.[57]

Industry officials followed the same line. Harry Warner, whom Nye had accused of producing more propaganda films than any other, proudly announced his opposition to Hitler. Nazism was "an evil force," he said, and "the world struggle for freedom was in its final stage." He advocated fighting side by side with England. The studio's anti-Nazi pictures did not have an ulterior purpose. As for *Sergeant York,* it was "a factual portrayal of the life of one of the great heroes of the last war," Warner said. "If that is propaganda, we plead guilty."[58]

Although denied the services of its cross-examiner, Hollywood gained an ally in Ernest McFarland, who took an unusually combative role for a freshman senator. "McFarland worked on Nye like a censor working on *Lady Chatterly's Lover*," chortled the trade's *Hollywood Reporter*. "Which of these pictures was the most objectionable? . . . " McFarland asked. Nye found it hard to answer. "It is a terrible weakness of mine to go to a picture tonight and not be able to state the title of it tomorrow morning," he said. "Somehow or other I have a rather lasting impression of . . . *I Married a Nazi*." Why was it bad? asked McFarland. Nye said he had not seen the picture "in a long, long time." Perhaps sensing the trap the Arizonan was baiting, Nye said he had relied in part on newspaper reviews. He said he had seen "three or four or five" others, but he could not name them. "Let me see if I can help you a little bit," said McFarland. "Did you see *Escape*?" More than titles had vanished from Nye's memory. Would you tell me a part of the story so I could try to remember? he pleaded. The North Dakotan's flounderings cast doubt on the indelible effects of propaganda.[59]

McFarland pressed after Nye like a school master exposing a student who had not done the day's reading. He enumerated pictures Nye had cited in his St. Louis speech: "*Convoy*. Did you see that picture?"

Nye thought he had.

"Do you remember anything in that picture that was particularly objectionable?"

Nye: "No; I am at a loss to call to mind any particular feature about it that led me to draw the conclusion which I have drawn." *Flight Command*? No. *That Hamilton Woman*? No. *Man Hunt*? No. *Sergeant York*? No.

The Great Dictator? Aha! Nye remembered that one. Why was it objectionable? "Why, it was a portrayal by a great artist, not a citizen of our country, though he has resided here a long, long while, that could not do other than build within the mind and heart of those who watched it something of hatred, detestation of conditions and of leadership that existed abroad."

Confessions of a Nazi Spy? Nye was confused between that and *I Married a Nazi*. "For the life of me I could not tell you which was which," he said. McFarland concluded that he must have based most of his criticisms on what others had told him. "I do not know that I would want to say 'most,'" Nye said weakly. " . . . But certainly the representations of others have played a large part in the conclusions that I have drawn, a considerable part."[60]

The verbal duel between McFarland and Nye turned into a disaster for the isolationists. The North Dakota senator looked ignorant, anti-Semitic, and rather too cavalier about Hitler.

The investigators were soon in full flight. The hearings even elicited useful advertising copy from the non-interventionists. Nye conceded that *Confessions* was an "exceedingly good" film. Tobey rather too generously called *Dive Bomber* "a very fine picture with no propaganda in it." Clark requested that *Flight Command* be striken from the list of questionable films. And *Sergeant York*, said Brooks, called for "allegiance to our country" and was not propaganda.[61]

Willkie's strategy worked brilliantly. Hays's "nothing but entertainment" defense required more than the usual willing suspension of disbelief that one had to apply to the movies. Willkie instead converted the issue from propaganda to a question of fact. He knew that the bulk of Americans, fearing war but abhorring Hitler, shared the movies' empiric view of Nazism. By linking the movies with print media, he made Hollywood appear mild by comparison and yet entitled to the same freedom from federal censorship. And by claiming that the industry was producing portrayals of the "world as it is," he wrapped the studios in the flag of patriotic service. Hollywood emerged as an unlikely hero.

The hearings were adjourned on September 26; on December 8, 1941, one day after Pearl Harbor, Clark announced their abandonment. Since the issue of interventionist propaganda was now moot, no report was issued.

This was a pity. Although the non-interventionist position had little credibility by the fall of 1941, the broad issue of how the movies' messages were determined was of lasting importance. By 1941 moviegoers were receiving a steady, one-sided dose of interventionist propaganda in various guises. The newsreels were strongly interventionist, with material ranging from battle scenes, to a British idyll (Winston Churchill being hailed by the troops or the "Duchess of Kent reviewing her women's corps"), to arms production by the "arsenal of democracy." One or more special defense shorts might follow. Then the feature might take up the chant with an anti-Nazi picture such as *Man Hunt,* idealization of the armed forces such as *Dive Bomber,* or an act of homage to outright involvement such as *A Yank in the R.A.F.* Even a "flyweight comedy" might include a casual but evident crack, as when the hero sneers at a wimpy rival who refuses to fight: "Oh, isolationist, eh?" The problem, in other words, was both smaller and larger than whether movies and newsreels were factually correct or whether interventionism was wise or wicked. The issue was control of the industry and the resulting exclusion of an important political perspective from the screen.[62]

Isolationist journalist John T. Flynn tried to make this point in a sober way during the hearings, but his effort was obscured by Willkie's fireworks. Flynn, who was research director for Nye's munitions investigation, served as associate editor of *Collier's* and chairman of the New York chapter of America First. "Sometimes the worst kind of propaganda is propaganda which is particularly true," he said. The danger stemmed from the reiteration of a single point of view. "There is censorship for you gentlemen to worry about," he said. It was not censorship by the isolationists but by the industry and the Hays office. Flynn had a cure: not censorship but antitrust. "Take that out of the hands of a monopoly," he said. "Break it up."[63]

Liberals, most of whom were interventionists, could agree with this much of Flynn's diagnosis. Attacking Hollywood was easy, said John McManus, film critic for the liberal New York daily *PM.* "It is vulnerable as a nest of monopoly, as a misuser of an artistic trust, as the foster-parent of bingo." The liberal press supported Hollywood not because of the "nobility of the movie magnates" but because "the context of the inquiry" and the isolationists' motivations made it suspect, said *The Nation.* "The films are still subject to the worst kind of censorship," it continued, "the censorship of private bigots." Norman Cousins of *Saturday Review* recalled that, until the pioneering *Confessions of a Nazi Spy,* Hollywood ignored Nazism almost entirely, even though "that material happened to represent a living drama that had already become a tragedy for millions of people." The liberal press thought the real subject of an investigation should have been the industry's internal censorship which had left it strangely mute for so long on the issue of fascism.[64]

Many people in Hollywood hoped the international crisis would bring about more social and political awareness in the movies. In *Foreign Affairs* Walter Wanger argued it was time to win "permanent and inviolable freedom of speech on the American screen." This would include the right to advocate social reforms, plead for peace, and "expound, emphasize and proclaim the virtues of the true American way."[65] Freedom of the screen still lay well in the future. Nevertheless, building on the interventionist footing belatedly dug in 1939–41, motion picture crews went on to create the most explicitly political films in Hollywood's history. Their chief concern was proclaiming "the virtues of the true American way"—a subject that sparked enormous controversy. Hollywood opinion overwhelmingly rejected isolationism in private, and, after the Senate hearings, found the isolationists an irresistible public target. Beyond that theme, the interpretation of America and the war was up for grabs. The industry watched with a mixture of eagerness and wariness as the Roosevelt administration tried to sort out what propaganda role Hollywood ought to play. The task eventually fell to the Office of War Information, which brought to the movie colony its rival production code.

III.

Will This Picture Help Win the War?

Does the picture tell the truth or will the young people of today have reason to say they were misled by propaganda?

—"Government Information
Manual for the Motion
Picture Industry," June 1942.

Americans during the period 1939 to 1945 confronted the possibilities of propaganda uneasily. Access to information is crucial to democratic citizenship; hence Americans have usually regarded propaganda, with its connotations of tainted information, with suspicion. Yet since total war requires mass mobilization, democratic governments find propaganda machines indispensable in maintaining civilian and military morale. The prominent political scientist Harold Lasswell wrote in 1927 that government management of opinion is an inescapable "corollary of large scale modern war." Some viewed propaganda as a positive alternative to coercion of the population.[1]

But for large numbers of Americans between 1939 and 1945, the World War I legacy reinforced the sense of propaganda as something alien and sinister. In 1917–18 the Committee on Public Information, better known as the "Creel Committee" for its chairman, progressive journalist George Creel, mounted a propaganda campaign that remains in some ways unsurpassed in the United States. The committee blanketed the country with posters, pamphlets, and "four-minute men," who gave rousing patriotic speeches in theaters and other public places. Creel could take some credit for whipping up nationalistic fervor to a frenzy—and much of the blame as well for its side effects: a "hate the Hun" campaign that contributed to distorted perceptions, persecution of German-Americans, and disillusionment after the war. During the 1930s the antagonism to propaganda was reinforced by the suspicion that British propaganda had helped maneuver the country into war in 1917.[2]

When war broke out in Europe on September 1, 1939, the United States was the only major power without a propaganda agency. The ubiquity and excesses of Soviet and Nazi propaganda were well known, as were their extraordinary successes. Josef Goebbels, proponent of the "big lie" technique, could claim some credit for both the extraordinary unity of the German people and the disarray of some of the Reich's neighbors. Propaganda had gone international by the late 1930's; not only Germany and the Soviet Union, but Italy, Japan, and Great Britain used various media to advance their causes beyond their borders. The sudden collapse of France in the spring of 1940 lent credence to hopes and fears about the possibilities of propaganda, for many observers attributed the republic's fall to a loss of will, induced in part by Nazi propaganda. Concern mounted that stronger efforts needed to be made to awaken faith in democratic values and awareness of their vulnerability.[3]

Film became an instrument of propaganda in its early years. Lenin considered film "the most important art," and popes, presidents, and press agents concurred. During World War I American films such as *The Beast of Berlin* and *My Four Years in Germany* touched off anti-German riots in some cities. D. W. Griffith turned his masterful touch to Allied propaganda with *Hearts of the World,* starring Lillian Gish, in 1918. The Soviet Union had its propaganda masterpieces such as Sergei Eisenstein's *Potemkin* while Nazi Germany could boast of Leni Riefenstahl's *Triumph of the Will.* In any consideration of propaganda, film took a leading role.[4]

Propaganda is a bit like pornography—hard to define but most people think they will know it when they see it. A widely accepted definition holds that "propaganda is the expression of opinions or actions carried out deliberately by individuals or groups with a view to influencing the opinions or actions of other individuals or groups for predetermined ends and through psychological manipulations." This broad definition, which emphasizes conscious efforts to influence opinion, is to be contrasted with education, which endeavors to present a more balanced discussion of all sides of the issues. Propaganda, as the French critic Jacques Ellul notes, is a pervasive aspect of modern life, particularly industrialized societies. It often has a factual, rational base; but the steady, pervasive repetition of this type of information creates a field from which the individual finds it hard to stand back and form an independent judgment.[5]

President Roosevelt, the consummate media politician of his day, tried to influence public opinion through his speeches and his manipulation of the news media. In part because of his efforts, the non-interventionist position never received equal time or space. He also employed the apparatus of the federal government, including J. Edgar Hoover's Federal Bureau of Investigation, to harass and discredit his opponents. But Roosevelt was loath to get too far in front of public opinion. Remembering the costly fallout from his "quarantine the aggressors" speech of 1937 and the dismal results when he tried to purge conservative Democratic senators in 1938, he did not want to risk his political capital in premature forays. In particular he wanted to avoid anything that looked like preparation for American intervention in the war before he was re-elected in 1940. He also remembered the criticism heaped on Woodrow Wilson and George Creel for the excesses of World War I propaganda. Too much blatant propaganda could well trigger a backlash that would undermine rather than advance his policy, and it would certainly create a furor on both sides of the aisle in Congress. As a result, propaganda policy evolved from a typically Rooseveltian melange of caution, indirection, duplication, half-measures, and ambiguity. By the fall of 1941 FDR had created a thicket of competing, overlapping agencies, none of them with a clear mandate.[6]

Roosevelt took his first step toward an official propaganda agency in late 1939 when he signed an executive order creating a new bureau with an ostentatiously innocuous name: the Office of Government Reports (OGR). Called "OGRE" by its critics, OGR employed a strategy of informational propaganda.

OGR was limited to serving as a clearing house for information about the defense program, whose operations were burgeoning, and to informing the executive branch about public opinion. The agency, for the most part, disseminated accurate, neutral information, while withholding adverse news. This information was placed in a context designed to build public confidence about America's growing military power. OGR's implicit intent was to create an atmosphere of assurance that would bolster the president's unfolding international policy. The office assumed that if such information were readily available, the private media could be counted on to use it—a strategy that worked well.[7]

OGR's head was Lowell Mellett, former editor of the *Washington Daily News,* now a presidential assistant. Mellett resigned from the Scripps-Howard chain because of its strident opposition to Roosevelt, whom he deeply admired. Though not a forceful personality—he picked up the nickname "white rabbit"—he kept FDR's loyalty. Mellett and his agency aroused considerable controversy. Congressional conservatives feared the agency would be a New Deal election vehicle and refused to fund it. Roosevelt had to reach into his own office funds to operate what became known as "Mellett's Madhouse." In 1940, however, Mellett successfully defended his budget request before Congress, and OGR became a fully funded part of the defense effort. Mellett went on to play a key role in the evolution of propaganda strategy in the film industry.[8]

FDR took a more explicit propaganda role in Latin America. In August 1940 he created by executive order the Office of the Coordinator of Inter-American Affairs (CIAA). This was safer for the president, since it involved foreign affairs rather than domestic politics. Roosevelt worried about Nazi penetration of the hemisphere—he circulated dubious maps showing a German attack on the United States working its way up from the bulge of Brazil—and made hemispheric defense a priority. The Office's head was John D. Rockefeller's grandson, Nelson D. Rockefeller. Film played an important part in CIAA's propaganda strategy. Its Motion Picture Division was headed by John Hay Whitney, Rockefeller's fellow multimillionaire and an important financial backer of *Gone With the Wind.* Whitney's money, connections, and experience in Hollywood gave him easy access to the top echelons of the movie colony.[9]

Roosevelt still moved cautiously on the domestic front. He took a tentative step in March 1941 when he signed an executive order to create a Division of Information within the Office of Emergency Management (OEM). This agency continued the informational propaganda strategy. Heading the division was Robert Horton, an aggressive former Scripps-Howard editor. Horton's division operated a central press room where Washington correspondents could get their fill of news releases and similar material on OEM's sixteen mobilization agencies. It also published *Defense*, a slick weekly magazine about American rearmament.[10]

OEM's Division of Information could not satisfy a coterie of administration interventionists, who advocated an inspirational propaganda agency. By March 1941, with FDR re-elected and the Blitz against Britain still raging, interventionists pushed for a strong propaganda agency. They argued that conscription, the recently passed Lend-Lease bill, and a military buildup were not enough. As Secretary of the Interior Harold L. Ickes put it: "I do not believe that armaments will be of much use to us if we do not have the will to use them and an understanding of why we are expected to use them." Vice President Henry A. Wallace even advocated borrowing heavily from Goebbels' tactics. The proponents of a much enhanced propaganda mission included such administration heavyweights as Secretary of War Henry Stimson, Secretary of the Navy Frank Knox, Attorney General Francis Biddle, Secretary of Labor Frances Perkins, and Assistant Secretary of War John J. McCloy.[11]

Some administration figures, chiefly Mellett and presidential press secretary Stephen B. Early, countered that it would be wiser to stick with informational propaganda. Reflecting their experience as journalists, they believed the disadvantages of inspirational propaganda outweighed its benefits. "There can be no government propaganda operating in behalf of national policy," Mellett said, "until there is an accepted national policy." The types of propaganda agencies being proposed were designed "to force action by Congress," but that would be bitterly resented on the Hill. The American news media were the best in the world, he believed. In areas where their reports were still carried, such as Latin America, they had a credibility unmatched by those of any other nation. Heavy-handed propaganda influence in these channels could only undermine their effectiveness. He was confident, in any case, that the tide of pub-lic opinion was running with the president, as evidenced by the acceptance of peacetime conscription and Lend-Lease. He ar-gued that the informational propaganda strategy of moving slowly and waiting for the public to recognize "conditions as they are" paid long-run dividends.[12]

Mellet's confidence in the success of the informational strat-egy reflected his reading of the pro-interventionist tenor of most news coverage in 1940–41. Hollywood movies and newsreels that dealt with international subjects were almost wholly inter-ventionist. On radio the equation was "completely in our fa-vor," Mellett found; only controversial speeches were evenly balanced. (The influence of the Federal Communications Com-mission was at work. Stations had to carry replies to controver-sial speeches because of the FCC's "fairness doctrine," but in other areas stations were aware that the Roosevelt administra-tion appointed FCC commissioners, who gave and withheld li-censes.) The press was more of a problem, which he attributed to publishers' antipathy towards the president. Even here, how-ever, the tide was turning. Except for "the naturally bad ele-ments," the press was "seeking ways of getting gracefully into line," Mellett said. "We can soon have the great majority com-mitted even to the point of enforcing some restraint of their own on the bad elements." This interventionist domination of the news media, attributable in part to the informational prop-aganda strategy, undercut the presumed need for more forceful propaganda—and indeed raised questions about the even-handedness of the media.[13]

The administration's efforts were augmented by private anti-isolationist groups. The best known was the Committee to De-fend America by Aiding the Allies, headed by William Allen White, the Kansas newspaper editor. After the White committee helped secure passage of early measures to aid Britain, the or-ganization lost its leadership position to Fight for Freedom, a more militant group composed of interventionist writers, jour-nalists, and clergymen. FFF sought an immediate declaration of war against Germany. Because of its extensive contacts with well-placed journalists, by mid-1941 FFF's message could be seen in countless newspapers and magazines, heard on nationwide radio hookups, and encountered at public rallies, petition drives, and street corner rallies. FFF tried to discredit major isolationist figures by giving them "the image of a Nazi, a Fascist sympathizer, or a dupe of the Axis." FFF's executive director was Ulric Bell, the aggressive former Washington bureau chief of the well regarded *Louisville Courier-Journal.* He later joined the Office of War Information in 1942 and carried his sharply anti-isolationist views to Hollywood, where he exercised great influence as OWI's overseas representative from late 1942 through 1943.[14]

The advocates of inspirational propaganda hoped their wishes were answered when the president created the Office of Civilian Defense (OCD) on May 20, 1941. He chose a political star to head the agency—Fiorello La Guardia, mayor of New York City. The "Little Flower" could deliver a flag-waving speech with the best of them. But his duties as mayor of the nation's largest city, chairman of the Permanent Joint Board on Defense of Canada-United States, plus a re-election campaign, left little time for a man of even his super-human energies. The efforts La Guardia devoted to his new job were limited chiefly to civilian protection, not morale-building. The Office of Civilian Defense became one of the most criticized preparedness agencies in the government.[15]

Made of much sterner stuff was the neutrally named Office of the Coordinator of Information (COI), created by executive order in July 1941. This represented Roosevelt's commitment to agitational propaganda or psychological warfare. After a long fact-finding trip for the navy, William "Wild Bill" Donovan convinced his old friend FDR that the United States needed an intelligence agency for foreign missions. COI would not only gather intelligence but engage in covert actions. Donovan's clandestine menu included black propaganda, the equivalent of what we now call disinformation—deliberate use of rumor, deception, and lies to generate confusion and defeatism among the enemy. Donovan intended to use propaganda as "primarily an attack weapon . . . often having with it the flavor of subversion." He saw propaganda as "the arrow of initial penetration in conditioning and preparing the people" for invasion, followed by fifth column work, commandos, and then invading troops. Such tactics demanded close coordination with the military services, and hence tight security. These activities could not be linked with a domestic propaganda agency, he argued, for that would compromise security, impair the effectiveness of psychological warfare campaigns, and "expose our plans and our methods to the enemy." The creation of COI was momentous, for it was the predecessor of the wartime Office of Strategic Services which, in turn, spawned the Central Intelligence Agency.[16]

Thrust into COI a month later was Robert Sherwood, who convinced his friend Roosevelt that the United States needed a voice abroad to counter the anti-American propaganda broadcast by the Axis. FDR authorized Sherwood to set up the Foreign Information Service within Donovan's COI. Sherwood's bureau eventually became the Voice of America. The playwright recruited leading talents, such as director-producer John Houseman, writers Thornton Wilder and Stephen Vincent Benét, journalist Joseph Barnes, and banker James P. Warburg. Sherwood promoted a strategy of inspirational propaganda that touted the glories of democracy and the American way of life. He also believed, however, that one of democracy's effective weapons was to admit failures as well as to glorify successes. He did not want to move into the agitational propaganda that Donovan favored.[17]

By the fall of 1941 the confusion in the propaganda and information sectors was intolerable. Criticism rose on all sides. Army Chief of Staff George C. Marshall complained of low morale among draftees, which he traced to apathy in the general public. FDR chose a temporary solution. He took away the morale-boosting functions from La Guardia's agency and placed them in a newly formed Office of Facts and Figures (OFF). Heading OFF on a part-time basis was Archibald MacLeish, the prominent poet and librarian of Congress. Ulric Bell became assistant director. The organization built a talented staff that included such people as Pulitzer Prize historian Henry Pringle and writer Malcolm Cowley.[18]

La Guardia and MacLeish took pains to disabuse reporters of the most obvious fact about OFF—that it was a propaganda agency. "There are three reasons why it is not," the mayor said. "The first is that we don't believe in this country in artificially stimulated high-pressure, doctored nonsense, and since we

don't, the other two reasons are unimportant." MacLeish insisted that OFF's sole purpose was to convey accurate information that would be neither "perverted nor colored." He
promised to avoid "bally-hoo methods." Unlike totalitarian
states, democracies could "take the people into the confidence
of the government," he said. OFF's job was to clarify and co-
ordinate, "to provide a basis for judgment," not to "control or
regulate." MacLeish promised, in short, what he called a "strategy of truth."[10]

Perhaps. No one expected MacLeish to turn into a Goebbels,
but suspicions lingered. Arthur Krock, the flinty Washington
correspondent of the *New York Times,* cautioned: "If OFF pipes
out the undiluted, uncolored facts, it will be the first government information bureau to do that." And in an editorial slyly
titled "Here's Where We Get OFF," the *New York Herald Tribune*
mused: "OFF is just going to superimpose its own 'well orga-
nized facts' upon the splendid confusion, interpret the interpreters, redigest those who now digest the digesters, explain
what those who explain what the explainers of the explanations
mean, co-ordinate the co-ordinators of those appointed to co-
ordinate the co-ordinations of the co-ordinated." There was no
ignoring the fact that OFF was set up to promote a particular
line of policy and that its "undoctored" facts would be placed
in a field bounded by those perceptions. OFF, while ostensibly
relying on information methods, represented a solid step into
the realm of inspirational propaganda.[20]

Pearl Harbor freed Roosevelt to deal forthrightly with the
propaganda situation. His first important step was to appoint
Lowell Mellett coordinator of government films on December
17, 1941. Motion pictures could be one of the most effective
tools in "informing" the public, FDR's executive order read. Besides overseeing the government's war-related films, Mellett was
to establish liaison with Hollywood and insure that the studios
implemented their pledge to help the war effort. OGR and later
OWI had no censorship power per se over Hollywood films. But
the filmland trade paper *Variety* presciently anticipated that
Mellett would attempt to have the industry "insert morale-building and citizenry-arousing themes in its films to promote the
war effort."[21]

Although Mellett's appointment made sense to Washington,

he was an unknown to Hollywood. *Variety* suggested two alternatives: Jock Whitney, who was well connected in the industry and wanted the job, or John Ford, the director, who had signed on with Donovan's Committee on Information. Mellett made a get-acquainted trip to Hollywood in mid-January 1942. Addressing a gathering of the War Activities Committee of the Motion Picture Industry, Mellett reaffirmed his belief in freedom of the screen. He praised the industry for alerting Americans to the danger of fascism, even before the war: "You couldn't have done more in your efforts to educate people. The government, of course, was pleased but we were unable to advertise what you were doing. Some misguided people [the Wheeler-Nye investigation] advertised the job you did. . . . Now we can help you in your work." The former journalist was perhaps too lavish in his praise of Hollywood's interventionist pictures, but he effectively stroked the out-sized egos in his audience.[22]

Mellett in effect proposed a deal. He wanted his office to be the clearing house for *all* dealings between the studios and the government. While this made administrative sense and was consistent with Roosevelt's order, it planted the seeds of a critical conflict, for the military branches would fight Mellett's coordination. In return the OGR chief promised to respect the interests of commercial theaters. Some twelve thousand theaters had agreed to accept any picture—chiefly shorts—bearing the seal of the War Activities Committee. "We have been mindful, and will continue to be, of the interests of the theatre owners," Mellett said. This was a fateful decision. Many industries, such as steel and automobiles, saw their entire production diverted from civilian to war-related goods. A takeover of part of Hollywood's production was contemplated by some government officials, notably by M. E. Gilfond, the Justice Department's public relations chief, and officers in the War Department's public relations branch. Mellett, however, reasoning by analogy from his newspaper experience, believed that the studios would cooperate with the propaganda program if the government did not interfere with the box office. Thus the propagandists and the movie makers embarked on an uneasy flirtation. The government needed Hollywood, but too much propaganda could wreck the movies' entertainment appeal— the very thing that made the studios attractive to the propagandists. On the other hand, the film makers sincerely wanted to cooperate, but not at the risk of hurting their profits. The struggle over the respective spheres of government and Hollywood reflected the difficulty in resolving the clashing imperatives of politics, profits, and propaganda.[23]

In April 1942 Mellett set up a Hollywood office. Heading the branch was Nelson Poynter, who was also unknown to the movie colony. Poynter, the thirty-nine-year-old publisher of the *St. Petersburg Times* and close friend of Mellett, did not follow movies. Mellett thought that his political understanding—Poynter too was an interventionist New Dealer—was more important than movie expertise. Poynter bent to his task eagerly, arriving in Hollywood in late spring and beginning a round of conferences with studio heads, producers, directors, and writers.[24]

The movie liaison office came under the Domestic Branch of the Office of War Information (OWI) when it was created in June 1942. Despite repeated appeals from MacLeish to clear up the propaganda "Tower of Babel," Roosevelt procrastinated until late spring. The Bureau of the Budget told him he simply could not go to the Hill with a budget that requested $41.7 million for five quarreling, overlapping agencies. That got the president's attention. He created OWI as an amalgam of all the propaganda bureaus except two. Displaying the colossal ambition epitomized in his remark "I never wanted to be *vice* president of anything," Nelson Rockefeller threatened to resign if CIAA came under OWI. The State Department backed him and his agency retained its independence. FDR also accepted Donovan's contention that the black propaganda and covert action he contemplated should not be part of a civilian morale agency because of possible security leaks. The Donovan organization began its growth into the free-wheeling OSS. Sherwood's Foreign Information Service was split off from Donovan's group, however, and became the core of OWI's Overseas Branch.[25]

Roosevelt wanted to announce the director of OWI at the same time he established the agency. Various names circulated, among them radio commentators Elmer Davis, Edward R. Murrow, William L. Shirer, Rex Stout, and Byron Price, head of the Associated Press. MacLeish, though agreeing to stay on for a time to head the domestic branch, took himself out of the running for the directorship. Roosevelt settled on the radio commentator "with the funny voice. Elmer—Elmer something." Davis, a novelist and journalist, had moved from isolationism to intervention. His commonsense views, delivered in the flat, slightly nasal Hoosier voice that the patrician president found slightly peculiar, inspired confidence. On June 13, 1942, the White House announced the creation of OWI and the appointment of its chief, Elmer Davis. The presidential order instructed OWI to undertake campaigns to enhance public understanding of the war at home and abroad; to coordinate government information activities; and to handle liaison with the press, radio, and motion pictures. Davis confessed he "felt like a man who had married a wartime widow and was trying to raise her children by all her previous husbands."[26]

He had inherited an unruly brood, one prone to get into embarrassing fights with the neighbors. To deal with films OWI relied on the Bureau of Motion Pictures (BMP), which had been transferred from the Office of Government Reports with Mellett as BMP chief. As part of OWI's Domestic Branch, the Bureau through its Washington office supervised the production of government propaganda shorts. The previously established Hollywood office, run by assistant chief Nelson Poynter, handled the volatile relations with the motion picture industry. OWI was not the Creel committee resurrected. Having learned from the experience of the World War I agency, the Roosevelt administration wisely separated the realms of propaganda and censorship. A separate Office of Censorship, headed by Byron Price, oversaw censorship of incoming and outgoing mail, films, and like material. The White House and the military services, through their control of information, exercised their own censorship. OWI officials had also learned that hate propaganda was counterproductive and that something more than flag-waving emotional pitches was necessary. That meant an emphasis on understanding the issues of the war—as OWI interpreted them. When asked what OWI's strategy would be, Davis replied simply "to tell the truth." Like MacLeish, Sherwood, and others, he believed that a strategy of providing accurate data would rally Americans and foreigners alike to the Allied cause. As might have been expected, however, "truth" and "accuracy" were elusive guidelines for a body of ideologically committed people at war. Deliberate falsification might be rare, but OWI was as interested in establishing a context of interpretation as it was in disseminating information.[27]

The ads were lurid even by Hollywood standards. A huge Japanese figure, blood dripping from its buck-toothed fangs, rose from the sea. His octopus tentacles swatted American planes from mid-air and crushed American ships on the high seas. Book now, the ad urged film distributors. Universal's hot new special, *Menace of the Rising Sun*, chronicled "Japan's Double Decade of Double Dealing." The film would tell Americans for the first time how "Japs repaid kindness with ruthless murder," how "Jap militarists played their filthy game of treachery," and how the "Japs had planned for years to stab the United States in the back." To Universal the nation of the Rising Sun was nothing other than the "Beast of the East."[28]

The blatantly racist *Menace of the Rising Sun* was representative of the latest swing in the picture cycle. In a mirror image of Hollywood's aversion to international themes before 1939, the movie industry now rushed to exploit the war as a backdrop for all sorts of pictures. The war became an all-purpose dramatic device capable of motivating any range of human emotion. The war itself took center stage in 72 pictures that OWI analysts classified as "war features" between December 1, 1941, and July 24, 1942.[29]

Hollywood's instant analysis embroidered the "stab-in-the-back" thesis. America was at war because the Japanese, conniving for years, attacked Pearl Harbor—nothing more. The drama of Pearl Harbor lent itself to movie colony formulae. Here was gangsterism on an international scale with America cast in the role of outraged innocent.

In picture after picture the legends grew. Twentieth Century-Fox issued *Secret Agent of Japan* starring Preston Foster and Lynn Bari. Foster is a disgruntled American running a cafe in Shanghai. Always ready to sell information to the highest bidder, he is convinced by Bari that he must join the war against Japan because he is an American. To OWI the film was "strictly the old spy hocus-pocus." The enemy is depicted as brutal and treacherous, but his "motives and ideology" are not examined. *Variety*, as OWI, found the film unconvincing and noted that "some of the Japs used in the pic act and look like fugitives from a Chinese laundry."[30]

OWI analysts found a repetitive pattern as they sat through screening after screening. *A Prisoner of Japan* (PRC, July 1942) dwelt on "the sadistic cruelty of the Japs, who kill an innocent native boy and a wounded American Naval officer for no apparent purpose other than to satisfy their blood-lust." *Remember Pearl Harbor* (Republic, 1942), which continued the stab-in-the-back refrain, was "totally unrealistic and quite devoid of any merit." *Danger in the Pacific* (Universal, 1942), told of American-British cooperation in discovering enemy bases in the jungles of "Paragelean." The enemy was "fiendish and diabolical." To reviewers for OWI the film obviously acquired its war significance "tardily and superficially; it might have been better if it had not acquired any at all." In *Halfway to Shanghai* (1942), Universal presented Burma as a "sturdy, self-reliant bulwark against Nippon." While the propaganda agency believed the film to be "fairly intelligent," it deplored the characterization of the Chinese as "silly, giggling, ridiculous" buffoons. The enemy were "the usual fanatic, Heil Hitlering heavies" and brutal "Japs." The film failed, however, because by the time of its release, Burma was under Japanese control.[31]

These anti-Japanese films represented only a small slice of war-related subjects. The war—that versatile, all-purpose dramatic device, capable of initiating any action in a variety of infinitely exotic backgrounds—fulfilled Hollywood's fondest dreams. In the movie makers' ceaseless quest for variety and spectacle, the war was a godsend. The studios quickly grafted the war upon their traditional formula pictures: gangster stories, screwball comedies, frothy musicals. Even Tarzan, isolated in his jungle fastness, enlisted for the Allies.

In *Tarzan Triumphs* (RKO, 1942) Nazi agents parachute into Tarzan's peaceful kingdom and occupy a fortress, hoping to exploit oil and tin. Johnny Weissmuller, a slightly flabby but still commanding noble savage, rallies his natives (all of whom are white) against the Axis. "Kill Nadzies!" Tarzan commands the natives. They nod eagerly. The Germans are so despicable even the animals turn against them. Tarzan chases the head of the Nazi troops into the jungle, and, just as the fear-crazed German officer frantically signals Berlin on his shortwave radio, Tarzan kills him. In Berlin the radio operator recognizes the distress signal and rushes out to summon the general in charge of the African operation. While Tarzan, Boy, and Jungle Priestess laughingly look on, Cheetah the chimp chatters into the transmitter. Ignorant of the fatal struggle in the jungle depths, the general hears the chimp on the radio, jumps to his feet, salutes, and yells to his subordinates that they are listening not to Africa but to Der Fuehrer.[32]

The Devil With Hitler was similar fare. In this Hal Roach slapstick comedy Hell's board of directors decides that Hitler should replace the devil. The tall, well-groomed Satan, who was spent a lifetime building his power in Hell, does not want a "flash in the pan like Hitler" usurping his position. He becomes Hitler's valet, and, after a great deal of difficulty, forces him to release two prisoners. By making Hitler do a "good deed" the devil could return to his rightful position as ruler of Hell. Mussolini appears as a pathetic tool of Hitler; a sneaky, simpering "Suki Yaki" enacts the stock Japanese.[33]

The Daring Young Man epitomized for OWI many of Hollywood's worst faults. The film turned racketeers into Nazi spies and used the war as background material for a grade "B" comedy. Playing the role of Jonathan Peckinpaw, Joe E. Brown wants to impress his girlfriend by joining the armed forces but is refused by all three branches because he is too short. To build himself up he starts bowling. He becomes an overnight sensation when a local gambler uses him as a stooge for a trick radio-controlled ball. Three Nazi agents discover they can send messages to German subs while standing near Peckinpaw when he bowls. FBI agents expose the farce and Peckinpaw is disgraced. But he redeems himself by single-handedly capturing the Nazis and winning the intertwined rewards of love of girlfriend and love of country: He is accepted into the army.[34]

A series of musicals appropriated the war for a backdrop as if it were simply the newest set on the backlot. Movies like *True to the Army, Star Spangled Rhythm*, and *The Yanks Are Coming* linked military uniforms and tearful goodbyes with typical musical hijinks. These pictures reflected Hollywood's insatiable appetite for novelty and its tendency to appropriate any noncontroversial subject for immediate commercial purposes.

But would these pictures help win the war? Emphatically

not, said OWI analysts. They found this trend in the picture cycle deeply disturbing. Despite the flood of anti-Axis films, no picture yet produced would "give us a true picture of our enemy," contended Dorothy Jones, OWI's chief film analyst, in July 1942. Virtually everything about the war was missing or muddled, she thought. Serious treatment of the war issues—whether in their international or domestic aspects—was all but nonexistent. If these pictures were Hollywood's down payment on its pledge to help the war effort, OWI intended to up the ante. The industry needed strong coaching, Nelson Poynter advised, to "raise its sights."[35]

"U.S. Will 'Cue' Hollywood," reported *Variety* in early May 1942. Poynter set up an office in the Taft Building at the corner of Hollywood and Vine, the crossroads of the movie colony. Plunging into a busy round of conferences with producers, directors, and writers, he sometimes attended fifteen story conferences in a week. Poynter's biggest problem at first, he recalled, was to convince the studios that he had no censorship power. He told the movie makers that the government simply wanted to help them fulfill their stated goals of boosting the war effort, and that he wished to be helpful. He downplayed informational shorts and stressed the importance of incorporating the government message in feature films. OWI could be most helpful in this process if it got to review scripts before production began. Poynter reassured the studios that the agency could not demand scripts and tried to keep his request on a basis of cooperation.[36]

The shift from shorts to features was important. While willing to produce four- to ten-minute information films on victory gardens, rubber conservation, or tank production, the industry was very uneasy about larding entertainment pictures with explicit propaganda themes. The studio moguls had definite ideas about what worked at the box office, and they resisted outsiders tampering with their time-proven formula. As *Variety* quoted an unidentified studio executive: "We don't want people whom we would not employ, because they are not qualified through experience and training, telling us what to do." The industry continued to fear that, whatever OWI's promises, the government would impose some form of censorship.[37]

OWI preferred to convert Hollywood, not censor it. The

agency hoped the studios would make some serious films dramatizing the issues of the war, such as the Four Freedoms. But OWI hoped to capitalize on the artfulness of Hollywood and the susceptibility of movie audiences, "spellbound in the darkness," to insinuate its message into the minds of an unsuspecting public. As Director Elmer Davis put it: "The easiest way to inject a propaganda idea into most people's minds is to let it go in through the medium of an entertainment picture when they do not realize that they are being propagandized." Entertainment pictures presumably could reach a mass audience impervious to carefully reasoned writing. OWI believed this could be accomplished if propaganda messages were "casually and naturally introduced into the ordinary dialogue, business and scenes which constitute the bulk of film footage." For example, crowd scenes might contain women in uniform, teenagers participating in war activity as part of their daily routines, and businesses displaying war posters, rationing notices, and other signs of a nation at war. By making the war pervasive in the depiction of ordinary lives, the movies would show that the country was united, with everyone participating equally. Despite Davis's call for a "strategy of truth," OWI prepared to manipulate cinema images in ways imperceptible to the public.[38]

Poynter carried OWI's message to the studios. A sample of his weekly logs from May and June 1942 shows him dealing with the upper ranks of the industry. At MGM he had a long session with Executive Producer Eddie Mannix in which he urged him to make fewer combat films and more on the war issues. Poynter suggested that MGM's proposed remake of *Lost Patrol* be used to dramatize the Four Freedoms in the Philippines, where the "pagan Igorots, Catholic Togalogs, and Mohammedan Morros—all colored—fought with white men." He urged producer Sam Marx to make a feature on short wave radio which he thought offered a great "opportunity for universal education." He also supplied official information for MGM shorts.[39]

At Warner Brothers he met with Jack Warner, Charles Einfield, Gordon Hollingshead, and Jerry Wald, among others. There he learned that the studio planned a film on Joseph E. Davies' *Mission to Moscow,* the controversial account of the U.S. ambassador to the Soviet Union from 1936 to 1938. Warners also planned a picture on a theme—the merchant marine—that would be "enormously helpful to the war effort." Released as *Action in the North Atlantic* with Humphrey Bogart in one of his lesser known roles, that picture too was destined for controversy.[40]

Lunching with David O. Selznick, Poynter was delighted to learn that the acclaimed producer of *Gone With the Wind* was ready to turn his talents to "the real epic of the Four Freedoms, pointing up the postwar aspects." At Universal he met with producers Bruce Manning and Walter Wanger and made suggestions on how to present the "Chinese angle." And at Twentieth Century-Fox he talked with Jason Joy, the studio's public relations chief, who informed him they were rushing to complete a picture about the evacuation of the people of Japanese ancestry from the West Coast. From Joy's description Poynter thought the film fit OWI's goals. He was in for a rude shock.[41]

In June Poynter addressed a Hollywood writers group and figuratively spanked them, and the industry at large, for not informing people about the real issues of the war. He praised a notable exception, *Mrs. Miniver* (MGM, 1942). It showed the British people forgetting class barriers in order to advance the war effort. Give us "a *Mrs. Miniver* of China or Russia," he appealed, "making clear to our people our common interest with the Russians and Chinese in this struggle." OWI would get versions of *Mrs. Miniver* for these other allies. But, as even OWI officials conceded after the war, *Mrs. Miniver* presented an idealized version of British life which, for propagandistic reasons, downplayed class cleavages.[42]

The newspaperman's contact with film makers reinforced his sense that Hollywood needed OWI's cueing. In the summer of 1942 Poynter and his staff assembled their suggestions in a "Government Information Manual for the Motion Picture Industry." The manual is a key document in understanding the relationship between film and propaganda during the war. More than a "how to" handbook, the manual was a comprehensive statement of OWI's vision of America, the war, and the world. That perspective derived from the liberal or left-liberal orientation of much of OWI's staff. Issued in loose leaf so that frequent up-dates could be incorporated, the manual affords an illuminating glimpse of how a key segment of American opinion understood the meaning of the war.

The only consensus about the war in America was that we had been attacked, that defeating the Axis was imperative, and that American might and right would triumph. That broad tent covered, however, sharp ideological cleavages about the nature of American right, and what American might should accomplish. Infinite shadings of opinion existed throughout the war, to be sure, but they tended to coalesce, like filings affected by magnetic forces, around two poles: Henry Luce's "American Century" editorial of 1941, and Henry A. Wallace's "Century of the Common Man" speech of early 1942. OWI marched under the banner of the common man. Wallace interpreted the war as a landmark in the revolutionary struggle for individual rights going back to Jesus Christ. The war was truly a struggle between light and darkness. America fought for the Four Freedoms worldwide. The vice president emphasized a decent standard of living for all, to be attained through government action in a mixed economy—in short, a world New Deal. Wallace wrote his speech as an answer to Luce. The publishing magnate wanted America to impose its power on the world for whatever purposes it saw fit; his blueprint was truly for a Pax Americana. He placed private enterprise ahead of social reform and evoked conservative constructs of stability, order, and economic freedom. In historian Norman Markowitz's phrase: "Luce had combined the Invisible Hand of Adam Smith with the benevolent imperialism of Rudyard Kipling to create the American Century."[43]

Believing every film was imbued with significance for the war effort, OWI asked film makers to consider seven questions:

1. Will this picture help win the war?

2. What war information problem does it seek to clarify, dramatize or interpret?

3. If it is an "escape" picture, will it harm the war effort by creating a false picture of America, her allies, or the world we live in?

4. Does it merely use the war as the basis for a profitable picture, contributing nothing of real significance to the war effort and possibly lessening the effect of other pictures of more importance?

5. Does it contribute something new to our understanding of the world conflict and the various forces involved, or has the subject already been adequately covered?

6. When the picture reaches its maximum circulation on the screen, will it reflect conditions as they are and fill a need current at that time, or will it be out-dated?

7. Does the picture tell the truth or will the young people of today have reason to say they were misled by propaganda?

The manual was a virtual catechism of the world view articulated by Wallace in his "Century of the Common Man."[44]

1. *Why We Fight.* If one word summed up the struggle it was "democracy." That flexible term was used to provide a comprehensive explanation of why the Allies fought; it embraced both domestic politics and society and the international order. Democracy divided the world into two camps. The Allies were *ipso facto* democracies. This was a war for survival, since defeat meant slavery for all. The stakes of the war were so high that no compromise was possible. The manual quoted Wallace: "There can be no compromise with Satan." When Roosevelt announced the doctrine of unconditional surrender in 1943, OWI easily incorporated the idea. Ever mindful of the disillusionment that seared America after Versailles, the agency taught that we fought for a "worthwhile peace." Total victory would bring forth a "new world"—a world of the Four Freedoms to be shared by everyone, including the defeated Axis. The globe was, to use the term popularized by Wendell Willkie's bestseller of 1943, "one world." That world was indivisible; democracy must be universalized or these freedoms would "always be in jeopardy in America." The new world would be the community of the open door, "dedicated to the free flow of trade, ideas, and culture." The war was a continuation of revolutionary struggle; 1942 was an outgrowth of 1776.

This was, then, "a people's war," OWI proclaimed. Everyone had a stake in it, regardless of class, ethnic, or religious identification: everyone contributed according to his or her ability. "Show democracy at work," the manual said, "in the community, the factory, the army." Avoid stereotypes, such as blacks in menial or comic roles. Show loyal aliens, "glad of a chance to support and help the free land of their adoption." Few aliens were fifth columnists; they should be depicted as helping the war effort of "the free land of their adoption." Although this was a war for survival, "a worthwhile peace" would follow, based on the Four Freedoms—freedom of speech and religion, freedom from want and fear.

2. *The Enemy.* The enemy was not the entire German, Japanese, or Italian people, nor even the ruling elites. "The enemy

is many people infected with a poisonous doctrine of hate, of might making right," said the propagandists. Enemies were ubiquitous. "This is total war," they wrote. "Everyone is either a friend or a foe." Abetting the fascists' spies and saboteurs, who could be readily unmasked, were the uncommitted, the pessimists, the buck-passers.

3. *The United Nations.* Thirty nations were allied against the Axis. The manual homogenized them into democratic societies which, whatever their peculiarities, shared a common anti-fascist goal. If an ally fell short of democracy, better to overlook that fact and concentrate on its contribution to United Nations victory. British imperialism was glossed over with praise for the empire's "magnificent battle." More difficult was Stalin's Soviet Union. "Yes, we Americans reject communism," said the manual. *"But we do not reject our Russian ally"* and its heroic contribution to victory. Chiang Kai-shek's China, so badly misunderstood in the United States, was transformed into "a great nation, cultured and liberal." It had been "fighting our war since 1933" and we would be "closely bound" with her "in the world that is to come." Trujillo's Dominican Republic, Somoza's Nicaragua, and the Union of South Africa stuck out awkwardly, but as smaller nations they did not require specific whitewashes. The Allies should be given their due; the U.S. should not be shown winning the war single handedly. The people of the United Nations should be neither "peculiar creatures essentially unlike ourselves" nor "patently American types . . . in a foreign locale." Demeaning stereotypes were to be avoided at all costs.

4. *The Home Front.* American democracy was not perfect, OWI acknowledged. The country had its underprivileged, but they were becoming "less underprivileged" and hence had a stake in the war's outcome. Government programs—New Deal measures, though not so identified by the manual—brought slum clearance, curbs on "vicious tenant farming," rural electrification, and advances for blacks.

Unity became the byword of the civilian war effort. The movies should show everyone sacrificing cheerfully for the war. This might extend from uncomplaining payment of taxes and purchase of war bonds to such mundane practices as carrying one's own sugar when invited out to dinner or giving up seats on trains and buses to servicemen. Volunteer activities should be lauded, not belittled. Women should be shown in pictures as stepping forward, becoming war workers, donning armed forces uniforms, and assuming jobs formerly handled by men. They should also be depicted as coping without their husbands or sweethearts, even leaving their children at day-care centers. From production centers a stream of war goods flowed, implicitly promoting confidence in ultimate victory. The theme of all types of workers and management bosses contributing to victory—and achieving harmony through labor-management committees—undergirded OWI's vision of a united home front.

5. *The Fighting Forces.* Although combat scenes naturally furnished an abundance of dramatic material, OWI urged the studios to use them for something more than melodrama. The agency hoped movies could stress all components of the armed forces, whether glamorous or not, show the careful training of G.I.'s, and prepare the public for casualties. The multi-ethnic platoon, "using names of foreign extraction" (what American names were not of foreign extraction?) and showing occasional black officers, would strengthen the impression of national unity. Finally, the public should be prepared for fatality lists by showing "why the sacrifice of their loved ones was worthwhile."

The OWI manual, augmented by revisions and "common law" decisions on particular films, constituted in effect a second code. Though not so rigorous or far-reaching as the Production Code Administration's canon, the OWI code served much the same function, instructing the moviemakers on the correct presentation of certain subject matter. The two codes coexisted uneasily, for they had different purposes. Both codes were designed to ensure that the movies reflected their sponsors' point of view, to be sure; but the challenge for the PCA code was more to remove material, that of the OWI to insert it. The two codes and the organizations interpreting them also differed in their political outlooks. They shared a certain conservatism in that they upheld the legitimacy and justice of American politics and society. OWI, however, demanded overt political positions while PCA tried to minimize them. And OWI through its embrace of the New Deal and the "Century of the Common Man" advocated a mild social democracy and liberal internationalist foreign policy that was anathema to the author of the PCA code and its chief interpreters. However, the PCA also recognized that the war created "extenuating circumstances" which would bring more violence and social and political subjects to the screen. Thus the explicitly political nature of the OWI code challenged an entrenched set of procedures, and thereby ensured controversy.[45]

Much of this potential for conflict was hidden in the summer of 1942. In a burst of patriotism the industry hailed the manual. Here was the recognition the movie colony had sought from the government. The manual was not filed and forgotten; the major studios duplicated copies or lengthy summaries of it for their staffs. The record of conferences between studio personnel and OWI indicates that many producers and writers gave it serious consideration as they planned productions. Not surprisingly, the manual, like OWI generally, found its friendliest response in liberal or leftist quarters. Warner Brothers was the most liberal studio and the most receptive. Nelson Poynter told the brothers Warner he was counting on them to blaze the trail in Hollywood. As a group writers were more left-leaning than the senior executives of the studios; some directors were also receptive.[46]

Even the writers and directors who were members of the Communist Party found the politics of the manual appealing. Some of them, such as Dalton Trumbo and John Howard Lawson, would become known during the Cold War as the "Hollywood Ten" when they ran afoul of the House Un-American Activities Committee. More politically conscious than many other writers, they were often chosen for war-related screenplays where they could put their expertise to work. This should not be misunderstood. There was little danger of "communist" ideas being slipped into wartime movies undetected. Whatever writers did, they were under the strict supervision of a top-heavy, usually conservative, studio hierarchy. Also, the Communist Party was in a phase in which its position was almost indistinguishable from that of European social democrats and advanced New Dealers. It was not that American liberals had moved left; it was more that, owing to the war, the Communist Party had temporarily moved right.[47]

What OWI was promoting in Hollywood, then, was an interpretation of American society and international politics that commanded assent from the center of the political spectrum to the left, but not necessarily from the right. That point of view, colored by wartime necessity and wishful thinking, raised as many questions as it answered. Consider the cornerstone of the edifice: "democracy." As a description of reality it fit only a few of the United Nations. As a measure of political aspiration, it was too specifically American to be extended to the myriad complexities of world politics. Faced with references to violence by the Spanish Loyalists in Paramount's *For Whom the Bell Tolls*, agency reviewers said: "Now it is necessary that we see the democratic-fascist battle as a whole and recognize that what the Loyalists were fighting for is essentially the same thing that we are. To focus too much attention on the chinks in our allies' armor is just what our enemies might wish. Perhaps it is realistic, but it is also going to be confusing to American audiences."[48]

OWI therefore retreated to a world of symbolism designed to evoke the desired responses. Concepts such as "democracy," "fascism," and "unity" conformed to what social theorist Robert Merton termed "sacred and sentimental" symbols—beliefs and opinions grounded in emotion, as is characteristic of patriotic and religious feelings. The use of such symbolism was all but irresistible because it seemed to evoke favorable results from large numbers of people. Therein lay the danger. Merton warned that so long as mass response was the goal, "the choice of techniques of persuasion will be governed by a narrowly technical and amoral criterion." This goal was dangerously manipulative because it encouraged "the use of whatsoever techniques work." Merton did not contend that all appeals to sentiment are manipulative. He offered, however, a distinction that is useful in interpreting OWI and Hollywood: "Appeals to sentiment within the context of relevant information and knowledge are basically different from appeals to sentiment which blur and obscure this knowledge. Mass persuasion is not manipulative when it provides access to the pertinent facts; it is manipulative when the appeal to sentiment is used to the exclusion of pertinent information."[49]

Through their use of sacred and sentimental symbols OWI and Hollywood tried to manipulate opinion by denying or clouding relevant information. The manual's seventh question correctly cited the heavy responsibility borne not only by Hollywood but also by OWI: "Does the picture tell the truth or will the young people of today have reason to say they were misled by propaganda?" The answer to that question, and its consequences, became clear as the sometimes competitive, but eventually collaborative, relationship between the propagandists and the commercial mythmakers unfolded.

The difficulty OWI would have in raising the studios' sights became apparent in mid-summer 1942 when Twentieth Century-Fox proudly released *Little Tokyo, U.S.A.* The propagandists were already disturbed by the general tenor of war-related films. *Little Tokyo* was guaranteed to offend agency reviewers. "Virtually everything in it," said Dorothy Jones, "is calculated to shiver the well-sensitized spines of the Office of War Information." *Little Tokyo* was a $300,000 "B" movie. But because of its treatment of war themes it became a milestone in the relationship between OWI and Hollywood.[50]

The film makers at Twentieth Century seized on one of the most dramatic, and controversial, aspects of the home front: the mass roundup and internment of people of Japanese descent on the West Coast. Although the studio obviously thought this picture would have box-office appeal, it also seemed to believe it was contributing to the war effort. *Little Tokyo* developed the theme that anyone of Japanese descent, whether alien or American citizen, was loyal to the emperor of Japan and a potential traitor to America. This interpretation ultimately brought the wrath of OWI down on the studio, but it was clear that the studio, to some degree, reflected what was in reality U.S. government policy.

Although the film was fictional, it employed a quasi-documentary style for verisimilitude. The studio rushed cameramen to the Japanese quarter of Los Angeles to shoot the actual evacuation. The army cooperated in the filming. Following the usual protocol, the studio sent its script to the chief of the pictorial branch of the War Department's Bureau of Public Relations for clearance. Approval was granted. This meant only that the script contained nothing offensive to the army, but Twentieth Century assumed that it had the government's blessing. There was only one hitch in completing the documentary footage. After the evacuation, Little Tokyo was dark and deserted, making shots of street scenes and nightlife there unobtainable. The resourceful studio decided to send its cameramen to Chinatown. Who would notice that the street signs had Chinese instead of Japanese characters? Besides, to Hollywood, all Asians looked alike.[51]

This handy assumption carried over to the casting. Chinese actor Richard Loo, who became famous for his portrayal of the sinister Japanese during the war, took the part of Oshima—a would-be hero in this film. The villainous Takimura was played by the heavily made-up Harold Huber, a bit-part actor tackling his first big role. He disliked the role but accepted it, according to Twentieth Century's press handouts, because of a sense of wartime duty. Screen press agents seemingly would stop at nothing if it could be turned to their advantage.[52]

For its basis the film accepted as true the charge by Martin Dies, Democrat of Texas and chairman of the Special Committee of the House on Un-American Activities, that 15,000 Japanese nationals were involved in espionage. It opened with an ostensibly factual prologue that took a swipe at one of Hollywood's favorite targets, the isolationists:

> For more than a decade, Japanese mass espionage was carried on in the United States and her territorial outposts while a complacent America literally slept at the switch. (Camera pans [to] shots of Japanese taking photographs of refineries, harbors, airports.) In the Philippines, in Hawaii, and on our own Pacific Coast, there toiled a vast army of volunteer spies, steeped in the traditions of their homeland: Shintoists, blind worshippers of their Emperor. . . . This film document is presented as a reminder to a nation which until December 7, 1941, was lulled into a false sense of security by the mouthings of self-styled patriots whose beguiling theme was: It can't happen here.[53]

The first character to appear is Ho Takimura, who oversees Japanese espionage in Southern California. Though American-born, he is loyal to the "Son of Heaven, our Emperor." In Tokyo he toasts "the end of the white man's domination." Dissolve to "Little Tokyo," where he explains to fellow Japanese-Americans that the Empire of the Rising Sun will soon carry out its carefully wrought plan to strike its "greatest enemy—the United States." He exults: "On a morning not so far distant the United States shall receive a rude shock—*before* breakfast." And on the morning of December 7 Takimura assures his fellow spies: "Nothing will go wrong. We have planned long and thoroughly. The first bomb will fall on Pearl Harbor exactly on schedule—

four minutes from now. . . . Here in California we will do our part." Then on to California and "the subjugation of the United States." A bit later, however, the Japanese conspirators worry that "mass evacuation . . . will defeat our plan of operation here." That comment closed the loop; the empire's best laid plans could be thwarted by the roundup of the Japanese population.

Enter the hero, a Los Angeles police detective with the all-American name of Mike Steele, played by Preston Foster, already a veteran of the "stab-in-the-back" sub-genre. Investigating a murder in Little Tokyo he gets nowhere as the belligerent Japanese play dumb. "Just try to get information from this Oriental bund around here," he fumes. But Oshima, a high school friend of Steele's, breaks with his community and agrees to help. The next time Oshima appears he is in the city morgue, minus his head. There was no mistaking the implication. The film depicted the Japanese-American community as "a single, unified body which works together at all times for itself and against America," said reviewer Dorothy Jones. "The penalty for loyalty to the U.S. is swift, certain, and mortal."

As Steele doggedly pursues his investigation the Japanese continue to stonewall. He encounters Mr. and Mrs. Okuna. (She is clad in a kimono, a visual clue implying disloyalty.) Neither of the Okunas can speak good English—another hint of potential treason—but they are steeped in their constitutional rights. They babble brokenly that Steele cannot enter their home without a search warrant. The scene suggested that, since the Japanese used the shield of constitutional rights for treasonous purposes, it was all right to strip them of this protection. Steele leaves them alone, but later he bulls his way into the home of a Japanese he suspects of having an illegal broadcasting unit. When it is objected that he needs a warrant, he responds: "The only warrant I need is my badge." Finally Steele cracks the Japanese spy ring. Disarmed, they march off to jail at gun point. No longer able to contain himself, Steele punches out Takimura and exclaims: "That's for Pearl Harbor, you slant-eyed. . . . " Inspired by the detective's direct action, his superior officer throws a haymaker of his own, and a minor character joins in the melee.

These illuminating scenes have opened the eyes of Steele's

naive girlfriend, a radio announcer with the effete name of
Maris Hanover, played by Brenda Joyce. So far she has played
the dupe, assuring her listeners that the arrival of the Kurusu
mission promises peace. But her boyfriend's single-handed defeat of one corner of the Japanese conspiracy brings her to her
senses. The story re-enacts the timeworn theme in which the
strong man of action wins over the bright but credulous female;
only missing were nuptials at the police station. The movie's
final scene, after shots of the evacuation, shows her broadcasting: "And so, in the interests of national safety all Japanese,
whether citizens or not, are being evacuated from strategic military zones on the Pacific Coast. Unfortunately, in time of war,
the loyal must suffer inconvenience with the disloyal. . . . Be vigilant, America!"

"Invitation to the Witch Hunt," cried OWI reviewers. *Little
Tokyo* preached hate for all people of Japanese descent, who were
shown as potentially disloyal. Oshima's helping Steele and Ms.
Hanover's reference to the loyal and disloyal were the only hints
that some Japanese-Americans were not traitors. This "rabidly
unbalanced" portrayal muddied the concept of the enemy.
Moreover, "one such film can open the floodgates of prejudice
. . . and can render the post-war re-absorption of Japanese-
Americans an almost insuperable problem," OWI staff feared.
The depiction of ostensibly peaceful Japanese farmers poised
for sabotage reminded the agency of "the familiar propaganda
line of the Associated Farmers of California, well known for its
fascist bias and its interest in taking over Japanese-owned land."
And Steel's flying fists and warrantless searches were simply ap-
palling. "Gestapo methods," despaired OWI. "Did somebody
mention that we are presumably fighting for the preservation
of the Bill of Rights?"[54]

The propagandists faced a dilemma. Here was a film that
revealed "a frightening misapprehension" of the war program,
in Jones's view. Poynter also disliked the picture, though not so
much as his reviewers. But what could be done? Twentieth Century-Fox would be loath to give up its investment in the movie,
or even to make very many changes, for they would be costly.
Since OWI was not consulted during the production process,
its leverage at the time of release was minimal. Poynter and Mellett nevertheless decided to go to the studio and ask for several

changes to "take most of the curse off." Takimura was to admit that not all Japanese-Americans were loyal to the emperor; Steele and Ms. Hanover were to refer to the large number of loyal Issei and Nisei. These requests irritated Jason Joy. The film was intended to make the audience hate only the disloyal, he contended. Joy reminded Poynter that the army had passed the script. Meanwhile the local board of the Office of Censorship had screened the picture and approved it for export. Who was OWI to complain? Nevertheless Joy agreed to make the changes, except for Ms. Hanover's closing speech; she had become visibly pregnant. The alterations were little more than cosmetic, however, and the film's release triggered a new round of protests. The War Relocation Authority, which ran the Japanese concentration camps, was "considerably disturbed." It was worried that widespread distribution of the picture would undermine its plan to resettle the Japanese, especially in the Middle West. The relocation agency asked OWI to try to have a new prologue incorporated which would say that the film had not been cleared with the government, had no official sanction, and should not be read as "a blanket indictment of all persons of Japanese ancestry, and especially not the citizens, who comprise two-thirds of the groups and whose average age is 23 years." Norman Thomas and Milton Eisenhower added their protests.[55]

Poynter went back to Joy, who rejected OWI's appeals. Joy emotionally declared that the propagandists did not advocate killing Japanese. Poynter merely tried to suggest that it was unhealthy for national morale if all Japanese were portrayed as disloyal and that it was the Japanese military, not all Japanese, who "must be exterminated." Joy insisted that the changes that Twentieth Century had already made for OWI were enough. Predictably he dismissed the suggestion that the picture not be distributed in the Middle West.[56]

Hollywood's bewilderment with OWI's strictures was perhaps understandable. The propaganda agency dared not insist that the studio kill *Little Tokyo*, even had OWI possessed that power, for that picture did not, in reality, contradict government policy. OWI might insist that racial stereotyping was bad, but it was precisely that type of racism that underlay the decision to intern the Japanese. It made no difference how long they were in the United States; it was felt that as a racial trait they maintained loyalty to the emperor. OWI could cite FBI reports that no acts of sabotage by Japanese had been detected on the West Coast, but War Department officials countered that their absence proved the existence of the plot—the Japanese were waiting for the right moment to strike with maximum effect! OWI might worry that *Little Tokyo* could "open the floodgates of prejudice," but the tender shoots of tolerance had already been drowned. OWI could argue that America fought for the Bill of Rights, but that brought no comfort to the internees of Manzanar and Tule Lake. As Secretary of War Henry L. Stimson, an advocate of the detention drive, conceded, the internment drove "a tremendous hole in our constitutional process." Hollywood, in short, was not out of step with government policy. It was OWI that heard a different drummer. Not for the last time would the propagandists find their assumptions at odds with the realities of American society and government policy.[57]

Little Tokyo, U.S.A. taught OWI an important lesson. If the agency wanted to be effective in Hollywood, it was imperative that it see scripts prior to shooting. Once a film was finished, it was too late. Could OWI get the studios to agree? After all, they willingly submitted scripts to the Hays Office and the military. But the Hays Office was a creature of the industry, and the military had resources the studios needed. OWI, which at this point offered little but moral suasion, might find that not enough.

Growing out of the *Little Tokyo* episode, OWI began taking a more active hand in advising Hollywood. Poynter had to play his role with care. Mellett cautioned his deputy that he should not put himself in a position where the industry considered him naive or a roadblock. "The best you can do ... is to urge ... the necessity for factual accuracy," Mellett said—"that and the greater persuasiveness of understatement or restrained depiction." In particular he hoped to deflect the "terrific" pressure to make "hate pictures." Such films might generate a fervent emotionalism, which might collapse or poison postwar relations. He believed the only lasting basis for victory and for peace was a firmly grounded understanding of the war issues. But factual accuracy, understatement, and restraint were scarcely Hollywood's usual methods. Whether a propaganda agency—whose objectives were not dissimilar from the movies'—would employ such an approach also remained to be seen.[58]

Access to scripts was in itself no guarantee of success. So long as OWI lacked real power even cooperative studios could thwart the propagandists, as another Japanese-related picture, Warner Brothers' *Air Force*, demonstrated. Jack and Harry Warner conceived of *Air Force* as a patriotic service. A $2 million "A" feature, it boasted top-rated talent: writer Dudley Nichols, producer Hal Wallis, and director Howard Hawks. Its leading men included Gig Young, Arthur Kennedy, Harry Carey, and John Garfield. The studio received full cooperation from the Army Air Force, arranged by none other than commanding general H. H. "Hap" Arnold, a personal friend of Jack Warner. Hawks used Nichols' shooting script only as a general guide. Capable as he was of walking off the set if he suspected studio interference, Hawks changed dialogue as he went so that the film bore "only a general resemblance" to the original script. An imperious director like Hawks added to OWI's woes.[59]

Air Force concerned the flight of the "Mary Ann," a B-17 Flying Fortress whose routine training flight from San Francisco on December 6, 1941, erupted into adventure and heroism when it encountered the Japanese attack on Pearl Harbor the next morning. Their flight became a voyage of discovery as they learned the full extent of "Jap treachery and brutality." In the end, however, they proved that American superiority would win the war.

OWI reviewed the script in October 1942 and found much to criticize. Although a better movie than *Little Tokyo, U.S.A., Air Force* revived the theme of disloyalty among all people of Japanese descent. These "traitorous fifth columnists" were depicted as "a major factor, if not the chief cause, of the early defeats suffered by American forces in the Pacific."[60] When the *Mary Ann* lands in Hawaii the crew is attacked by "local Japs." In Honolulu the local C.O. observes:

> We had plenty of trouble here too with the *friendly* Japanese. (Grimly) Three trucks arrived from Honolulu at seven thirty this morning—delivering supplies. When the first Jap plane showed up they slammed across the field and wrecked every airplane in sight. Cut the tails off all but three of our fighters.

On to Wake Island, where the crew of the "Mary Ann" discovers more "Jap" treachery. The Wake Island commander tells
them:

> Same thing here. If we'd had our twelve fighters up, we'd have smeared
> them on that first attack. But we were listening on the shortwave to Tokyo
> telling us about Mr. Sakuro Kurusu's peace mission to the United States.
> I've studied all the wars of history, gentlemen, but I've never come across
> any treachery to match that.

Finally at Clark Field in the Philippines they learn that local
Japanese set brush fires to guide their bombers. A disgusted
American soldier adds: "That ain't all they done, neither. They
cut our telegraph lines—just before that first sneak attack." The
obvious implication was that Clark Field could not receive
warning of the impending attack, which was not true. A horrified G.I. exclaims: "Chee, dat ain't war dat's moider."

As a complement to disloyal Japanese-Americans, the film
shows the Japanese military as bloodthirsty savages who operate
outside the bounds of civilized warfare. In one scene the Japanese machine-gun an American as he tries to parachute to
safety. Frustrated by their inability to respond in kind, an American flier bursts out: "We're getting kicked around all over the
place by a lot of stinkin' Nips." His desire for revenge is requited when they hit a Japanese plane. He yells with joy: "Fried
Jap going down!" Certain language in the film required Warner
Brothers to run the gauntlet to get the required Production
Code Administration seal of approval. Joseph Breen instructed
the studio to delete Garfield's heartfelt "Damn 'em! Damn 'em!"
as well as "lousy," "hell," and "hellhole." Not even total war entitled American ears to hear "damn" or "hell"—"fried Jap," yes,
but not "lousy."[61]

By contrast Americans are shown as civilized. When Corporal Weinberg wonders why Congress has to vote for war—
"Don't dey know we're *already* in it?"—Sergeant White corrects
him: "Listen, any buck-toothed little runt can walk up behind
Joe Louis and knock him cold with a baseball bat—but a clean
man don't do it. Your Uncle Sammy is civilized: He says, 'Look
out, you sneaks, we're gonna hit above the belt and knock the
daylights outa you!'"

OWI was increasingly exasperated with this post-Pearl Harbor reflex. The agency reminded Warners that the vast majority of Japanese-Americans were loyal. It was time to move beyond the stereotyped view of the enemy. Hollywood should stop showing the war "in terms of revenge against a buck-toothed little runt ... and cease regarding our enemy as a sort of un-sportsmanlike international footpad." The enemy was fascism, "a system which seeks to enslave the world." Nor was America going to win the war by itself; victory would be an Allied effort.[62]

But OWI was again left in the position of the critic without power. The Army Air Force approved the film for distribution at home and abroad. "Warners had to have Air Force approval, but they could get along without ours," observed Lowell Mellett. "The alleged Japanese saboteurs or potential saboteurs formed part of their story thread, which was thin enough at best, and when they finally got the okay of the Air Force they were in no mood to make any further changes." The movie attracted some protest when it was released in March 1943. Norman Thomas and Columbia sociologist R. M. MacIver complained of the unfair and inaccurate portrayal of Japanese-Americans. However, until the propaganda agency had muscle as well as moral suasion it could be ignored.[63]

The experience of *Air Force,* coming on the heels of *Little Tokyo,* moved Mellett to bolster OWI's clout. Trying to interfere with domestic exhibition would open OWI to charges of censorship and provoke a political storm that probably would endanger the agency. Mellett's strategy was indirect. He decided his Hollywood office needed a representative of OWI's Overseas branch to bolster Poynter's representations. The overseas representative would create less controversy, for the government's right to censor material sent abroad was assumed. And as Mellett pointed out, "it would hurt like hell" if a picture were limited only to domestic exhibition, since foreign showings often made the difference between profit and loss for the studios. Chosen for this new position was Ulric Bell, the former head of Fight for Freedom. Like Poynter he had no movie experience except as a customer.[64]

Mellett also reasoned that if he could establish a liaison with the Office of Censorship he might be doubly effective. If this strategy worked, OWI would exert leverage with the studios similar to that possessed by the military and the Hays Office. OWI, too, would exercise a sort of censorship which would affect not only foreign audiences but American viewers as well. Mellett and Poynter, who would have vigorously resisted such moves with their newspapers, took this fateful step warily but firmly. Their action would be controversial but it would eventually lead to a remarkable convergence of interests between the propaganda agency and the citadel of popular culture.

IV.

OWI Takes the Offensive

For the benefit of both your studio and the Office of War Information it would be advisable to establish a routine procedure whereby our Hollywood office would receive copies of studio treatments or synopses of all stories which you contemplate producing and of the finished scripts. This will enable us to make suggestions as to the war content of motion pictures at a stage when it is easy and inexpensive to make any changes which might be recommended.

—Lowell Mellett to studio
heads, December 9, 1942

We know how it turned out, and so it is hard to imagine it might have been different. In retrospect the American war machine seems so powerful, its industrial capacity so awesome, its scientific prowess so elegant, that the outcome of the war must have been a foregone conclusion. It was not so early in the war. The first year of the American conflict constituted a period of almost unrelieved bad news. "We could lose this war," said OWI chief Elmer Davis in his first summation on the war, in mid-August 1942. America had never lost a war, but that was a statement only about our ancestors, he said. And they were never up against this kind of war—"total war, in which defeat by our enemies means destruction." Though many Americans had made great sacrifices, as a nation we were only "ankle deep in the war." We could win the war, "but we are not winning it yet."[1]

Pearl Harbor, Wake, Bataan, Corregidor, Manila and all the Philippines, Singapore, the linchpin of the British Empire in Southeast Asia—outpost after outpost fell, and it was even feared for a time that General MacArthur had been captured. On the Russian front, the Nazis swept the Russians before them and aimed a major thrust at Stalingrad. The battle for that city would be the battle for Russia; few were willing to bet on the Russians. In Africa, Rommel drove toward El Alamein, seventy miles from Cairo, threatening to seize the Suez Canal and cut the British Empire in two. On the other side of the ledger one could point to the defensive victory at Midway, which seems more important in retrospect than it did at the time. There was also the electrifying, almost unbelievable, news of Jimmy Doolittle's raid on Tokyo; but the damage American fliers inflicted was more psychological than substantial. Both hopeful events were immortalized in film—Midway in John Ford's gripping documentary *The Battle of Midway,* the Doolittle raid in *Thirty Seconds Over Tokyo.* Nonetheless a year of bad news made an indelible impression. Many would agree with Archibald MacLeish when he reminisced: "[the fear] that we could have lost that war, and were within inches of losing it, never left me in Washington."[2]

The gloom deepened as Americans felt the first unaccustomed pinches of wartime rationing, news censorship, and curbs on freedoms. Cries of mismanagement of the war effort and demands for an immediate second front fouled political discourse. Voters vented their anger on November 8 by throwing out nearly one hundred incumbent members of Congress—a stunning referendum against the Roosevelt administration and its conduct of the war to date. Though not as visible as a presidential landslide, this congressional avalanche altered the political terrain in its own way. By the spring of 1943 Malcolm Cowley wrote in *The New Republic* of "the end of the New Deal" and the possibility that, without too much more change in structure or personnel, "a fascist state could be instituted here."[3]

The tide of war began to shift about October or November of 1942. "This is it," people sang out. The United States mounted its first offensive in the European theatre, in North Africa, on November 6, and though the news from Kasserine Pass was bad, we were finally giving it to the Nazis. We scored a victory at Guadalcanal. And there was another morale-boosting event of great symbolic significance—Eddie Rickenbacker, the World War I ace, was found alive after drifting for twenty-four days on a raft. We could feel at last that victory would be ours, perhaps as early as 1944. But the eventual, horrifying costs were already beginning to be sensed.[4]

In such an environment, OWI's Bureau of Motion Pictures viewed Hollywood films with mounting frustration. The very first question it had asked the studios to consider—"Will this picture help win the war?"—sounds absurd in retrospect. But in that grim year of 1942 propagandists as well as film makers took the question with deep seriousness. Every act seemed to bear on the war. Increasingly frustrated with Hollywood's performance, Lowell Mellett and Nelson Poynter decided that drastic measures were needed to bring the industry in line with OWI's propaganda program.

As the summer of 1942 wore on, the Bureau strengthened its liaison with the studios. Poynter or his deputy, Warren Pierce, met frequently with top executives. At 4 p.m. on Mondays, Wednesdays, and Fridays, for instance, Poynter had a standing appointment with the MGM brass. The fiasco of *Little Tokyo, U.S.A.* had taught the Bureau's staffers that vigilance in the scripting stage paid the biggest dividends. Script review became a major part of the office' work. The five-person analysis section wrote detailed reviews of scripts submitted by the studios. Poynter or Pierce edited these analyses and used them as the basis for discussions with the producers. An internal operations analysis concluded that the reviews were "an excellent wedge" with which to insert OWI's ideas into the script. "The effect of our efforts . . . becomes more apparent every day," it stated, as more scripts and films incorporated OWI suggestions.[5]

The acceptance of OWI's ideas was far from automatic, however, in mid-1942. Hollywood and OWI were still testing each other. Though script reviews might provide an opening wedge, the full extent of OWI's leverage had not yet been determined. The Bureau of Motion Pictures felt particularly frustrated in dealing with pictures that had been in production before the formation of the agency but were now reaching the screen with explosive results.

One of the hottest issues for BMP that summer erupted over MGM's "Man on America's Conscience," which triggered a bitter row over what was perhaps the most frightening domestic issue: race. Although one might think it was the American black who troubled the nation's conscience, Metro wanted to rehabilitate the reputation of President Andrew Johnson (1865–69). Abraham Lincoln's successor enjoyed a certain vogue before the modern civil rights movement as the embodiment of the slain president's presumed generosity toward the South and as a champion of reunion. Largely overlooked were Johnson's opposition to black voting rights, his support of the notorious black codes that regimented blacks' behavior, and his opposition to programs for the economic advancement of the freed slaves. By contrast the Radical Republicans of the Reconstruction era, particularly Pennsylvania Congressman Thaddeus Stevens, were painted as vindictive partisans who put the South "to the torture." Southern white supremacists found this interpretation appealing. So did the movie industry. Wanting to protect the box office from southern film censors, Hollywood adopted the region's white supremacist view, typified by the idealized plantation society of *Gone With the Wind.* Blacks had been relegated to the most degrading stereotypes, as represented by Stepin Fetchit and worse.[6]

The screenplay for "The Man on America's Conscience" was crafted by John L. Balderston, a liberal screenwriter who yielded to studio demands despite his own convictions; the script made Andrew Johnson the hero and Thaddeus Stevens the heavy. Balderston, who had scripted the 1931 classic *Frankenstein,* turned his considerable talent with monsters to the character of Stevens. The champion of black rights emerged as a crippled, demonic figure, who cajoled Johnson, a helpless alcoholic, into a reversion to drunkenness. Stevens even consorted at cards with John Wilkes Booth, and was thus implicated in President Lincoln's assassination! The inconvenient fact of slavery simply evaporated. After the Civil War the former slave owners returned in glory to their plantations and to their rightful place in the Union.[7]

MGM thought it was simply making another "biopic," a framework on which to hang one of Louis B. Mayer's beloved costume dramas. But this material was social dynamite in the tense racial atmosphere of World War II. In 1943 racial tensions exploded into rioting in Detroit and other major cities. OWI wanted to dampen racial conflict, which both threatened wartime unity and gave the Axis fodder for its propaganda mills.

The agency also worried that movies such as this Metro travesty would further antagonize blacks, who displayed considerable skepticism about America's rhetoric of democracy. Blacks despised the Nazis' racism—a phenomenon they understood, they said, because of their experience with "minor Hitlers here." But early in the war they displayed a marked tendency to identify with the Japanese as fellow people of color. A survey of Harlem blacks carried out by the Office of Facts and Figures in early 1942 found that 49 percent of respondents believed they would be no worse off if Japan won the war. Eighteen percent actually thought a Japanese victory would improve their lot. OWI correctly interpreted such findings as reflecting a desire to see American society "changed not conquered." Blacks were overwhelmingly loyal to the United States, despite their status as second-class citizens. Blacks had to "fight for the right to fight," said Walter White, head of the National Association for the Advancement of Colored People (NAACP). But when they finally won that right, they had to fight in segregated units. The armed forces even segregated blood plasma by race, and German POWs were allowed to dine in restaurants that were off limits to black American G.I.'s. The black press during the war called for a "Double V"—victories over both the Axis abroad and Jim Crow at home.[8]

"The Man on America's Conscience" became a crucial test case of OWI's power with the studios and its commitment to racial justice. Its Bureau of Motion Pictures joined an informal alliance of blacks (led by Walter White) and white liberals and leftists in Hollywood who pressed for greater sensitivity on racial issues. Though many of Hollywood's veteran black performers feared change because the old stereotypes were their meal tickets, a new generation demanded, in Lena Horne's words, that "the Negro be portrayed as a normal person." Wendell Willkie played a uniquely influential role as both chairman of the board of Twentieth Century-Fox and special counsel to the NAACP. More liberal on racial issues than Franklin Roosevelt, Willkie gave a fiery speech to studio executives in early 1942 in which he pointed out the offensiveness of racial stereotypes and their danger to the war effort. Willkie and White circulated among the tables at the annual Academy awards din-

ner, visited studio commissaries, and met privately with industry leaders in their campaign to have Hollywood depict "the
Negro as a normal human being and an integral part of human
life and activity." Many industry officials pledged to cooperate.
White believed that "some extraordinarily fine things are in
prospect in the moving picture world . . . a new concept of the
Negro." His optimism was premature.[9]

The controversy over "The Man on America's Conscience"
highlighted the problems to be overcome, and OWI's willingness to buckle under pressure on the race question. The agency
had learned of the inflammatory screenplay from a studio leak
that appeared in *The Daily Worker.* Alarmed, Mellett asked MGM
for the script and passed it on to White. The black leader was
appalled. Not only did much of Steven's villainy have no basis
in fact, but the idealization of Andrew Johnson ignored that
president's callous disregard of black rights. White cited W.E.B.
DuBois' *Black Reconstruction in America* and similar scholarly
works to demonstrate the promise inherent in the Radical Republicans' program. The eventual failure of Reconstruction led
directly to the "evils which curse the South today," said White.
He asserted that the picture would do "enormous injury" to
black morale by its seeming endorsement of white supremacy.[10]

White's learned citations predictably made no impression
on MGM. And OWI was interested not in conducting a history
seminar but in the practical politics of 1942. Despite the recent
pledges by the studios and by liberals, blacks found themselves
outgunned by MGM and ultimately abandoned by OWI.

The OWI and its Bureau of Motion Pictures were both seriously concerned about the film, but on different grounds.
Mellett told MGM that no one should do anything that was "apt
to cause disunity or even bad feeling." He asked the studio to
change the picture enough to avert trouble; if that were not
possible he hoped MGM would withhold the picture until the
country emerged from the present crisis. MGM protested bitterly, demanding to know whether "a minority in the country
shall dictate what shall or shall not be on the screen through
the Mellett office?" Only war secrets should be considered suppressible, the studio contended. This was a reasonable argument in the abstract, but it lacked credibility coming from an

industry which kowtowed to the Legion of Decency and to the Southern censors, and blue-penciled material likely to be offensive to a variety of pressure groups.[11]

However much OWI staff wanted to improve the portrayal of blacks in the movies, the war came first. So Nelson Poynter of BMP's Hollywood office told a disappointed Walter White that it would be "a mistake to make a major issue of this film." Poynter explained: "We want to encourage the studios to make films with real guts, films that can cause complaint from pro-Fascist minorities; therefore, I think we have to . . . register our complaints and be willing to lose a battle and win a war." The black minority could be sacrificed for OWI's larger war propaganda goal.[12]

But some adjustments were suggested concerning the movie role of Thaddeus Stevens, his character, motivation, and historical interpretation. OWI's view had been limited by its inadequate understanding of the black perspective, and in this it was not alone. In the 1930s and 40s awareness of black history and culture was minimal, even among supporters of black rights. Many historians still sharply criticized Reconstruction, and viewed the Civil War as a tragic, avoidable mistake. Dorothy Jones, OWI's most perceptive social critic, was told by Frank M. Garver, a Civil War historian at the University of Southern California, that scholars almost uniformly viewed Andrew Johnson favorably. Stevens, on the other hand, was considered a "half-crazy fanatic" who was obsessed with punishing the South and did not "give a snap for the Constitution." Dorothy Jones concluded that the script reflected contemporary historical interpretations. The controversy's origins in *The Daily Worker* provoked a further question: was Thaddeus Stevens perhaps more a hero of the left-wing rather than of blacks? OWI concluded that he was. Poynter quoted screenwriter Balderston: "Stevens was for chasing the Kulaks off their land and this is very appealing to the Communists." Poynter reasoned that it was not Stevens' championing of black rights that excited the Communists, but rather his desire to expropriate Southern landholders. Poynter and other BMP staffers felt the Communist Party wanted to exploit the issue to gain black support.[13]

MGM reluctantly agreed to reshoot parts of the nearly finished film—an expensive operation. Stevens, portrayed as a villain in the original version, now emerged as a sincere, if mis-guided, figure. The revised picture tried to focus on issues of principle, but with the embattled president clearly representing superior virtue. The changes did not go very deep. Released with the less provocative title of *Tennessee Johnson*, in its new form the picture was yet another variation on a favorite Hollywood theme—the success story.

In the opening scenes the shackles are struck from the feet of Johnson, a runaway apprentice, and he begins his rapid climb from small town tailor to political grandee. His dutiful wife rep-resents his better nature. "A white man without property is a mudsill," he says. "We were all mudsills once," she responds. She helps him see that he should champion the common man. Johnson devotes his career to fighting those who complain he is "rousin' up the white trash and makin' levelin' speeches." As president he applies an ostensibly even-handed idea of equality. When he grants amnesty to white Southerners, he declares: "Here at this desk where Lincoln freed the slaves, I now free their masters." Shrewdly wary of Stevens, he fends off the pro-posal to give blacks "forty acres and a mule"—a notion de-signed to make Stevens seem purely vindictive. Stevens, played by Lionel Barrymore, who "was originally conceived to look like the shaggy one of the Three Stooges, was slicked up a little," said *PM*'s film critic John T. McManus. The picture contains just four blacks—all of them docile servants in Washington, D.C.— and all of two lines hinting at slavery. The finished product was an early instance of what later became a frequent tactic when Hollywood faced OWI's racial strictures: writing out. If blacks were portrayed in an offensive manner, it was easier to elimi-nate them than to change the treatment.[14]

OWI was greatly relieved when it saw the release print. In-stead of a threat to national unity, *Tennessee Johnson* had become, in Mellett's words, "a forceful dramatic exposition of the de-velopment of democratic government in this country." The film stressed the importance of achieving change through the ballot box rather than through violence. This was, of course, an ironic message for American blacks who were systematically excluded from voting, often through violence. But "ballots not bullets" fit OWI's emphasis on democracy. *Tennessee Johnson* was also an allegory of "the little man in our society"—the very embodiment of the log-cabin-to-White House myth that OWI wanted to beam to the world. The picture meshed neatly with OWI's stress on unity, but it did so only by distorting and minimizing the central issue of race.[15]

Few shared OWI's upbeat assessment of the picture. Blacks and some leftist supporters were appalled. A star-studded cast of protesters, including Ben Hecht, Zero Mostel, Harold Clurman, Lee Strasberg, Canada Lee, Vincent Price, and Dorothy Gish, signed a petition that asked OWI to "do everything in its power to have it scrapped." The black sociologist E. Franklin Frazier denounced it as a travesty and suggested that "perhaps white America needs this form of hypocrisy to survive." Even the patient Walter White began to question the value of the alliance with Hollywood liberals and with OWI.[16]

OWI personnel were disturbed by their experience with *Tennessee Johnson*, despite what they considered a successful outcome. To Poynter and his colleagues it seemed that the studios were still not taking their wartime responsibility seriously enough; any subject, even one apt to exacerbate disunity, was as always fair game for Hollywood. Mellett had hoped Metro would shelve *Tennessee Johnson* indefinitely. Since reshooting parts of completed pictures was expensive, the only way to prevent a reoccurrence was to get hold of the scripts early. Metro's contention that "only war secrets should be suppressible" was also troubling, for OWI thought its mandate was much broader than that. *Tennessee Johnson* became another bead on OWI's string of the studios' malfeasance.

Whatever the studios' shortcomings, the *Tennessee Johnson* episode raised troubling questions about OWI itself. The agency, fortunately, stopped short of an effort to suppress the picture, though had MGM taken the hint and withdrawn it Mellett would have shed no tears. Elmer Davis had promised a "strategy of truth." In this case, however, what concerned the propagandists was not the truth, however elusive that might be, but political expediency. The agency's primary goal was national unity. It hoped to achieve that by altering *Tennessee Johnson* enough to avoid offense to blacks, but without threatening the white majority. If those objectives were incompatible, however, black rights would be jettisoned, much as the studios caved in to Southern censors. This was an ominous portent. For the truth about any number of subjects—the Soviet Union, China, or the American home front—did not conform to OWI's image of what Hollywood ought to show. Whether more leverage for OWI would yield greater accuracy on the screen seemed increasingly in doubt.

In its single-minded desire to project a unified, fully mo-bilized America, the Bureau of Motion Pictures then targeted what seemed an unlikely offender: *Palm Beach Story*, a hilarious satire on the idle rich. This screwball comedy was written, di-rected, and produced by Preston Sturges, the acknowledged master of the genre. Starring Claudette Colbert and Joel Mc-Crea, the picture was released by Paramount in November 1942. The movie focuses on the marital woes of socialites Tom and Gerry Jeffers, whose ardor has cooled considerably after five years of life together. They owe several hundred thousand dol-lars back rent on their New York apartment, and Tom needs money to develop a landing net that will revolutionize aviation. Gerry wants to get a divorce in Palm Beach but lacks the train fare. Using her long legs to good advantage, she gets a deaf wie-ner manufacturer to shower her with gifts and money. Enroute to Florida she becomes the mascot of the Ale and Quail Club, a group of millionaires heading south in their private railroad car. Drinking huge quantities of ale, they practice for the quail shoot by making the stereotypical wide-eyed, knee-knocking porter toss up crackers, which they pulverize, along with the railroad car. Terrified, Gerry flees the Ale and Quail Club. She meets another millionaire, John D. Hackensacker III, who takes her to Palm Beach on his yacht. He falls in love with Gerry; his sister flips for Tom. All ends happily as Gerry returns to Tom, and the Hackensackers marry Tom's twin brother and Gerry's twin sister.

To OWI the picture was no laughing matter. Even if Amer-icans recognized it as fantasy, BMP reviewers thought it might still do considerable mischief abroad. To Dorothy Jones *Palm Beach Story* was "a fine example of what should *not* be made in the way of escape pictures." Set in early 1942, its giddy disre-gard of war sacrifices in that dark year made it "a libel on Amer-ica at war." Marjorie Thorson entered a long catalog of offenses. "We are shown only unbridled extravagance, fantastic luxury, childish irresponsibility and silly antics on the part of those who

should, by virtue of wealth and position, be the economic leaders of a nation at war," she complained. Although Breen had
made Sturges cut Gerry's divorces from eight to four, American
morals still seemed "incredibly cheap." "Do we want Europeans
and Latin Americans to believe this is typical of American domestic ideals?" Our English and Russian allies were insulted.
Princess Centimillia describes her foppish gigolo Toto as "English—a primitive type" and thinks his strange Slavic patois is
Baluchistani. The army too was insulted when the princess suggested a ride to Ft. Myers, where they might put Toto in the
army.[17]

Thorson was particularly emotional on the subject of transportation. The destruction of the private railway car by members of the Ale and Quail might be humorous in peacetime, but
"this is 1942, we are at war, there is an acute rolling stock shortage, and there's nothing funny about the misuse or destruction
of a war essential," she wrote. "Furthermore, useless civilian
travel has presumably been abandoned for the duration." Ditto
Hackensacker's 300-foot yacht. He doesn't enjoy it but feels
obliged to take it for "an occasional joyless sail." The government had much better uses for the craft and its sailors, she
stated. OWI analysts believed that foreign audiences would mistake the picture for reality, and the contrast between their pri-
vations and the luxuries and irresponsibility of *Palm Beach Story*
would generate a resentment "that would gladden Hitler's
heart."[18]

If evidence were needed of OWI's tendency to take the war
and its responsibility—both very serious matters, to be sure—
to an exaggerated length, surely this was it. Even in the context
of 1942 it is hard to see *Palm Beach Story* as anything but harmless escapist entertainment. If foreign audiences accepted every
Hollywood picture as a depiction of American reality they must
have been confused indeed. For America was then not only the
sybaritic world of *Palm Beach Story* but also the chintz comfort
and sober domesticity of Andy Hardy, the homespun individual
heroics of *Mr. Smith Goes to Washington*, the treacly goodness of
Shirley Temple, and the western's restatement of law and order.
Moreover, foreign viewers may have absorbed a much more
positive message about America than the literal-minded propagandists anticipated. Hollywood's worldwide influence on

fashion, manners, and morals was much remarked, and seems to have given foreigners an image of America as a land of promise, plenty, and freedom—not a bad message to convey in a war against fascism. Perhaps some foreign viewers even stopped to think that here was a country that could still satirize itself. Hollywood's sense of humor may have been one of the great unrecognized assets of the public-opinion war. Even deadly serious subjects can be taken too seriously.

Since *Palm Beach Story* could scarcely be said to contain any military secrets, the Office of Censorship approved it for export. That further disturbed OWI. Mellett and Poynter increasingly believed the censorship agency was too lenient. *Palm Beach Story* encouraged them to press for a tighter censorship code which would take OWI's interests into account.[19]

BMP reviewers also were upset by what they saw at a screening of Warner's *Princess O'Rourke*, which attempted the difficult task of blending war issues with comedy, humanizing the president, and showing Americans doing their part for the war. The producers had not shared the script with OWI and trouble resulted. Poynter insisted: "I assure you I have not lost my sense of humor," at the same time that he was lamenting that Warner Brothers, "with its high sense of responsibility," would do this. Just imagine, he said, what "ill-conceived atrocities" would be committed by other studios "that are recklessly using the war for background incidents in an opportunistic attempt to capitalize on the war rather than interpret it."[20]

How had Warners offended? The Red Cross women had "resounding and ridiculous ranks," and when one of their friends served as the training dummy they pounced upon the unwitting victim with "sadistic glee" and displayed a presumably comic ineptitude with bandages and blankets. The women in a civil defense unit delighted in staging too frequent air raid drills. (OWI objected not to the stereotyping of women but to the lampoon of war activities.) Foreign royalty who appeared vitiated from centuries of in-breeding seemed interested primarily in perpetuating themselves and their investments, and their duties seemed to consist primarily of attending flower shows. A princess breathed the blithe assurance that "we will come back into our own again—we always do." This touched off a predictable OWI mini-lecture on the generally noble qualities of European

nobility, from their devotion to the allied cause to their willingness to give up their thrones if that should be the will of the
people after the war.

Nor did the U.S. government fare well enough. The president—a very busy, high-minded man in wartime, OWI thought—
appeared as a "busybody" intent on marrying off an heiress to
a foreign throne without the consent of the government. He
even accepted a dollar as a tip from a boy who mistook him for
a guard. The Secret Service were the traditional stupid flatfoots.
Finally—and this Poynter put in capital letters—the episode in
which a State Department official used his pull to help a young
man avoid induction was "one of the most serious, demoraliz-
ing things in the whole picture." This was probably the most
inadvisable part of the film, although the ridicule of women
might be at least as offensive. The rest of this catalog of
transgressions reflected hypersensitivity.[21]

Poynter enjoyed political lampoons, but he thought that
even such a "skillful satire" as *Of Thee I Sing* might be "inadvisable" in wartime. And that went for other subjects, especially
films showing problems in American society. Though Poynter
praised *The Grapes of Wrath*, he opposed making such a film in
wartime. If Hollywood too often used the war as simply another
backdrop for stale genre pictures, OWI allowed the lens of war
to distort its judgment about whole classes of films.[22]

Balanced against these problem-ridden movies, BMP took
heart from pictures that reflected its influence. On December
4, 1942, an OWI platoon with high expectations marched into
a Metro screening room to watch the release print of *Keeper of
the Flame*. Early in the summer of 1942 the agency had been
asked to "supply the thinking" for the picture, one of the few
pictures to deal with domestic fascism. The film told the story
of Robert Forrest, a wealthy industrialist who had carefully cul-
tivated an image of Americanism but intended to launch a fascist coup. Little of this was evident through the first nine reels.
One of the less remembered entries in the long series of Hepburn-Tracy duos, *Keeper of the Flame* had all the appearance of
a conventional murder mystery combined with a love story.[23]

Reporter Steve O'Malley, played by Tracy, returns from Europe to cover the funeral of his hero Forrest, head of the Forward America Association, and decides to write the great man's

life story. But something is wrong. Forrest's male secretary has the unmistakable sinister air of a movie villain. The widow, Christine Forrest, played by Hepburn, is attracted to O'Malley but remains uncooperative. The circumstances of Forrest's demise seem improbable: He was killed on his own estate when his car plunged into a ravine whose ridge had been washed out in a cloudburst. An atmosphere of brooding mystery deepens, complicated by the false clues that are the mystery writer's stock-in-trade. One day O'Malley sees smoke rising from the "arsenal," an old stone building where Forrest worked alone. He and the secretary rush to the building, where Mrs. Forrest nervously assures them she is only burning old love letters. O'Malley, realizing that she is in trouble—the secretary has received orders from Forward American headquarters to kill her, for she knows too much—persuades her to tell him all she knows.

Mrs. Forrest bursts into a long soliloquy in which she admits complicity in her husband's death. She knew the bridge was washed out but did not warn him because she finally realized the truth behind the image—her husband was America's number one fascist and was on his way to give orders to his saboteurs to strike. She bursts out:

> Everyone worshipped him. No, no, the image of him. The image that had been carefully built up ... , built up with a terrible purpose. When I discovered what that purpose was, I had to destroy the image. No, I had to destroy the man to save the image. Yes, that was it.... He grew to despise the people.... He felt that we were all beneath him.... When Robert began to change, I saw the face of Fascism in my own home. Hatred, arrogance, cruelty. I saw what the German women were facing. I saw the enemy.

She shows O'Malley a sheaf of articles attacking Catholics, Jews, blacks, and labor and subtly appealing to the Ku Klux Klan. She reveals a stash of money, the names of wealthy contributors to Forward America, and the names of the men who were to be America's first storm troopers.

The morning she pieced the story together she went riding to collect her thoughts. Looking at the washed-out bridge she knew Forrest would be killed unless she warned him. But she did not "because it came to me that clean death in the rain was the best thing that could happen to Robert Forrest." She prayed: "Let him be killed that he may not mock those who had trusted him and destroy them as he had destroyed me." O'Malley asks her help in writing the story—the true story—of Forrest and Forward America. She demurs. Wouldn't it destroy the people's faith in their hero? "He wasn't their hero—he was their enemy, and they must know it," O'Malley explodes. "People are not children. Sometimes they act like children if you get them scared or confused, but down in their hearts they know—they're not afraid. They want the truth, and they can take it."

Smoke begins to fill the windowless stone crypt. The secretary has set it afire. He rushes in and shoots Mrs. Forrest, and fires at the reporter but misses. Mrs. Forrest dies in O'Malley's arms. The secretary escapes but is struck and killed by an automobile. O'Malley goes on to write the sensational story of the Forrest case. The picture moves swiftly to a conclusion with a newspaper showing Mrs. Forrest's portrait and the caption "She Died for Her Country," and a close-up of O'Malley's book, *Christine Forrest: Her Life,* which dissolves into a fifteen-second shot of the American flag billowing in the breeze.

"Here were my war aims," recalled the scriptwriter, Donald Ogden Stewart, "which coincided, I believed, with those of Roosevelt and all good Americans." OWI's enthusiastic sextet concurred. "A splendid contribution," read their review. The propagandists thought the picture helped clarify that the fascist threat was not simply military but economic and political. Americans needed to know that native fascism, "one of our most powerful enemies within," would stalk the country "in a guise of Americanism." If the people knew the truth they would do the right thing.[24]

Keeper of the Flame did indeed reflect the war aims of OWI, liberals and leftists, such as Stewart, the wealthy, Harvard-educated writer who joined the Communist Party in the 1930s. The film dramatized some of the core assumptions of the Popular Front perspective: the wealthy and powerful were the source of a possible fascist takeover; they would generate group hatreds, particularly of minorities; and the people could be trusted to do the right thing, if only they were told the truth. But these were not the war aims of all Americans. Nor was the film's message as unambiguous as the Hollywood BMP contingent seemed to think. Lowell Mellett did not share their enthusiasm for the picture and even pointed out that Robert Forrest had the dem-

agogic qualities that Franklin Roosevelt's detractors attributed to the president. And Louis B. Mayer, who others thought
had Forrest's traits, was shocked at the film's identification of
the rich with fascism and stormed out of the screening. For OWI,
Mayer's was an ominous departure.[25]

The Bureau of Motion Pictures found the picture "exciting"
and guaranteed to stoke the "fighting spirit." Reviews were
mixed, however. *Keeper of the Flame* may have lured some unsuspecting fans to the theater, but even the most star-struck fans
must have realized they had been propagandized by the time
they heard Hepburn recite OWI's thinking.[26]

If *Keeper of the Flame* dealt with ominous domestic tensions,
Pittsburgh (Universal, 1942) was chiefly a vehicle to keep John
Wayne, Randolph Scott, and Marlene Dietrich before the public. Discussions with CIAA representatives helped transform it
from a conventional love and action picture with Pittsburgh as
a vague backdrop into a movie with notable war propaganda.
Not that the romance disappeared. Dietrich played Josie, a
"hunkie" who is determined to escape the squalid life of a Polish miner's daughter. She becomes, in fact, the woman as redeemer when she marries Cash Evans (played by Scott); her good
sense and better nature prove instrumental to his soaring success as a steel baron. If Cash is the good industrialist, Pittsburgh
Markham (played by the Duke) is the bad magnate—unscrupulous, cruel to labor, interested only in himself and bigger
profits. He breaks Josie's heart by marrying the daughter of a
wealthy steel operator and, predictably, having married for all
the wrong reasons, begins his slide from grace. Cash and Pittsburgh are partners at first, but Cash cannot stand his ruthless
tactics. Their partnership dissolves in a fierce fistfight in a mine
shaft. Pittsburgh's wife divorces him, and her father ruins him
financially. Penniless, he slinks into Cash's huge coal works as
a common laborer under an assumed name.

But Pittsburgh Markham is redeemable; the war makes
everyone put aside petty personal grudges for a greater cause.
Josie, Joe Malneck, the labor organizer, and Doc Powers, head
of the research department, are working on wartime manpower
problems at Cash's plant. Here labor, science, and women are
symbolically joined in behalf of the war. They discover Pittsburgh's real identity, and when Cash fires his defeatist produc-

tion manager, he hires his old partner-rival in his place. (This was a favorite theme. King Vidor's 1943 epic, *An American Romance,* used war production demands as the device to reconcile a feuding father-and-son industrialist team.) At a giant rally in the company yards, Markham-Evans coal products receives the Army-Navy "E". Cash lauds Pittsburgh Markham, Malneck, and the thousands of determined workers. He delivers an impassioned speech about the war and every American's stake in it, and the enthusiastic workers troop back to their jobs to set another production record.

Pittsburgh gets low billing in any John Wayne or Marlene Dietrich retrospective. The picture was strictly run-of-the-mine. The stars' flat performances failed to bring much life to one of the tritest plots in cinema; further, the semi-documentary treatment of the coal and steel industries and their role in the war effort weighed down an already slow-moving picture. The *Hollywood Reporter* and *Motion Picture Herald* advised distributors to emphasize the duel between Wayne and Scott over Dietrich. Since the film was shot off-the-cuff with only a rough script, OWI reviewers remained in the dark until they saw a release print in late November 1942. They praised the film's "earnest" contribution to the war effort and applauded the way it linked coal and steel with war production. They noted, however, that much of the dialogue had been "culled directly" from their manual for the industry, and would have been improved "by translation into terms more directly and simply relating to the characters, situations and background." Poynter pressed Mellett to see *Pittsburgh* without fail and to give him his "hard boiled reaction." Mellett did: "The propaganda sticks out disturbingly." Propaganda was scarcely being put over on audiences who did not know they were being propagandized. As propaganda made further intrusions into an entertainment medium, a backlash began building in Hollywood's executive suites.[27]

The competing demands of entertainment and propaganda heavily colored *So Proudly We Hail,* a Paramount production which was to have an important effect on BMP's relations with the studios. *So Proudly We Hail* was a major production that told the story of heroic army nurses at Bataan in 1942. The picture starred Claudette Colbert, Paulette Goddard, Veronica Lake, and Sonny Tufts. Producer-director Mark Sandrich, best known for his Fred Astaire–Ginger Rogers musicals of the mid-1930s, sent the first script to the Motion Picture Bureau in October 1942. OWI reviewers Marjorie Thorson and Dorothy Jones were ambivalent. They thought it had great possibilities for the propaganda program, but required a lot of work with writer Allan Scott. They wondered, too, whether a production laced with gore and hopelessness would have the right upbeat message upon release in mid-1943, when Americans would be deep in combat.[28]

So Proudly We Hail blended war and romance. Though a story of women nurses, the picture is enclosed in a male frame—narration by a military doctor. A group of nurses ship out for the Philippines in November 1941, only to get caught in the aftermath of Pearl Harbor. Although their convoy is hit, they reach the islands and carry on their profession under grueling conditions. Their camp is shelled by the Japanese, despite their prominently displayed Red Cross flag. They make a successful retreat only because Olivia (Veronica Lake), whose fiancé was killed by the enemy, sacrifices herself for the larger group—a frequent movie wartime gesture. She arranges her long blond hair over her shoulders so that the Japanese will think she's an innocent woman, pulls the pin on a grenade, stuffs it into her clothing, and walks toward the oncoming Japanese. The grenade explodes, wiping out the enemy as well as Olivia, and her comrades escape. Eventually the order comes to evacuate to Corregidor; they are finally plucked from the island fortress and returned home.

Though Olivia's love ends in death, the others are more fortunate. Joan (Paulette Goddard) falls in love with Kansas (Sonny Tufts), the quintessential hayseed football player turned marine—the kind of guy who will return home, make a fair amount of money selling insurance, and spend the rest of his life reminiscing about his war days. The chief romance is that of Lt. Janet "Davey" Davidson (Claudette Colbert) and Lt. John Somers. Despite regulations forbidding nurses to marry, they are wed in the Philippines by a chaplain, with the blessing of the nurses' commander, Capt. "Ma" McGregor. Duty calls; the next day John leaves for Mindanao in an effort to get desperately needed quinine. Then the news comes that he is missing in action. Davey suffers a nervous collapse. On the voyage home she rallies from her trance-like state when the doctor-narrator reads a letter from John, telling her he is safe and enclosing the deed for the little farm where they will live in peace and plenty after the war.

Poynter had high hopes for the picture, since it made a serious attempt to deal with the issues and highlighted the neglected role of women at war. He also thought this might be an opening wedge at Paramount, which had shared few scripts with OWI. Poynter sent Sandrich a long memo urging the producer to "lift your sights even higher." A Chinese character in the film implied that America alone would win the war. Instead of picturing ourselves as "Lady Bountiful," we should remember how much we owe our allies, Poynter said. Hollywood's conventional demeaning treatment of Asians needed to be tempered. The Chinese were referred to by the insulting term "Chinamen"; Filipinos were "clucks" who had to be beaten before they would fight. The frequent references to Japanese as "apes," "yellow," "monkeys" and the like were disturbing. OWI felt racial epithets distracted attention from the fact that the real enemy was ideological, not racial; they also tended to play into the hands of those who wanted to make this a racial war. OWI's women reviewers seized on the derogatory portrayal of women. The nurses seemed most concerned with having a man around; if he wasn't, they collapsed. "The worst feminine characteristics have been emphasized," said Poynter. "The girls" quarreled with each other, gossiped constantly, grew "petulant under any strain," were insubordinate, and ignored regulations against fraternization with enlisted men.[29]

Poynter turned screen writer as he tackled the war issues, all-important to OWI. Scott's script already reflected several OWI themes—the people's war, the promise of lasting peace, the failure of isolationism. John's closing speech included language culled directly from the OWI manual. Evidently sensing an opening, Poynter pressed Sandrich to incorporate still more material and even suggested detailed dialogue changes. This flight to the typewriter cost Poynter dearly, for it aroused the ire of Paramount's chief, Y. Frank Freeman, who had ample clout in Hollywood and Washington. Poynter breached one of the industry's taboos by suggesting actual wording; this was too great an intrusion on the studio's control. Moreover, Freeman,

a conservative Georgia banker, theater owner, and cola distrib-
utor, viewed OWI as subversive. "I found him ignorant, bigoted,
reactionary and malignant," recalled producer-director John
Houseman. "His main preoccupation as studio head, seemed to
be to make sure that no 'niggra'—male or female—ever came
into contact, on the screen, with a member of the Master Race."
When Hollywood charged the Bureau of Motion Pictures with
too much interference in the creative process, Freeman had a
smoking gun.[30]

The damage this episode caused, and what Poynter's sug-
gestions reveal about OWI, merit extended quotation. In Scott's
final script, dated November 21, 1942, the chaplain's Christmas
Eve sermon began: "You must forgive me for being sentimental.
We are a sentimental people and proud of it. Despite the fact
that our enemies deride us for it, it makes us the stronger."
Pointing out that it was ironic to even talk about "Peace on
Earth" with a world at war, he continued:

> Sometimes it is fated that some generations, some people, like us gath-
> ered here, must live for the future. Christ did. It may be our destiny. We
> will be forgotten as He is occasionally ... but through us there *will* be
> peace on earth, good will toward men! We will see to it that there is! We
> must! It's a gift we must give the future, and perhaps because it is a gift
> we may not touch it ourselves. And now—God bless us every one.[31]

This speech, already rhetorical and overwritten, was not
enough for Poynter. He still felt the film was suffused with fu-
tility. He sent Sandrich a detailed memorandum on how to recast it, making the argument more explicit and wrapping the
Allied cause in the ultimate benediction—God's will:

> 1. The chaplain is doubly moved because war is now breaking out all
> over the Pacific at Christmastime.... The whole concept of Militarism—
> the doctrine of force which Fascism represents violates the Christ ideal.
> ... Peace on Earth, Good Will Toward Men is not just an ideal of broth-
> erly love as propounded by Christ. It represents collective security....
> 2. What is democracy? It's not just a political mechanism.... It is [a]
> way of life based on the premise that each one of the two billion indi-
> viduals in the world is important and entitled to a break.... A high
> sounding description of this is called "the dignity of man" which includes
> a Chinese coolie, a Filipino farmer or a Malayan cocoanut picker.
> 3. Democracy has been on the march since Christ. Christ was a revo-
> lutionary because He said that each individual is important.... Century
> by century the combination of the Christ ideal and modern industry and

communications have freed more and more individuals. This now gives rise to what the Vice President has called the "Century of the Common Man."

4. If I were a chaplain making such a speech, I couldn't help but become sentimental, especially on Chrismas Eve. I would acknowledge that we are a sentimental people, and by God, I would boast about it. The Fascists think purely in rational, mechanical, communications terms, but we think in human terms. We actually believe in the Christ idea. . . . Millions of Tiny Tims say and mean it—"God bless us, every one."

Thus we do have FAITH—*faith in ourselves*, not a blind faith, but faith in ideals which we have seen progress. . . . We have such faith in these, such faith in ourselves . . . such faith in mankind that we are tough about it and, by God, we will fight for it because we are dead without it. . . . We don't think in heroic terms of our contribution to future generations. . . . War is merely an extension of this continuing fight that we all believe in. . . .

Finally, the chaplain sees that this war is a religious war . . . , a conflict between the followers of the doctrine of force and the doctrine of mankind. When Joe Louis said, "This is God's war"—he said a mouthful.[32]

Poynter's own mouthful was indigestible. It was possible to imagine this passage on the editorial page of a tabloid newspaper, but the film would have stalled dead. Steeped in a literary culture, Poynter had little sense of how to recast ideas for film.

Poynter was also dissatisfied with nurse Janet's explanation of why we were in such a predicament at Bataan, even though it embroidered OWI's theme that isolationism was to blame.

Why——are those ragged, sleepless, starved, sick men stumbling through the most humiliating defeat in American history? Because we have no quinine, and the things that go with quinine: big guns, and troops, and food, and a responsibility to the world we live in. Why? Because old men said we were impregnable between two oceans. . . . Who should we have listened to—our President? or those who smugly told us the smug things we wanted to believe in?

Poynter proposed instead a medical analogy:

We thought we were living in a part of the world that could not be affected by all the pestiferous, political spots elsewhere in the world. . . . If Bubonic Plague broke out in Manchuria, we would have donated millions of dollars to eradicate it because we knew that it might ultimately infect America, but when a political plague broke out there by invasion, we would not have been willing to do something about it. We had to wait until this plague spread out further and further until it hit Pearl Harbor.[33]

This speech too was impossible. Production would have ground to a standstill as Miss Colbert tried to get through "pestiferous, political spots." Sandrich and Luigi Luraschi, head of Paramount's censorship department, were mystified by Poynter's suggestions. But they promised to incorporate as many of them as possible. Like his earlier ideas, they would "definitely bear fruit" with "change[s] you can see in the script." But they warned him that it would be hard to get them all in without seeming "preachy."[34]

Preachy, indeed! In trying to comply with OWI's guidelines, Scott had already weighted his script with more propaganda than it could bear. Witness the closing scenes, drawn almost directly from the OWI motion picture manual.

A doctor reads John's letter to Janet explaining why this war is different.

> You were kids from all walks of life—all classes—all kinds of people. ... This is not a people's war because civilians also get killed. It's the people's war because they have taken it over and are going to win it and end it with a purpose—to live like men with dignity, in freedom. (Slow dissolve from Janet's imperturbable face to John writing the letter in a drab bar.) People who brought the war will try to take the peace once we've won the victory. [But] a small voice is growing across all boundaries ... : it's what Jane said, what Rosemary felt, and Olivia. It's what made Kansas cry. It says: "This is our war now, and this time it will be our peace."

Janet's dead look brightens to one of intelligence. John ties the war to the personal level—love and abundance:

> I am enclosing a deed to that little farm I told you about. It is now in your name. I'll wait for you there, or if you are there first, wait for me. Thank you, thank you my darling for my life.

Eyes luminous, Janet affirms: "We *will* be back." The nurses return home, sailing under that wartime symbol—the Golden Gate Bridge, sun streaking through the clouds—as music swells and a poster calling for nurses is superimposed.

The picture was released in June 1943. Poynter could not resist a congratulatory note, with the merest hint of auctorial pride: "It's beautiful!" he told Sandrich and Scott. "*So Proudly We Hail* demonstrates what film can do toward interpreting the war without sacrifice of dramatic and entertainment values, when it is in the hands of gifted and conscientious men." BMP reviewer Peg Fenwick lauded the movie as the first to show women's contribution to an active war front, and a testament to their ability to fulfil their "obligation" to the war effort. One of Paramount's biggest pictures in 1943, it ran with a trailer in which the army nurses corps appealed for volunteers.[35]

So Proudly We Hail remains notable as the only wartime hit to focus in a significant way on women in combat. Nonetheless the picture's seriousness was severely undercut by its lapses into stereotypical conventions of a woman's place. In the traditional female role of nurses they perform courageously, but what motivates them is not their work—or even the war—but men. (In *A Guy Named Joe,* released in 1943, a woman takes a heroic role as a pilot, but the ghost of her former lover, played by Spencer Tracy, guides her to her target.) Olivia's self-sacrifice, which is triggered by what the Japanese have done to her fiancé, suggests that since she has lost her man, life isn't worth living anymore. Davey Davidson ignored military rules against marriage—love overrides all—and at the movie's end lapses into a profound depression from which she can be roused only by a letter from her husband. *So Proudly We Hail* continued the "snide movie attitude toward women," said Manny Farber of *The New Republic.* "The theater owners get their cheesecake in hunks so great that much of the movie hinges on Miss Goddard's black nightie." No one would stand for a picture in which male soldiers were so dependent on the opposite sex.[36]

Perhaps the wartime public would not have accepted sharper challenges to gender roles. We will never know, for Hollywood showed little interest in breaking out of its male-dominated formulae, and the Bureau of Motion Pictures, though showing increased sensitivity to changing female roles later in the war, found the studios resisted recognizing women's contributions to the war in any but conventional categories. As it was, the pressure the Bureau exerted on Paramount contributed to the budding crisis between OWI and Hollywood.

By the fall of 1942 Mellett and Poynter had learned two things. Left to its own devices, Hollywood would continue to make films which, they believed, harmed the war effort. On the other hand, intervention by the BMP staff in the script stage could produce significant improvement. Although the general trend of pictures was improving, the studios' cooperation was confined to specific instances. BMP officials, backed by OWI brass, decided to take the offensive.

OWI felt increasing pressure to produce results in Hollywood. Though Poynter's office might be heartened by pictures that were due to be released some months later, the public at that same time was only seeing movies that perpetuated deplorable trends. M. E. Gilfond, director of public relations for the Department of Justice, detected little change in the movies. He urged Mellett to lay out a comprehensive program that Hollywood should be asked to accept, regardless of whether or not it was good business. Why treat Hollywood with kid gloves when we were telling every citizen and every industry what to do? Gilfond said: "The question of free speech . . . in the entertainment world is not particularly valid." Bosley Crowther, film critic for *The New York Times,* concurred: "Our films are still making mistakes which arise from a way of thinking that belongs to another world." OWI also felt heat from abroad. The agency frequently received reports about the bad impression American movies created in foreign countries. James Reston, a London correspondent for *The New York Times,* filed a representative critique. Why did the government make special films for foreign distribution, he asked, but still allow "Hollywood to put across, day in and day out, the most outrageous caricature of the American character?"[37]

Concurring with Reston's lament, Mellett hit upon a solution—by his admission, "a drastic one." OWI should ask the Office of Censorship to bar bad pictures from export. He approved of such a move in "the more outrageous" cases. "It would hurt like hell" if a picture were withheld from export, for in many cases foreign exhibition still made the difference between profit and loss. In time the Hollywood product would improve for both foreign and domestic audiences. "Personally I would welcome any effort toward saner depiction of American life," Mellett said.[38]

He urged Poynter to establish relations with the Los Angeles Board of Review, the local branch of the Office of Censorship. "Are you being called in on any or many productions?" he asked. "Is the relationship sufficiently close to assure your ability to prevent the export of a picture in which the national interest is flagrantly ignored, etc., etc., etc.?" Poynter in reply suggested that, if he could not get a producer to cooperate, he would use "the club of censorship" in important cases. Mellett agreed that OWI should invoke censorship, though in a subtler fashion.[39]

Poynter quickly set up a luncheon with Watterson Rothacker, the head of the Los Angeles Board of Review. Rothacker's experience lay in the executive side of the industry. A pioneer in film technology, he was vice president of Martin Quigley's movieland publishing empire when he was handed the government's scissors. An industry man, Rothacker sympathized with the studios' desire for maximum export opportunities. In this he was aided by the censorship regulations handed down by his superiors in Washington. This code barred export of films only if they contained scenes or other information of direct military value, such as shots of battleships or factories. There was no clause under the code at this time to ban films which might be interpreted as mocking American life, such as *Palm Beach Story* or *Princess O'Rourke,* or which might offend foreign sensibilities. Poynter watched in dismay as Rothacker, though claiming he wanted to be helpful, stuck to the letter of the code and wrote export permits for these and other "actrocities."[40]

Mellett and Poynter decided that the way to get the censor's ear was to have a representative of OWI's overseas branch augment the Bureau of Motion Pictures' Hollywood office. Poynter would still run the shop, but the man from Overseas could more credibly and subtly carry OWI's objections to Rothacker. In mid-November 1942 Ulric Bell, who by now had become a special assistant to Director Davis, was dispatched to Hollywood to assume this role. Poynter hoped that the new representative would receive official status as a member of the Board of Review's advisory committee. This position did not materialize, but Bell, more forceful than Poynter, put his combative instincts to work in Hollywood.[41]

Bell applauded the results Poynter had achieved thus far, but he also found many films to be objectionable. He particularly loathed gangster pictures. A large number of "lousy jobs" were in production, he decided. He objected to Paramount's *Lucky Jordan*—"one of those racketeer things"—in which for no reason the gangster shed his old life and emerged a war hero. Warners' *Truck Busters* had gangsters stealing war material and then making a killing selling it on the black market. The censor passed both films for export. As Bell began trying to win over Rothacker, he made gangster movies his special target.[42]

Bell's efforts fit the larger strategy to bring the studios, as well as other government agencies, in line behind OWI. Thoroughly frustrated, Poynter complained that most producers were "merely throwing a sop to the Mellett office—a sort of 'play a game with their government,' as they do with the Hays Office censorship—[to see] how far they can go without getting into trouble." The studios also played government agencies off against each other, in particular using military approvals against OWI objections. "There is just too damn much confusion" in Hollywood's relations with the government, Poynter told Mellett. "It's got to be resolved in Washington 'on the highest levels'—as youse Bureaucrats call it." Unlike the Production Code Administration and the military, both of whom backed their desires with very real economic power, BMP had to rely on persuasion and patriotism. Poynter's solution was to add a bit of compulsion by having OWI officially designated as the sole clearing house for Hollywood's contacts with the U.S. and foreign governments. On October 21 he sent his boss a draft letter which informed the studios that all such contacts should be channeled through OWI.[43]

Elmer Davis and his assistant directors, at their staff meeting 10 days later, gave Mellett the green light to take after the studios. But Mellett kept Poynter's draft letter in his desk drawer for the time being. He chose first to deliver a strongly worded speech at a major industry forum, the annual meeting of the National Board of Review in New York City on November 12, 1942. Drawing bold headlines in Hollywood, his speech received recognition as an event of national importance: it was excerpted in *The New York Times*. Mellett attacked the "plague" of double features, known as "dual bills" or "duals." He scorned them for wasting chemicals needed for gunpowder production and for taking up screen time that was needed for informational shorts. Duals were only part of Mellett's concern. He also demanded better war pictures. He conceded that the industry had improved somewhat and he stressed that entertainment pictures were essential, but these films must eliminate "care-lessness and false conceptions" from "all pictures that touch on the war," he said. Too many movies showed all Germans as "Hit-ler-heiling blockheads" or suggested that "any American cor-respondent, given the aid of a good-looking blonde," could win the war while the rest of us "sit in a theater three or four hours a day and cheer." Anything that encouraged people to think the war was this simple was "a very great disservice to the country." The times required "effective pictures to aid the war effort." BMP staffers had been saying much of this for months. What was new was Mellett's going public and charging a powerful, self-obsessed industry with not shouldering its share of the war effort.[44]

Hollywood's response was predictable. The *Motion Picture Herald* countered that duals were necessary to develop new stars. As for the industry's patriotism, the *Herald* embroidered the ar-gument dear to trade publications in every industry: we are very patriotic, we alone know how to make our product, and we can best serve the war by doing things the way we want to do them without outside interference, especially from bureaucrats. Al-though the trade papers optimistically (and wrongly) guessed that Mellett spoke without Davis's blessing, they worried that OWI was up to something serious.[45]

Mellett stunned the industry with a letter to all the studios on December 9, 1942. He told the studios "it would be advisa-ble" and in their interest to routinely submit finished scripts, and even treatments and synopses of proposed productions, to his Hollywood office for review. "This will enable us to make suggestions as to the war content of motion pictures at a stage when it is easy and inexpensive to make any changes which might be recommended," he wrote. Since OWI's expansive def-inition of war content touched even John D. Hackensacker III's yacht, Mellett was casting a broad net indeed. He also wanted the studios to routinely allow the Hollywood office to screen pictures in the long cut. Although rather late to add material, this review would give OWI a chance to recommend cutting any material "harmful to the war effort." In addition, Mellett asked the studios to channel all contacts with the armed forces and foreign governments through OWI and to inform him of any previous contacts with foreign governments he did not know about. With these demands, Mellett had taken a fateful, and risky, step. Although the movie makers had given the Production Code Administration the very powers of review that OWI now demanded, never before had a government agency sought such a sweeping overview of film content.[46]

"CENSORS SHARPEN AXES," screamed *Variety.* The *New York Times* headlined its page-one story: "Movies Must Submit Scenarios to the OWI." This was the biggest government news in Hollywood since the antitrust consent decree of 1940. Harry Warner, who thought his studio had been operating very much as Mellett wanted, assured him of his full cooperation. The bulk of the industry, however, responded with alarm. The producers' association met for several hours to debate the issue. Opinion was divided. Some saw it as a move toward direct censorship. William Goetz, who ran Twentieth Century while Zanuck was in the army, claimed Mellett wanted "complete censorship over the policy and content of our pictures." Others surmised it was a trial balloon to see how far the industry would go to comply. Within a few days most of the industry lined up in solid opposition to Mellett's demand.[47]

Ulric Bell cast his shrewd newsman's eye over "the ruckus out here" and pronounced it "kindergarten stuff." Most of the producers had been submitting treatments and scripts anyway, he noted, but the Mellett letter had given some of them "an excuse to go on what amounts to a sit-down strike." A showdown loomed. "Lowell either will have to be backed up or he will have to be relieved," Bell said.[48]

Mellett's letter placed OWI on the defensive. Davis held a press conference on December 23 in which he defended Mellett and insisted the agency had no power of censorship. "We can make suggestions . . . and if a man does not want to follow those suggestions, why, that is his look-out," Davis said. He attributed the furor to Hollywood's being "a very excitable place" and to the "imaginative" talents there. The letter, according to Davis, involved nothing more than a continuation of the "service" OWI was providing the industry. The Hollywood press, no strangers to palace intrigue, divined a rivalry between Mellett and Davis. Their headlines read: "MELLETT TRIAL BALLOON BURSTS" (*Reporter*) and "DAVIS SMACKS MELLETT ORDER" (*Variety*). Whether or not this was so, there was no mistaking the marked shift from an "advisable" studio assent to government review to an assent that was "purely voluntary," as Davis, Mellett, and Poynter explained the letter.[49]

From the long perspective of Hollywood censorship, the industry's inflamed response to the Mellett letter seemed a bit unreal. The BMP head was only asking for what the studios found advisable to do routinely with other industry and government offices. The studios submitted all screenplays and finished pictures to the Production Code Administration; and dozens of state and municipal censorship boards passed on the suitability of movies. Further, the industry cooperated eagerly with the army and navy; it often yielded to the pleas of outraged pressure groups; and it packaged scenes with black entertainers so that Southern censors could delete them without affecting the continuity of the film. Since 1940 the studios had passed scripts and films dealing with Latin America to the Coordinator of Inter-American Affairs. And on occasion, as with *Idiot's Delight,* film makers had even submitted scripts to foreign fascist governments. But now, when its own government in wartime asked for similar access, Hollywood was outraged. The industry had surrendered its virtue long ago. Bosley Crowther noted that the industry had asked Roosevelt to set up a liaison office such as OWI and had tacitly accepted Mellett's advisory authority. In his view the studios needed more government advice, not less. Of the 60 or so war-related pictures he saw in 1942, not more than 20 "could be accepted as respectable representations of plausible events." "A national war effort involves some motivation from a central source," he said.[50]

Despite a brave attempt at a united front in OWI, Mellett and Poynter faced a growing backlash within the agency. In time they would be the main casualties of OWI's late autumn offensive. Gardner "Mike" Cowles, Jr., the head of the agency's Domestic Branch, now worried about the Bureau of Motion Pictures. He agreed that Mellett's letter could easily be construed as an attempt at censorship. Cowles maintained his own channels of information with Hollywood. A personal friend of some important movieland figures, he also relied on Jean C. Herrick, *Look's* Hollywood correspondent. His informants told him that the producers objected not only to the possibility of censorship but also to OWI's operators. "There is an almost unanimous opinion among important producers" that Mellett and Poynter were "incompetent to advise on changing scripts," Herrick reported. "They will never be able to obtain healthy cooperation from the Motion Picture Industry." He urged "a complete house cleaning." Herrick's proposed solution, mimicking that of important industry figures, was to appoint a Hollywood heavyweight to run the bureau. The obvious choice was Mayer, the most powerful man in the movie colony, but Herrick conceded that this Hoover Republican would not be acceptable to the administration. Other possibilities were Walter Wanger and Hal Wallis, but neither had the necessary clout. Herrick thought a possible compromise might be Frank Freeman, but the White House would find the Georgian no more acceptable than Mayer.[51]

The Bureau's ideological leanings also aroused resentment. Mellett passed on a friendly warning to Poynter that his staff should guard against "straying too far afield in the realm of ideology" with sympathetic movie figures. The conservative upper ranks of the studios had become aware of OWI's left-liberal leanings.[52]

The damage was considerable. Mellett sent his protegé an avuncular but cheerless letter at year's end. "The revolt in Hollywood . . . is a more serious matter than we have admitted even to ourselves," Mellett began. He had been sobered by a long talk with Freeman. The Paramount executive claimed he did not object to OWI's suggesting general themes. But he adamantly opposed the agency's dealing directly with his employees, chiefly writers and directors; all contacts had to go through his office or his representative. He also insisted that BMP refrain from suggesting "details of treatment." Freeman had been deeply offended by Poynter's suggested speeches for the chaplain and nurses in *So Proudly We Hail*. The moguls' control of their shops remained fundamental. Mellett found Freeman's emotional outburst a "revelation" and feared the studios would demand "a sacrificial goat"—Poynter.[53]

Mellett sided with Freeman on the issue of "monkeying with his creative talent." Pride of authorship had skewed the Hollywood branch's assessment of some pictures. "You boys and girls have been pretty proud of the job done on *Pittsburgh* and *Keeper of the Flame*," he continued. "Catching both of them cold, as I did, I was shocked by the way the machinery creaked." Reviewers noticed the propaganda; some liked it, others did not. *Pittsburgh* fared badly at the Washington box office, which might be attributable to the propaganda. If pictures were commercial failures, said Mellett, "we will get the blame" and Hollywood will resist incorporating OWI's themes. Poynter agreed that he had gone too far in writing dialogue and promised to desist.[54]

In reality "great things" had been accomplished, Mellett continued, and even more was possible. He advised his deputy to modify his operation in any way that might be necessary. In time, Mellett said, "they will be coming back to us." He added a postscript: "May I add that if I didn't think you had done and will continue to do a great job, I wouldn't be able to write you in this fashion." Poynter had already found 1942 to be a trying year; with Mellett's reprimand, scarcely softened by the congratulatory P.S., Poynter's year ended on an even bleaker note. Not only did he face recurrent opposition from industry figures, but his boss had taken him to the woodshed for the way he had carried out a strategy they had mutually agreed upon. The chastened Poynter approached the studios more cautiously.[55]

By early 1943 the squall blew itself out. The studios, except for the recalcitrant Paramount, resumed submitting scripts to OWI's Hollywood office on a regular basis. But Mellett and Poynter were seriously weakened in movieland, and the affair consumed some of the Domestic Branch's dwindling capital on Capitol Hill. Ironically, however, OWI's position in Hollywood was eventually strengthened. Ulric Bell moved into the spotlight, forcefully presenting the dangers that ill-considered pictures posed abroad, and lobbying hard with the Office of Censorship. The attitude of OWI's Hollywood office had been transformed. At first the somewhat diffident bureau believed the industry would come around on the basis of patriotic appeals. But as the propagandists watched Hollywood perform against the backdrop of the increasingly terrible war, they grasped the weapon they would have found abhorrent in the summer of 1942—the club of censorship. Interwoven with economic realities, censorship laid the basis for an eventual resolution of the conflict between propaganda and mass entertainment.

V.

Shakeout in Hollywood

No one has yet advanced an argument in support of producing a picture known in advance to be doomed to domestic exhibition exclusively.

—*Motion Picture Herald*,
August 14, 1943

As if OWI did not have enough trouble in Hollywood merely dealing with the studios and the Office of Censorship, the agency also had to contend with the Army and the Navy, who had long enjoyed a cozy liaison with the studios. The Bureau of Motion Pictures wanted to be the sole spokesman for the government with the studios. Otherwise, as Poynter had pointed out in the fall of 1942, its effectiveness would continually be undercut by the military, which did not share OWI's objectives. The military, like the Office of Censorship in 1942, limited its advice to Hollywood to military matters, avoiding the larger war issues on which OWI focused. Yet the studios could use military approval to deflect OWI criticism. As Ulric Bell vigorously pressed his case with the Office of Censorship, BMP tried to shoulder the military aside.

The industry and the armed forces had cooperated for many years. Almost any time a picture involved the armed forces in a major way, the producing studio sent the script to the War or Navy Departments. The military checked partly for propriety, to insure that the services' uniforms, insignias, and traditions were accurately represented. But of course much more was at stake. If the picture was not harmful to the military's interests, the services would provide personnel and equipment to assist

113

in staging battle and camp scenes. The savings in production costs could be enormous. The cooperation of the armed forces often determined whether or not a picture would be made. Virtually every movie made in the 1930s and 40s that dealt with a military subject enjoyed the cooperation of the armed forces, and most Hollywood pictures treated the military favorably. *All Quiet on the Western Front* was distinguished by its rarity. In World War II, when armed forces cooperation became extremely important for Hollywood, the industry was well aware that a smoothly running system was in place with the military. Neither the armed forces nor the studios wished to see OWI disrupt it.[1]

The upstart propaganda agency's problems in dealing with the military became evident early. In the spring of 1942, Warner Brothers picked up on Mellett's suggestion that someone make a film on the heroic, but less glamorous, merchant marine. Producer Jerry Wald began work on a picture, originally titled "Torpedoed," that was to be released as *Action in the North Atlantic* starring Humphrey Bogart. Poynter promised Warners that he could get the navy to provide whatever the studio wanted for the picture. Wald sent him a long wish list, including footage on convoys to Great Britain and the Soviet Union, convoys under attack by submarines and airplanes, and convoys' defense systems. He also wanted to put a camera aboard a freighter as it joined a convoy and steamed across the Atlantic, and to interview sailors. Months passed. Production lagged. Poynter had trouble delivering the goods. A frustrated Wald concluded that there was "quite a lot of political intrigue going on" with the army and navy opposing Mellett's operation. Warners did not want to get into the middle of it. Finally Hal Wallis told Wald to go back to the old system and send scripts "for clearance" to the military branch in question.[2]

Poynter's first attempt to establish the Bureau of Motion Pictures as the central clearing house for relations between Hollywood and the government ended in failure. The information Wald wanted was too secret for release. This was scarcely surprising. Merchant marine losses were heavy in 1942, the convoy system was a lifeline for Britain and Russia, and convoys' defense tactics were ultra-secret. The navy, moreover, shared little of OWI's enthusiasm for prompt news reporting. Not until some months had passed did the navy admit the extent of the losses it suffered in the battle of the Coral Sea, in May 1942. As Elmer Davis put it: Admiral Ernest King, chief of naval operations, believed that in war information "there should be just *one* communique. Some morning we would announce that the war was over and that we won it." The army proved somewhat more cooperative than the navy, and the release of military news improved as the war wound on—some suggested it was because there was news of victory instead of a string of defeats. But one of the first lessons OWI learned in Hollywood was that military branches in wartime would be formidable opponents to a civilian agency that wanted to coordinate war propaganda.[3]

To be on the safe side, Warners submitted scripts to both OWI and the Navy in June 1942. The BMP propagandists were encouraged. The script, by John Howard Lawson and W. R. Burnett, offered a "graphic picture of the convoy system," and its bringing together of diverse Americans for a crew suggested that America was "a composite of the best of all nations, races, and creeds." On the other hand, the reviewers thought the screenplay treated the navy disparagingly by showing a pompous admiral and a captain unable to sink an enemy vessel. Ironically, however, the navy did not find the portrayal of its men objectionable, and Warners sailed ahead disregarding OWI. The Bureau scored with another objection. A black pantryman in the film asked why he should fight for the Allies. The implication seemed to be that "he had nothing to hope for in white America." Lawson answered the question symbolically by having a white sailor die protecting him from German bullets. But the black character remained a pantryman, and the inference was that he would continue to be a pantryman "unless by some miracle, he became another Rochester or Joe Louis." The next draft of the script simply eliminated him, sidestepping the issue. OWI acknowledged this, but the new draft seemed preferable to the original treatment. OWI happily noted that the second version corrected the mistakes in the first draft, and the film was "completely in line with the Government's War Information program."[4]

Released in April 1943, *Action in the North Atlantic* was an excellent example of the attempt to combine OWI messages with the conventions of the Hollywood adventure film. It starred Humphrey Bogart as first mate Joe Rossi and a stolid Raymond

Massey as Captain Jarvis. The movie is framed by messages from Franklin Roosevelt. In the opening message the president says: "The goods *will* be delivered by this nation, which believes in the tradition of DAMN THE TORPEDOES, FULL SPEED AHEAD!" The action opens with Bogart leaning on the railing of the ship, shrouded in thick fog, describing in his tough-guy voice the ship's cargo: gasoline. He winces—that darn tooth is acting up again! He's too busy womanizing in port to see a dentist. Soon the tanker slips out to sea with its vital cargo. The ship is intercepted by a German submarine, which scores a direct hit. Fire engulfs the vessel. The survivors, huddled in a lifeboat on a flaming sea, are rammed by the submarine. The U-boat's ghoulish crew laughs uproariously and photographs the results. The survivors scramble into a life raft. "Go on, laugh ya apes!" cries the captain. "I swear to God our time is comin'. . . . We'll hunt ya down and slice ya like a piece of cheese!" They can't hear you, a sailor tells him gently. "But God can," he says quietly.

Adrift for eleven days in the tiny raft, they are finally rescued and return to a media welcome in New York City. Jarvis is reunited with his wife, who in her quiet inner fortitude is everything the stalwart wartime wife is supposed to be. She tucks him into his twin bed, softly kisses him goodnight and, out of range of his hearing, allows herself a few gentle sobs. His dog, a symbol of fidelity, sleeps beside his bed.

Meanwhile in a waterfront dive Joe Rossi is belting down straight whiskey in an effort to drown his toothache. He encounters Gus, the stereotypical loudmouth, who persists in describing the convoy he saw leaving port. Here was a perfect opportunity for the message that "loose lips sink ships." Joe warns him to shut up. He won't. The inevitable happens. Joe punches him out with a couple of swift jabs. Then the intrepid first mate gathers up the prize—the willowy black-gowned singer—and departs.

With Joe and the chanteuse ensconced in the production code's sexual never-never land off-screen, the scene shifts to a hiring hall along the docks. Pulaski, a survivor of the shipwreck, says loudly that he's not shipping out again. He has a pregnant wife—"I want to bounce my kid on my knee." Besides, nobody cares about the merchant marine. O'Hara, another survivor

(William Bendix), raises his fist to punch him out. A companion restrains him. That's what we're fighting for—free speech, he says. Then he turns to Pulaski. "But your thinking is cockeyed," he says. He has a family too. "So you want a safe job! Go ask the Poles, the Czechs, and the Greeks. . . . The trouble with you, Pulaski, is you think America is just a place to eat and sleep in. You don't know what side your future is buttered on." O'Hara rips Pulaski's union button off his jacket. Just then a crew call is announced for one of the new Liberty ships. O'Hara and his companions rush to the hiring window to sign on, leaving a sobered Pulaski, alone at his table, thinking about democracy and peer pressure. Pulaski gets up, smiles, and joins up again.

Here were OWI's ideals translated by John Howard Lawson into the language of the waterfront. And if anybody missed the point, the next scene—a graduation ceremony for a merchant marine officer class—underlined it with a short homily from the instructor about the importance of the merchant marine. People do care about the merchant marine, Pulaski.

The survivors from the first sinking are reunited on the new Liberty ship, whose comforts fill them with awe. Sailing to Canada to form a convoy, they join a symbolic parade of allied ships—first a Soviet ship, then a Dutch ship whose captain lost his family in the German destruction of Rotterdam. Jarvis opens his sealed orders. They are destined for Murmansk. "There's no bigger job than this," says Joe.

In depicting action at sea, the moviemakers walked a tight rope between the propaganda need to inspire confidence by showing sailors as competent, and the cinematic demand for action. After a German submarine hits one ship, a major battle ensues with a wolf pack. A U-boat picks up the Liberty ship but can't quite get it because, as the distressed submarine captain exclaims, these Liberty ships "zind zu schnell." The U-boat tails them for hours. Jarvis decides to risk his ship for the good of the rest by leading the sub away from the convoy. "We're on our own now," he says. It is a long black night laced with tension. Joe suggests they shut down all engines to throw the U-boat off their track. The submarine blacks out too. For hours the two vessels drift in a silent deadly game of tag. Joe's strategy works. The submarine captain finally radios that the Liberty ship has eluded him and asks the Luftwaffe for a dawn patrol off Nor-way.

German pilots locate the lone ship and strafe it. The ship's antiaircraft gunners return the fire and down a plane, which crashes into the ship. The captain is hit in the leg; after digging out the slug, Joe takes over. The patrol leaves. It falls on Joe to handle the burial at sea of eight men killed in the raid. He says: "Any one of us could be lyin' here and somebody read the book over us and be tossed in the sea. That ain't what's important. A lot more people are gonna die before this is over, and it's up to the ones who come through to make sure that they didn't die for nothing." The crew recites the Lord's Prayer, and the bodies are slid into the deep. Cut immediately to a shot of the ship, battle-scarred but triumphant, steaming majestically ahead. With wartime propaganda rhetoric clothed in Bogart's inimit-able style, the film visually symbolizes the eventual victory for which these sailors died.

The ship's speed falls to a mere six knots, making it vulner-able to the dogged submarine. A torpedo strikes the ship. "Wir haben sie! Wir haben sie!" cries the ecstatic U-boat captain. But Joe's resourcefulness surfaces again. The damage is serious but not fatal. He orders the crew to set fire to the ship and sends an SOS indicating they are abandoning her. He bets that this will fool the submarine captain and he will not waste another torpedo, but instead will surface. He is right. The submarine surfaces. In a dramatic sequence the Liberty ship, engulfed in smoke, bears down on the U-boat and rams it. The German cap-tain, so cool and in control earlier, screams in terror as he drowns in his flooded compartment. Soon planes flash through the sun-dappled clouds. A moment of apprehension. They are—Russian planes.

The film moves swiftly to its denouement. The vessel limps slowly but heroically into Murmansk. "It's a miracle," exclaims an officer. "That isn't a miracle—that's American seamanship," retorts the convoy's admiral. Throngs of Russian women and children (the men are at the front) cheer wildly: "Tovarich!" "Tovarich!" A sailor tells a puzzled compatriot: "That means comrade—that's good." The puzzled crewman understands and joins in: "Comrade! Comrade!" Cut to a reflective Joe Rossi on

Hollywood in its golden age was at the vortex of conflicting political, moral, and economic pressures. To keep the movies clean, noncontroversial, and profitable, the moguls set up a "czar," Republican politician Will Hays (left), shown here introducing the dour Yankee president Calvin Coolidge and Mrs. Coolidge to Hollywood glitter, personified by "America's sweetheart" Mary Pickford, and to the top of the corporate power structure, Louis B. Mayer. To protect Hollywood's worldwide market, Hays, assisted by Joseph Breen (seated below) and Geoffrey Shurlock, strictly enforced a censorship code that purged not only moral lapses but political controversy. *(Margaret Herrick Library/Academy of Motion Picture Arts and Sciences)*

In *Confessions of a Nazi Spy* (1939) (above), Hollywood's first genuinely anti-Nazi film, George Sanders, playing a dedicated follower of the Führer, tells his eager disciples that the Third Reich's spies have penetrated the United States. Charlie Chaplin's triumph, *The Great Dictator* (1940) (below), lampooned the pretensions and vulgarity of Hitler and Mussolini. Chaplin, playing the parts of both Hynkle, dictator of Tomania, and a Jewish barber persecuted by the Nazis, discusses affairs of state with Napaloni, dictator of Bacteria (Jack Oakie). *(Museum of Modern Art/Film Stills Archive, hereafter MOMA)*

As the United States edged toward war, Hollywood movies took an increasingly interventionist line. In *Sergeant York* (1941), a glorification of World War I hero Alvin York, Gary Cooper courts "Miss Gracie." The wholesome sixteen-year-old Joan Leslie fit the role of a shy, Bible-reading hero's wife better than the original suggestion, 1940s bombshell Jane Russell. *(MOMA)*

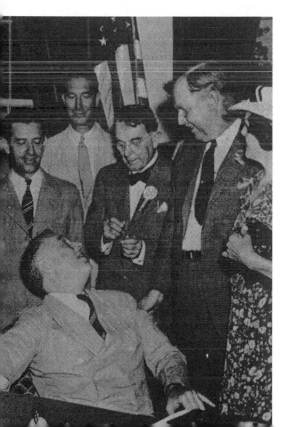

Eager to swing Hollywood behind his war policies, Franklin D. Roosevelt greets the real Alvin York (right), visiting the White House for a special screening of *Sergeant York*. FDR liked the film except for all the killing. *(MOMA)*

The controversial job of carrying out Roosevelt's mandate to mobilize the movies for war fell to four journalists. The popular radio commentator Elmer Davis, shown delivering his weekly wartime address, headed the Office of War Information. Lowell Mellett (bottom left), a former Scripps-Howard editor, headed OWI's Bureau of Motion Pictures in 1942–43. Ulric Bell (bottom right), a Washington correspondent, used the club of censorship and the carrot of foreign profits to make the studios listen to OWI. Nelson Poynter (seated at desk), the publisher of the *St. Petersburg Times,* took a lot of flack as OWI's first film liaison man in Hollywood. *(Franklin D. Roosevelt Library, National Archives/Still Photo Division, Nelson Poynter Memorial Library/University of South Florida—St. Petersburg, and Louisville Courier-Journal and Times)*

Japanese treachery instantly became a staple of wartime movies. In *Air Force* (1942) (Above), a film marked by crude racial epithets, the crew of the bomber *Mary Ann* listen in horrified disbelief to the news of Pearl Harbor. From left, John Garfield, George Tobias, and Harry Carey. *Little Tokyo, U.S.A.* (below), justified the incarceration of anyone of Japanese descent, including American citizens, on suspicion of treason. The hero, Los Angeles police detective Mike Steele (Preston Foster), gets nowhere in his investigation of "this Oriental bund" until he employs his flying fists. OWI disliked the picture and stepped up its demands that the studios submit screenplays to it before shooting began. *(MOMA)*

Opposition to the Third Reich might take the heroic form of a resistance leader, Kurt Müller (Paul Lucas) (above), confronting a Nazi sympathizer, Teck de Brancovis (George Coulouris) at left. His wife Sara (Bette Davis) is an equally committed anti-fascist, but her mother is unprepared for this turn of events in *Watch on the Rhine*. Among his other attributes in the beloved *Casablanca* (below), Rick (Humphrey Bogart) was a dedicated anti-fascist beneath the cynical exterior, as his pianist Sam (Dooley Wilson) and Sidney Greenstreet well knew. *(MOMA)*

Two films that spelled trouble for OWI were the Hepburn-Tracy duo *Keeper of the Flame* and *So Proudly We Hail*, a salute to nurses on Guadalcanal. Christine Forrest (Katharine Hepburn) explains to newspaper reporter Spencer Tracy why her husband, "America's number one fascist," had to die. OWI liked the picture's politics, but Louis B. Mayer stormed out of the preview. Poynter's attempt to write dialogue for nurse Janet (Claudette Colbert), carrying out her duties perfectly coiffed and rouged, plunged the agency into trouble at Paramount. *(MOMA)*

the bridge. What's the matter? Jarvis asks. "I'm just thinking about the trip back," says Joe. It was the best line in the picture.

The ending is framed with the voice of FDR intoning "we shall build a bridge of ships. . . . Nothing . . . shall prevent our complete and final victory" as a parade of mighty ships rolls down the slipways and the American flag waves smartly over the sea.

Action in the North Atlantic delighted those involved in war propaganda. Poynter lauded it as "intelligent propaganda for the cause of the United Nations." Jack Warner was awarded the Maritime Service victory flag when the movie premiered in New York City. Henry J. Kaiser, the ship-building wizard, thought it was such a morale builder he wanted to show it to all his war workers. The film rang many of OWI's bells—the role of the allies, the importance of the merchant marine, the responsibility of civilians at home (whether they were stalwart wives or drinkers in bars who ought to keep their mouths shut), the need for everyone to do his part, the toughness of the enemy, and the certainty of eventual victory. Appearing in 1943 at the height of American-Russian friendship, the film gave the Soviet Union added prominence. Parts of it would be an embarrassment to Warner Brothers after the war; the "tovarich" scene is often omitted from the movie when it plays on television.[5]

As entertainment, *Action in the North Atlantic* was less successful. *Time* judged it a "pulp-fictional log . . . of heaving, buckling studio sets . . . directly in the line of descent from 'The Perils of Pauline.'" The propaganda was blatant, even if it went down more easily in Bogart's laconic, worldly-wise persona. Although the structure of the film is too pat to generate much real tension for viewers, the documentary techniques lent some visual interest. And it did have Humphrey Bogart.[6]

OWI was able to have some influence on *Action in the North Atlantic*, but little on the strictly military issues. Not surprisingly, the studios deferred to the military, with whom they had a long-term understanding—a relationship reinforced by the primacy of the military in wartime. As part of the effort to augment its influence with Hollywood, which culminated in Mellett's letter of December 1942, OWI tried to make the armed forces clear pictures through OWI—an impossible task in wartime.

The War Department's extravagant praise of Hollywood triggered the propagandists' campaign. " 'FILM INDUSTRY IN WAR 100 PCT.' COL. WRIGHT SHOUTS PRAISE OF HOL-LYWOOD," read a banner in *The Hollywood Reporter* in the un-mistakeable style of movieland trade sheets. Col. W. Mason Wright, head of the motion picture division of the War De-partment's Bureau of Public Relations, abandoned the passive voice of militarese for movie puffery: "No matter what we want from Hollywood, we get it—and quick. We do not even have to ask. Hollywood comes to us. . . . The tremendous value of Hol-lywood's part in the war is inestimable." The industry thrived on this sort of praise, and the studios could flaunt the War De-partment's encomiums whenever OWI complained about their lack of cooperation.[7]

Poynter gagged when he saw the interview. "The movie mak-ers would rather be told how wonderful they are" than face up to their responsibility "for creating better understanding of The Issues of this War," he said. The matter of who interpreted gov-ernment policy to Hollywood—the military or OWI—needed to be clarified. Poynter sent Mellett a draft letter on October 21 which informed the studios that all contacts with the U.S. and foreign governments should be channeled through OWI. Poyn-ter's draft amplified a letter President Roosevelt had sent to var-ious government agencies in August in which he told them to compose their differences behind closed doors rather than washing them in the public prints. The president's letter im-plied that government agencies should cooperate with OWI in matters pertaining to motion pictures, but it did not order them to do so.[8]

Elmer Davis tried to lend whatever muscle he had. On De-cember 3, 1942, he sent letters to the secretaries of War and the Navy asking them to channel all their contacts with Hollywood through OWI. Davis had sallied forth on a Quixotean tilt. His letter was passed down the chain of command to General Surles, the Army's PR chief, who said the close contact between the army and Hollywood dictated army involvement in every stage of production. "Only the Army can decide whether the pro-posed treatment is an appropriate depiction of the Army," he declared. OWI would be at best an intermediary, not "a useful collaborator." The agency suffered a similar rebuff from the Navy. This fruitless gambit reminded OWI that, unless the president intervened, civilian agencies in wartime were at the mercy of the military.[9]

In early January 1943 the military relented somewhat from Surles' original dismissal of the request, and a protocol for handling treatments, scripts, and finished pictures was initialed by OWI, the Army, and the Navy. Under its terms producers would submit any material dealing with the armed forces to the propaganda agency at the same time as it was submitted to the Army or Navy. The military agreed to consult with OWI about matters of general policy before approving or rejecting the material. The agreement stipulated that "of course ... OWI exercises no 'right' of clearance"; the procedure was simply to offer the civilians a forum to review pictures for general war policy. This was a limp agreement indeed. OWI now sat in the conference room, but it remained to be seen whether OWI representations would be taken seriously by the Pentagon.[10]

Some agitated Hollywood executives worried that even this tepid arrangement signaled an OWI "invasion." A committee headed by Paramount's redoubtable Frank Freeman, president of the Association of Motion Picture Producers, drafted an alternate plan designed to reduce OWI's influence in two ways: It limited the mandatory OWI review to materials submitted to the army and navy (all else remained voluntary), and, instead of passing recommendations to the army, BMP would convey them directly to the studios. In this way the propagandists would have little opportunity to influence the army or navy to veto a picture, and the studios retained their freedom of action. The producers noted that their procedure afforded them OWI's advice but avoided any implication of OWI censorship.[11]

Hollywood's worries about OWI working through the military were exaggerated. The armed forces public relations offices found the propagandists chiefly a nuisance. Ulric Bell detected few practical results from the new consultation procedures. Mellett still complained in May 1943 that the army was "damn determined that we shall have practically nothing to say about their motion pictures."[12]

Indeed the industry soon had to worry about a much more

serious "invasion" of its territory than OWI. The army began to threaten Hollywood's heartland—commercial exhibition—and the industry found they had an unlikely ally in Lowell Mellett. The subject was the "Why We Fight" series, a seven-part epic of the origins and first years of the war, produced for the army by one of Hollywood's finest, Frank Capra. The prominent director of such 1930s favorites as *It Happened One Night* and *Mr. Smith Goes to Washington*, Capra enlisted in the Army soon after Pearl Harbor. The army gave him the rank of colonel and put him to work making indoctrination films for the troops. The success of the first installment of the "Why We Fight" series—*Prelude to War*, which won an Oscar for best documentary of 1942—raised the possibility of commercial release through regular movie houses. Capra's number one fan, Franklin D. Roosevelt, endorsed the idea. The army was eager for the Capra series to reach the public, but it also had a bigger target. General Surles hoped the series would be an opening wedge that would enable him to "introduce any Army film, a reasonable amount of them" to commercial distribution. How far the army's PR chief wanted to go was not clear, but Drew Pearson claimed that the army intended to take over 25 percent of screen time. Industry officials treated the "Why We Fight" issue warily. They did not want to be accused of being deficient in patriotism, but they intended to protect their commercial interests.[13]

Mellett emerged as the principal opponent of the army's scheme. He told FDR it was "one of the most skillful jobs of movie making I have ever seen"—and hence all the more dangerous. He believed the chief effect would be to leave audiences in a state of "nervous hysteria"—"bewildered rather than fired to a clear purpose." That might win the war, but it wouldn't help much in "making a saner world after the armistice." Mellett thought it ran counter to OWI themes at some points, and his agency, which was supposed to be the central clearing house for such efforts, had not been consulted. "This is the third instance in which a Hollywood director, put in a service uniform and given the government's money to spend, has come up with a finished Hollywood product that has evaded scrutiny by the OWI," he said. John Ford did it with *Battle of Midway*; Darryl Zanuck tried with North Africa but the army scotched his effort.

"I hate to have to spend so much of my time seeking to outwit these boys," Mellett told the president. The BMP chief envied the resources at Capra's command and resented the military's evident desire to run the war without OWI.[14]

Even worse, Mellett feared the army's heavy hands would unravel his carefully knit pattern of cooperation with the movie industry. He had tried to buy Hollywood's cooperation by pledging that the government would not release feature-length pictures in competition with theirs. In return the industry promised to consult on feature pictures, to allow government shorts to be shown in movie theaters every other week, and to screen Hollywood's own patriotic shorts in alternate weeks. Mellett believed Washington could no more force movie theaters to show government pictures like *Prelude to War* than it could demand that newspapers print government copy. Besides, most "Why We Fight" films ran from 50 to 60 minutes each. This was fine for boot camp indoctrination but exactly the wrong length—midway between a short and a feature—for commercial theaters.[15]

Mellett soon became the heavy to the army. The issue, which arose in October 1942, dragged on until mid-March 1943 as OWI and the army negotiated changes in *Prelude to War* and the terms of its release. In March, *A World At War*, which Samuel Spewack made for OWI, completed its critically and commercially successful run. It was the only full-length documentary OWI asked theaters to exhibit. Army officials thought they now had the green light to exhibit *Prelude to War*. But OWI raised new objections. "That's that God-damned Lowell Mellett," exploded Under Secretary of War Robert Patterson. "I talked to Elmer Davis 3 or 4 days ago and he told me that by all that was holy, they would be shown and there'd be no more fooling about it and now there is more fooling about it." Was Davis the boss of his shop or was Mellett? Patterson demanded to know. General Surles phoned Cowles, who felt "violently" that the picture should be released to theaters. "I'm going to get Lowell over here late today and get through with his damn letter-writing and get the picture out," Cowles said. That seemed to break the log jam. Mellett agreed to present the picture to the War Activities Committee, the industry group that coordinated the offering of shorts. He insisted on certain changes; a new version contained a long introduction by Secretary of War Stimson and closed with a panorama of United Nations troops and flags.[16]

The War Activities Committee told the army, in effect, that despite its technical excellence there was no market for its picture. The Committee reinforced Mellett's point that feature-length documentaries had limited appeal. *Prelude to War* suffered the further liability that its subject, the origins of the war, had already been covered by documentaries such as Paramount's *World in Flames* and March of Time's *Ramparts We Watch*. They played in only half the houses which showed the Committee's program, even though their material had been more timely than *Prelude*'s. If moviegoers in 1943 were interested in the war, they wanted to see current developments, not old news. They were not the captive audience with which the army was familiar.[17]

But the War Department juggernaut ground on toward its goal. Under Secretary Patterson fired off a hot letter to Davis blaming Mellett for the six-month delay. Assistant Secretary of War John J. McCloy followed with a "Dear Lowell" letter. Whenever he asked why the series was not shown in public, he wrote, he was told "Lowell Mellett opposes it." "I cannot believe," McCloy continued, "that there is *any* consideration that would justify not showing these to the public." The public relations generals toyed with releasing to the press the story of Mellett's opposition, or even getting a congressional resolution demanding the series be shown in public. These measures proved to be unnecessary. After two days of fruitless searching, Surles finally tracked down Francis Harmon, vice president of the War Activities Committee, in a meeting with Davis and Mellett. "That's fairly significant ... finding all three of them in a huddle," Surles said.[18]

The resistance of OWI and the industry was at an end. The War Activities Committee agreed to distribute the picture, now billed as "The Greatest Gangster Picture Ever Made." Harmon knew this leap of showmanship might shock some people. "But it may get some girls from the 5 and 10 in to see this picture," he said. "That's our problem—we know the educators and the conservative people like it—now if we can lure the chewing-gum crowd, we'd better do it." People seemed to prefer fictional gangsters, however; *Prelude to War* was not a box office success. Some army officials accused the industry of sabotaging the picture, claiming that Hollywood could attract "large audiences to lousy pictures when they felt like it." But the real reason Americans did not line up for *Prelude to War* was probably that they wanted their war current or not at all.[19]

The "Why We Fight" controversy demonstrated that, in the end, a civilian agency usually loses to a determined military organization in wartime. But OWI had gone to considerable lengths to preserve Mellett's original deal of no interference with feature exhibition by the industry—a point that was reassuring to Hollywood. The box office failure of *Prelude to War* deflected demands for commercial release of other films in the series. By the spring of 1943 the relations between OWI and the military had been clarified. The propaganda agency had not managed to get the military to defer to it in dealing with Hollywood; that was probably a chimeral aspiration. But the possibility of further military intrusion into OWI's domain in Hollywood had been stopped, giving the agency potentially wide latitude.

Using to the full his influence as a representative of OWI's Overseas Branch, Ulric Bell made the most of that opportunity. He was greatly helped by the tougher line that began to emerge in the Office of Censorship. In late summer of 1942 the Censorship Bureau's New York Board of Review, which scrutinized newsreels, issued a stringent supplement that set a more urgent tone. It warned: "Don't show pictures of unsavory aspects of American life—gangsters, slums, hopeless poverty, Okies, etc., and in particular violations of American wartime restrictions, such as rationing, gasoline and rubber rules, etc." The newsreel censors also forbade "empty and vainglorious boasts" about American wealth and power. Through the fall of 1942 OWI urged the Censorship Office to extend similar restrictions to feature pictures.[20]

On December 11, 1942, the Office of Censorship issued a new code that fulfilled many of OWI's desires. The new regulations' appearance at the same time as Mellett's controversial letter to the studios was coincidental. Interestingly, though Hollywood dug in its heels over Mellett's requests, it uttered scarcely a peep about the censor's new rules. Those rules banned anything having to do with factories, military equipment, or easily identifiable terrain, from being sent abroad without explicit approval from the Censorship Office, the military, or both. The December code's biggest departure was in the portrayal of American society. A key clause prohibited showing "labor, class or other disturbances since 1917 which might be distorted into enemy propaganda." If these were incidental in a dramatic production they might be allowed. Similarly "scenes of lawlessness or disorder in which order is restored and the offenders punished" might be approved if lawlessness was not the main theme of a picture. Gangster pictures were the most troubling example of this type of film. The censors believed such productions discredited the American political system in the eyes of foreigners, but they were not banned *per se*. Westerns escaped. "The bang-bangs survived the governmental psychoanalyzing with flying colors," said the *Hollywood Reporter*. "Since the law and the hero and his good American horse always triumphed in the end, the westerns were accepted as good, though innocuous, screen salesmen of the American way."[21]

The new code would prove very helpful in steering studios away from the type of pictures that had troubled the Bureau of Motion Pictures for some time, and in keeping such pictures home if the studios persisted in making them. Bell liked the changes and wanted the code tightened still more, particularly to curb the gangster pictures he loathed. Poynter, on the other hand, feared the Office of Censorship was going too far. "We certainly do not want to try to convince foreign peoples that we have achieved Nirvana," he said. Poynter and Bell were soon at loggerheads over the degree of Nirvana the movies should reveal.[22]

Bell redoubled his efforts to convert Rothacker. Together they endured *Dixie Dugan*, which Twentieth Century had made despite BMP's objections. In a Charles Ruggles burlesque of the air raid warden, the comic chased an incendiary bomb as it burned from floor to floor. "It is a very poor way of dealing with a very serious part of the war effort," Bell sniffed. But displaying more detachment than OWI moviegoers usually did, he recognized that it was such a poor picture it wasn't worth protesting. Even Jason Joy "groaned" through it. "No audience would be very much concerned about anything other than walk-ing out," Bell said.[23]

He pressed his case, however, with an unlikely production, Republic's *London Blackout Murders*. This "B" picture offended Bell on several counts: Londoners "might recoil" from the "suggestive" title. It was also implied that the British govern-ment would consider a separate peace with Germany. An over-worked doctor uttered the "completely irresponsible line" about his work during a blackout: "I had to amputate a woman's leg last night. Instead, I cut off her head." And Lend-Lease took "an unnecessary side-swipe" when a character remarked, "We still have whiskey—if they don't start sending *that* to the Ameri-cans." But Rothacker passed the picture. BMP reviewers saw it a few days later and asked for a number of changes. Despite assurances that the film would be altered, nothing was done. Rothacker stuck to the letter of the code unless he was "fortified from every possible angle," said Bell.[24]

The overseas liaison officer went to the top and enlisted Elmer Davis to ask Byron Price, Director of Censorship, to over-rule Rothacker. But Price could not agree that "suppression should go the lengths Bell has suggested." Movies should not be banned for "every crack . . . which someone might think of-fensive to someone." Price then pointedly reminded Davis that the policy was to exercise "great liberality" with outgoing ma-terial "on the theory that the people of the United Nations could take it and that the enemy would find ways to distort devel-opments anyway." It was going pretty far to ban a murder story just because it contained "some ridiculous material." Ironically, the country's chief censor read the self-styled advocates of the Four Freedoms a lesson in freedom of expression.[25]

Undaunted, Bell continued to press his case. In March 1943 he composed a list of 21 films—mostly "B" pictures—that had been passed by the censor despite his objections. Some of these used only a rough script and hence were less open to OWI in-fluence before shooting, but in other cases studios simply ig-nored the bureau's objections. Producers often engaged in "a hide-and-seek race . . . to get the censor's okay before they show their stuff to OWI," Bell complained. A case in point was RKO's *I Walked With a Zombie* which he tried for six weeks to get a look at but was always told it was not ready. A better picture than its title suggested, *Zombie*'s treatment of voodoo in the West Indies alarmed Bell because it seemed to draw a sharp line between whites and blacks. The film was a good deal more ambiguous than Bell's reading allowed; some of the whites, including a missionary doctor, acknowledged the efficacy of voodoo. Bell did not wish to take any chances with this unusual bit of anthropological relativism. On February 4 the studio invited OWI to screen it—one day after Rothacker approved it for export.[26]

Bell did not contend that all 21 movies should be barred from export, but each contained objectionable material he wanted corrected. He carried on a vendetta against gangster pictures. The prime offender was RKO's *Mr. Lucky*, a Cary Grant vehicle released in the spring of 1943. Months later he complained it "still stands as about the worst picture, from our standpoint, I have seen here."[27]

The picture had one of those only-in-Hollywood origins. Milton Holmes, a tennis pro at the Beverly Hills Tennis Club, wrote it when he was down on his luck and, in a moment of optimism, showed it to Grant, who liked it. The matinee idol plays Joc Adams, a crooked gambler who wants to clear out on his gambling boat for Cuba, only to be stopped by the sudden arrival of a 1A draft card. But Joe Bascapolous, possessor of a 4F (ineligible for the draft) card, dies; Joe Adams wins the dead man's card at dice and assumes the dead man's identity. He is at his wit's end as to how to raise the $6,000 stake he needs to start his own gambling operation, until Dorothy, an icy young New York society woman (Laraine Day), badgers him for $50 for a ticket for war relief. Aha! Why not set up a rigged casino at her ball and abscond with the proceeds? But gambling is illegal, and she won't hear of it, of course—until she begins to fall in love with him. She melts; the news of gambling at the ball turns relief tickets into the hottest numbers in town.

Then a letter arrives from Joe Bascapolous's mother in Greece. Adams takes it to a Greek Orthodox priest for translation. He is deeply moved as the priest reads the simple but affecting account of the German invasion. Adams has a conversion experience in the cathedral, visually emphasized by no fewer than four changes of lighting on his face. He can't doublecross the war relief—we're going to run it on the level, he tells his startled cronies. His archrival, Zepp, shoots him as he leaves with the proceeds; though wounded he gets the money to relief headquarters. Meanwhile he has given his boat to war relief. He sails with it to Europe, leaving Dorothy behind—he's not the kind of guy for her. When he returns, having joined the merchant marine, she's waiting for him on the fog-shrouded pier.

From one point of view *Mr. Lucky* offered a positive theme. It was the story of personal regeneration under the combined influence of a noble woman and the war effort—a favorite wartime theme. The cynical, selfish Adams, who will do everything he can to avoid the war, begins to change into a more human individual. The tragedy of Greece convinces him that this is his war after all. The plot is rather implausible and Adams' conversion rather contrived, but thanks to Grant's street-wise characterization, the picture is entertaining. Much of George Barnes's camera work is excellent, particularly the way he capitalized on the fluid possibilities of the medium. In scenes in the war relief office, the camera moves deftly across and around partitions to pick up fragments of conversations, coincidences, and inadvertent eavesdropping.

In a superb sequence Adams learns to knit. Dorothy is trying to break down male prejudices against some aspects of relief work. "I don't knit," says Adams, his masculinity offended. But to prove his sincerity he reports to the knitting instructor, who coos, "We'll educate those little pinkies." Adams grimaces as an elderly society woman takes his hands in her beringed fingers, tells him earnestly you spell it "P-U-R-L," and takes him through the drill. As Adams gains in dexterity he is moved to a store window to display his talents. A crowd of men press against the window watching in disbelief. His sidekick, Cronk, rushes in aghast to get his boss out of there. "Where's your moral bravery?" Adams retorts. He makes Cronk sit down and learn to knit. Cut to the boat, where Cronk leans over a crap table showing the other men how to knit. Subsequently whenever he waits in the car to drive his boss, he nonchalantly passes the time knitting, surrounded by disbelieving male crowds. This sly dig at machismo is rare and Grant carries it off superbly. The film also took a crack at the pretensions of charity-ball society. Adams' gambling setup is what gets them to turn out for the relief ball. Perhaps writer Holmes had had his fill of this set at the tennis club.

The fun and positive virtues in all of this were invisible to Ulric Bell. He objected to the emphasis on the "sordid side of American life" and the "inaccurate representation" of the country. He intensely disliked the draft dodging scenes and the imputation that relief activities got poor responses and had to resort to illegal gambling. OWI wanted to show every sector cheerfully doing its bit for the war. He told Rothacker the draft dodging treatment was so bad there would be "public repercussions." RKO toned down the draft-dodging dialogue for foreign release, and the censor, rejecting OWI's protests, gave it an export license.[28]

Bell got some support for his interpretation of the picture, though not for censorship, from Manny Farber of the *New Republic*, who titled his review "Method in Its Badness." He likened the skillful treatment of the "vulgar story" to "a bad salad with an intelligent dressing." But most viewers took the picture for what it was—sheer fun, with a rather improbable conversion scene. *Time* happily noted the "discovery" that you could say flat out "what nearly every man secretly feels about the draft"—provided the bad guys said it. So frank were some of the comments that audiences giggled loudly when a stern-visaged Uncle Sam appeared on a recruiting poster. Of 69 preview cards returned at showings in Riverside, California, only two questioned the draft dodging or gambling. Most of them liked Cary Grant—that seemed to be the essence of their comments.[29]

Surely in this case the censor was right. *Mr. Lucky* contained some scenes of perhaps questionable taste, but it was hard to imagine the dire consequences Bell feared. One of the things that set democracy apart from fascism was the freedom to laugh at oneself. That was probably better propaganda than a sheaf of Christmas Eve sermons about Christ and democracy.

A lesser known picture, *Lucky Jordan* (Paramount, 1942), raised similar issues for Bell. Lucky Jordan, played by Alan Ladd, tries to dodge the draft and swindle the army. But when Nazi agents beat up Annie, a gin-swilling, pan-handling grandmother who had befriended him, Jordan undergoes a conversion similar to that of Joe Adams. He sees the evil of Nazism, helps round up a spy ring, and meekly returns to the army. Nazis beating up a defenseless grandmother—wasn't this analogous to Hitler's aggression? Perhaps, but it was too subtle a parallel for Bell and OWI reviewers, who wanted Jordan to announce his awakening with a soliloquy on global politics.[30]

Some films projected potentially harmful impressions of foreign affairs. Warners' *Desert Song*, a remake of the old warhorse of 1932, showed French oppression in North Africa. Scenes of French torture in the original version were cut, but Bell still thought the picture "could be most detrimental" to the Allies in North Africa. Two cloak-and-dagger releases from Warner Brothers, *Background to Danger* and *Adventure in Iraq*, which had aroused OWI criticism in the script stage, remained objectionable to Bell because they exploited the war for trite spy antics. Paramount's *Road to Morocco*, which Milton Eisenhower upon a return from a visit to his brother on the North African front said "simply must not reach North Africa," received Rothacker's approval nonetheless. With the Allied invasion in progress, however, the studio recanted and assured the censor it would not ship the film to North Africa without OWI's consent. Metro's *Assignment in Brittany*, though an "excellent" portrayal of the French Resistance, contained a gratuitous opening scene in which a Free French officer stabbed an Arab.[31]

Bell was troubled by the manner in which America was portrayed, in particular by the emphasis on lawlessness, and by the number of scenes that ridiculed the war effort. Monogram ignored OWI objections and produced *Clancy Street Kids* around youth as hoodlums. Universal's comedy *Hi Ya Chum* showed a town dominated by gangsters; defense workers were easy prey for crooks. Universal's *Cowboy in Manhattan* featured gangsters and suggested that lynching was "a standard method of distributing justice in Texas." In RKO's *Petticoat Larceny* law officers were "stupid and inefficient;" in Paramount's *True to Life* the satiric portrayal of air raid wardens could have been omitted from export prints; in Columbia's *Junior Army* American youths came off as "poor sports, snobs and bullies." Bell believed the way to stave off export disasters was to have Washington headquarters rule that Rothacker could not pass on a picture until he received a recommendation from OWI, Overseas Branch.

The code was too limited, Bell complained. He wanted it "widened considerably."[32]

For Bell, the ardent interventionist, Hollywood's exploitation of "the sordid side of American life" was unpatriotic. These pictures might undermine support from the Allies and offer the enemy material with which to blacken America. Bell did not want to run these risks in a total war. Democratic freedoms are always precarious in wartime, and he believed far-reaching curbs were acceptable because of America's peril.

Poynter disagreed sharply. "Fascist methods need not be used to defeat the common enemy of Fascism," he said. Though he had been concerned about the movies' treatment of American life, he now thought Bell and the Office of Censorship were going too far. He conceded that Hollywood had unduly emphasized glamour and gangsterism in the past. The danger was that in trying to correct this imbalance, OWI and the censor were pressuring Hollywood into presenting "a distorted, dishonest picture of sweetness and light in America that becomes incredible to a foreign audience."[33]

Poynter identified three chief problems as a result. First, labor relations. Hollywood's traditional aversion to showing strikes was reinforced by the censorship code of December 1942, which banned scenes of labor strife since 1917. He suggested that "an honest interpretation" of the labor scene would counteract Axis propaganda. By year's end American industries would produce more munitions than the rest of the world combined. "Our labor policies cannot be all wrong and accomplish such results," he said. Second, lawlessness. Poynter thought movies could show American institutions meeting social and political problems and hence reaffirm faith in democracy. Less concerned about the export of *Mr. Lucky* than was Bell, he noted that some people thought gangster pictures might actually help counteract Axis propaganda that Americans were soft. Third, the black market. Poynter wanted to use Hollywood to mobilize opinion against black markets and in support of rationing. Censorship regulations were unclear, so studios tended to avoid the subject rather than risk trouble. Ironically this probably harmed the war effort by suggesting that "America is having too easy an experience in this war."[34]

Freedom in American pictures would inspire other demo-

cratic peoples. Everybody knew that every country had problems with lawlessness, black markets, labor strife, and antisocial
behavior. It would be a show of strength to admit that America
had not solved all its problems but was making progress dem-
ocratically. "If OWI's policy is the 'strategy of truth,' " he said,
"isn't it necessary to make a sacrifice hit now and then?" Poynter argued partly from a journalist's belief in freedom of expression. But he also thought his position would assist the war effort. The purpose of a sacrifice hit, after all, is to advance the
runner. Unless present trends were reversed, he feared that the
drift toward escapist comedies, musicals, and fantasies would
"become so excessive that the screen will not be as valuable a
weapon as it otherwise can be."[35]

Bell countered that relations with the studios had never been
better, which he attributed largely to the emphasis placed on
the foreign angle. Producers did not dispute the government's
right to "supervise material sent abroad in wartime." He accused Poynter and Mellett of undercutting him on certain pictures, including the by now notorious *Mr. Lucky*. On only one
point did he agree with Poynter—that the two sections were on
divergent courses and OWI headquarters needed to straighten
out the tangle. In December, Bell had praised Mellett and Poynter for bearing the brunt of pioneering with Hollywood, but
now he called their work a "botch." "Poynter can't work with
me and I won't work with him," Bell said. Poynter sensed the
initiative slipping from him. "We have lost control of our own
staff," he confided to Mellett. If reviewers made incorrect judgments he could not get them to make changes. Bell refused to
attend Poynter's Saturday morning staff meetings. The situation was intolerable; the office could have only one boss.[36]

Poynter described the conflict to Mellett as a clash between
Bell's wish to use the "club of censorship" and "our philosophy
of free communications." Poynter seemed to have forgotten his
eagerness to have Bell join the Hollywood office and carry
OWI's desires to the Office of Censorship. Bell wanted to say
America had no significant problems; Poynter was willing to
acknowledge some of them, so long as films showed democracy
solving them. The Overseas Branch representative went further
than Mellett and Poynter wished, but having once invoked censorship to aid propaganda, the Bureau of Motion Pictures found

it hard to turn it off. Together censorship and propaganda, by reinforcing each other, form an especially dangerous combination, for they make complete that denial of "access to pertinent information" which Robert K. Merton identified as the hallmark of the manipulation of opinion. OWI's strategy stopped well short of the total perversion of information that characterizes totalitarian societies, but the "strategy of truth" was badly twisted by the perceived exigencies of total war.[37]

OWI was in deep trouble by the spring of 1943, in both Hollywood and Washington. Riven by internal feuds, the Domestic Branch made an inviting target for the resurgent conservative coalition in Congress. When the political shakeout was over, OWI would find the overseas policy was its ace in the hole.

The tone of the organization shifted markedly in the early months of 1943. Bell's approach in Hollywood had its parallels in personnel and programatic shifts at Washington headquarters. Those who believed in an emphasis on serious, reflective analysis of the war—Mellett and Poynter considered themselves among them—were put increasingly on the defensive by people who skirted the deeper issues of the war in favor of slick, superficial techniques borrowed from the world of advertising. The conflict was most acute in the writers' section of the Domestic Branch. When Archibald MacLeish left OWI at the end of 1942, Mike Cowles became head of the Domestic Branch. He was less the writer-intellectual and more the publishing executive, attracted to the splashy displays, short sentences, and simplified concepts that characterized *Look*. When he reorganized the Domestic Branch in February 1943 the writers began reporting to William Lewis, a former CBS vice president. The graphics section, which often collaborated with the writers, came under Price Gilbert, a former vice president of Coca-Cola. The writers lost much of their autonomy, and Cowles dampened their initiative by limiting their efforts chiefly to writing materials requested by other government agencies. Although OWI claimed only to be interpreting government wartime policy, the writers could scarcely lift a pen without appearing to take sides on some controversial issue and hence offending some politically potent group. Perhaps personally uneasy about the writers' politics, Cowles found their output politically damaging. The publisher and his new deputies increasingly stressed the short, pungent imagery of American advertising, which was less politically suspect.[38]

To many OWI veterans this direction was intolerable. Henry Pringle warned that it was driving creative talent out of the organization. Several writers resigned when Cowles refused to permit publication of a controversial pamphlet on food shortages. Francis Brennan, former head of the Graphics Bureau, quit, rapping the agency's new tendency "to make necessary civilian actions appear palatable, comfortable, and not quite as inconvenient as Guadalcanal." Reading Brennan's statement, MacLeish concluded OWI was "no longer very much interested in the innards of the war." The graphics staff made their distaste for the new regime clear by circulating a poster around the office: The Statue of Liberty raised not her torch but four bottles of Coca-Cola. The caption read: "The War That Refreshes: The Four Delicious Freedoms."[39]

The dispute went public when Pringle, Brennan, Arthur Schlesinger, Jr, and several others fired a broadside in April justifying their resignations. "There is only one issue—the deep and fundamental one of the honest presentation of war information," they said. Promotional techniques had their place, but OWI was dominated by "high-pressure promoters who prefer slick salesmanship to honest information." It was impossible now "to tell the full truth." OWI was being turned into "an Office of War Bally-hoo." To be sure, OWI's record for telling "the full truth" had long since been compromised. But the tendency to avoid the ideological aspect of the war, to sugarcoat unpleasant realities, and to package wartime issues as though they were soap and soft drinks could only mean a further dilution of public understanding. The new direction betrayed a growing suspicion that the public, whether American or foreign, could not be trusted to make up its own mind.[40]

In touching so many controversial issues, OWI had done something to offend almost everybody, and the change of course came too late to save the Domestic Branch. OWI's enemies gave chase as the listing vessel tacked to the right. In the War Department General Surles and his staff chortled over the troubles reflected by the writers' wrangle. On Capitol Hill conservative Republicans and southern Democrats launched an attack: a parade of senators and congressmen rose to denounce a particular pamphlet that had offended their constituents or an activity that violated American values.[41]

Two themes ran through the hearings and floor fights. One was the ingrained suspicion of artists and intellectuals that American politicians and men of affairs harbored. The other was the feeling that OWI was too liberal. Republican Representative John Taber of New York denounced the agency as "a haven of refuge for the derelicts." One representative bore in on writers who were being paid more by OWI than they could earn in civilian life. His prime example was Robert Riskin, who, according to the congressman, was being paid a munificent $4,000 a year in comparison to his $2,000 civilian salary. Riskin had been earning $2,000 *per week*, Sherwood corrected him. The congressman, undeterred and unabashed, continued his roll call, leaving a corps of talented writers wondering why they had abandoned their regular high-paying jobs for service in a war effort that repaid their patriotism with miserly checks and congressional vilification.[42]

The New Deal had effectively been stalled since 1938 by a combination of conservative opposition and Roosevelt's increased attention to foreign affairs. In 1942 the president told a news conference that Dr. New Deal had been replaced by Dr. Win-the-War. Mobilizing its increased strength after the 1942 elections, the conservative coalition moved from a holding action to an attack on existing liberal programs. A host of New Deal agencies were eliminated and others severely cut back. With its roster of liberal to leftist artists and writers, the OWI Domestic Branch not surprisingly was caught in the anti-New Deal barrage. Joe Starnes of Alabama informed the House that the OWI message had a "distinct state socialistic tinge." Representative Allen of Louisiana singled out the pamphlet *Negroes and the War*—criticized by blacks and racists alike—as an attempt to glorify one race over another. "For God's sake, give us unity in this country and let us get on with the war," he cried. Republican Senator Rufus C. Holman of Oregon unfurled the first issue of *Victory*, OWI's overseas magazine, and denounced as Democratic electioneering its article on "Roosevelt of America—President, Champion of Liberty, United States Leader in the War to Win Lasting and Worldwide Peace." The critics had a point. How neutral a propaganda agency should, or could, be in propagandizing its own people was a genuine question. The way the critics raised the issue, however, suggested they were less interested in that philosophical problem than in how it might be turned to partisan advantage.[43]

Had members of Congress delved into the Bureau of Motion Picture's manual for the motion picture industry they no doubt would have felt their charges confirmed. Twelve months of controversy in the movie capital exacted a political toll. Representative Robsion of Kentucky condemned Mellett's "censorship" of Hollywood. Poynter believed that Frank Freeman worked behind the scenes with Senators Walter George and Richard Russell of his native Georgia to kill the motion picture office. Whether Poynter was correct was unclear. As head of the Motion Picture Producers Committee in Hollywood, Freeman sent telegrams to the key Congressional committee chairmen expressing the producers' support of a continuing liaison effort. That did not necessarily mean, however, that he wanted Mellett and Poynter to run it.[44]

Even if the Georgia conspiracy did not exist, there was no doubt that Poynter's operation had rubbed Hollywood conservatives the wrong way. Martin Quigley drew the line clearly in a long, signed editorial in the *Motion Picture Herald*. One problem, he said, was that the OWI motion picture division had few people with experience in "the *business* of motion pictures." They were interested instead in the "arty" aspects of film. An indefatigable promoter of Hollywood as a business producer of "pure entertainment," Quigley fought anything that disrupted commercial interests.[45]

What really raised his ire was OWI's liberalism. He conceded that the Bureau was a useful conduit of government information about the war. The source of "misunderstandings," he claimed, lay in the bureaucrats' pushing "their cherished readjustments of the social, economic and political order." He was offended that OWI chastised MGM when the Parliament scene in *Random Harvest* failed to include Labour members "wearing baggy and unpressed trousers, denim shirts open at the neck and exposing hairy chests and that sort of thing." The industry wanted only to cooperate with the war effort. OWI bureaucrats were a "clique of self-authorized policy makers . . . [who] would run the nation, and the world, their peculiar and militantly divergent way."[46]

Quigley had a valid criticism about the propagandists' interference in some pictures, notably *So Proudly We Hail*. In other instances, such as *Random Harvest*, his criticism attempted chiefly to discredit liberal and leftist opinion and to reassert the studios' traditional prerogatives. To Quigley and his crowd the Labour party was even more anathema than the New Deal, and they were not going to give it favorable play if they didn't need to. The quarrel was not really about entertainment—OWI's suggestion in this case did not hurt the film's dramatic qualities—but ideology.

OWI could count on a few friends, notably the liberal Representative Emmanuel Celler of Brooklyn, but they were not enough. A House committee recommended funding the domestic branch at 40 percent of the 1942 level. The whole House went the committee one better by voting, 218 to 114, to kill domestic operations altogether. The Senate too was hostile but not so heavy-handed. An administration loyalist, Senator Joseph O'Mahoney of Wyoming, proposed an amendment to cut appropriations from the existing $7,625,000 to $5,500,000; his suggestion failed, 40 to 34. The Senate then halved his proposed appropriation, to $2,750,000. In conference House members whittled the figure to just $2,125,000—only 27 percent of the authorization for the branch the previous year. Eight hundred OWI staffers were fired as the domestic work force dropped from 1,300 to 495. The Senate had maneuvered adroitly. As Davis pointed out, it provided just enough money to avoid "the odium of having put us out of business and carefully not enough to let us accomplish much."[47]

Poynter tried desperately to keep his office alive. Enjoying independent means, he even offered to serve without salary. These efforts came to naught. Mellett left OWI, though he continued to serve in a vaguely defined capacity as a presidential assistant into 1944. Poynter, now nicknamed "disapoynter," took solace in a vacation in Mexico.[48]

Their departure made possible a reorganization which enhanced the interests of both OWI and the studios. The domestic side abandoned liaison efforts with the studios and limited it-self to the production of information shorts. In a remarkable turn of events Stanton Griffis, chairman of Paramount's exec-utive committee, took Mellett's place and operated chiefly as a figurehead. Political opposition had gotten rid of Mellett and Poynter and squeezed the domestic operation into the harm-less, noncommercial realm of shorts. Indeed, Griffis made clear to his fellow executives that his main objective was to protect the industry.[49]

But OWI's liaison activities in Hollywood did not end; they were, if anything strengthened. The reviewing staff simply moved over to the Overseas Branch in place of the Domestic Branch and continued operations without missing a reel. The operation now had a single head—Poynter's nemesis Ulric Bell. The hobbling of the domestic branch, though a personal defeat for Mellett and Poynter, ironically strengthened the OWI's hand in Hollywood. No one in the industry denied the government's interest in policing what films were exported. Freed from Poyn-ter's opposition, Bell strengthened his ties with the censor. He benefitted, too, from OWI's growing influence abroad. As allied armies liberated potential markets, Hollywood's interest perked up. For now the propaganda agency could use something be-sides patriotic appeals in negotiations with the studios—on the one hand, the club of censorship, on the other, the carrot of reconquered markets.[50]

Hollywood "has shed no shackles, as a result of the closing of the domestic OWI branch, but has reduced by one-half its chances of achieving a Houdini," said the *Motion Picture Herald* in mid-August 1943. The industry was no longer looking for magical escapes, however. Even the *Herald* was shifting from its inveterate anti-OWI line. It was true, after all, the paper de-cided, that Mellett and Poynter were "a fount of information, suggestion and counsel, not a seat of censorship." But while most producers still felt they themselves were better qualified to judge what was appropriate for American audiences than were bureaucrats, the foreign market was a different matter. Only the boldest producer would "set himself up as better qual-ified to judge what is good or bad for the inhabitants of neutral and reoccupied countries . . . than an official in the confidence of the heads of government."[51]

Bell's bureau now operated as an "advance guard of the Office of Censorship," the *Herald* continued. The BMP spoke with a single voice—Bell's. His representations could be put solely in terms of a movie's effects in foreign countries, which made Rothacker, the Los Angeles censor, more comfortable. Bell noted happily that Rothacker consulted with him "morning, noon and night" and followed his recommendations in almost all cases. In quick succession the censor denied foreign audiences such gems as *Fugitive from a Prison Camp*, *The Great Swindle*, *The Batman*, *Hillbilly Blitzkrieg*, *Sleepy Lagoon*, and *Secret Service in Darkest Africa*. Bell took a certain grim satisfaction in reports of the negative impression *Lucky Jordan* created in Sweden. The censor almost certainly would not have passed it now, he said. The major remaining difference between OWI and the Office of Censorship concerned westerns. When Bell protested *Buffalo Bill*, Rothacker noted with dry understatement that the picture's depiction of whites mistreating the Indians had a factual basis, and since it was set before 1917 he could not touch it. If it was history it didn't have to be the United States of Nirvana.[52]

Pictures denied an export license—"that highly profitable detail," in the words of the *Herald*—could recoup their negative costs through the U.S. market. But profit-making institutions are not in business just to cover their costs. As the *Herald* pointed out: "No one has yet advanced an argument in support of producing a picture known in advance to be doomed to domestic exhibition exclusively." Pictures with export licenses could follow "the troops into the reoccupied countries as they are opened up" and "the world . . . returns its screens to the use of American product." It was simply "dollars-and-cents sense for producers to shoot at the greater and growing market."[53]

Each mile of territory recaptured in Europe and Asia by the Allied armies brought the interests of the government and Hollywood closer. The government was eager to use approved films as a weapon in its cultural reoccupation of Axis-held countries—and audiences in those nations were eager to see American movies again. The Allies had no more than landed in Sicily when the *Motion Picture Herald* announced that "Italian theatres will show American pictures almost as soon as the smoke has settled in the wake of invading armies." OWI's help was invaluable. It exhibited films which had its seal of approval and held the money in trust for the companies. As the executives increasingly realized that OWI wanted "only to be helpful, their attitudes change[d] remarkably" said Robert Riskin. In "brutal honesty," he continued, the industry's "unprecedented profits" produced a level of cooperation from the agency that surprised even the studio chiefs. OWI foreign operatives were so solicitous of Hollywood's prerogatives that Riskin reported by mid-1944: "An unsavory opinion seems to prevail within OWI that the Motion Picture Bureau is unduly concerned with considerations for commercial interests."[54]

The shakeout in OWI in mid-1943 had brought a rapprochement between businessmen and bureaucrats. To feed the wartime sellers' market, Hollywood increasingly sacrificed artistic standards for short-run commercial objectives, leading industry figures such as Samuel Goldwyn and John Houseman to lament that during the war the studios "came closer to producing movies by assembly-line methods than at any other time in its history." The resulting pattern resembled the dominant pattern of the rest of the wartime American economy. Government and industry discovered that they needed each other; the advancement of political and economic interests went hand-in-hand. And the anticipated expansion of American political influence after the war increased the profit-making potential of American business. From a mixture of patriotism and the profit motive, Hollywood became a compliant part of the American war machine. Freedom of the screen was not an issue for the studio heads: an industry that had feared "enslavement" by Lowell Mellett was already in thrall to Joseph Breen. When OWI, like PCA, showed that censorship would be "smart showmanship," the industry was only too eager to cooperate. The results were visible in all areas of Hollywood production—the home front, the allies, the enemy, and the hope for a peaceful postwar world.[55]

VI.

Home Front:
Defining America

The fact that slavery existed in this country is certainly something which belongs to the past and which we wish to forget at this time when unity of all races and creeds is all-important.

—OWI script review of
"Battle Hymn,"
August 20, 1942

The war touched all Americans, and some of its effects were profound. Nearly ten percent of the country's population served in the armed forces. For them, and for their loved ones, the threat of death was a harrowing reality. But the war was omnipresent in lesser ways too. It drastically altered the way in which many people made a living. The war boom ended a decade of depression and put more money in more pockets than ever before. "The men and women on the production line and in the home are as much a part of the battle front as the soldier in the battle zone," said OWI in its manual for Hollywood. That bit of praise contained a truth that the propagandists did not intend: The production line claimed more casualties than did the battlefield. Even the mundane aspects of daily consumption reminded one of the pervasive effects of the war: spreading oleo instead of butter on your morning toast, carpooling and using public transportation because of rationed tires and non-existent new cars, cutting back consumption of meat, riding all night sitting on your suitcase because the train was overcrowded, relatives saving sugar for weeks so Dick and Mary could have a wedding cake. Of course the war's disruptions in the Continental United States paled by comparison with the death and devastation endured by millions of Europeans and Asians. Nonetheless, to the stock line "Don't you know there's a war on?", changes both large and small provided a ready answer.[1]

The home front had the stuff of drama. Hollywood found there a rich lode in the altered lives of its customers. OWI saw there a vital story of democracy mobilized for war. "It's everybody's war," proclaimed the Bureau of Motion Pictures. Thus the studios and the propaganda agency turned to the home front in their quest, one for profits, and the other for propaganda messages. If there was one subject the Hollywood moguls were convinced they knew, it was America. Their success was based on their ability to intuit the subliminal wishes of the vast public. They thought the public wanted upbeat stories with happy endings about people who were beautiful, witty, and successful, but not so far removed from a middle class norm as to make it difficult for audiences to identify with the characters on the screen. That idealized portrait of America was fine with OWI, which wanted to project a picture of a prosperous, wholesome, democratic America. Some flashpoints of controversy remained between the studios and the agency, however, chiefly over the exploitation of social problems such as gangsterism and juvenile delinquency. For the most part Hollywood and OWI found that they could use similar sacred and sentimental symbols in the pursuit of profits and propaganda.[2]

The studios willingly complied with BMP's request that movies show everybody cheerfully doing his or her bit for the war. Films showed citizens making little sacrifices without complaint—buying bonds, donating blood, volunteering for the Red Cross, putting up with rationing. And even such a cinematic staple as screeching tires was toned down in Preston Sturges's *The Miracle of Morgan's Creek* to avoid a reprimand from OWI about wasting rubber. Each sector of the economy—management and labor, in industry as well as on the farm—received respectful attention. (Although liberals and leftists had often attacked business in the 1930s, OWI propagandists cooled their criticism because they wanted to show all sectors mobilized for war.) The depiction of mass mobilization extended to the youngest citizens. OWI sent out a special bulletin on the "children's war" which gave hints on how to depict kids collecting scrap, cultivating Victory gardens, and saving nickels and dimes for war bonds.[3]

Everyone could agree on such innocuous, if heartwarming, symbolism. But when OWI called for a sympathetic treatment of the New Deal's mildly social democratic goals, the agency ran into the buzzsaw of polarized wartime politics in the film community. Although it is sometimes assumed that, during wartime, "politics is adjourned," domestic political jockeying continued unabated during World War II. Liberals feared the end of the New Deal in 1943, but hoped that Roosevelt would lead a liberal revival once victory was assured. Conservatives seized on the war as a way to cut back New Deal programs they found abhorrent and to build toward a future takeover of the federal government. Hollywood reflected these currents. In 1944, a leading liberal organization, the Hollywood Free World Association, staged a huge dinner at which Vice President Wallace was the featured speaker. Screenwriter Dudley Nichols headed the assemblage, which included such guests as California Governor Earl Warren, Walter Wanger, Olivia De Havilland, and Walter Huston. The day before that event cinema conservatives flexed their muscle with the announcement that a new Motion Picture Alliance for the Preservation of American Ideals had been formed, headed by MGM producer Sam Wood. The Alliance, which played an important role in the red-baiting and black-listing episodes of the Cold War, boasted among its founders such men as Walt Disney, Gary Cooper, Victor Fleming, King Vidor, and its officers eventually included such luminaries as Ward Bond, Charles Coburn, Hedda Hopper, Adolphe Menjou, Robert Taylor, and John Wayne.[4]

OWI's message thus produced conflict with some moviemakers. Insisting that this was a "people's war," not a racial or class war, agency analysts linked political freedom with the economic security promised by the New Deal's rudimentary welfare state. They praised FDR's steps toward economic justice, invoking the popular period symbols of Boulder Dam and the Rural Electrification Administration. Strongly pro-labor, they hailed the unions' contributions to worker solidarity and the wartime production boom. And the BMP's manual for Hollywood anticipated the most radical speech Franklin Roosevelt ever made—his 1944 State of the Union address in which he sketched "cradle to the grave" social programs similar to those implemented after the war by the British Labour government.[5]

The liberal propagandists hoped to reassure workers about their place in the postwar economy. Fear of a postwar depression loomed, and debate raged over how to organize the economy. Industrialists and conservatives gave primacy to the role of business. OWI stressed the role of government and labor and gravitated toward Vice President Henry Wallace's formula of "sixty million jobs." They envisioned a postwar world of abundance, fed by American productive power; if the U.S. economy continued to be geared for maximum production, as it was by the government during the war, there would be work for all, including minorities. In OWI's vision all Americans could "contribute constructively toward making the postwar world a world of plenty and security." Freedom from want went hand in hand with freedom from fear.[6]

BMP's largely female reviewing staff was sharply attuned to what women meant to the war effort and what the war meant to women. They urged the studios to show women taking the place of men on the job and putting their children in day-care centers. Perhaps drawing on their own experience, these analysts argued that "American women are finding new expression in jobs they have assumed." Women were not going "to return 'en masse' to the kitchen" at war's end. They were entitled to "ample opportunity and equal pay." The BMP staff urged Hollywood to find ways to interpret these new roles for the public. Hollywood could place a woman in a welder's mask easily enough—it was a new form of costume drama—but women's "new expression" was a much more threatening challenge to Hollywood's trite portraits of women and family.[7]

Another minority—blacks—posed an even bigger challenge, not only for the film makers but for OWI. The propaganda agency recognized that the persistence of second class citizenship undermined black morale and called into question American preachments about the Four Freedoms, but it argued that progress was possible in a democracy. The demands of profit and propaganda made it all but impossible to deal forthrightly with race on the screen.

OWI's aims earned ready support in Hollywood's liberal quarters, particularly from some of the radical writers. But trouble could erupt when the agency departed from its generalized goals about widespread participation in the war effort and tried to promote its New Deal philosophy. One of the most significant home-front pictures, King Vidor's *An American Romance* (MGM, 1943), provoked several clashes over its celebration of rugged individualism—a message befitting a founder of the Motion Picture Alliance.

Though largely forgotten today, *An American Romance* was an important wartime production. The film was very expensive, costing about $3 million, and it attracted much attention. Its semi-documentary depiction of American industrial might excited OWI. The film also received unique high-level encouragement from the Department of Justice. Attorney General Francis Biddle and M. E. Gilfond both read the script and kept a close eye on the production's progress. They made little attempt to influence the screenplay, but bolstered Vidor's sense that a home-front picture was an important contribution to the war effort. Many critics found it to include some of the most compelling use of technicolor to that date.[8]

For Vidor, an able craftsman and dedicated innovator, the picture was the culmination of a long-held personal dream. As a young director he asked Metro's wunderkind Irving Thalberg what themes most excited him. Thalberg replied: war, wheat, and steel. Captivated by that vision, Vidor essayed war in his 1925 silent classic, *The Big Parade*. Although he never had an opportunity to do wheat, his chance to do steel came in World War II. His ambition fitted in well with his belief that he could serve the war effort by making a picture on the contribution of American know-how to the arsenal of democracy.[9]

Vidor blended his story of steel with a Horatio Alger formula. The result was, originally, a paean to American industry and to industrialists—the embodiment of the American dream. But that vision angered OWI, particularly because it included a negative portrayal of labor unions. The film was based on Vidor's original story, which he had laid out in the summer of

1941. By the time shooting began the screenplay had received the ministrations of no fewer than twelve writers. The credits finally attributed the screenplay to Herbert Delmas and William Ludwig (the latter a frequent contributor to the Andy Hardy series), based on original material by King Vidor. For a title the director toyed with the worshipful "Man of Tomorrow" and the highly suggestive "The Magic Land." Vidor settled finally on the simple but grand "America." When OWI objected that no one movie could encompass all of America, Vidor chose "An American Romance." This had the advantage of suggesting a love interest, though anyone who ponied up two bits expecting to see much romance would have felt short-changed.[10]

Vidor submitted a completed script to OWI in November 1942. In this version Stefan Dangosbiblichek arrives at Ellis Island virtually penniless, but his strong arms and his earnestness are so convincing that he is allowed to stay in the United States. He walks—yes, walks—to Minnesota, where a cousin gets him a job in the iron mines. His name truncated by a boorish mine foreman, Steve Dangos soon sets himself apart from his fellow workers by his intellectual curiosity. Fascinated (like Vidor) with steel, he follows the ore to Chicago, where he signs on with a steel mill. He quickly rises to foreman. He also marries Anna, the Irish school teacher he awkwardly courted in the iron country. Dangos meets Walter Clinton, an automobile manufacturer. Small world! Clinton happens to be a railroad engineer who had befriended him on his lonely trek to Minnesota. Dangos and Clinton go into business to produce a fast, streamlined car that threatens to make every other automobile obsolete. The banks set him up with a huge automated plant—and then sell him out. A man without a job, he decides to see America. Finally he and Anna decide to live out their days in an orange grove in California. War erupts. Clinton pleads with him to join forces in producing airplanes on the same mass-production scale they used to make cars. Dangos demurs until two of his sons, both navy pilots heading for secret battle stations, convince him this is everybody's fight. He phones Clinton, and the old Dangos know-how soon has fighters and bombers rolling off the assembly line in record time.[11]

This script set off alarm bells in the OWI suite in the Taft Building. "This story is a deluxe automobile edition of Horatio

Alger," complained Marjorie Thorson, "and if Henry Ford had written it, it could scarcely express the Ford philosophy more clearly." American industrialists were the heroes; bankers were the heavies. Labor existed only as a mute mass; unions were vaguely sinister. But the agency desperately wanted a picture on the home-front production miracle, and the script suggested a potentially fascinating depiction of industrial power, saluted the contributions of immigrants, and highlighted American freedom of opportunity. With reorientation it could be made into "one of the most useful of 1943."[12]

Thorson entered a long catalog of changes that OWI wanted. In keeping with the idea of a "people's war," she suggested some drastic changes to moderate the glorification of management and to enhance the role of workers. "Implicit in the story," Thorson pointed out, "are many leaves from the classic but discredited American myth" that anybody with ability and determination can become an executive. The depression should at least be recognized. Equally serious was the treatment of labor unions. Dangos' first job in the steel industry appeared to be as a scab. Later, when workers staged a sit-down strike at his auto plant, Dangos dispersed them with armed guards and tear gas. Here were echoes not only of Henry Ford but of the Hollywood brass as well. The studios fought unions bitterly in the 1930s, though not as violently as Ford, and returned to the offensive after the war. As OWI feared, these scenes encouraged lurking suspicions that labor was radical, violent, and untrustworthy. "This is a fascist tactic pure and simple, tending to divide one group of Americans from the other," Thorson said. OWI insisted that labor be treated more sympathetically.[13]

A more general anxiety for OWI was that Dangos seemed unaware of American values, or unimpressed by them. Although there were repeated appeals to freedom and opportunity, they seemed to mean nothing to him but "freedom to make lots of money." When Dangos is urged to take out citizenship papers, he snorts that the only thing he would get for that was the right to vote. The hero even seemed too busy to have much of a family life. OWI hoped he would come to a more complete understanding of American freedoms. Interestingly enough, OWI's concerns had an echo in a critique written by Anne

Wormser, a Metro script doctor, who also noted that Dangos' single-minded drive for economic success left his spiritual side undeveloped. Inadvertently Vidor hinted at the psychic costs of the scramble up the ladder. Neither Metro nor OWI was interested in this ironic commentary on the American dream.[14]

Wanting to give only "the best impression of American Industry," Vidor intended to show that working on an automobile assembly line was "exciting and pleasing." Through a trick of cutting he stepped up the pace of the assembly line he had filmed at a Chrysler plant. An alarmed Chrysler vice president feared Vidor would produce another speed-up stunt similar to Charlie Chaplin's famous sequence of the production line run amok in *Modern Times*. Quite the contrary, Vidor assured him: Chaplin "will not like what I have done, which is against all of his method of characterization of his 'little man.'" Where Chaplin showed a frazzled worker dominated by the machine, Vidor composed a hymn to the assembly line in which workers fit harmoniously.[15]

OWI officials reacted strongly against Vidor's vision. Together with the director's treatment of unions, the script seemed to suggest the domination of labor by machines and their managers. They considered that point of view dangerously akin to the totalitarian ethos with its repression of the working class by an industrial elite. They argued that, with democratic unions, industrial progress could bring an "affinity of man and the machine." Poynter and Thorson saw unions as not merely economic bargaining units but agents for humanizing the means of production.[16]

OWI's suggestion did not go down easily at Metro. E. J. Mannix "yelled and screamed," Poynter said, and charged that OWI was trying to force the studio to make a "'new deal picture.'" "Metro doesn't want to make controversial subjects," the MGM executive said. Poynter defended himself by saying he didn't think the "continued growth of democracy" was controversial. But in the eyes of Louis B. Mayer, OWI's suggestions were politically tainted.[17]

A number of meetings between Poynter, Vidor, and studio officials brought some results. The studio realized that the harsh treatment of labor had to be changed. Screenwriter Gordon

Kahn wrote a scene in which Dangos returned to his factory as a 76-cent-an-hour lathe operator and joined the union, but only when it signed a no-strike pledge for the duration. This was too improbable even for Hollywood. Instead, Vidor decided to have Dangos leave the company after his entire board of directors turned against his anti-union policy.[18]

An American Romance was finally released in October 1943, nearly two-and-a-half years after work began. "I really think we've got something big this time," said a pleased King Vidor. The film was of epic length. When preview audiences squirmed at its original length of 15,600 feet, Vidor cut nearly 2,000 feet. The final product earned praise from OWI for its "fascinating" depiction of American industrial might and its improved (if not wholly satisfactory) story of American life.[19]

The film interweaves two dominant American themes—immigrants and industry. *An American Romance* is a sort of immigrant's progress. The picture opens in mythic fashion. A ship looms out of the primeval ocean mists. Masses of immigrants huddled against the rail peer intently into the void. The clouds lift over a sun-streaked New York City as the strains of "America" build to fortissimo. As Steve Dangos's eldest son was to say later: "Nothing is impossible for us in this land."

Steve's life embodies the dream. After his determined trek to Minnesota, he gets a job in an open pit iron mine through his cousin—quickly, effortlessly; there is work for all. Steve is astonished when he receives six dollars for his first week's work. "I like this country. Already rich man," he says. He buys new boots. Not only is the immigrant upwardly mobile, he takes his part in the consumer society. Throughout the picture each raise in pay affords Steve a new house and an increasing abundance of consumer goods. Befriended by Anna, the proverbial goddess school teacher, Steve learns to read, an opportunity denied him in the old country. The good life promises not merely material bounty but the benediction of the spirit.

Still under the sway of European class distinctions, Steve only slowly realizes America's infinite opportunity. He listens with disbelief at a Fourth of July rally as a political spellbinder promises that "your son can become president." Anna assures him it's true. Steve's ambition extends no further than becoming boss of the steam shovel. Anna erupts: Is that all! Don't you want to make steel! Is that why you left the old country? To dig in a hole? "I thought you wanted to climb to the sky!"

Steve begins his rise. He follows the ore boats to the steel mills of Chicago. He sees the steel-making process he read about in Anna's encyclopedia. Each segment is lovingly documented in Vidor's technicolor; the steel workers perform an almost choreographed ritual before the brilliant blazing backdrop of the giant furnaces. Unfortunately, to later viewers the ore-into-steel sequence seems too much like an animated encyclopedia article better suited to a high school social studies class than to the Saturday matinee.

Steve signs on at the steel plant—again, work is plentiful—and within a year is promoted to foreman. He understands that climbing the ladder means deferring gratification. When he and Anna marry he takes only a day off. Some day, he promises, when the kids are grown, we'll take "fine trip." So long as the hero is working and rising that day will never come. He is blessed nonetheless with a devoted wife and five children. The first is a girl—a great disappointment to him. "Girls must be born, too," he sighs philosophically. The next four children are boys. They bear the names George Washington Dangos, Thomas Jefferson Dangos, Abraham Lincoln Dangos, and Theodore Roosevelt Dangos—a living Mount Rushmore. The sons carry the immigrant's progress into the second generation. George Washington is valedictorian of his high school class. Thomas Jefferson has an intellectual, aesthetic bent and discusses God and nature with his mother.

The children also provide a lesson in Americanism. Over his father's protests George Washington enlists in the army in World War I rather than go to college. He helps his father see the necessity of his service and convinces him to apply for citizenship, which Steve has always been just a little too busy to do. Steve and Anna, dressed in their Sunday best, practice the citizenship catechism and pledge of allegiance. Just as they are ready to leave a telegram arrives informing them of George's death. Anna emits a muffled cry. Steve steels himself and comforts her: Don't cry, Anna. We should be proud of Georgie, he says. With great feeling they recite the pledge of allegiance together, and then leave for the ceremony. Steve has given up his first-born son for his adopted country. Thus the movie instructed the audience in how to bear the grief of the loss of sons—stoically and with the knowledge that death was meaningful.

The immigrant's progress is the personal counterpart of America's rise to industrial dominance. *An American Romance* idealizes the America of heavy industry. Blast furnaces, belching locomotives, elongated ore boats, rivers of molten metal, infernos of steam and smoke—all become a visual representation of the might of an industrial society whose war-making capacity surpasses that of all others. The evolution of the automobile symbolizes industrial progress. The original hand-cranked model undergoes a metamorphosis in Steve Dangos's fertile brain and becomes the sleek streamlined model which by the 1930s had come to represent the utmost modernity. The film glories in the mastery of man over the environment. The narrator describes an open pit mine in Minnesota's Mesabi mountain range—the mine is an immense gash of reddish earth. Here once stood a town and a hill, he says, but we have dug enough ore to fill the Panama Canal twice. To a post-1960s audience such scenes convey environmental depredation; to a World War II audience, however, steam, steel, and smoke were meant to convey prosperity and power.

Vidor's movie represents visually his belief in the harmony between humans and machines. He acknowledges the dangers of the industrial age. In the iron range a new man is almost scooped up in the steam shovel's bite of earth—but he escapes to the laughter of his fellow workers. In an accident in the steel mill Steve Dangos is suspended for a time over a fiery pit of molten steel—but he survives thanks to an acrobatic rescue. One of his prototype cars turns over in a test run—but the driver emerges without a scratch and offers the off-hand line: "Swallowed my gum." Vidor acknowledges the issue of the human costs of industrialization only to reassure viewers that the perils are manageable by reducing them to the stylized stunts and sight gags familiar to movie audiences. He implies the dangers are not serious. The speedup scene on the automobile assembly line reinforces the machine's benignity; the workers swing to their tasks swiftly, effortlessly, and cheerfully as automobiles take shape almost magically before our eyes.

Like the physical danger of industrial work, the question of labor organization is transformed from peril to harmony. When Steve's nascent factory is about to be snuffed out for lack of credit, cousin Anton, the original immigrant, appears almost as a genie from a lamp and offers his savings. Let's all be partners, cries an inspired worker. Foregoing wages, plant employees pitch in to build a model car. Exhibited in a national auto show, it secures the financing the fledgling company needs. It's "our dream come true—a wonderful magic dream," says a labor spokesman.

The Dangos firm grows into a corporate giant. But Steve cannot adjust to changing conditions. He refuses to recognize the union; there can be only one boss, he says. Thomas Jefferson Dangos tries to reason with him. The workers will not make unreasonable demands, he says, for that would force the company into bankruptcy and destroy their jobs. Neither side can win in a strike, he continues; "force is no substitute for wisdom." But Steve remains adamant. A three-month strike ensues. Finally the entire board, including son Thomas and cousin Anton, presses Steve to meet the union halfway. Howard, now the union president, offers his hand to Steve and points out: "Efficient production demands cooperation between labor and management." Steve declines the hand and goes into retirement. Desolated, he sinks into a leather chair in the empty board room. He has even broken with his second son over the labor issue. There is nothing left to do but go home to his devoted, understanding wife.

An American Romance thereby taught a lesson that both OWI and Vidor could live with. Labor and management were not antagonists; they shared similar objectives. Steve's son is used to underscore the point. Though he graduated from college with an engineering degree, he enters the company as an ordinary worker. He explains that he wants to learn practice instead of theory and wants to get to know the men. Thomas Jefferson Dangos celebrates American pragmatism over alien theory, reenacts his father's rise (albeit with practically effortless swiftness), and carries his empathy for the working class to management's high councils. He is the epitome of the enlightened business executive who understands that recognition of unions is a matter of both justice and efficiency. In contrast to the earlier scripts, unions are no longer sinister; they have become the housebroken moderates of the New Deal ideal. OWI's lesson was clear: Goodwill between management and labor would ensure maximum productivity for the common war effort.

Indeed the war provides a means to resolve the economic and familial tensions raised in the film. Old animosities fade as people find unity in a cause greater than themselves. The government needs planes built faster than they've ever been built before. Dangos's old company experiences trouble converting to aircraft production. A labor-management committee concludes this is a job for Steve Dangos. Son Thomas persuades his father to come out of retirement. Steve takes Thomas home to mom, who is baking a chocolate cake; they partake of this sacrament of reunion. Together father and son iron out the production kinks. Planes, not cars, now take shape before our eyes; men—and notably women—bend eagerly to their tasks to the beat of snappy music. Finished bombers flow from an assembly line and soar aloft. Variations on "America" swell as Steve and Thomas Jefferson Dangos, beaming broadly, watch a sun-washed sky fill with planes for victory.

Under the watchful eye of the Bureau of Motion Pictures, *An American Romance* has been transformed from a paean to rugged individualism into a celebration of management-labor cooperation. The immigrant industrialist was still the hero, but his success was now contingent on a new acceptance of moderate unions. The picture invoked the liberal vision of a harmony of interests in society. Wartime realities belied this rosy picture. The high rate of worker deaths and injuries refuted Vidor's light-hearted treatment of industrial perils. Management-labor conflict remained intense. Worker alienation, though mitigated in the 1940s by the sheer joy of having a job after a decade of depression, was a growing problem. But in *An American Romance* OWI liberals and Hollywood conservatives achieved an uneasy truce under the exigency of war.

Like Vidor, David O. Selznick brought an epic sweep to *Since You Went Away*, his essay on the sacred and sentimental symbols of home-front America. A single household serves as a microcosm of the war effort. The film remains in its symbolic grandeur and grandiloquence the ultimate summation of the home front. OWI watched his production eagerly and found that he intuited many of the ideas they wished to convey. Although Selz-

nick was more conservative than the BMP staff—at a Los Angeles rally for Republican presidential nominee Thomas E.
Dewey in 1944, he charged that bureaucracy was strangling the
country—he and OWI worked well together nonetheless, for his
focus on the vicissitudes of a single household skirted most of
the political tensions that surrounded King Vidor.[20]

Selznick brought prodigious energy and a formidable talent
for organizing mass spectacle to the film, his first since the phe-
nomenally successful *Gone With the Wind* (1939) and *Rebecca*
(1940). The show business cliché "no expense has been spared"
was apt for once. Selznick poured $2.4 million—about the same
expenditure per minute of running time as for *Gone With the
Wind*—into the production for his Selznick International Pictures. He wrote his own script, a 290-page monster that was re-
putedly the longest the movie colony had seen. While many producers dared not exceed forty days of shooting, Selznick took
127, not including time for retakes. His company fiddled for
four days until the heavens cooperated with just the right cloud
formation to complement a country love scene. He dragged a
huge statue of Abraham Lincoln from a local high school in
order to enhance a graduation scene. Among the 205 speaking
parts was one for Lionel Barrymore, who though starred, appeared for only 90 seconds in the release print, and another for
Charles Coburn, who received $25,000 for an extra scene that
was later cut.[21]

Selznick assembled a strong cast. Claudette Colbert played
the lead as mother Anne Hilton, who holds the home together
after the departure of husband Tim for the war in January 1943.
Jennifer Jones, coming off an Oscar-winning performance for
her first film role in *Song of Bernadette*, played seventeen-year old
daughter Jane. (She became Selznick's wife in 1949, after his
divorce from Irene Mayer Selznick, daughter of the MGM chief.)
Shirley Temple grew up to age thirteen as the other daughter,
Brig. Joseph Cotton was superbly cast as Tony, the debonair perennial bachelor whose world-weariness cannot conceal a sentimentality as deep as that of the others. Monty Woolley turned
Colonel Smollett into a variation of the crotchety boarder he
immortalized in *The Man Who Came to Dinner*. His grandson,
Corporal Smollett, a feckless youth destined for martyrdom, was
played by Robert Walker. Agnes Moorehead was cast as Mrs.

Hawkins, a selfish society matron. And transposing the role of the archetypal mammy from the Civil War to the current conflict was, of course, Hattie McDaniel.

These prodigious resources did not guarantee success—witness Vidor's *An American Romance*. But Selznick, whom some termed Hollywood's Barnum, knew how to deploy his resources. He had an innate sense not of what America was but of what Americans wanted to be. He became the ideal interpreter of OWI's wishful images. The symbolism and sentimentality of *Since You Went Away* help explain why the picture was a topical smash but suffers badly out of its context. Its dream portrait of American life throws into high relief the happy coexistence of entertainment and propaganda.

"This is a story of the Unconquerable Fortress: the American Home ... 1943," reads a caption as the film opens on a cheery blaze in the fireplace of the Hiltons' home. The camera moves lovingly over the cliches of domesticity: an empty leather chair, a grand piano, a desk with the fish caught by Tim and Anne on their honeymoon, bronzed baby shoes, family pictures, his pipe, and the emblem of fidelity—a sad bulldog. This is the American home of everyone's dream. A seven-room brick colonial on a gracious street in an Ohio city—the emblematic Midwest again—it befits the status of Tim Hilton, advertising executive.

Anne comes in and says softly: "This is the moment I've dreaded—coming back to our home alone." Tim has been gone for an hour. She didn't want him to go, but he had assured her they would look back upon the experience as their greatest adventure. "I have no courage and no vision, Tim," she says. We suspect that her sense of self will change. Now she steps into her role as mother and pulls herself together as her two daughters come home from school.

The first part of the film is a virtual compendium of OWI-approved vignettes of American life as changed by the war. Amne rents out a spare room to Colonel Smollett. The man who comes to breakfast fusses endlessly when the eggs are not to his liking. The women treat his crabbing as yet another little sacrifice for the war; besides they have ideas about how to use their feminine wiles to reform him. The devoted Fidelia has to seek work elsewhere because Mrs. Hilton can't afford her now but returns each day to cook and scrub after hours, refusing to take money. Scenes around town identify the war's impact. A steak house is out of steak; Mrs. Hawkins arranges a dance for the men at Chamberlain Field and imports twenty girls for partners; the coast highway (Lake Erie never looked so inviting) is deserted; Brig cultivates her victory garden with an artless enthusiasm that is meant to be cute. When a girl doesn't want to date a man who isn't an officer, Tony gently corrects her, pointing out that G.I.s do most of the fighting.

The family's long train trip to have a brief rendezvous with Tim offers several opportunities to drive the propaganda points home. Their train sits in a siding as seemingly endless troop and supply trains thunder by. This is not the self-indulgent pleasure travel of *Palm Beach Story*. But some people still haven't gotten the word. In the crowded dining car a businessman grouses: If we're late I'll miss the biggest deal of my life. A navy man with an amputated arm says: "I've got plenty of time from now on." Brig frets to the conductor: Can't we get this train moving? I'll miss my pop! Your pop will have a lot better chance of coming home if these supply trains get through, he says. European refugees tell how they got no meat or milk when the Germans moved in. Quick cut to a plump society woman who, in the midst of devouring corn on the cob, spits out that "it's simply outrageous" they're serving only two meals a day in the diner.

Because of the delays, the family misses Tim. Tearfully they read the message he left. In a scene shot from behind the three walk slowly into the shadows of the cavernous lobby. On the long ride back they find a wounded soldier with a mother and her baby. Brig falls asleep on the shoulder of a kindly older woman whose daughter was a nurse at Corregidor. Jane, who wanted to get a war job but was blocked by her mother, is inspired to become a nurse's aide. Anne now agrees. Cut to the capping ceremony where Jane, with shining face and sun glinting off her white cap, recites the Red Cross pledge. Brig is upset because she herself is only doing "kid's stuff" for the war—gathering salvage, rolling bandages, and selling war stamps.

In subsequent scenes an affluent woman is heard to say: "I swear I can't tell any difference between it and butter." A sailor ponies up five months' pay for war bonds. And a wealthy man insists it "suits me if they tax me 100 percent!" Judging from the howl that went up—from Hollywood executives among others—when the government proposed to tax away all income above $25,000, this well-heeled gentleman had more war spirit than most.

Back home they get a telegram that Tim is missing in action. Anne faints, rather artificially. That night the three cuddle together as Anne goes through family albums. The dog offers his head for her to cry on. Dissolve to a church service, where Barrymore mixes patriotism with religion.

Meanwhile a romance has been developing between Jane and Bill Smollett. He makes one of the classic transitions of war films—from a sensitive young man troubled about the morality of killing and worried about his own courage to a brave soldier convinced of his cause. Smollett so far had been a great disappointment to his martinet grandfather, who glories in the family's string of officers going back to Yorktown. Young Smollett's development—treated as a process of normal maturation—is assisted by Jane, the woman as facilitator and redeemer. "You're fine and strong," she says. "You're just sensitive, that's all." After a talk with her he summons his strength for the role of American warrior. Playing women's role as mediator, Jane and Anne also try to bring some reasonableness to the colonel, who threatens not to see the family disgrace off at the station.

Bill and Jane spend a last afternoon together in the country. They walk hand in hand through a field under Selznick's perfect sky. A storm looms. They kiss passionately, illuminated by lightning. They seek shelter in an old barn, where they become engaged.

Bill leaves on the midnight train. Jane says she'll meet him in New York tomorrow, get married, and have a baby! Bill, the sensible male, says no—wait until the day after the war. He stands in the vestibule as the train begins to move. She runs frantically to keep pace as the train gathers speed. She throws him her class ring. He throws her the watch Grandpa gave him, a watch handed down from an ancestor who was killed at Vicksburg. She reads the inscription—"To William G. Smollett, who will lead men to glory on the battlefield"—and bursts into tears. Breathless, Grandpa arrives at the station two minutes late.

A few months later Bill, inevitably, is killed at Salerno. Jane tries to pretend the telegram is a mistake but Anne cautions, no, it's better to face it. "Cry your heart out," mother says. "A wonderful boy loved you, Jane—that doesn't happen to everybody." Jane composes herself and helps make dinner. She offers to take the colonel his supper, but this time he joins them. He now understands that Bill is someone to be proud of. He reflects on how fortunate it was that Bill knew Jane. "The good die first," he says.

Jane is not going to college. Instead she works in a veterans' hospital. The scene is idyllic and suffused with hope, in line with OWI's wish to show programs assisting veterans resume normal lives. Dr. Sigmund Golden, a kindly German emigré psychiatrist, works patiently with "a fine young man who must have another chance at life." To Jane he says, don't you have someone you'd like to do this for? "We must not live in the past, my child," he says. "There's a whole wide broken world to mend."

But some people remain blind. The last segments of the picture present several lessons in democracy and the importance of everyone doing his or her share. Mrs. Hawkins upbraids Jane for being an aide and mixing with all sorts of young men who . . . Jane cuts her off: "Who lost their arms and legs? . . . and I don't think breeding entered into it." "Bravo, Jane," shouts the colonel. Mrs. Hawkins persists: There must be women more suited for that type of job. "There aren't women more suited," says Jane, "and women who might help, like you, Mrs. Hawkins, think you're doing your part if you attend a canteen dance for your own pleasure. Please don't worry if our precious well bred hands come in contact with their mangled bodies. We'll survive, even if they don't." Jane and Brig burst into tears and run upstairs. Mrs. Hawkins is shocked, and turns to Anne: Are you going to let your daughter talk to me that way? she demands. Those things should have been said long ago, Anne retorts. "I'm ashamed . . . that I've even known you." She assails her for hoarding, cheating, and "all the other unpatriotic things you've done." Mrs. Hawkins storms out.

Now it's Tony's turn to add his voice for democracy. He's too worldy wise to join the armed forces for noble reasons like Tim. But working on musicals seemed petty with a war on, and, besides, he was looking for excitement. He laughed at the Four Freedoms. But he couldn't laugh off one single corny phrase:

"Home Sweet Home." Ironically it is the bachelor who voices, possibly wistfully, the theme of the American home.

Anne realizes she has been living in a dream world. She goes to work as a welder—another woman who welds all day without mussing a hair. The factory affords her a lesson in democracy. She develops a friendship with a Czechoslovak woman whose name was "like nothing we ever heard at the country club." The immigrant tells her story, recounts her trip to the Statue of Liberty—a popular wartime symbol—and tells Anne: "You are what I thought America was."

The closing sequence unites everyone on Christmas Eve, except for Tim. Pan to his empty chair. The celebration is interrupted by a phone call: Dad is safe and coming home. The final scene is shot from outside the snow-covered house. In silhouette we see Anne and her daughters hugging each other in the dormer window. The camera dollies backward to take in the whole house. To the strains of "Adeste Fidelis" a caption appears: "Be of good courage, and He shall strengthen your heart, all ye that hope in the Lord."

OWI and critics generally recognized *Since You Went Away* as the definitive cinematic statement about domestic life during the war. Ulric Bell praised the "corking story." William Cunningham, Bell's successor in the Bureau of Motion Pictures, thanked Selznick for his "splendid cooperation with this office." The agency thought the depiction of American life especially valuable for overseas audiences. The blending of the war with personal growth held particular appeal for the propagandists. Bill Smollett becomes a hero worthy of his family; Jane Hilton loves, loses, and attains mature womanhood; Anne Hilton is shaken out of her sheltered country club set; Mrs. Hawkins gets her comeuppance; Colonel Smollett surrenders the persona of the grim disciplinarian; even Tony comes to acknowledge that this war is for an ideal. The main characters' personal growth parallels that of the nation, from the isolationist dream world to the stern realities of international responsibility.[22]

Most critics enjoyed the picture. "It's a pip," said *Newsweek*. Although conceding that the film was short on intellectual content, *Life* thought it captured "ordinary American thinking" in a way that was "genuinely heart-warming" for people who were "personally involved." Even critics such as Agee, who preferred a different style, confessed to enjoying it and gave Selznick a certain guarded praise.[23]

But even in the midst of war several critics called attention to those flaws which make *Since You Went Away* a squirm-inducer for postwar audiences: the dripping sentimentality, the too ob-vious manipulation of viewers' emotions, the sheer self-indulg-ence that threatened to overwhelm the intimate story. An anon-ymous critic in *Theater Arts* thought Selznick's "concentrated barrage" on the audience's emotions dissipated the many fine scenes and high-level acting. *Commonweal*'s Philip Hartung wished Selznick had been more sparing with the "theatrical corn" and the sob-drenched goodby scenes. He also thought the picture needed to be drastically shortened, starting with the Christmas Eve cable that ended the film "on a false note." "There are many of us who are of good courage and have strong faith, but who will not receive cables on Christmas Eve telling us our sons or fathers are safe after all," he said. Nonetheless *Since You Went Away* would remain "the definitive home-front movie . . . until a realist comes along to show us what life is really like in America during World War II."[24]

Yet there lay Selznick's brilliance. The film triumphed pre-cisely because it was not realistic. With Hollywood's slickest touch he wove together the sacred and sentimental symbols of American life and set them in the national shrine: the middle class home. The Hiltons' is transposed up a notch to the upper middle class, but so much the better. Selznick captured, without irony, how middle class Americans saw themselves. Though Hol-lywood thought servants were commonplace, only 6 percent of Americans enjoyed their services in 1940. In 1944 pollsters found that 98 percent of the population described themselves as economically middle class and 88 percent as socially middle class.[25] The genius of Hollywood was its ability to capture not American reality but American aspirations and make them seem real. "Until a realist comes along. . . . " But neither Hollywood nor, for that matter, OWI wanted a realist. *Since You Went Away* succeeded because it was a dream portrait by those living the dream.

Many families were not, of course, blessed with the movies' miraculous return of father, son, or loved one. Early in the war

OWI began urging Hollywood to help prepare audiences for the death of loved ones. One of the first films to do this was *Happy Land*, a Twentieth Century production released in late 1943. In contrast to the industrial brawn of *An American Romance* and the urbanity of *Since You Went Away*, the suggestively titled *Happy Land* invoked the sacred and sentimental symbols of a tranquil small town in Iowa, given the name Heartfield. Although America was a predominantly urban nation, the social cohesion and wholesome values of small town life—however compromised in reality—still cast a nostalgic glow for OWI and Hollywood. To this Grant Wood garden of virtue *Happy Land* added the complication of the death in battle of the local druggist's son. Upon its release *Happy Land* earned OWI's praise for "the most effective portrayal of straight Americana viewed to date."[26]

Happy Land was based on a story by MacKinley Kantor, who specialized in sentimental Americana. OWI watched the film's development carefully. Early versions suggested that America was fighting simply in self-defense; the propagandists worried that there was not enough idealism in the picture. Most of these concerns were eventually solved to OWI's satisfaction by writers Kathryn Scola and Julian Josephson. Kenneth MacGowan, whose next picture would be *Lifeboat*, was the producer; the director was Irving Pichel, whose wartime credits included such uneven pictures as *Secret Agent of Japan*, *The Pied Piper*, and *The Moon Is Down*.[27]

The picture's documentary-style opening invokes every cliché of small town life: Main Street, haying in the nearby fields, and—reminiscent of *Our Town*—Marsh's drug store as social center. (The town is Santa Rosa, California, whose Midwestern sobriety appealed to Hitchcock for *Shadow of a Doubt*.) Druggist Lew Marsh, played in painfully stolid fashion by Don Ameche, closes down for the day and walks home to a grand old Victorian house. His aproned wife (Frances Dee) greets him and sets a table of rib-sticking meat balls and scalloped potatoes. *The* telegram arrives: Their only son, Rusty, has been killed in action in the navy.

Although Agnes Marsh bears up fairly well, Lew sinks into despondency. His minister assures him that "Rusty died a fine death. He died for his country." "What was Rusty's country?"

Marsh shoots back. "He never had a chance to live ... never went anywhere—just went to school—worked for his dad—never had a home of his own or a boy of his own to worry about—or make a scooter for. It isn't right. It isn't fair." On Sunday morning the minister prays for consolation, but Lew's spot in the pew is vacant. He is staring at the tree trunk in the backyard where Rusty carved his initials.

As hymns swell in the background—presto! Gramps, dead twenty-one years, appears. He has gotten a special dispensation from the "authorities" to come down and help out. Gramps coaxes Lew to take a walk around town. A series of flashbacks ensue, building an image of family and community. Corporal Lew Marsh returns from World War I to a cheering crowd. His romance with Agnes begins over a sundae at Gramps' drug store. Little Rusty is taken to Gramps on his death bed. The scene suggests an immutable cycle of life and death. The boy stares at Gramps' Grand Army of the Republic service flag on his tombstone; his mother assures him there will be no more wars. That's the way to bring up American boys, says Gramps. "Not thinking about battles and conquests" but to enjoy "the homely simple things right here." Dissolve to a cornfield, where, in a perhaps inadvertent irony, Rusty and his pals are playing a rather warlike game of cowboys and Indians. Rusty grows up. He goes through every all-American rite of passage: Boy Scouts, football star, track star (he fell in the state meet but got up and finished), church youth group (where he was mainly interested in the girls), hired hand in his father's drug store. His is one of the most antiseptic adolescences imaginable. He seems never to have questioned anything, never been tempted to duck into the pool hall or peek at a Hollywood pinup, never cussed or swigged anything stronger than sarsaparilla.

His life reinforces the notion of the American rural community—*Gemeinschaft* on the prairie. An old farmer comes in for a $2.25 prescription but has only 35 cents. Rusty makes up the rest from his piggy bank. He makes friends with two poor kids from Dakota who've only tasted ice cream once in their lives. They get a free cone. Lew sends food to them, and Agnes goes over to set up housekeeping.

Rusty knows he belongs here. He considers going to the University of Iowa. He chooses instead to go to pharmacy school in Des Moines so he can come back to the store. (Was the state university too subversive for Main Street?) In Heartfield everybody has a place; everyone pitches in to help the less fortunate. This is America, the movie says, but it also seems to say this could be the world.

War erupts in 1939. The lone black in the film, the town's night watchman, emerges from the shadows of the nether world to deliver the lesson: "This ain't no World War No. 2. It's the same old war. The Kaiser was yellin' for a place in the sun, and this crazy man he's screamin' for ... well it's the same thing—weasel talk. Same old bunch of gangsters and killers out to make slaves of the rest of Europe." Rusty understands and volunteers for the navy before Pearl Harbor. His bus pulls away from Main Street for the last time.

To stirring patriotic music Gramps says: "As long as kids can play cowboys and Indians in the corn ... "—he pauses, plucks a four-leaf clover and gives it to Lew, who yields his first smile— " ... join Boy Scouts and do a good deed every day, eat ice cream, go to high school, play football, picnic in Briggs Woods, and take an honest-saved $1.90 ... it'll be worthwhile." Lew thanks him for the walk around town. "Rusty did lead a rich life," he says. But he still cannot bring himself to say the other things Gramps wants him to say. "I'll always wish he's back."

Gramps goes back to heaven. Lew returns to the store and takes a new interest in his work. Tony, a sailor—a friend of Rusty's—comes to the store. He has no family. Lew takes him home, where he tells the story of Rusty's sacrificial death. Rusty was carrying another man up from sick bay when the torpedo hit; if he'd just been looking out for himself he might have made the deck and survived. Lew offers him a glass of loganberry wine made by a little old lady in town. Lew, Agnes, and their surrogate son Tony drink a sacramental toast.

The story and the cinematic treatment coexisted uneasily. The photography was by the rising talent Joseph La Shelle, who won an Academy Award the next year for *Laura*. His unromantic, matter-of-fact camera work, complemented by restrained editing, captured the town's simple dignity. For devotees of realism, such as Agee and Farber, his photography offered great promise for serious pictures. Agee went so far as to say that the work of La Shelle and Alfred Valentine in *Shadow of a Doubt* took up "the Magna Carta for American films from the cellar corner where it was tossed along with the lost thirty-two reels of 'Greed.'"[28]

Interestingly enough, OWI's analysts, with their attention fixed on the story line and dialogue, failed to notice that La Shelle's photographic approach presented their image of America with winning authenticity. They found the message in the self-sacrificing Rusty, Gramps' moralizing, and Lew's ultimate conversion. As preachy as *So Proudly We Hail* and as contrived as *Keeper of the Flame*, the heavy-handed *Happy Land* reeked with propaganda. OWI's predilection for overt sermonizing instead of a matter-of-fact documentary, which would have allowed audiences to make up their own minds, betrayed a lack of faith in the "strategy of truth."

Tender Comrade (RKO, 1943) transposed the intertwined issues of loss of loved ones and the meaning of America to a feminine key. OWI was delighted. Ulric Bell reported "all cheers and hosannas" for it. His staff termed it "the most effective and moving screen portrayal" of the role of women in the war and praised its presentation of the issues. The production drew on the talents of unlikely collaborators. Two future members of the Hollywood Ten were involved: Dalton Trumbo wrote the script and Edward Dmytryk directed. Ginger Rogers, dancer-turned-would-be-serious actress, assumed the lead role of Jo Jones. OWI watched the film making eagerly, and found Trumbo, like many of the more radical writers in Hollywood, responsive to its coaching.[29]

Tender Comrade would have been deservedly forgotten in a 3 a.m. television slot after the war had it not been for the Trumbo-Dmytryk involvement. RKO thought it was doing the war effort a good turn, only to be hit with the charge during the Cold War that the film contained communist propaganda. An anguished Mrs. Leila Rogers, a member of the Motion Picture Alliance for the Preservation of American Ideals, charged that her unsuspecting daughter had been forced to speak Trumbo's insidious line: "Share and share alike—that's democracy." That idea, she said, was communist! In the World War II context that line just seemed like good propaganda as four working women pooled their resources.[30]

The story is a simple one. Chris Jones (Robert Ryan) goes

to war. His new wife, Jo Jones, gets a job in an aircraft factory. To save money and raise their living standard—she and three other women decide to pool their earnings and rent a big old house instead of "rathole" apartments. (This is as close as Hollywood and OWI get to dealing with the serious problem of the wartime housing shortage.) Jo gives birth to a son. Chris is killed. Jo explains to their son that Dad died to give him a better break. As in *Happy Land*, the sorrow of death is requited by the knowledge that the cycle of life and death goes on through the male line—with a surrogate son in *Happy Land*, with a real son in *Tender Comrade*.

The Ginger Rogers vehicle featured women perhaps more prominently than any other war-related movie. And while Trumbo and RKO no doubt conceived of it as a tribute to women on the home front, the picture of women that emerged was decidedly ambiguous. Trumbo, though a Communist Party member, did not break out of the Hollywood hokum about women. Perhaps delighted just to have women featured prominently, OWI reviewers seemed not to notice how the picture undercut the feminist argument they advanced in the manual. On the positive side women were shown volunteering for war work and making those little sacrifices which indicated to OWI a cheerful acceptance of war's discomforts. They understood how daily activities that might seem trivial fit into the larger picture. From time to time they got the good speeches—which were usually reserved for men—about the war issues. Rogers took the news of her husband's death with a soldierly stoicism and understood how his death, however painful to her, was necessary for a better world. But *Tender Comrade*'s clear implication, contra the Bureau of Motion Pictures, is that when the men come back to the factory women will shuffle back to the kitchen.[31]

Though ostensibly a tribute to women, *Tender Comrade* undermines its positive appeal with trite movie conventions about women. Jo is "a possessive, dominating shrew," erupted Manny Farber, "whose cruel, selfish and over-indulgent love and concept of marriage should cure a lot of soldier-home-sickness." When one of their husbands returned from the war all of the women "devoured [him] before your eyes," he said. Farber's exaggerated fear of the castrating female was worthy of Philip Wy-

lie's flaying of "momism." In his over-reaction one might nonetheless detect a clue to the picture's failure to establish women,
even in wartime, as independent people with lives of their own.
The women of *Tender Comrade* are still dependent on their men
and indulge in the pettiness that composes part of the demeaning stereotype of women.[32]

Glamour remains an obsession. Women aircraft workers are
perfectly coiffed and attired in smartly-cut work clothes, and
emerge from the day's riveting without a smudge. (In *So Proudly
We Hail* Veronica Lake and compatriots managed to fight the
Japanese without mussing their hair.) Work apparently is all
right so long as it doesn't interfere with women's real concern:
beauty. This feminine urge undermines the war effort as some
of them hoard lipstick or try to circumvent rationing, until they
are shamed into compliance.

But more basic than anything else is that life revolves around
your man. Chris and Jo have a terrific fight before he leaves for
the war. He insists that she must not get a job. Though she fights
his demand momentarily, she gives in when he agrees to drop
overtime work. "I don't want money," Jo says. "I only want you."
It's all right to work during the war when he's gone, but presumably she will hang up her designer hard hat and return mer-
rily to the kitchen. Even the hardbitten Barbara, who's "seen a
lot," comes around, though it takes her husband's injury on the
Yorktown to transform her. She groused about rationing as "just
a pain in the neck." Now she realizes "I'm just a big no-good
dame!" She had vowed she'd never "knuckle down to any man,
no matter how good he was," she says. "[But] If I ever get that
guy in my arms again, I'll knuckle down to that man, Jo." When
Doris's husband returns safe and sound, all the housemates flock
around him and cook their specialties for him. In the picture's
closing moments, as Jo fights back the tears, her comrades tell
her to think of him and be strong. She promises to bring up
their son according to Chris's program. Through the boy she
will live.

While the picture was wrestling, however unsuccessfully,
with women's roles, it gave several war issues a thorough, and
rather blatant, verbal airing. The film connects everyday household management with the global struggle. The housekeeper
for the four wives, a refugee from Dresden, refuses to patronize

a blackmarket butcher—he's "taking food right out of the mouths of the U. S. Army!" she says. It's just a little thing but it leads to big things, she says. She knows. "Once in Germany we had a democracy. . . . We let it be murdered." A housemate confesses to hoarding no fewer than 127 tubes of lipstick. This true confession prompts a lecture from Jo: "All that metal and all that grease!" What if twenty or thirty million other women did it? "Anyone who hoards is a heel."

This exchange leads to bigger things dear to OWI's agenda. Barbara asserts that we would not be in this mess if we'd just minded our own business. "Our guys are out fightin' in countries they never even heard of for a lot of foreigners who'll turn on us like a pack of wolves the minute it's over," she says. You ought to be ashamed, Jo retorts. "Do you know where that kind o' talk comes from! It comes straight from Berlin!" Every time "you even think it you're doublecrossing your own husband." We make mistakes, sure. Germany and Japan can't stand mistakes. "Go to Germany, go to Japan, and the first time you open your trap the way you have tonight you'll find a gun in your stomach. You're the kind o' people Hitler counted on when he started this war."

The war is not just for high-sounding ideals but for a better life, reminiscent of the Four Freedoms. Jo explains this to their son after she gets the telegram. "You see, little guy, I know the ropes." She plans his life, as Chris had planned it before he left. He wanted his boy to go to college and he wanted to support him to be a doctor, lawyer, musician, or whatever he wants to be. Your dad "went out and died so you could have a better break when you grow up," Jo continues. He didn't leave you any money—no million dollars or country clubs. "He only left you the best world a boy could ever grow up in. He bought it for you with his life . . . a personal gift to you from your dad." Don't ever let anybody say he died for nothing. As tears glisten in Jo's eyes, Chris says in a voice-over: "Free to live with you, enough food and our own home. That's what the war's about, I guess." Jo continues: "Grab it right in your hands, Chris boy, and hold it high." She kisses the baby. To her husband's picture she says: "Don't worry, Chris. He'll grow up to be a good guy." She puts the picture in the crib facing the baby.

Jo closes the bedroom door and starts downstairs. She begins to break down. She hears her housemates' voices. "Come on, Jo. Head up. Take it on the chin like a good guy, like a soldier's wife should." She pulls herself together, straightens up, walks resolutely downstairs and out of the picture. Dissolve to clouds and then Chris and Jo, tiny figures hand in hand beneath a vast sky, as music swells in triumph.

This mawkish ending to a didactic picture was the last straw. James Agee called it "one of the most nauseating things I ever sat through." Preview audiences concurred. "Ending was *awful!* Too much propaganda!" exclaimed a viewer from a preview in Glendale. "Bored!" shouted a comment card from Pasadena. "The PROPAGANDA touch was so honeyed it was sickening," said another Pasadena viewer. "If you could re-do all that part of it, you might have a picture." Another patron felt as if she had attended a lecture on "why we are fighting this war." These audiences were scarcely being propagandized without knowing it, as Elmer Davis had hoped. Indeed one viewer urged RKO to stick to entertainment and let the Office of Price Administration and OWI combat the black market, little realizing perhaps OWI's role in entertainment films.[33]

In both *Tender Comrade* and *Happy Land* the experience of loss is tied to the meaning of America. Both pictures instruct Americans in how to experience war death. For one of life's most personal moments they provide a political meaning. The model they create is based on the code of the stiff upper lip, combined with the promise of regeneration through sons or surrogate sons. The model virtually denies a moment of grief. Moreover, in *Tender Comrade* the male production heirarchy extends this stereotypically male code to women: Jo is not even allowed tears.

Both films dealt with a deeply serious subject and one very much on the public's mind. Yet neither mounted a treatment worthy of the theme. Doubt, anger, grief—these most understandable human emotions were subverted by the worst prepackaged conventions of propaganda and formulaic entertainment.

Ironically, OWI's Overseas Branch in New York, which controlled the shipment of films to liberated areas, concluded in April 1945 that *Tender Comrade*'s propaganda was unsuitable. This office decided that the five women's living standards were too lavish to be shown in countries that had experienced war-times destitution. These analysts objected to lengthy discussions of the bacon ration (people in other countries had forgotten what bacon tasted like, they said), the desire for a real fireplace instead of the gas-fired substitute, and the cornucopia of baked oysters, stuffed cabbage, fish steak, pumpkin pie, and whipped cream spread before Doris's husband. Most of all "the cheap and obvious propaganda" backfired. "Any people who need such cheap peptalks on the most elementary sacrifices could not possibly know what this war is all about," they said. RKO was caught short from all angles. It had larded an entertainment picture with propaganda and received high praise from OWI's Hollywood branch, only to find its most earnest efforts dismissed as not consistent with the overseas effort.[34]

Miles away from the earnest domesticity of *Tender Comrade* and *Happy Land* was the madcap, satirical, yet ultimately America-affirming Oakridge, California, of Preston Sturges's *Hail the Conquering Hero*. Sturges, one of the genuinely individual talents in Hollywood, had enjoyed some success as a Broadway playwright and Hollywood writer. Then from 1939 through 1944 he wrote and directed eight pictures, several of which, *The Great McGinty*, *The Lady Eve*, *The Miracle of Morgan's Creek*, and *Hail the Conquering Hero*, rank among the masterpieces of screwball comedy. Sturges satirized politicians in *McGinty*, feminism in *Eve*, and motherhood in *Miracle*. In the timely *Hail*, which he considered his best picture, he tackled hero-worship and politics, among other themes. *Hail* had a turbulent production history. The picture was finished in December 1943, but Paramount's chief of production, B. G. "Buddy" DeSylva, insisted on cutting the talkier passages. When a preview in February proved disastrous, Sturges, whose contract with the studio had expired by now, offered to return without pay, write a new ending, do four days of retakes, and restore the integrity of the original. The desperate studio agreed, and *Hail* climaxed his most creative period. Finally released in August 1944, the film enjoyed some critical acclaim but indifferent box-office success.[35]

Hail the Conquering Hero brought to perfection the Sturges trademark—a combination of frenetic, practically slapstick, energy with an extremely deft visual and aural satirical touch. The picture suffered, however, from the director's characteristic last-reel letdown, which, in the case of *Hail*, introduced a sharp shift in tone and added ambiguity to his message. Sturges's trouble in ending his pictures has been the subject of speculation by both contemporary and subsequent admirers; it robbed *Hail* of what could have been its most potent message.

A morose Woodrow Lafayette Pershing Truesmith, played by Eddie Bracken, a Sturges discovery, is spending a lonely evening in a bar. The son of Sgt. "Hinky Dinky" Truesmith, who was killed at Belleau Wood in 1918, he has a terrible sense of failure because his chronic hay fever left him 4F. He has been pretending to his mother that he was overseas while he was really working in a war factory in San Diego. Several marines, led by Sgt. Julius Heffelfinger, a friend of Woodrow's dad, arrive at the bar and decide to take him home as a hero of Guadalcanal to please his mother. Now the frolic begins.

Woodrow arrives to a hero's welcome in Oakridge. The mayor, Everett Noble, starts to deliver a bombastic speech welcoming him "home to the arms of his mother." One of the brass bands, thinking this is their cue, strikes up a tune; not to be outdone the other bands break into their numbers. Soon we have an Ivesian medley of bands marching and blaring all at once "Let Me Call You Sweetheart," "There'll Be a Hot Time in the Old Town Tonight," and "Mademoiselle From Armentiers." A bewildered Woodrow returns home, where his mother keeps a shrine, complete with ever-burning candles, to the memory of his father. "Now I have two heroes," says his beaming mother. The town takes up a collection to pay off his mother's mortgage. A fund drive begins for a monument that would show Hinky Dinky and Woodrow shaking hands and the inscription "Like father, like son." How am I going to get out of this? worries Woodrow.

Worse is to come. A committee, headed by the judge, comes to visit. "I guess I deserve it," he says, expecting the worst. "Of course you do," they say, anticipating the best. "We're going to do it right here," they smile. "Not in front of my mother!" he all but shrieks. The judge looks serious. There's "something rotten in this town," he says ominously. Woodrow looks deeply worried. The town is full of slackers, tax evaders, people who don't buy bonds, the judge continues. The town's motto— "business as usual"—is dishonest in wartime. The committee wants him to take Doc Bissell's place. "But I'm not a veterinary," Woodrow cries. "I hardly know one end of a horse from the other." No, no, they say, take his place as a candidate; we want you to run for mayor.

The speechless hero is led out onto the front porch, where he confronts a throng of well wishers and a band strikes up "For He's a Jolly Good Fellow." He begins a halting speech, the meaning of which completely escapes the crowd. "Ladies and gentlemen, I wish I were dead," he says. "I love my mother very much." (A natural flair for politics, says one of the pols.) "I really don't deserve it. . . . The medals that you see pinned on me you could practically say were pinned on me by mistake. . . . I've known all of you all my life. I've mowed your lawns. I delivered milk for your babies. . . . " (That line's remarkable, says a pol. He could be president!) "Nothing would be dearer to my heart than to be worthy of the honor you have offered me. I wish I could accept it." (Cheers!) "I'm no hero." (Cries of No! No!) "I haven't had Dr. Bissell's long experience with animals." (Laughter.) "There's the man for you. I thank you." (The finest political speech since Bryan and the crown of thorns, says one pol.) Back in the kitchen Woodrow gulps cooking wine to steady his nerves. "I'm not running for mayor," he says with finality. He tries to escape his predicament by arranging for a fake call ordering him back to his marine base, but that fails.

Woodrow takes a sentimental walk with Libby (Ella Raines), his old girlfriend. They broke up when he ostensibly went to war, and she got engaged to Forrest Noble, the tall, good looking son of the mayor, who's 4F—and glad of it—because he too has hay fever. (Libby seems to like men who sneeze a lot.) Woodrow tries to tell her the truth. "I'm a phoney," he says. "I've never been in Guadalcanal. I've never won any medals—or even been in the marine corps really. Understand? But she refuses to understand. She pats him on the shoulder, tells him he's had a hard day, and that she will love him always. The townspeople, too, refuse to hear.

As scriptwriter Sturges is now in a dilemma. He has effectively, sometimes brilliantly, satirized the creation and acceptance of heroes. But how is he going to resolve the situation? The truth, seemingly, must come out, but with what results? The hero is poised on the knife edge of the fickle mob.

Sturges is wrestling with the ability of the mythology of war to mislead, but, as will become clear, he shrinks from its full implications. Although the motivations of Woodrow and the marines are estimable, it is easily evident how wartime heroism could be manipulated for political purposes by unscrupulous parties. (Only a year or two ahead lay the distortion of war records by men like "Tail Gunner Joe" McCarthy.) Such issues had already been much on Sturges's mind in *The Miracle of Morgan's Creek*, released a year earlier. In that picture he wanted to have Dr. Upperman, a minister, express the moral stand, warning young women against promiscuity with soldiers, but the passage also suggested his larger concern over wartime popular hysteria. Through Upperman Sturges wanted to say that "all is not gold that glitters, that the young are impetuous, that war time is a thoughtless time and that in any large group of good men there are of necessity some fools and scoundrels . . . and against these I warn you. Beware of the spell cast by jingling spurs, . . . the hasty act repented at leisure, . . . of confusing patriotism with promiscuity, of interpreting loyalty as laxity." (The passage was cut by the studio.) In *Hail* it is not sexual promiscuity but mental laxness against which Sturges seems to warn.[36]

Yet having spent the first two thirds of the picture building this warning, he is unable to carry it through. At his giant campaign rally Woodrow confesses all, mixed with a condemnation of the townspeople's blindness. Doc Bissell tried to serve you, Woodrow says, "only you didn't know a good man when you saw one, so you elected a phoney instead—until a still bigger phoney came along and then you naturally wanted him." Cured of his fear, Woodrow reveals that he's 4F and plaintively expresses his inability to live up to his father's ideal. "If I could reach as high as my father's shoestrings my whole life would be justified. . . . I've told you all this because too many men have bled and died for you and for me to use this lie any longer. . . . It's no use telling you I'm sorry because—I wish I was dead." He looks at his mother, her head bowed and in tears. "That's all," he murmurs and exits the flag-decked stage.

Sgt. Heffelfinger jumps to the rostrum. "What that kid just done takes *real* courage," he says. He explains how the whole thing happened. We met him in this bar, see, and. . . .

Libby finds Woodrow packing to go away. She has returned

her ring to Forrest and goes back to Woodrow, her true love. They leave for the train station. There they find the sergeant leading a big crowd under the "Welcome Woodrow" banner. "What is this—a lynchin'?" he trembles. Though he doesn't know it, the townspeople have come there because they love him even more. When the pols tried to give the nomination back to Bissell, the doctor refused. He'd never seen a more convincing display of honesty, Bissell said; besides, it wasn't a bad thing for Woodrow to have done those things for his mother. So they came to the station to catch Woodrow before he caught the southbound. The marines swing aboard the train's rear platform. The locomotive accelerates to the beat of the Marine hymn. The marines wave to the cheering crowd. Cut to an angelic Woodrow, who forms the marine slogan—"Semper Fidelis"—with his lips. Cut back to the diminishing rear end of the train, which dissolves into the shrine of his father.

Woodrow has won back his sweetheart and the love of his townspeople. Once again Hollywood's happy ending celebrates the upright individual hero. It is Mr. Truesmith goes to Oakridge. The people, recognizing finally the good and the true, throw out the windbag mayor for the youthful idealist. But there is little reason to believe this ending. Sturges's view of the small town throughout most of the movie suggests a group of smallminded followers who are easily seduced by political shams. Woodrow's fear of a lynching party is not unreasonable; this sort of public does not like to find out that its heroes are fake. Nor is Woodrow's election as mayor an unmixed blessing. Everett Noble deserves to be thrown out, but the hero for a day, however honest, has no obvious qualifications for the job. The best choice—Doc Bissell—is once again passed over. Moreover, Sturges presents an ambiguous view of military heroism. He satirizes it in the first part of the picture—the shrine to Hinky Dinky and the general's statue—but switches to an affirmative vision with Woodrow's confession and "semper fi."

Artistically the ending of *Hail* is unsatisfying, but it was sufficiently upbeat to earn kudos from OWI as "a good picture of working democracy in America today." (It was ruled unsuitable for distribution in liberated areas, however, because of fears it might be misinterpreted.) The problematic conclusion recalled the critique by James Agee, who admired Sturges's work but felt his endings almost always betrayed a fear of "intactness and self-commitment." And Richard Corliss wrote: "Too often, Sturges's artistry would carry a film until the last reel, when the happy hack would take over, turning the fade-out into a cop-out." Both critics thought his films reflected the artist's division between his bohemian adventuress mother, Mary Desti, and his successful stockbroker stepfather, Solomon Sturges.[37]

Whether or not Sturges in his films was playing out some deep-seated ambivalence towards his parents, he was deeply committed to art, and chafed under the studio system and the constraints of the production code. To an irate parent whose children had seen *The Miracle of Morgan's Creek* he wrote: "It is this very habit of confusing the theatre with an ice cream parlor which has caused so much unnecessary misunderstanding." The attempt to make all motion picture plays suitable to all ages had "so emasculated, Comstocked and bowdlerized this wonderful form of theatre" that many adults simply ignored it. "It is my intention," he said, "someday to bring you Ibsen, Shakespeare, Moliere, yea even Sophocles, Aristophanes and others who did not write for children in a chain of adult theatres or at least theatres with adult hours." He had few choices for the ending of *Hail the Conquering Hero*. Whatever his own probably deeply ambivalent feelings about his subject, the moral strictures of the PCA and the political constraints of wartime left him little alternative but a last-reel affirmation of America.[38]

OWI welcomed pictures such as *Since You Went Away, Happy Land*, and *An American Romance*, but they wanted more of them. Dorothy Jones, BMP's chief reviewer, after the war lamented the fact that feature films "did little to dignify and interpret for American audiences the home-front war." She particularly objected to the appropriation of the war as a backdrop for comedies and romances. Though Hollywood often looked upon the war as simply another theme to exploit, Jones's complaint seems like a case of tunnel vision.[39]

OWI's reviewers always had trouble with comedy that touched on the war—witness *Palm Beach Story* and *Princess O'Rourke*. When Laurel and Hardy threatened to start cutting up, the Bureau of Motion Pictures was on guard. "Home Front," a Laurel and Hardy screenplay filmed as "Nothing But Trouble," raised some sensitive issues. As might be imagined, the plot with

its complications and improbable twists is impossible to sum-
marize. In essence the duo hire out as a chef and butler—the
slapstick possibilities were infinite—and while making dinner
and being fired and rehired manage to save Christopher, boy
king of a mythical Balkan country, from being poisoned by his
evil regent. The original treatment contained three major
transgressions which MGM executives agreed to change after
protests from OWI. Laurel and Hardy originally returned from
Yokohama on a prisoner-of-war exchange deal—a subject strictly
off limits because of the heated emotions on that subject. The
king was determined to rule, which risked offending the anti-
monarchical partisans; so the country was transformed to a
mythical land in which citizens had the right to choose their
form of government. A railroad magnate in league with the regent intended to build railroads in the country after the war;
that was dropped to avoid the imperialistic implications. In addition a scene in which the young king and President Roosevelt
swapped stamps from their collections was eliminated. MGM no
doubt thought the scene was cute, but OWI guarded the president's image carefully. The propagandists feared that some of
these references might be taken as reflections of official policy,
but even with Oliver Hardy's attempts at frustrated dignity, the
duo would have remained strictly unofficial.[40]

Although OWI thought the home front was intensely dramatic, it was in reality a pretty tepid subject by comparison with
other war themes. Two contrasting screenplays that did not advance to the filming stage illustrated the problem. "One Destiny," written by Tess Slessinger and Frank Davis for Twentieth
Century-Fox in early 1943, was one of OWI's favorite scripts.
The proposed film showed how various sectors of yet another
mythical Iowa community came to understand the necessity for
wartime unity. Craig, given a draft deferment to stay on the
farm, makes townspeople understand that he isn't yellow, just
doing an essential job; he even rallies local businessmen to close
their shops and pitch in with the harvest. Sylvia, who has been
turning Craig down, decides she loves him after all and they
plan to get married—after the war, of course. Congressman Sam,
a party hack, undergoes conversion to enlightened representative when his only son is killed in combat. The writers adopted
most of OWI's numerous suggestions, and the propaganda an-

alysts proudly felt that Twentieth Century's good sense had improved not only the war messages but the dramatic content as well. This may be doubted. Had this variation on *Happy Land* been filmed, Craig, Sylvia, and Congressman Sam would have drowned in dextrose.[41]

"Night Shift" was the converse of this bucolic vision, and OWI argued strongly against its filming. Warner Brothers, which was more attracted to social problem themes than other studios, purchased the rights to the novel of the same name by Marita Wolff. The screenplay was a sort of *Tobacco Road* set in a squalid factory town. The characters toiled in a factory that was a death trap and found their lives a dead end. Their lives, said BMP, were "filled with trouble, loneliness, death, insanity, drunkenness, infidelity, and gangsterism." Little wonder that someone thought this would make a salable movie. OWI liberals might well have applauded such a novel five years before, but in the midst of a global conflict they saw it as a threat to the war effort. They feared that the picture would substantiate Axis propaganda about the decadence of American life. Nelson Poynter urged Warners to show how these problems were being solved through the democratic process and thus enhance "the glorious story that we have to tell about our country."[42]

The studio tried. By 1945 several writers had produced a packing case full of different treatments and scripts. They gradually changed the emphasis from the quasi-Marxist story of alienated workers in the depression to a story of individualism triumphant in a postwar world without limits, if only people had faith in themselves. Warners decided not to film any of the screenplays, probably in part because of OWI's objections in 1943 and the swing away from serious pictures later in the war. Praise for *An American Romance*, condemnation for "Night Shift"—thus did the perceived needs of war alter the liberal ethos from identification with the working class to support for the needs of the state.[43]

Though studios tended to avoid films about social problems, some found the surge in juvenile delinquency during the war an irresistible subject. Latchkey children wandering the streets of boomtowns, kids locked in cars in factory parking lots while their parents worked, children chained like animals to their trailer homes—all bespoke the disproportionate burden

the war dumped on children and teenagers. Adolescent violence rose dramatically. Like the characters Preston Sturges had
in mind, teenage girls, some only twelve years old, decorated
bus and train stations and became known as Victory Girls and
Patriotutes. Tracked down by vice squads, they protested that
they were only performing a patriotic service—keeping up military morale.[44]

Monogram's low-budget *Where Are Your Children?* appalled
BMP reviewers with its "sensational portrayal of a young girl's
downfall, youthful drunkenness, orgiastic dancing and necking,
a seduction resulting in pregnancy, a stolen car, a joy ride, a
murder, an attempted suicide and the repentant older generation." Here clearly was something for everyone. (This description was actually a bit on the sensational side itself, for the
watchful eyes of Joseph Breen would not have allowed something quite so sensational as OWI described.) Since the movie,
like most "poverty row" productions was shot with only a rough
script, OWI had little chance to influence it. The agency exacted
its dues, however, when it got censor Rothacker to demand that
about 10 percent of the film be cut in order to get an export
license. Americans might be thrilled or chilled by these adolescent antics, but foreign audiences saw a considerably tamed
younger set. Under similar OWI pressure, RKO modified the
screenplay for its own picture on juvenile delinquency. Originally titled *Youth Runs Wild*, it became first *Are These Our Children?*, then *The Dangerous Age*. It was finally released with the
admonitory title *Look To Your Children*, and included a series of
"stock shots showing how the Boy Scouts, 4-H Clubs, city play-
grounds and similar institutions are combatting juvenile problems." Just as the PCA refused to show systematic corruption,
so too OWI was willing to acknowledge social problems only if
the movies showed a solution.[45]

This combination of Hollywood imagination and OWI propaganda was fundamentally misleading. Social services, never
adequate, tended to be cut rather than expanded during the
war. What the head of Vassar's Child-Study Department said of
the Victory Girls might have been extended to a generation:
They were another category of "war casualties."[46]

The most serious home-front problem—the portrayal of
blacks—did not lend itself, however, to the facile solutions of

the juvenile delinquency pictures. As the furor over *Tennessee Johnson* indicated, Hollywood found it difficult to abandon its time-worn demeaning portrayals of blacks. As Dalton Trumbo said, the movies made "tarts of the Negro's daughters, crap shooters of his sons, obsequious Uncle Toms of his fathers, superstitious and grotesque crones of his mothers, strutting peacocks of his successful men, psalm-singing mountebanks of his priests, and Barnum and Bailey side-shows of his religion." OWI's Bureau of Motion Pictures regretfully concurred. In an analysis of the depiction of blacks in wartime movies in 1943, the bureau concluded that "in general, Negroes are presented as basically different from other people, as taking no relevant part in the life of the nation, as offering nothing, contributing nothing, expecting nothing." Blacks appeared in 23 percent of the films released in 1942 and early 1943 and were shown as "clearly inferior" in 82 percent of them.[47]

OWI wanted to improve the movies' images of blacks. Continuation of the traditional stereotypes confounded the agency's attempt to show America as an ideal democracy. The biased portrayals undermined black war morale at home and hurt America's image abroad. But there were clear limits to how far the Bureau of Motion Pictures would go on this issue. OWI had been pleased with the outcome of *Tennessee Johnson*, even though black spokesmen found the picture offensive. The propagandists hoped to clean up the worst examples of racial stereotypes and to introduce positive black characters if that could be done without too much trouble. But the agency would not go beyond these minimal steps, and if often fell short even of these.

The easiest way for Hollywood and OWI to deal with racial problems was "writing out"—simply eliminating a potentially troublesome character. The Motion Picture Bureau counseled just such a strategy when it read the screenplay for MGM's projected "Battle Hymn." The script showed some blacks in a Maryland household during the Civil War who would probably be perceived as slaves, so the bureau recommended they be omitted. "The fact that slavery existed in this country is certainly something which belongs to the past and which we wish to forget at this time when unity of all races and creeds is all-important," said BMP reviewer Dorothy Jones. Metro complied. When the presence of a black pantryman called attention to military segregation in *Action in the North Atlantic*, Warner Brothers cut him out at OWI's suggestion. Black servants disappeared from *An American Romance*. The extent of writing out is hard to gauge, but it was probably extensive: membership in the black actors' union fell by 50 percent during the war, suggesting that their opportunities were much reduced.[48]

In the remaining roles blacks sometimes attained an equality that OWI could applaud. Two of the strongest roles were in two of the best wartime movies—the legendary *Casablanca* (Warners, 1943), and *The Ox-Bow Incident* (Twentieth Century, 1943). Though still in the cinematic ghetto of the entertainer, Sam, played by Dooley Wilson, is relatively equal as the piano player in Rick's *Casablanca* cafe. In *The Ox-Bow Incident* Leigh Whipper plays a minor but important role as one of a handful of men who hold out against the lynching of men who turn out to be innocent. OWI found the "excellent characterization of a Negro," as well as the triumph of the judicial process, reason to recommend the film for export.[49]

Blacks escaped conventional limits more fully in combat pictures than in any other genre. They played heroic combat roles in *Crash Dive* (Twentieth Century, 1943) and *Sahara* (Columbia, 1943), although the former followed the navy's policy of limiting blacks to menial tasks in the early part of the war. MGM's *Bataan* (1943) offered perhaps the greatest departure, with Kenneth Spencer adding a black face to a baker's dozen of ethnically diverse G.I.s. He is almost equal. He is present for discussions of strategy, although his contribution is not about how to defeat the enemy but a vague affirmation of faith in the United States. He dies as heroically as the other soldiers in the face of the overwhelmingly superior Japanese force. Yet subtle implications of inferiority remain. "He spends a good part of his on-screen time humming 'St. Louis Blues,'" notes historian Daniel Leab. When he sets an explosive charge, he depends on the instructions of his white partner, who is entrusted with pushing the plunger. Ironically, Hollywood's ability to create a mythical world gave blacks a better deal than did real life, for there were no integrated combat units at this time. Yet OWI applauded these depictions of blacks, for they symbolized the unity of colors and creeds fighting for America. The situations being depicted involved artificial communities, and not reality:

the U.S. armed forces were "integrated" on the screen many years before they were actually integrated on the battlefield.[50]

Alfred Hitchcock's *Lifeboat* (Twentieth Century, 1944) also included a notable black character under conditions similar to combat—a diverse group of passengers from a torpedoed liner put aside their differences in order to survive an ordeal in a lifeboat. The picture makes one solidly affirmative gesture when the steward Joe, well played by Canada Lee, is offered a vote on a crucial decision. Joe seems surprised at this benevolence, as well he might be. The positive gesture is undercut, however, when he abstains from voting, perhaps indicating that he cannot really exercise such judgment. Hitchcock undermines Joe in other ways too. He logs less time on camera than the others; he is treated patronizingly; his original nickname was Charcoal; he is an adept, if reformed, pickpocket; and he clings to a rather simplistic religious faith. OWI recognized that Joe was intended as a sympathetic character, but these problems contributed to its ruling that the film should not be sent to liberated areas. *Lifeboat* allowed a black person to integrate a space under extraordinary, life-threatening circumstances, but even here the baggage of Jim Crow persisted.[51]

The limits of Hollywood's understanding of blacks, even after Willkie's and White's efforts to heighten film makers' consciousness, were underscored by *Since You Went Away*. Selznick conceived his magnum opus on the home front as a tribute not only to white working women but to blacks as well. But this salute seemed like more of the same old stereotyping. Selznick included a few blacks in crowd scenes, as OWI wished. The most important black character, however, was the symbolically named Fidelia, the stereotypical maid played by Hattie McDaniel. By sheer force of personality McDaniel dominates the scenes in which she appears; indeed she may well be the most memorable character among these insipid WASPs. While making allowance for eighty years of economic change, and transposing the scene from a Georgia plantation to a Northern urban household, Fidelia is still the faithful black servant of *Gone With The Wind*. She is as devoted to Mrs. Hilton as her predecessor was to Miss Scarlett. Fidelia returns regularly after hours "to get in her day's measure of malapropisms, comic relief, mother wit, and free labor," said James Agee. She "satisfied all that anyone could possibly desire of a Negro in . . . restive times." OWI failed to notice these shortcomings as it celebrated Selznick's sentimental version of the home front.[52]

The propaganda agency was equally insensitive to the black perspective in musicals that featured blacks. When the armed forces were on parade instead of at war, Hollywood resuscitated one of the worst show-business stereotypes—the minstrel show—in Warner Brothers' *This Is the Army*. A painted backdrop of zoot-suited blacks, made up as for a minstrel show, looms over a Harlem street whose Orchid Club gin mill exemplifies white impressions of the black capital as an entertainment mecca. The real "Brown Bomber" Joe Louis in uniform salutes as the black soldiers do a snappy song and dance number, "That's What the Well-Dressed Man in Harlem Will Wear." "Mr. Dude" has stashed his top hat and tails. Instead for the duration

> When's he's struttin' down the street with his sweetie pie.
> Suntan shade of cream or an olive drab color scheme
> That's What the Well-Dressed Man in Harlem Will Wear.[53]

Here was the black man not as worker, father, or solid citizen but as lover, playboy, and flashy dresser—and the war as fashion show. In the all-male revue the soldiers dress in drag when women are needed. White G.I.s don the garb of Little Bo Peep and southern belles; significantly, black soldiers are done up as whores and tramps. The blacks break into the inevitable tap dance and, turning on their stereotypical rhythm, put the whites to shame. But there is no phony integration in this picture. *This Is the Army* is as segregated as the real army of democracy.

Two all-black musicals from 1943 highlighted the dilemma of the black star locked in the confined assumptions of the entertainer. *Cabin in the Sky* (MGM) and *Stormy Weather* (Twentieth Century) featured strong performances by outstanding stars, but, like Hattie McDaniel, the very framework of these pictures perpetuated the position of blacks as essentially a people apart. *Cabin in the Sky* combined comedy, music, and the trite image of black religion as one step removed from picturesque superstition. The Bureau of Motion Pictures worried that blacks were presented as "simple, ignorant, superstitious folk, incapable of anything but the most menial labor." OWI's Washington headquarters dismissed such worries and thought the picture was just good fun.[54]

Stormy Weather dramatized the life of Bill "Bo Jangles" Robinson and featured Lena Horne in her first big role. OWI called attention to the film's implied segregation but concluded it could not "possibly give offense to any group." Walter White, however, objected that Lena Horne was forced to do "vulgar things" that producers would not dare impose on white actresses. He feared that Hollywood reinforced stereotypes of blacks as "primitive barbarians who never step short of extremes" in sexual matters. Latter-day audiences, fed on the wide-open sexuality of movies and television, find Horne sexy rather than vulgar. White nonetheless had a point; in the context of World War II, such roles reflected a subtle racism.[55]

Horne was ambivalent about such casting. On the one hand wartime movies gave her an immense following among blacks—and among whites too. A black academician recalled her own feelings when she saw the picture as a North Carolina teenager: "I didn't know all that stuff was going on—I just wanted to look like Lena Horne." Some whites date their first impression of "black is beautiful" from *Stormy Weather*. The title song became her trademark. On the other hand Horne, while managing to avoid the maid or jungle roles she had feared, had trouble getting the dramatic parts she coveted. "I became a butterfly pinned to a column singing away in Movieland," she said.[56]

For some liberal reviewers such pictures were, as Manny Farber said of *Cabin in the Sky,* "well turned decorations in something which is a stale insult." Hollywood's proclaimed good intentions would merit respect, he said, only when "it brings out a movie where the central figures are Negroes living in a white majority." Walter White dreamed, too, of a serious treatment of black life. Early in the war he tried to interest several producers in a sort of early day *Roots* that would trace black history from an African tribe to modern professional success. Other people of color had had their day on the screen. Irving Thalberg poured all of MGM's resources into a classic, if cliché-ridden, panorama of Chinese life: *The Good Earth* (1937). But no producer would take White's bait. Screen images at the end of the war strongly resembled those OWI had found in 1943. A Columbia University study in 1945 found that of 100 black appearances in wartime films, 75 perpetuated old stereotypes, 13 were neutral, and only 12 were positive. The "new concept of the Negro" that White had expected did not materialize.[57]

OWI did not dare propose such a film, for in dealing realistically with black history it would challenge the propagandists' vision of a united, democratic America. They settled instead for vague, safe hints of incremental change, designed to suggest that democracy would bring eventual progress in race relations. The agency's sacred and sentimental symbols were thus deployed on the racial front to imply that blacks were full participants in American life while they remained in fact a people apart. Until the Four Freedoms became a reality for American blacks, their loyalty and their imagery would be the subject of manipulation by their self-styled allies.

During the war OWI and Hollywood joined forces to tell Americans how to think about the often bewildering changes they were experiencing in their daily lives. They defined an America of infinite promise, in which the sacrifices of today bought security and prosperity for tomorrow. That message of reassurance masked a host of problems and anxieties that did not lend themselves to cinema clichés. By emphasizing the promise of American life to the exclusion of its performance, Hollywood and OWI narrowed the permissible bounds of opinion. To be sure, the propaganda agency encouraged greater openness in some areas, such as recognition of labor's contribution. The major thrust, however, of the combination of OWI and Hollywood was to foster a belief that social problems are chiefly the result of individual deficiency, that they are ephemeral and easily solvable. By excluding information from the public, wartime movies contributed to the impoverishment of dialogue about American society.

VII.

Putting the Russians Through the Wringer

War has put Hollywood's traditional conception of the Muscovites through the wringer, and they have come out shaved, washed, sober, good to their families, Rotarians, brother Elks, and 33rd Degree Mason.

Variety, October 28, 1942

In late April 1943 four thousand people gathered in Washington, D.C., for a gala premiere of Warner Brothers' proud new offering, *Mission to Moscow*. The crowd, composed of political figures, socialites, and hard-boiled journalists, enthusiastically hailed the picture. The public premiere followed a special private screening at the White House for President Franklin D. Roosevelt and his inner circle. A dramatization of the book of the same name by Joseph E. Davies, the United States ambassador to the Soviet Union from 1936 to 1938, the film skilfully combined fiction, half-truths, and documentary techniques. American-Soviet friendship stood at its height in the spring of 1943, the year the Red Army turned the tide on the Eastern front and Roosevelt, Churchill, and Stalin met for the first time, in Teheran. The film fed a genuine hunger on the part of millions of Americans to know more about their heroic but little understood and still mistrusted allies. To the Roosevelt administration, which had been deeply involved behind the scenes in the production of the film, *Mission to Moscow* would help bolster an uneasy alliance. The picture airbrushed out most of the nasty

185

features of Stalin's regime, delivered an all-out pummeling to American isolationists and British appeasers, and attributed an almost super-human prescience about world affairs to Roosevelt, Stalin, and Joseph E. Davies.[1]

But the cheers that greeted the film's premiere faded almost instantly. From the moment the picture went into general release it was surrounded by some of the bitterest controversy ever attached to an entertainment film. Upon reflection virtually no one believed *Mission to Moscow* rendered Soviet reality accurately—or even American politics faithfully. The film became the most notorious example of propaganda in the guise of entertainment ever produced by Hollywood. In 1947 Warner Brothers was so worried by the onset of the Cold War that it ordered all release prints destroyed. Yet during World War II the film had its share of passionate and highly placed defenders, if not for its accuracy then for its intentions.[2]

Although *Mission to Moscow* was the most blatant example, a pro-Russian picture became an indispensable proof of a studio's sincerity towards the war effort. Practically every studio had its Russian film; most of them were released in 1943—early enough to capitalize on American gratitude for Soviet military successes and not so late as to be clouded by the growing fears of what those triumphs would mean for the postwar era. MGM offered a musical salute with *Song of Russia;* United Artists' *Three Russian Girls* provided gender balance for Columbia's *Boy from Stalingrad.* RKO completed a somewhat ambiguous *Days of Glory* in 1944, and Columbia weighed in with the last word, *Counter-Attack,* in 1945. However, *Mission to Moscow* and Samuel Goldwyn's *North Star* were the two films which, whatever their artistic shortcomings, marked the apogee of pro-Soviet sentiment in American media.

The appearance of movies favorable to the Soviet Union was the most striking example of the plasticity of reality under wartime demands. Hollywood paid little attention to the Soviets before World War II, and when it did the Russians fared badly. In part this reflected popular perceptions of Russia. The Bolshevik revolution of 1917 froze American opinion in an anti-communist stance, and Washington did not establish diplomatic relations with the Soviet regime until 1933. Public attitudes warmed somewhat in the early 1930s, particularly in intellectual circles, when the Soviet five-year plans seemed to be working better than Western capitalism. There was a nest of communists and fellow travelers in the film colony in the 1930s. Because of the structure of the industry, however, they had virtually no chance to inject their politics into their products. Thus a major current of artistic and intellectual opinion in the 1930s was not documented in American motion pictures. Hollywood capitalists, who were busy fighting labor unions in the 1930s and cranking out scurrilous pseudo-documentaries to defeat Upton Sinclair's bid to become Socialist governor of California in 1934, remained unsympathetic to the Soviet experiment.[3]

Moreover, even in those few instances when studios wanted to depict Russia more favorably, they faced determined opposition after mid-1934 from Joseph Breen. In 1934 the prominent director Lewis Milestone wanted to make *Red Square,* a sympathetic treatment of Soviet life, but he was warned off in no uncertain terms by Breen. (Milestone finally got his chance to do a Russian picture in World War II.) An economic factor reinforced the Soviet blackout in Hollywood: there was no market for U.S. films in Russia. Concern for its box office in Hitler's Germany and Mussolini's Italy during the 1930s had made the studios wary of offending those governments, but Stalin's Soviet Union enjoyed no economic clout. Any possibility of a tolerant treatment of the U.S.S.R. was squelched by the stunning Moscow purge trials and executions of the late 1930s and then the devastating Nazi-Soviet nonaggression pact of 1939, which left all but the most doctrinaire communists reeling.[4]

The best known prewar film dealing with Russia was Ernst Lubitsch's sleek comedy *Ninotchka* (MGM, 1939), famous as the picture in which Garbo laughs. The film contrasts glamorous Paris with the drab, oppressive Soviet Union. Garbo plays Ninotchka, a humorless, hard-bitten Communist official who had killed a Polish lancer when she was sixteen. The original script, by the great team of Ben Hecht and Charles MacArthur, limned a Ninotchka reared in Soviet society, who held the standards of bourgeois society in contempt. She looked upon love as merely a "biologic urge." Although Joseph Breen shared the script's loathing for Soviet life, he refused to permit such a treatment of sex, even if it reinforced the picture of demonic communism. A bitter controversy ensued, but finally the studio and PCA reached agreement in a screenplay by crackerjack writers Charles Brackett, Billy Wilder, and Walter Reisch. Ninotchka still thumbs her nose at bourgeois conventions but love is not profaned.[5]

She comes to the French capital to check up on three male Soviet bureaucrats who are supposed to be conducting negotiations but are steadily succumbing to the luxury of capitalist, decadent Paris. She scorns Paris fashions for a trip to the waterworks. But then she meets Count Leon, an aristocratic White Russian emigre, played by Melvyn Douglas, and, after the requisite protests, falls in love. The allure of Paris, the high-living center of the capitalist West, proves to be too much. Ninotchka dances, drinks her first champagne, revels in the use of lipstick, excitedly models a floppy hat, and falls in love with Count Leon, who crowns her with the grand duchess's tiara. And she laughs. Not Marxist pieties but the flowering of human instincts amid capitalist luxuries make her happy.

Alas, she is recalled to squalid Moscow. Leon's love letters are censored. But socialist economics can thwart true love only temporarily. Ninotchka is dispatched to Constantinople, again to whip the three bungling bureaucrats into shape. She discovers, however, that they have defected and opened a restaurant. There Leon steps from behind a pillar. Ninotchka melts in his arms, and she too defects. In typical fashion Hollywood suggests that the erstwhile party dominatrix has found what every woman wants—a man of her own and a life of luxury. The picture slyly suggests that the Soviet system is not only dull and oppressive but against nature.

America's attitude toward the Soviet Union began to undergo a change on June 22, 1941. On that day—one of the most momentous in modern history—Hitler unleashed his panzer divisions against Stalin, still his partner. The Red Army reeled in the face of the Blitzkrieg. By late autumn the German legions were pounding on the gates of Leningrad and Stalingrad and were training their binoculars on the glittering spires of the Kremlin itself. The Third Reich straddled Europe from the English Channel to the Ukraine and unfurled the swastika across North Africa. Germany seemed on the verge of a decisive victory over Russia, which would leave Hitler free to turn full force against Great Britain.

Now Americans wanted to know more about this strange, distant country which had become, willy nilly, an ally in the fight against fascism. Winston Churchill, the Tory enemy of communism, set the tone for much public thinking in Britain and America. "The Russian danger is . . . our danger and the danger of the United States," he said, "just as the cause of any Russian fighting for his hearth and home is the cause of free men and free people in every quarter of the globe." By an eighteen-to-one margin Americans told George Gallup's pollsters that they wanted Russia to defeat Germany. That December, while the battle for Moscow was raging, Pearl Harbor formally put Americans in the same antifascist boat with the British and the Russians. Yet many former isolationists, economic conservatives, and Roman Catholics remained deeply suspicious of the Soviet Union. The Russians, to be sure, would never become allies in quite the same way as the British or, remarkably enough, the Chinese, but millions of Americans were now ready to listen to a new interpretation of the U.S.S.R.[6]

Joseph E. Davies, easily the most sympathetic ambassador the United States has sent to Moscow, provided that interpretation with his hugely successful *Mission to Moscow* bestseller in late 1941. A native of Wisconsin, Davies had been a leading corporate lawyer, and had also played an active role in Democratic Party politics. Woodrow Wilson had named him commissioner of corporations. Aggressive, able, and ambitious, Davies made the most of his years in Washington. He became friends with another upward bound Wilson political appointee, Franklin D. Roosevelt, then assistant secretary of the navy. And he married Marjorie Post Hutton, heiress to the multi-million dollar Postum fortune.[7]

Davies was only the second U.S. ambassador to the Soviet Union. When the United States opened diplomatic relations with the Soviet Union in 1933, Roosevelt had tapped another friend from Wilsonian days, William Bullitt, to serve as ambassador. Bullitt had seemed like an ideal choice. He had been sympathetic to the Bolshevik revolution, advocated establishing relations with the Lenin government from the start, and married Louise Bryant, lover of the radical journalist John Reed, upon the latter's death. (Reed was the author of the classic *Ten Days That Shook the World*.) But Bullitt's marriage soured (it ended in divorce), and so did his opinion of Stalin's Soviet Union.[8]

Eager to improve relations in 1936 after the Bullitt debacle, FDR turned again to Wilsonian Washington. He called Davies away from Mrs. Davies' summer retreat in the Adirondacks and asked the flabbergasted capitalist solicitor to represent the United States in Moscow. Though innocent of diplomatic experience, Davies could not turn down an insistent president and personal friend. The embassy staff found Davies a trial, as foreign service professionals often regard political appointees, and they considered him naive about Stalinist realities. For his part the envoy regarded the staff as too suspicious and politically conservative. He made every effort to improve U.S.–Soviet relations, whatever the abuses of Stalin's regime. The ambassador left Moscow for the easier climate of Brussels in June 1938 and returned to Washington as a special assistant to the secretary of state in January 1940.[9]

The Nazi invasion of Russia in June 1941 restored Davies to the limelight. He quickly began compiling his book. Believing the effort would quell suspicion of Stalin and help develop interventionist sentiment, Roosevelt encouraged the idea, and Under Secretary of State Sumner Welles allowed the use of confidential State Department documents. The manuscript was largely the product of Davies' "ghosts," Spencer Williams and Stanley Richardson, who had been journalists in Moscow in the 1930s. Davies' ghosted prose was not memorable; America's leading literary critic, Edmund Wilson, compared the style to that of Warren Harding. But no matter. *Mission to Moscow* was the right book at the right time. It was published on December 29, three weeks after Pearl Harbor. To Americans still trying to make sense of the dramatic and perplexing events which, in less than six months, had transformed America and Russia from bitter enemies to comrades in arms, Davies' inside story had the ring of truth. His first-hand account, buttressed by hitherto inaccessible documents, seemed to make sense of these topsy-turvy developments. The book sold 700,000 copies, was translated into thirteen languages, appeared in the then novel paperback format selling for two-bits, and was treated by the *New York Times* as a major news event in its own right when the paper excerpted it. President Roosevelt inscribed his copy: "This book will last."[10]

But to gain the maximum impact the book had to be made into a movie. Stories varied about who approached Warners to make the picture. Davies said that, having received overtures from various studios, he contacted Harry Warner—with FDR's blessing. The Warners said that Roosevelt, at a White House dinner, had appealed to them directly. Regardless of who initially involved the studio, the film enjoyed unusual White House backing. Davies leaped at the chance. Everyone wants to be in pictures—not least a wealthy former ambassador who loved the limelight. Warner Brothers' sterling political credentials made it the obvious choice for FDR and Davies. On July 3, 1942, they bought Davies' movie rights for $25,000, a decent but not princely sum. Warners generously granted Davies script control, one of the most coveted chits in Hollywood. The studio promised to get his approval of "the basic story." Davies would use that pledge, plus his connection with FDR, to exert a good deal of influence over the final product.[11]

The principals began work on *Mission to Moscow* with enthusiasm. Ringmaster was a new producer, Robert Buckner, a one-time correspondent for a British newspaper, who had reported briefly from Moscow and Ethiopia. He earned his spurs at Warners by writing several screenplays, including those for *Knute Rockne—All American*, which featured Ronald Reagan in one of his most famous roles, and the James Cagney vehicle *Yankee Doodle Dandy*. A Southern conservative, Buckner later described *Mission to Moscow* as "an expedient lie for political purposes" and claimed to have objected frequently, but without avail, during the filming. At first he was charmed by Davies—"a great fellow and very helpful," he said—but he soon found the ex-envoy mainly meddlesome. The director was Hungarian-born Michael Curtiz, who had collaborated with Buckner on *Yankee Doodle Dandy* and had just finished the immortal *Casablanca*. Curtiz, who had directed more than 100 Hollywood films (among them a spate of Errol Flynn thrillers) in his long career, could be a virtual dictator on the set. Yet he seems to have shown little interest in the political shoals that lay all about him.[12]

The venture got off on the wrong foot. Davies' first choice

for a writer was Robert Sherwood. A three-time winner of the Pulitzer Prize for drama, Sherwood had left the theater to serve as a Roosevelt speechwriter in 1940. The playwright also knew the ropes in Hollywood, where he had done the screenplays for *Idiot's Delight, Abe Lincoln in Illinois,* and *Rebecca.* Combining political awareness and cinematic savvy, Sherwood would have been ideal. But in 1942 he could not leave his post as associate director of OWI. Instead Davies called on Erskine Caldwell, who was well known for social protest books such as *Tobacco Road* and *You Have Seen Their Faces,* and who had reported on the Russian front. But Caldwell had no experience as a screenwriter. Everyone despaired of his treatment and script for the first third of the picture. He was "well paid and excused."[13]

In desperation Warners turned to one of the best writers in its stable: Howard Koch. In 1938, as a writer for radio, he had scripted the vivid "The War of the Worlds" for Orson Welles' Mercury Theater. He was, however, exhausted from his work on *Casablanca,* and wanted to go East to visit his ailing father. But in a highly unusual audience with both Warners, the writer yielded to their patriotic importuning. Though concerned about social problems, Koch knew little about the Soviet Union, and he had not read *Mission to Moscow.* That was just as well. Davies was determined to provide the interpretation—and his ideas of drama as well. In early September Buckner and Koch spent two days in conference with the former ambassador at his camp in the Adirondacks—"an island kingdom, self-sufficient like a fief of feudal days," said the screenwriter. Two weeks later the ambassador fired off a twenty-four page single-spaced memo full of suggestions, objections, and changes. Two major issues concerned the guilt or innocence of the defendants in the purge trials, and the Soviet invasion of Finland in 1939. The producer recalled that Davies insisted on the guilt of the accused, and also denied that the U.S.S.R. had invaded Finland. Whether Davies made such demands is not clear, but he concurred with the results.[14]

Formal involvement by the Soviet government was slight. Maxim Litvinov, the Russian ambassador to the United States, wanted the film to succeed. He asked Nicholas Napoli, head of the Soviet Artkino, to provide assistance with stock shots and the like; Napoli obliged. Litvinov and his English wife, Ivy Low, spent a week vacationing at the Davies' retreat before production began. The dinner table talk must have been fascinating as the Davieses and the Litvinovs looked forward to their portrayal in a major American motion picture; unfortunately no record was kept. Perhaps because of Davies' involvement, the Soviet embassy apparently did not read the script, as it did with some other wartime pictures about Russia. When controversy erupted over the picture, Soviet agents could not be blamed. *Mission to Moscow* was an American show.[15]

Davies kept Roosevelt abreast of *Mission's* progress in two meetings at the White House in October and November, and he cleared the FDR voice simulation with the president, whose unusually high degree of interest in the picture continued.[16]

The ambassador's extraordinary personal role complicated OWI's involvement. OWI readers liked the script; Koch's dramatization sounded many of the propagandists' notes. The agency's chief concern was to build trust in the Russians. When OWI's Hollywood liaision office found polls indicating a trend to believe that the Russians were indeed trustworthy—a trend that gained momentum with each Red Army victory—it passed the information on to the studio. Citizens were asked: "After the war is over, do you think Russia (England, China) can be depended upon to cooperate with us?" The percentage answering yes grew from 38 percent in February 1942 to 51 percent in August. That was gratifying to OWI. In August twenty-four percent said no, and 25 percent claimed to have no opinion. These percentages stayed roughly constant until the end of the war in Europe. But the other half of the ledger worried OWI analysts, especially when the response about Russia was contrasted with the 72 percent positive that England enjoyed and the whopping 86 percent that China boasted. (Eighty percent of those polled thought we should continue to cooperate with Moscow after the war and 78 percent thought we would, with only 7 percent saying we wouldn't.) For OWI the important point was to emphasize that the Soviet Union would fulfil its treaty obligations.[17]

The issue of trust bore directly on the pivotal decision of how to depict the purges. For dramatic effectiveness Koch, following Caldwell, decided to telescope the multiple trials into one. However defensible as an artistic strategem, the decision also had political overtones. It tended to heighten the conspiratorial aspect and thus added credibility to Stalin's charges. The more basic issue was what lay behind the trials. Stalin's prosecutor charged that the defendants were traitors who had been engaged in a massive conspiracy to sell out the Soviet Union to Nazi Germany. Despite confessions from the accused, few foreign observers believed these allegations. Davies' 1938 dispatches contended that some of the defendants had conspired to overthrow Stalin—in a "dramatic struggle for power" between Stalin and Trotsky, he said. That was a controversial judgment in itself, but still a far cry from the traitor thesis. By 1941, however, Davies had come to accept the whole package. In his book he said he now understood why there were no fifth columnists in the Soviet Union: they had been purged. The film turned on this very point.[18]

OWI's Poynter had reservations about this treatment and tried to introduce a more subtle approach. In early December he held a long conference with Buckner and then sent him a memo. He thought the picture tried to show that Stalin was for collective security and that the "Russians are an honest people trying to do an honest job with about the same total objective as the people of the United States." But the script's trial sequence trivialized that approach by making Trotsky "a mere quisling," intent simply on betraying Russia to Hitler. The OWI representative suggested, instead, that the Trotsky-Stalin split was a product of their differences over fomenting communist revolutions internationally. Believing the Soviet Union would continue to face implacable hostility from a capitalist world, Trotsky wanted world revolution. Stalin, however, wanted to focus on making communism work in the Soviet Union. By stimulating fear of revolution, the communist internationals gave Hitler and other dictators a pretext to sell themselves as saviors from communism. "Perhaps Stalin saw this," Poynter continued, and realized that he could not develop good relations with the U.S. and Britain until he abandoned "international meddling." "Perhaps he saw that the best possible Russian propaganda abroad was a healthy, progressive Soviet."[19]

Poynter's view had its problems. He took a rather benign attitude towards Stalin's excesses and went to some lengths to play down the Soviet Union's international propagandizing. But he at least gave more historical depth to the trials, which in the Davies–Warners version had the flavor of a rather crude spy story, and he helped make sense of the Popular Front era. But OWI's interpretation was too complex for Davies and Warner Brothers; the ambassador's own simple framework was politically and cinematically convenient.

As important to OWI as the interpretation of Russia was the film's treatment of international relations leading to the war. Although *Mission to Moscow* is remembered chiefly for its view of the Soviets, to World War II audiences its laceration of appeasement and isolationism was equally notable. Poynter and his staff found Davies, Buckner, and other principals receptive as they pressed for a heavy attack on the isolationists at several meetings while the shooting progressed and again when they viewed the incomplete rushes in January 1943. Two of OWI's favorite themes emerged strongly: The folly of the isolationists, who are made to seem a small, diabolical band thwarting the people's will, and Roosevelt as father-protector, apostolic successor to Woodrow Wilson, carrying the torch of collective security.[20]

Davies appears at the beginning of the film as a sort of American Everyman, identifying himself with the common person and the democratic tradition in which each person makes up his own mind. "If I were down there in the audience with you," he continued, "I'd want to know some things about this guy to assess his judgment and biases." Davies invokes the Horatio Alger theme. He is the archetypical American who's made it, loves his country, remembers where he came from, and (most importantly) can be trusted not to be hoodwinked by the communists. He invokes his "sainted mother," who was an ordained minister; his own religious convictions are "basic"—no off-beat creeds or suspicious practices for him. He lauds our free institutions, free enterprise, and competitive society. No disposition toward funny collectivist notions or state-run economies lurk in Davies' mind, "But while in Russia I came to have a very high respect for the integrity and the honesty of the Soviet leaders."[21]

The camera mats down to the foreword of Davies' book shown in bold, clear handwriting. In a close shot the ambassador's impersonator, Walter Huston, speaks directly to the audience and drops the mask of impartial observer. No national leaders have been "so misrepresented and misunderstood" as those of the Soviet Union between the wars, he says. The sequence leading to war begins in June 1936 . . . and as we see a series of stock shots of the League of Nations Palace in Geneva, Huston introduces Haile Selassie, Emperor of Ethiopia. Dressed in simple white tropical tunic and black cape, Selassie, played with dignity by black actor Leigh Whipper, recounts the Italian aggression against his helpless and unaided country. He warns that only collective security can halt fascist aggression.

The first delegate to seek recognition when Selassie finishes is Litvinov. Over a growing din of protest among the Axis delegates and reporters, he pleads: "There is no security for *any* of us unless there is security for *all*. That was the faith and lifelong work of the great man who created this assembly . . . *The League must live! It must be strong!*" As Litvinov speaks the camera follows delegates who are departing in protest. They walk past a statue of Woodrow Wilson, on which the camera focuses as Huston's voice-over continues: "The voice of the League founder was still, and the voice of his followers went unheeded. Soon a disillusioned world began to listen to another voice." Dissolve to Hitler in pantomime making an impassioned speech, followed by graphic newsreel footage of the Ethiopian invasion, Spanish Civil War, and Japanese invasion of China, building to a crescendo of marching, bombing, and strafing.

In the first few minutes the film traced the origins of World War II as a failure of appeasement and isolationism. The picture linked the Soviet Union's support of collective security with the idealistic vision of Woodrow Wilson. By implication Davies stands for Wilsonianism. Haile Selassie, although known to later generations as a corrupt and backward ruler, was a resonant symbol for wartime Americans. From the film one would never know that the United States was not a member of the League, that Washington did nothing to help Ethiopia, or that FDR accepted without protest the Neutrality Acts which were the cornerstone of isolationism.

Mission to Moscow sculpts Roosevelt, however, as an omniscient internationalist. Against a stock shot of the White House Davies' voice-over continues: "There was one man who foresaw what they meant—the president of the United States . . . He had called me to the White House just as I was about to leave on a vacation." They talked over old times. As they gaze reverently at an autographed picture of Woodrow Wilson, Roosevelt says: "The man who gave us our start, Joe. One of these days the world will catch up with him." Enough of reminiscence. FDR tells Davies he wants him to become ambassador to the Soviet Union. "But Frank, I'm not a diplomat," he protests, dumbfounded. (In real life Davies may have been taken aback at the destination, but not at being offered a major ambassadorial post, which, it was said, he had been promised in return for the substantial help he and his wife gave FDR's re-election campaign.) Roosevelt explains that he doesn't want a diplomat but "a sound American businessman who will get me the hard-boiled facts." It was no time for obsolete diplomatic niceties but for hard-headed American can-do. I get plenty of expert opinions, the president continues. Your job is to get me the right answers. This isn't a job. "This is a mission." Davies looks tensely at Roosevelt. He accepts.

The real-life mission left for the Soviet Union in January 1937 with the Davies family sailing for Bremen on the *Europa*, taking with them 25 refrigerators full of frozen food, including 2,000 pints of frozen cream. Stories differed on whether the family feared they would not find decent food or whether Davies' bad stomach required such precautions. The script's oblique reference to the giant stash riled the Davieses. It was cut out with the cryptic note from one studio official that the "milk had been dropped overboard." Warners knew better than to show the family yacht, *Sea Cloud*, a massive steam-and-square-rigged vessel which later, said *Time*, "bugged the eyes of Leningrad."[22]

The ambassador and his family had actually stayed in Germany for less than a week, but the script extended their stay, giving the film makers ample opportunity to hint of things to come. Even stereotypical German efficiency acquires sinister overtones, as every aspect of daily life is regimented to advance Hitler's war aims. Russia is a happy contrast. The Davies family is excited when it arrives at the remote border town. Simplicity, informality, and naturalness etch a sharp contrast with the rigid, militaristic society the Davies family had just left. An open, handsome army major welcomes them to the Soviet Union and offers them refreshments. Having breakfasted on ersatz eggs in Germany, the travelers fall upon an appetizing assortment of tea, cakes, and sandwiches. Good food, like straight talk, is an index of political rectitude. "Mmmm——," says Davies, savoring a pastry. "You know, I think I'm going to like this country." It is love at first bite.

Davies takes Soviet eavesdropping in stride. He calms an alarmed embassy staff member who wants to rip open the walls and ceilings to detect possible bugs. Maybe the Soviets have reason to be suspicious, Davies says; the Italian embassy was a nest of foreign agents. Besides, he doesn't say anything outside the Kremlin "that I wouldn't say to Stalin's face," Davies avers. And if there are microphones—well, "*let* 'em hear. We'll be friends that much faster. . . . Anyway, it's much too expensive" to rip up the walls. (To plain speaking, Davies adds parsimony.) The family is a bit uneasy over being followed everywhere by GPU agents. Are they protecting us or watching us, they wonder? "Probably a little bit of both," says Davies with a smile. The dreaded surveillance apparatus had to be acknowledged in some way, but this light touch reduced it to little more than a harmless idiosyncrasy. The film does not turn the Soviet Union into a Western-style democracy, but in keeping with the wartime propaganda approach to America's allies, it despicts happy citizens and a benign government to suggest the people really support the state.

Hollywood also lightens the impression of a dull, oppressive Russia by suggesting the emergence of a consumer society with widely available luxury goods—much like the film colony's image of America. Several scenes were created to satisfy Mrs. Davies' desire for a larger role for her character. She visits a cosmetics factory, run by Mme. Molotov, commissar of the cosmetics industry. A display worthy of Fifth Avenue contains an assortment of creams, powders, perfumes, and lipstick. Mrs. Davies is delighted and surprised. I studied the cosmetics industry in Paris, Mrs. Molotov informs her. "But I didn't realize that luxury trades were encouraged in the Soviet Union," says her American guest. Mme. Molotov smiles: "We discovered feminine beauty was not a luxury." Mrs. Davies laughs: "I guess women are no different the world over. Primarily, they want to please their men." The women discover they have much in common. Mme. Molotov says she prefers running an industry to merely social duties. Mrs. Davies reciprocates with the news that she had run her father's plant and now helps her husband in his work. They laugh. "Here we had the impression American women were ornamental and not useful, and you thought that our women were useful and not ornamental," says Mme. Molotov. This would have been news to Ninotchka.

These light-hearted moments fade quickly. The somber side of the mission comes into focus at the Americans' first diplomatic ball, a glittering affair in an ornate tsarist palace, as Litvinov, who has just been telling Davies that German agents are working to create havoc within Russia, is interrupted by an aide. An explosion has occurred at a major defense plant, leaving several hundred workers dead. It looks like sabotage—the fifth such incident in a few weeks. Several scenes follow showing the arrests of leading figures: Bukharin and Krestinsky, both former members of the Politburo; Yagoda, former head of the secret police; and Marshal Tukhachevsky, deputy people's commissar of defense. (In a remarkable example of cinematic liberty the marshal disappears from a box where he is watching the ballet with the Davies family.) The envoy says he'll keep an open mind and prepares us for the guilty verdicts by telling newspapermen: "Maybe when the truth comes out, you'll find it stranger than fiction."

Full filmic resources are used to suggest visually the guilt of the accused. They are seated together in a cramped box in the courtroom. The lighting and camera angles favor Vyshinsky, the prosecutor, and Davies, who sits taking notes. Vyshinsky extracts astounding confessions from the defendants. They admit that, led by Trotsky, they had conspired with Germany and Japan to bring about the defeat of the Soviet Union so that their own group would come to power. Germany was to receive part of the Ukraine; Japan was to get the Soviet Union's maritime province and oil in the event of a war with the United States.

Bukharin's confession is the emotional climax of the trial. The other prisoners are visibly affected by his statement, which concludes: "My hope is that this trial may be the last severe lesson in proving to the world the growing menace of Fascist aggression and the awareness and united strength of Russia. . . . What matters is not the personal feelings of a repentant enemy, but the welfare and progress of our country." The court orders the prisoners to be shot and their personal property confiscated. The other diplomats turn to Davies for his verdict: "Based on twenty years' trial practice, I'd be inclined to believe these confessions."[23]

There it was. Now *Mission to Moscow* had bought the party line that Trotsky and the Old Bolsheviks had engaged in a massive traitorous conspiracy with the Allies' enemies. This went far beyond Ambassador Davies' contemporary dispatches of 1937–38, in which he placed the trials and confessions in the context of a power struggle between rival Kremlin factions. The film reflected instead his hindsight of 1941, based on circumstantial evidence. By implication the picture accepted some measure of Stalin's terror as necessary. More than anything else, it was the picture's interpretation of the trials that gave it enduring notoriety. It was one thing to view Russia through rose-colored glasses. Most people could accept that as a contribution to wartime unity. But to translate the purges into a cornerstone of the Allied war effort—that was too much.

Nor did the travesty end here. Davies decides to awaken the American government to the world peril. Dissolve to a close shot of the ambassador dictating a cable to Secretary of State Cordell Hull. "There is no longer any question in my mind that these defendants ... were guilty of a conspiracy with the German and Japanese high commands to pave the way for an attack upon the Soviet state," Davies says. Thus the purges were an essential move to protect the country. The army is "unquestionably loyal"—indeed, strengthened by the purge of traitors. Davies added that Litvinov told him the Soviet Union was prepared to cooperate with Britain, France, and the U.S. in a strong stand against Germany's anticipated moves in Austria and Czechoslovakia. A troubled but now enlightened Secretary Hull looks up from the telegram and telephones the president.

Wipe to Roosevelt giving his famous "quarantine" speech. "When an epidemic of physical disease starts to spread, the community approves and joins in a quarantine of patients in order to protect the health of the community against the spread of the disease," he intones. "War is a contagion. . . ." As he speaks we see several reaction shots. The common people listen intently and approvingly—a group gathered around a taxicab listening to the car radio; a farmer, his wife, and hired hand on the porch of a farm home; workers in front of a small radio at a factory workbench. Cut to a wealthy club where well-fed members listen with half an ear to a huge radio. One member gestures contemptuously as if to say, "Some more New Deal nonsense." Another member nods and turns back to his newspaper. Roosevelt concludes: "America hates war. America hopes for peace. Therefore, America actively engages in the search for peace."

This sequence, so historically flawed, compounded the travesty. Davies not only accepted the confessions but went on to parrot the conspiracy thesis to Washington. Although the Red Army performed heroically, most historians believe the purges drastically weakened it. By its juxtaposition of Davies' dispatch with the quarantine speech, the film tried to suggest that he had inspired Roosevelt's notable address—a point for which there is little evidence. And the film makers overlooked the minor chronological problem that the trials of Bukharin, Krestinsky, and Yagoda took place in March 1938, some months *after* FDR's speech. Perhaps no other sequence in this propaganda picture swerved so far from the truth, inventing words that were not spoken, and restringing chronology.

Nor were the visual innuendoes of American politics accurate. The club members fit OWI's model of the domestic fascist—wealthy, anti-New Deal, isolationist. The film suggests that "the people" were ready to follow their leader, had their authentic voice not been subverted. In fact, however, isolationist sentiment could be found in all sectors of the public. Disappointed in the tepid public response, Roosevelt avoided risking his popularity with any more quarantine speeches.

As Davies' mission draws to a close, he and Litvinov exchange expressions of mutual esteem at a farewell stag dinner. Then, while the ambassador pays his final calls on Kalinin and Molotov, a door opens and Stalin appears. Everyone present is surprised, for it was highly unusual for Stalin to meet with foreign diplomats. Davies toasts Stalin: "I believe history will record you as a great builder for the benefit of common men." The Soviet dictator modestly gives the credit to Lenin, who conceived the five-year plans, and to the people, who carried them out.

He and Davies retire to a large, austere conference room. In one of the most memorable scenes from the movie, the two men sit on opposite sides of a long conference table, with a giant map of the USSR behind Stalin. The outlook for peace is very bad, they agree. Hitler has just invaded Austria, and they anticipate that the West will surrender Czechoslovakia to him without a struggle. Stalin pins the blame on "reactionary elements in England, represented by the Chamberlain government." They intend to build up Germany, push it into war with the Soviet Union, and then, when the combatants have exhausted themselves, step in and make peace to advance their own interests. Would Russia fight Germany over Czechoslovakia if France and England support Prague? asks Davies. We have a treaty with France to do so, Stalin replies, and we have "never repudiated a treaty obligation." The ambassador concurs: "Your past record speaks well for the future." But, Stalin adds portentuously, we will not be the cat's paws of others. "Either we must be able to rely on our mutual guarantees with the other democracies or ... well, we may be forced to protect ourselves in another way." The Russian urges Davies to awaken America and Britain to the peril. Davies agrees.

The rest of the movie is a sustained attack on British appeasement and American isolationism, mixed with a defense of the Soviet policy of 1939–41. Stock shots show the German army goosestepping, the Munich conference, and Chamberlain returning to the London airport waving his worthless piece of paper from Hitler and announcing "peace in our time." Then follow shots of the German takeover of Czechoslovakia. Davies' efforts to awaken the British government to the folly of appeasement get nowhere. Finally he goes to the country home of Winston Churchill, played by a look-alike Dudley Field Malone, a well known lawyer. Davies impresses upon the English leader that, though the Soviets know they will have to fight Germany eventually, "a temporary nonaggression pact would give them more time to prepare." Churchill concurs. But what about America and the Neutrality Acts? he counters. The ambassador assures him he will tell Americans the same thing. Davies says: "Unless we stand together against Hitler, we're very apt to have to fight him alone."

Davies' journey to the English countryside served to complete the triumvirate of Allied leaders. According to the movie, Stalin, Roosevelt, and Churchill understood that war was coming. These father-protectors would have saved the world from war had they been able to act. Stalin was blocked by British and French appeasers, Roosevelt by isolationists; Churchill was out of the government. What's more "the people" would have understood. Though thwarted in the 1930s, these leaders now stand united as rescuers.

Back home Davies' attempt to arouse Congress meets with indifference. Hollywood clichés cast legislators as small-minded and complacent. One Congressman reads a book while Davies talks; another cleans his finger nails with a pocket knife. There is even an echo of Idaho Senator William Borah's famous miscalculation—that he had better information than the State Department and there would be no war in 1939.

That opinion had just been uttered when we dissolve to a dateline of September 1, 1939, interrupted by a roar of artillery as Germany moves against Poland. Stock shot of the white cliffs of Dover, the wartime symbol of British invincibility. Then the Soviet Union is suggestively linked with the allies, even in 1939. The map shows the Nazis, but not the Soviets, gobbling up other countries. Davies explains that the Russian leaders remained suspicious of Hitler and tried to buy time for further armament. They "asked Finland's permission to occupy strategic positions against Germany and offered twice the territory in exchange," he continues. "But Mannerheim, Hitler's friend, refused and the Red Army moved in by force."

This remarkable sequence adopted the Soviet line and simply turned history upside down. The Soviet invasion of Poland was ignored and its attack on Finland, which most people considered naked aggression, was justified as a step in Stalin's master plan to fight Hitler. These gross distortions had no basis in fact. Indeed, Stalin apparently was totally stunned by the Nazi invasion of the U.S.S.R. in 1941, which caught the Soviet military by surprise. But in the midst of the war propagandists found it necessary to keep this information from the public. Instead they wove the events of 1939–41 into the heroic tapestry of Allied resistance.

Having cleaned up the image of the Soviets, the film turns on the isolationists. The last few minutes of the picture—a dramatic, fast-moving sequence of cuts and dissolves with vivid scenes and fiery dialogue—contrast sharply with the preceding leaden pace. Although *Mission* is usually remembered chiefly for its distortions of Russian reality, the attack on the isolationists contains the most powerful footage. The isolationists appear ignorant, cowardly, and even pro-fascist. They taunt Davies on his speaking tour with their familiar arguments: "Russia's as good as licked!" Stalin might switch colors overnight and rejoin the fascists. If I had to choose between Hitler and Stalin, I'd choose Hitler. Germany and Japan are good customers—we can do business with them. Let Russia and Britain come to a negotiated peace with Hitler. It's not our fight. We're safe between our oceans. . . .

Patiently, urgently, sometimes emotionally, but always with authority, Davies refutes their points. For each fleeting point made by the isolationists he receives several sentences and favorable camera angles. "Russia is the world's last rampart against Fascist slavery," he says. The Russian people will hold; they will adopt a scorched earth policy and defeat the "Nazi hordes." Simulated snow flakes fall over the map, the German advance grinds to a halt, and the Soviet counteroffensive begins, proving Davies' point. In answer to the isolationists' cynical "no business of ours" formulation, Davies invokes the symbols of America, religion, and freedom. America cannot be "an island of Christian individualism in a sea of totalitarian dictatorship," he says. "You can't negotiate with evil."

A chorus sings softly in the background "you are your brother's keeper." As retreating German infantrymen are swallowed up in fog, Davies in a voice-over invokes "the heroes of all nations who have given their lives in this, the people's war." The fog gives way to a bleak, snow-swept Russian battlefield, where a soldier stands guard before endless rows of crosses. The Soviet scene dissolves to a British sentinel and to crosses in North Africa, then to a Chinese, and finally to an American against the sea and jungle of Guadalcanal. We pledge "to you, the unborn generations yet to come," says Davies, "to work for peace, and justice, and the dignity of man so that you can answer Cain's angry cry, "Am I my brother's keeper" with "yes, you are." Long shot of the sky swept clear of the clouds of war. The chorus swells: "You are, yes, you are, you are your brother's keeper, now and fore'er, you are—"[24]

This grossly overdone, sentimental ending leaves latter-day

audiences groaning or snickering, but its creators found it an impressive ending to a moving film. Jack Warner lapsed into paroxysms of self-congratulation unusual even in the debased genre of Hollywood press agentry. To FDR's aide Marvin Mc-Intyre, Warner declared the picture to be "a fabulous success because it tells much of the truth." *Mission* would always be remembered for pointing out "adroitly" what could have happened to the country had not FDR been president. Davies basked in the production, and his pride grew as time went by. In August 1945, as the clouds of the Cold War gathered, he congratulated Koch on "the extraordinary dramatic quality, the movement, the insight in interpretation." Watching the picture again in 1947, as the picture figured prominently in HUAC's Cold War inquest into Hollywood, he still stood by the film's dramatic qualities and political judgments.[25]

OWI reviewers were as enthusiastic about *Mission* as any wartime film, for both its political and dramatic qualities. The final feature review deserves extended quotation:

> MISSION TO MOSCOW is a magnificent contribution to the Government's War Information Program, as well as proof of the potency of the motion picture as a means of communicating historical and political material in a dramatic way.... The whole field of international relations, Axis intrigue and the shameful role of the appeasers of the Axis in the past decade is illuminated for us. The presentation of the Moscow trials is a high point in the picture and should do much to dispel the fears which many honest persons have felt with regard to our alliance with Russia.... MISSION TO MOSCOW pulls no punches; it answers the propaganda lies of the Axis and its sympathizers with the most powerful propaganda of all: the truth. The possibility for the friendly alliance of the Capitalist United States and the Socialist Russia is shown to be firmly rooted in the mutual desire for peace of two great countries. The condition for world peace is shown to be the international unity of all the freedom-loving peoples of the world, without exception.... It is to be hoped that MISSION TO MOSCOW will have immediate release and the widest possible distribution.[26]

Ulric Bell confided to Robert Sherwood that the film had its "shortcomings," probably meaning the purge trials. But those flaws paled by comparison with the picture's contribution. Said the former head of Fight for Freedom: "It is a socko job on the isolationists and appeasers—the boldest thing yet done by Hollywood." Nelson Poynter told Davies he was "delighted" with the film. He thought it would be powerful proof that the American government wanted to correct twenty-five years of adverse propaganda about the Soviet Union.[27]

For Poynter and Bell *Mission to Moscow* had significance beyond its own story—it gave OWI added leverage in its duel with the industry. Poynter noted: "It is significant that private companies, not just United States government films are being made to interpret Russia to the American people." Bell found the picture would be a great help in getting Hollywood to tackle important issues.[28]

Mission to Moscow underscored how wartime political considerations supplanted the usual application of the PCA code. Breen objected that some of the political judgments were questionable, particularly the criticisms Stalin leveled at Britain and France. Ostensibly PCA was still worried about offending foreign audiences, though Breen no doubt found the movie's politics personally distasteful. Buckner brushed Breen's criticisms aside. The producer pointed out that Davies approved the lines and intimated that the ambassador spoke for the State Department. Moreover, the studio had been "in close touch" with OWI, which also gave the script its blessing. "In the face of all this, it seems to me that we ... can do little but approve the material ... ," Breen said reluctantly. But the PCA chief, in close touch with those sectors of opinion that mistrusted the partnership with Russia, reminded Jack Warner that there was another school of thought on the Soviet Union. Breen warned that "considerable protest" would probably greet the picture.[29]

Indeed, a tide of protest erupted when *Mission to Moscow* opened. The picture had its defenders, though more for its good intentions than its entertainment qualities. Support and opposition came from predictable quarters. *The Daily Worker* lauded the picture. Feisty Harry Bridges, president of the International Longshoremen's Union, believed it took "plenty of real guts" to make such a picture. In time "the average person" would say: "'The Warner Brothers knew the score when many others were asleep.'" From the right William Randolph Hearst, himself no stranger to the uses of propaganda, telegraphed: "Your film, Mr. Warner, gives 'the other side of the case'—the communist side—quite completely." Eugene Lyons, the disillusioned Marxist who now edited *The American Mercury,* termed the picture "grotesque" and gave it a 4F for political intelligence. No one intended to interfere with Hollywood's freedom to put out whatever pictures they wanted to make, he told former president Hoover. "But it is a different matter when our government seems to put its stamp of approval on a piece of totalitarian propaganda." Hoover agreed. Yet the war scrambled political lineups. A resolution praising the studio's "integrity, courage, and patriotism" arrived from the War Advisory Council of the Los Angeles County Council of the American Legion.[30]

Film critics were divided over the picture. Predictably enthusiastic praise came from Jack McManus of the liberal *PM*. *Mission to Moscow* was "the most significant film to come out of Hollywood in 25 years," he averred. "It is the first clean break with Hollywood's persistent policy of silence or deceit about the Soviet Union." Some praised the semi-documentary techniques which, said Bosley Crowther of the *New York Times*, lent a "realistic impression of fact." Others, such as Kate Cameron of the *New York Daily News*, disliked the heavy reliance on dialogue. "Nothing happens in the film," she said, "nothing but talk." And Irving Hoffman of the *Hollywood Reporter* fed the industry's lust for self-congratulation: The motion picture industry "added many an inch to its stature this week."[31]

More thoughtful movie critics were appalled at the picture. "Now I'm ready to vote for the booby prize," said Manny Farber of *The New Republic*. "Not one character" emerged, he said. The film made up its own facts, and it credited Davies with predicting every world event of the period. As a movie it was "the dullest imaginable." Not even Russian singing and dancing came off with any verve. "This mishmash is directly and firmly in the tradition of Hollywood politics," Farber concluded. "A while ago it was Red-baiting, now it is Red-praising in the same sense—ignorantly. To a democratic intelligence it is repulsive and insulting."[32]

James Agee agreed the picture was "a mishmash . . . a great glad two-million-dollar bowl of canned borscht, eminently approvable by the Institute of Good Housekeeping." Agee was glad to see the "conservatives" pinned for their responsibility for the war and the Soviet Union praised for its desire to destroy fascism. "The rest is shameful rot," he said, pointing out that in the movie there was no difference between the U.S. and the Soviet Union, "except that in Russia everybody affects a Weber and Fields accent and women run locomotives and you get tailed by a pair of harmless comics who claim to be GPU men." But in a telling twist, Agee did not think the problem was simply Hollywood. *Mission to Moscow* "indulges the all but universal custom of using only so much of the truth as may be convenient." Those who use such techniques insult themselves and their audiences alike, and those who accept and excuse such tactics "insult and endanger themselves still again, from within." The immediate pragmatic effect might be irresistible. "But the deeper effect is shame, grief, anaesthesia, the ruin of faith and conscience and the roots of intelligence; and the real end, as should be reasonably clear by now, is disaster." Rather than being beguiled by the half-truths and falsifications of *Mission to Moscow*, OWI analysts should have pondered Agee's warning.[33]

The issues raised by Agee reflected widespread concern about the film in politically minded intellectual circles. Dwight MacDonald spearheaded a letter signed by luminaries (many of them with leftist leanings) such as Alfred Kazin, Edmund Wilson, Max Eastman, Horace Kallen, Sidney Hook, James T. Farrell, A. Philip Randolph, and Norman Thomas. They claimed the movie "falsifies history and glorifies dictatorship" and compared its glorification of "The Leader" to totalitarian propaganda techniques. The most powerful critique was penned by John Dewey, America's leading living philosopher, and Suzanne La Follette, cousin of former Senator Robert La Follette and a prominent magazine editor. They had headed an international commission inquiring into the purge trials in 1937–38; the commission had come to the widely-accepted conclusion that the charges and confessions were false. Dewey and La Follette condemned *Mission to Moscow* as "the first instance in our country of totalitarian propaganda for mass consumption." They pointed out the myriad inaccuracies and outright falsifications in the movie. They took pains to point out the inconsistencies between the film's outlook and Davies' own words of 1937–38. He had written that the terror was "horrifying," and every family feared a "nocturnal raid by the secret police." But the Soviet Union of the movies was "gay, even festive," they noted, and the citizenry displayed "a happy confidence" in the regime. They hoped American-Soviet cooperation would continue after the war, but only on a basis of "a genuine understanding of the differences in our political system," not on the "basis of Soviet propaganda."[34]

What troubled them even more was that such propaganda tactics contributed to a growing "moral callousness." The crisis in morals was, they argued, "the fundamental issue in the modern world." The film was not a patriotic service but instead an assault on "the very foundations of freedom. For truth and freedom are indivisible."[35] What better evidence of the insidious inroads of propaganda than Davies' falsification not only of external reality but of himself? And yet, as perhaps they were unwilling to recognize, a war for freedom created through its own momentum forces that undermined, distorted, and falsified the truth.

Less explicitly political, and hence less overtly controversial, was *The North Star,* a Samuel Goldwyn production of 1943 based on a script by Lillian Hellman. *North Star* traced its origin to early 1942 when Harry Hopkins, FDR's alter ego, approached Hellman about doing a documentary with on-the-scene photography. Excited by the idea, she began planning with two of Hollywood's top talents—director William Wyler and Gregg Toland. Wyler, winner of an Academy Award for his direction of *Mrs. Miniver,* built a reputation as one of the most innovative directors. Toland, who brilliantly photographed *Citizen Kane* (1941), was perhaps the industry's leading cinematographer. The Soviets, through none other than Foreign Minister Molotov, agreed to cooperate. The team of Hellman, Wyler, and Toland had immense promise. Various delays ensued, however. Then Wyler enlisted in the Army Air Force, where he made two important documentaries, *The Memphis Belle* and *Thunderbolt.* Hellman decided she didn't want to do a documentary with anyone else. Instead she and Goldwyn agreed on what she later described as a "simple, carefully researched, semi-documentary movie" that would be shot on his ten-acre backlot. Whether the research was careful would soon be disputed. But Hellman's script reflected her sound sense that simplicity and a documentary style would best capture in human terms the heroic resistance of ordinary Russians.[36]

But that would not have been Hollywood. The studios might

turn out an occasional film, in which simplicity of treatment complemented the subject matter. More often Hollywood found the lavish production number irresistible. Peasant dramas were especially vulnerable to the disjuncture between thematic material and the overdone productions they received. It was almost as if the studio chiefs, fearing the subject matter would not play, felt they had to compensate by heaping on more glamour. Besides, they had armies of technicians to keep busy to justify the overhead. Even a master such as Irving Thalberg could not resist the temptation in *The Good Earth.* Hellman insisted *North Star* "could have been a good picture instead of the big-time, sentimental, badly directed, badly acted mess it turned out to be." As if to prove it she took the unusual step of publishing the screenplay in 1943, complete with an introduction by literacy critic Louis Kronenberger attesting to its virtues.[37]

Goldwyn's "big-time treatment" weighted down the script with an over-abundance of talent. Edward Chodorov, who had collaborated on the script of *Dodsworth* in 1936, was brought in to doctor Hellman's screenplay. Lewis Milestone, a capable, Ukrainian-born director, got his chance to do a Russian picture—with the playwright's blessing, he claimed. Milestone found it hard to resist reaching for grandeur with his favorite technique, the tracking shot. Associate Producer William Cameron Menzies supplied some of the grandiloquent touches he had employed with more success as art director for *Gone with the Wind.* Perhaps the most problematic judgment was the decision to make the first part of the film into a musical. Despite the considerable talents of composer Aaron Copland and librettist Ira Gershwin, the musical numbers were alternately silly and wooden. Copland's score sounded like a slick version of *Appalachian Spring* with Russian flourishes. Gershwin's lyrics, such as "we're the younger generation and the future of the nation" and "the dreams we cherish/will never perish," seemed borrowed from a bad operetta.[38]

OWI reviewers praised Hellman's script as "a magnificent job of humanizing the plain people of Russia." The peasants sparkled with "wholesome values," a desire for peace, and pride in the nation's accomplishments since the revolution. In line with the prevailing propaganda posture, the readers suggested that the film make clear that Soviet leaders understood conflict with Germany was inevitable. OWI attributed this to the two systems' "utterly different" ideologies—another reflection of its view that only totalitarian systems were aggressive. The propaganda agency also urged the movie makers to show the desire of the two lead youngsters, Tanya and Damian, for the Soviet Union and the United States to work together for collective security. The Soviet embassy in Washington read the script and offered only minor suggestions. Neither OWI nor the embassy objected to the film's setting, a collective farm in the Ukraine. In the rush to salute the Russian allies, the film overlooked the fact that many Ukrainians, still restive because of the millions of deaths suffered during the forced collectivization of agriculture in the 1930s, at first welcomed the Germans as liberators. In other parts of the Soviet Union, however, the scorched earth resistance was certainly a fact.[39]

The North Star opens in a Ukrainian peasant village. Except for the icon in the dining room and the picturesque rooflines this could be Iowa or Oklahoma. (It is really a collective farm, but the sole explicit reference is easy to miss.) A group of kids who have just graduated from high school is about to set off on a hike to Kiev on holiday. The date is June 20, 1941, and the radio reports German troop movements along the border. The juxtaposition of the ebullient adolescents with the viewer's knowledge of the meaning of those military maneuvers creates an atmosphere of foreboding. Oddly enough, although the Soviet Union has been at war for nearly two years, all seems normal.

We are treated to a round of peasant songs and dances and introduced to two symbolic older figures. One is Karp, a pig farmer played by Walter Brennan, who dispenses unlettered but shrewd wisdom. The other is Dr. Kurin, played by Walter Huston. Kurin is the embodiment of medical humanism and scholarly rectitude. A "famous man of science" who studied at Leipzig, he achieves a Tolstoyan transformation by settling in this out-of-the-way village to serve the common people and to write.

The peasant celebration finally completed, the youthful hikers set out for Kiev, and Karp for market. Suddenly the sky darkens with war planes. Grinning broadly, a German aviator strafes Karp's truck. The noble peasant is killed but not before admonishing his sons to get the guns out of the truck and get them to "our men." Karp is buried beneath a wide sky, to surging music. The band of hikers takes cover in a ditch. They regroup and begin a rear-guard action against an advancing column. Damian is blinded, a girl is killed. Kolya, a fighter pilot played by Dana Andrews, carries out a suicide mission.

The village is bombed with heavy casualties. The villagers do not stop to mourn but organize spontaneously and take oaths as guerrilla fighters. As the German army moves toward the village, a woman marches resolutely from her house, lifts her kerosene lamp to the thatched roof, and sets it afire. The village is engulfed in flames. "Another burning village!" an officer exclaims. "A hard people to conquer."

The invaders' medical officer, the overbearing Dr. Col. von Harden, played by Erich von Stroheim in a recreation of his World War I roles of the evil German, establishes a field hospital in the village. The children are given a good supper at the hospital. In a gripping scene they are taken one by one and forced to give blood transfusions. One child dies—too much blood has been taken. Dr. Kurin can stand it no longer. He demands to know how a fellow doctor can do such things. Von Harden represents the elitist German who exudes contempt for the Nazis but nonetheless goes along with them. He shrugs: "I do not like much of what I've done for the past nine years." Kurin explodes: You pretend to be civilized, but "men like you . . . to me you are the real filth . . . men who do the work of fascists while they pretend they are better than the men for whom they work . . . men who do murder while they laugh at those who order them to do it." Kurin shoots von Harden's assistant and then shoots the "civilized" doctor colonel.

The villagers flee. As they look back from their wagons they see their beloved village consumed in a tower of flame. Marina, transformed from a tittering, incompetent girl into a defiant woman, holds the blinded Damian in her arms and affirms: "We are putting the old life behind us so that we can fight for a new one. Wars do not leave people the same. All people will learn that and come to see that wars do not have to be. They will make this the last one, a free world for all men. The earth belongs to us the people. If we fight for it. And we will fight for it."

OWI was delighted with *The North Star*'s "magnificent contribution" to American-Russian understanding. The confrontation between Kurin and von Harden showed "the appeaser, most dangerous kind of Fascist, recognized as such and made to pay the price." Especially compelling to the propaganda office, with its populist leanings, was the lesson of ordinary Russians who rise spontaneously to fight for their homeland and for world peace. The Soviet government is virtually absent from the movie. There are a few references to the district commissar and to the army off somewhere in the distance, but they have little bearing on "the people," who organize spontaneously. As in other resistance pictures, the Russian peasants, face to face with fascism, instinctively understand. This message fit Hollywood formulae neatly. In many westerns it is the people who organize to get rid of the bad elements; they often have to overcome the mayors or sheriffs, who like appeasers or isolationists, are ineffective or even in league with evil. As in *Mr. Smith Goes to Washington,* the average person will do right and has the capacity for heroism.[40]

The way reviewers assessed the picture said a good deal about not merely their political attitudes but their appreciation of the possibilities of popular cinema. William Randolph Hearst ordered a smear campaign against the film. His directive reached the *New York Daily Mirror* in the midst of a press run carrying critic Frank Quinn's praise of this "notable tribute to a notable ally." To comply with the directive from San Simeon, the editors stopped the presses and inserted Jack Lait's denunciation of the film as "pure bolshevist propaganda" by a screenwriter who was "a partisan pleader for Communist causes." For the embittered Hearst seemingly nothing positive could be said about the Soviet Union or its people, despite their undeniable contribution to victory.[41]

But other critics, including many who vigorously opposed the Popular Front, praised *The North Star.* Whereas *Mission to Moscow* reeked with politics, the Goldwyn film packaged its message in ostensibly human terms. The resolutely middle-brow *Life,* in photojournalism the counterpart of Hollywood, bought the romanticized treatment of the common people. Luce's editors hailed the film as "an eloquent tone poem" and even proclaimed it the picture of the year. The Goldwyn touch even won over Martin Quigley. In a column headlined "Valour—Without Politics," the *Motion Picture Herald* editor stressed the producer's skill in skirting political controversy. Quigley warned that the Soviet Union occupied an "anomalous, aloof and special position among the United Nations" and presented problems "not yet clarified." Goldwyn's success, the publisher claimed, lay in presenting "an objective, vibrantly human and immediate story of people"—without politics.[42]

Myriad objections could be raised to this formula. For one thing, despite Quigley's ostensible even-handedness, a story about ordinary Russians probably could not have been made between mid-1934 and mid-1941. Moreover, Goldwyn practically barred politics—a vital part of human experience—from the script. The bouquets from Quigley and *Life* suggested how successful Goldwyn had been in diluting a politically charged subject so that it proved acceptable to the widest possible audience.

This was exactly what troubled the perceptive James Agee. He duly noted the "all but unprecedented" effort to portray ordinary Russians. The trouble was the picture "drowned in ornament." Resources more appropriate to screen romances were employed "to make palatable what is by no remote stretch of the mind romantic." The product was "one long orgy of meeching, sugaring, propitiation." He found the characters "stock," their lines "tinny-literary," their appearance "scrubbed behind the ears and 'beautified,'" the action sequences "stale from overtraining," the camera work "glossy and overcomposed." The problem—a frequent lament of Agee's—was not simply the commercial nature of American film but the inability of the studios to respect their audience and, in turn, the viewers' complicity in Hollywood's condescension towards them. He contrasted *The North Star* with documentaries, especially British productions, that trusted the audience and gave it to them straight. Agee did not contend that every production had to be an art film; he enjoyed romantic commercial pictures as much as the next person. But *The North Star,* as he pointed out, reflected one of wartime Hollywood's chief shortcomings, which indeed it shared with OWI's movie analysts—the inability, with rare exceptions, to match tone to subject matter. It was a failure of taste; it was also a failure of political nerve.[43]

Russian leaders appear to have viewed *The North Star* with

hilarity mixed with a keen appreciation of its propaganda potential for the masses. When Lillian Hellman visited the U.S.S.R. on an official cultural mission in 1944—a tour probably made possible by her role in *The North Star*—she found that in the Soviet capital the film was viewed as "a great joke." She did not elaborate. It seems likely that Soviet officialdom and the intelligentsia found the Hollywood interpretation of the peasantry rather humorous and may have realized all too well the divergence between the movie's interpretation of Ukrainian resistance to the Nazis and the actual course of events there. "But I guess outside Moscow there were some simple peasant folk glad to find themselves so noble on the screen," Hellman concluded. Red officialdom may have snickered, but it nonetheless capitalized on the propaganda potential of *The North Star* and *Mission to Moscow*, both of them enjoying wide circulation in the war-ravaged country. The Goldwyn production played to 50,000 people in a single theater in Siberia in twenty days.[44]

The other films on Russia produced between 1942 and 1945 presented variations on the same themes—indigenous resistance, a modern, happy Russia, and fraternity between Americans and Russians. OWI had an ample role in several of them, and it generally approved of the results.

If one studio would try to turn the grimness of war into a musical it would be Metro. It offered *Song of Russia*, built around the romance of a fictional composer (played by Robert Taylor, for whom Lowell Mellett got a postponement in his navy service because of the picture's importance to the war effort) and a young pianist (Susan Peters). OWI applauded as the performers' touring offered a panorama of a modern Soviet Union, peopled by industrious folk who liked to relax after hours to Jerome Kern tunes in glittering nightclubs. Although the screenplay was written by two members of the Communist Party, Paul Jarrico and Richard Collins, the couple gets married in a church ceremony conducted by Orthodox priests. The performers decide that the cause of Allied understanding requires their musical talents in America, where they transfer their conjugal music-making after the Nazi invasion. *Song of Russia* turned "the neatest trick of the week," said *Newsweek*, "leaning over backward in Russia's favor without once swaying from right to left."

MGM managed to make its contribution to the Russian cycle with torrents of Tschaikovsky. If we look back to *Ninotchka*, Metro was now singing a different tune.[45]

An American-Russian romance also served as a symbol of international rapprochement in United Artists' *Three Russian Girls* (1943). Howard Koch, drawing presumably on his experience in *Mission to Moscow*, did the screenplay, assisted by Aben Kendel and Dan James. American aircraft engineer John Hill (Kent Smith) is injured when his test plane strays into a dogfight with the Luftwaffe. He falls in love with nurse Natasha. She 'knows duty takes precedence over love and volunteers for battlefield service, where she is badly injured. John too understands the priority of service over personal life and returns to the United States for military duty.[46]

OWI found the first script a valuable contribution to humanizing the Russians. Unfortunately the second version erred so much in Americanizing the characters that the propagandists feared it would offend foreign audiences. At the agency's urging producer Gregor Rabinovitch went back to the original screenplay. The film's ending still seemed to suggest, however, that American understanding of other peoples was limited to the idea that everbody else just wanted what America had. Visiting Natasha in the hospital on his way home, John rhapsodizes about pumpkin pie and Thanksgiving in Nebraska and assures her they will meet again . . . as all the people of the world gather around one great big table for the first Thanksgiving after victory. It is Henry Wallace's pint of milk a day with all the trimmings.[47]

In *Days of Glory* (RKO, 1944) love and resistance are joined. Demonstrating that tributes to the Russians could cut across political lines, *Days of Glory* was written by the conservative Casey Robinson. (His recent films had included *Kings Row, This is the Army*, and *Now, Voyager*.) Robinson's screenplay was a vehicle for his wife, the Russian ballerina Tamara Toumanova, and Gregory Peck, whom it launched toward stardom. A prima ballerina of the Moscow Ballet, Nina (Toumanova) gives up her art as her understanding of the war grows, and becomes a determined fighter in Vladimir's (Peck's) guerrilla force. Together they meet death.[48]

But the idealization of the resistance, like Americanization, could go too far. Columbia's first Russian contribution, *Boy from Stalingrad,* showed the flame of resistance alive among a band of adolescents, who practically on their own keep the Germans from closing the ring around Stalingrad. One minute these kids seemed to be playing cowboys and Indians, the next they were thwarting the Wehrmacht. This was too much even for OWI. The enemy was too powerful for child's play.[49]

The last pro-Russian film of the war, Columbia's *Counter-Attack,* had the misfortune to be released in spring 1945, just as the end of the war in Europe deflated its topical appeal. John Howard Lawson, soon to be a member of the Hollywood Ten, adapted the script from a Broadway play by Janet and Philip Stephenson. Lawson's major political alteration was to change the young woman, played by Marguerite Chapman, from a German nurse to a partisan; politics aside, the shift made better dramatic sense. The story focuses on Kulkov (Paul Muni) and his female sidekick who keep several Germans at bay for three days until they are rescued by the advancing army. Reflecting the movie's origin as a stage play, *Counter-Attack* is confined to a basement and is rather talky. Director Zoltan Korda (of *Sahara*) and cinematographer James Wong Howe, facing a challenge similar to Hitchcock's in the confined space of *Lifeboat,* achieved a kind of spare vitality. Critics divided over whether the result was absorbing or whether audiences would emulate Kulkov in trying to fight off yawns. OWI moviegoers found the picture slow by American standards but thought that might be an asset with overseas audiences.[50]

The propaganda agency found *Counter-Attack* useful to the information program, in particular the unusually realistic acting of the Russian and German parts. OWI worked closely with the receptive Lawson. He was attuned to key OWI objectives—the average Russian's understanding of Nazi ideology, his appreciation of America, the promise of a postwar world of freedom, and even the treatment of Nazi prisoners in accord with the Geneva convention. Lawson changed several points when OWI feared a shift in audience sympathy if the Russians appeared to be too willing to "sacrifice lives for objectives." Some of these points were lost as the release print downplayed ideology for action. Particularly striking was the lessening of emphasis on Soviet-American understanding. This outcome suggests that someone in the studio hierarchy astutely sensed the growing apprehension about the Russians late in the war, or perhaps blue-penciled these sentiments because of his own views. In any case even so committed a communist writer as Lawson was powerless to prevail.[51]

Nonetheless a powerful visual salute remained at the film's conclusion, thanks to Howe's brillance. Russian tanks thunder across an underwater bridge the Soviets have built at a key river crossing. They seem virtually to skim over the water, and their path is illuminated by silvery moonlight streaming from a black sky—as if they were led on a holy mission with divine assistance.

Hollywood's process of "putting the Russians through the wringer," was part of the larger trend on the part of mass media and politicians to systematically distort the image of the Soviet Union for propapaganda purposes. When Cold War politics focused attention on the question of "who 'collaborated' with Russia," the real answer was not some nest of traitors or fellow travelers but "almost everybody." From 1942 through 1944 American opinion makers turned mental cartwheels to justify the alliance with the Soviet Union, even though many of them had been virulently anticommunist drum beaters prior to June 21, 1941, and would return to that comfortable posture after the war. The media and the government might have limited themselves to explaining the circumstances that had made the tie with Russians necessary, praising the undeniable contribution they made to the victory over the Axis. Instead, such mass circulation anticommunist magazines as *Saturday Evening Post,* *Collier's,* and *Reader's Digest* did a 180-degree turn and now embraced the very system they had so recently reviled. The *Post's* wartime coverage of the Soviet Union came almost entirely from the sympathetic Edgar Snow. *Reader's Digest* excerpted *Mission to Moscow,* even including the envoy's post-invasion justification of the purges.[52]

The single most telling example is the special issue that *Life,* then at the height of its influence, devoted to the Soviet Union on March 29, 1943. This issue was the equivalent in print of the pro-Russian movies. It adopted the same ostensibly objective documentary techniques, repeated essentially the same pro-Stalin line, and employed some of the same characters. Stalin himself, who in a notably benign portrait had graced *Life's* sister publi-

cation *Time* as "man of the year" just three months earlier, rated
the cover. Henry Luce's editors presented Soviet history as, in
essence, a chapter in modernization, Russian-style. Lenin became "a normal, well-balanced man who was dedicated to res-
cuing 140,000,000 people from a brutal and incompetent tyr-
anny." The U.S.S.R.'s great strides in industrial and
infrastructure development won praise. "It is safe to say that no
nation in history has ever done so much so fast," *Life* said. There
were costs, to be sure, but the magazine found justifications for
them. "Whatever the cost of farm collectivization, in terms of
human life and individual liberty, the historic fact is that it
worked"; Russian farmers were "content." We should not "get
too excited" about the state's control of information; if Soviet
leaders said it was necessary "to get this job done, we can afford
to take their word for it for the time being." A chart of Soviet
political organization, similar to those used in high school civics
books, showed power flowing upward from the masses. The
NKVD, successor to the GPU, was "a national police similar to
the FBI" whose job was "tracking down traitors." And who
should be the centerpiece of the issue, as expert on both Soviet
internal and external affairs, but Joseph Davies. "A notable success with both nations," according to *Life*, his "shrewd reports"
to the State Department presented a "true picture" of Russian
affairs. Despite the fact that those cables had differed markedly
from his post-1941 ruminations, the ambassador with the blessing of Time, Inc. repeated the same views he had beamed from
Warner Brothers' screen.[53]

The Russians were "one hell of a people," who "look like
Americans, dress like Americans, and think like Americans," *Life*
concluded. Of the farmers in *The North Star*, OWI wrote: "We
see them as people—like ourselves." That, indeed, was the implicit message of the American media, whether on the screen
or in print. The Soviet Union received the ultimate tribute of
American politics and media—they are a modern country, just
like us. Hence we should be able to trust one another and mould
a free postwar world. It is of course hard to be against greater
recognition of our common humanity—a quality in all too short
supply in 1943 or in any other year. But international relations
cannot be understood simply as an exercise in one-on-one understanding, tremendously valuable though that is, nor as a

modern morality play in which good and evil change roles from year to year.[54]

The origin and outcome of the era of Soviet-American friendship should shed light on the postwar controversy over communist influence in the motion picture industry. To frame the issue narrowly: Did Communist Party members and sympathizers determine, or have a significant influence on, the content of films dealing with the Soviet Union? The answer is a clear no. A few CP members and sympathizers worked on the pro-Soviet pictures. Of the Hollywood Ten only John Howard Lawson worked on one of these movies. But they did not suggest the subjects, and one sympathizer, Howard Koch, accepted an assignment on *Mission to Moscow* only under pressure from the studio heads. Most of their wartime script writing was far removed from the Soviet Union and communism. Their products had to run the gauntlet of the capitalist studio hierarchies, and their efforts often earned enthusiastic prase from various non-leftist sources, even from Martin Quigley in the case of *The North Star*.[55]

A broader issue involves the question of who actually controls mass market images. The pro-Soviet films that turned out to be so embarrassing later can be traced to the patriotism of studio heads or the importuning of political figures or a combination of the two. The Office of War Information assisted the process. The Production Code Administration, wisely relaxing its prewar political strictures, allowed these pictures to be made with nothing more than an occasional murmur. The studio chiefs retained control to the last cut; from all indications Jack and Harry Warner, Samuel Goldwyn, and most other studio chiefs were pleased with these products. *Mission to Moscow,* the most overtly political and most scandalous picture, owed its interpretation of events chiefly to Joseph Davies, not to a member of the Hollywood Ten. While Davies' loyalty was beyond question, a few questioned his judgment in 1943, and some noncommunist leftists were among his leading critics. Moreover, Hollywood's brief love affair with the Russians was but a facet of a pervasive trend in the national mass media. Similar arguments, similar images, and similar personalities were employed to make a politically inspired point. It would have happened had there been not one communist in Hollywood; indeed, it occurred largely without them. For a time the interests of communists in the film colony converged with the mainstream, but this was temporary, coincidental, and not of their making.[56]

The pro-Russian pictures are thus proof not that communist influence in the media was profound but rather that it was trivial. The studio heads, like their counterparts Henry Luce or William Randolph Hearst in the print media, established a position and had employees who willingly carried out their wishes. They were less concerned with giving the public what it wanted (as the Hollywood adage went) than with giving the public what they thought it needed. Mass media images thus underwrote a particular political line. They had less to do with a realistic appraisal of actual conditions than with transient political needs, and they were altered as political currents shifted. Wartime propagandists, whether in the public or private sectors, contributed to one of the most notable failures of American public life: an interpretation of the Soviet Union formed chiefly from mass-produced myth.

VIII.

Democrats Old and New: "Classless" Britain and "Modern" China

This emphasis on Chinese disunity and internal strife is particularly unfortunate today when it is important to acquaint audiences in all parts of the world with a new and unified China.

—OWI script review of
Keys of the Kingdom,
Jan. 19, 1944

Mrs. Miniver swept the Academy Awards for 1942. A characteristically lavish MGM release, the film garnered three of the most prized Oscars: best picture, best actress (Greer Garson), best director (William Wyler). The public loved the picture. It was a box office smash in both America and Great Britain. A U.S. poll in 1942 ranked *Mrs. Miniver* and *Wake Island* as the two favorite movies that year; women especially liked the Greer Garson portrayal. A well-made though not brilliant film, *Mrs. Miniver* was probably an inevitable success. Garson and her leading man, Walter Pidgeon, provided ample star power. Director Wyler, a three-time Oscar winner, was one of Hollywood's best. Perhaps equally important was the fact that the movie had the ideal message for the times. The character of Mrs. Miniver, a courageous mother who holds her family together in the teeth of the Blitz,

symbolized in personal terms Britain's lonely heroism in stem-
ming the Nazi tide. *Mrs. Miniver,* like *Since You Went Away,* projected an appealing fantasy—the upper middle class family as
war-inconvenienced democrat. Like *Mission to Moscow,* though
in a less political vein, *Mrs. Miniver* was intended to familiarize
audiences with the valiant story of one of America's allies.[1]

The MGM picture was not only a favorite with the public,
but OWI's Bureau of Motion Pictures considered it a model
propaganda piece. "Give us a *Mrs. Miniver* of China," Nelson
Poynter implored studio executives in June 1942. The Miniver
treatment produced a sentimental, warm-hearted response, but
whether it would enlighten the public about complex international problems, as the bureau hoped, was doubtful.[2]

Britain and China received an extraordinary outpouring of
American trust during the war. Though significant pockets of
suspicion remained about Soviet intentions, Americans overwhelmingly believed, according to an OWI poll in mid-1942,
that the British and Chinese could be counted on to cooperate
with us after the war: 72 percent said yes for Britain and an
astounding 86 percent did so for China.[3] This poll revealed as
much about our own view of America as it did about how we
believed our allies viewed us; in effect Americans were saying
that their vision of the postwar world—whether that of Luce's
"American Century" or Wallace's "Century of the Common
Man"—was shared by other right-thinking countries. That, of
course, was the point—Americans believed they shared with the
British and Chinese an essentially compatible vision. Unity was
the watchword. President Roosevelt met with Winston Churchill and Chiang K'ai-shek in Cairo in 1943 in a symbolic show of
solidarity. Churchill and Madame Chiang spoke to standing
ovations at joint sessions of Congress. Trying to eliminate a per-
ception of differences among the allies, OWI homogenized
America's quite diverse partners, to the detriment of our understanding of the complex world scene.

OWI worried that Allied unity could be undermined by a
recrudescence of Anglophobia. The Motion Picture Bureau's
manual noted there was a "tendency to be critical of the British." Though Americans probably felt as positive towards Britain as toward any country, the bureau realized that for both
historical and contemporary reasons opinion could be ambiv-

alent. The strong fraternal ties between the U.S. and Britain dated from the turn of the century, when influential opinion makers in both countries sensed that the Empire's interests were compatible with America's, soon to be the mightiest industrial power. Those ties, augmented by skillful British propaganda, had helped propel America into World War I. In August of 1941, Roosevelt's secret meeting with Churchill off Newfoundland, where the Atlantic Charter was issued, underscored the profound identification felt between some Americans and Britishers even before the United States formally entered the war. As the war ground on, Roosevelt and Churchill cemented their countries' alliance with a personal friendship that was most unusual among heads of state.[4]

Problems remained, however. First there was Ireland. The British domination of Ireland engendered continuing bitterness among Irish-Americans and some anti-imperialists as well. Massachusetts Representative John McCormack sold the Lend-Lease bill to his Irish constituency as a bill to save the Vatican, not England. Then there was imperialism itself. The sun would soon begin to set on the British Empire, but it had not in 1941. Even among American Anglophiles there was considerable opposition to the empire. Isolationist sentiment between the wars had promoted the idea that the United States had gone to war in 1917 to save the British Empire and warned against a repeat in 1941. Among many liberals and blacks independence for India was a priority. The future of the empire was probably the single most contentious issue between FDR and Churchill, with the American president sometimes needling his Tory counterpart. Lastly, many Americans viewed Britain as a class-ridden society that was not truly democratic in spirit. Though the British upper classes fascinated Americans, they also produced an opposite reaction. Roosevelt thought Britain's trouble was "too much Eton and Oxford," a reference to upper class domination of British life. Like many Americans FDR was both Anglophile and Anglophobe—attracted to England culturally but deeply sceptical about her politics.[5]

Hollywood fed on British imperialism and class distinctions, and the empire afforded a setting for innumerable swashbuckling pictures. With an eye more toward the box office than diplomacy, the movie industry wanted to revive its imperial epics during the war. The topicality of the Pacific war combined with the romance of Rudyard Kipling, the empire's arch-poet, was seemingly irresistible. RKO wanted to re-release *Gunga Din,* Metro to reissue *Kim.* Citing the dangers such pictures posed for Allied unity, Lowell Mellett appealed to the studios to drop these plans, and they agreed. The empire caught OWI liberals in a bind between their personal distaste for imperialism and their professional commitment to selling the war. Since the Tories seemed determined to hold onto the empire, the propagandists resorted to a favorite tactic with embarrassing subjects—ignoring them.[6]

Hollywood's delight in portraying the British upper classes also had to be corrected. *How Green Was My Valley,* which won the 1941 Academy Award for best picture, was a rare exception with its depiction of the Welsh common people, industrial strife, and environmental ruin. Imperialism and aristocracy both threatened OWI's image of democracy. The propagandists' advice to Hollywood blended British heroism with democracy. "Where would we be today if Britain had not continued to resist in the critical year when she stood alone, unprepared, and without allies, against the Axis?" BMP asked. It urged the studios to stress the "stubborn resistance" of the British after Dunkirk. Britain was also part of the "people's war." BMP asked Hollywood to "fight the unity-destroying lies about England." In particular it urged the industry to tone down the typical image of a land of "castles and caste" and drop the stereotypical, monocled, "bah jove" Englishman. As a "comrade in arms" England fought for the same things America did—"a just and lasting peace and a world governed by law and order." The "castles and caste" were just harmless anachronisms. For propaganda purposes British society had to be democratized and its empire written out.[7]

Mrs. Miniver, though produced before OWI got into the act in Hollywood, embodied these themes for British society. The film introduces us to an "average English middle class" family in 1939, when England is composed of "happy, carefree people, who worked, played, and tended their gardens." We are forewarned, however, that they will soon be involved in a "desperate struggle for survival." The story begins on a busy street in London, where Mrs. Miniver, on a sudden impulse, asks the conductor to stop the bus. She rushes into a store to buy the expensive hat she had seen earlier. Her prewar occupation is established: Mrs. Miniver is a professional consumer.

On her train ride to her suburban home she encounters Lady Beldon, the local aristocrat, who is wonderfully played by Dame May Whitty. Lady Beldon grouses constantly about the middle-class women she has encountered all day trying to buy things they cannot possibly afford: "I don't know what the country's coming to—everyone trying to be better than their betters—mink coats and no manners—no wonder Germany's arming." The English class system is established.

At the train station the local stationmaster, Mr. Ballard (Henry Travers), asks Mrs. Miniver if he could see her for a moment. He takes her into his office where he shows her a beautiful rose that he has spent years breeding. Ballard wants to enter the rose in the local flower show and respectfully asks if he can name the rose "Mrs. Miniver." She is taken aback, flattered, and consents. Ballard is delighted and tells her that he appreciated how nice she has always been to him over the years— always speaking to him and all that. Mrs. Miniver, unlike Lady Beldon, cares for people and does not distinguish between classes. Mrs. Miniver is a democrat.

The next scene introduces Clem Miniver, an architect. He is sitting in a fancy sports car in front of the Miniver home trying to bargain a better price for the car from the salesman. When the man won't lower the price Clem gives in and buys the car. The house is massive. They have two full-time servants, whom they treat with a dignity close to equality. They are consumers and good communicators as each worries how to tell the other about their purchase. Clem tries to establish that the old car is dangerous but finally blurts out that he bought a new used car—a very expensive one. Mrs. Miniver is delighted because the car will make her hat look trivial. As they are getting ready for bed—twin beds, and Clem's pyjamas are buttoned to the neck—Mrs. Miniver models her new hat. Dressed in an elegant nightgown, she is strikingly beautiful and erotic. Clem praises her beauty and then, as the code required, flips off the light, turns his back to her, and falls asleep.

Vin, their oldest son, returns from his first year at Oxford, where he has learned social consciousness. He thinks the car was a waste of money. Over dinner he waxes indignant about the class system. "Look about you! What have we? As pure a feudalistic state as there ever was in the ninth to the fifteenth centuries! I'm appalled!" The parents treat Vin with tolerant amusement. The young man's idealism is a phase all young people go through. But the point the movie is making is that England was in a state of transition. Lady Beldon represents the old school: everyone in their place. The Minivers, the new emerging middle-class, are much more democratic in their views. And the next generation, Vin, is receiving a democratic and egalitarian education at Oxford. If England had a class system in the past it surely would not survive the emerging generation. England was an evolutionary democracy.

Enter Lady Beldon's granddaughter Carol Beldon, played by Teresa Wright. She is a bit embarrassed and hesitant. The Minivers are puzzled. Carol blurts out her concern. It's about the new rose named after Mrs. Miniver. Lady Beldon has always won the rose award without competition. Miss Beldon asks Mrs. Miniver is she could suggest that Mr. Ballard withdraw his rose so her grandmother can again win first prize. Before the startled Mrs. Miniver can respond, young Vin brings his new-found ideals of democracy to the front. Must Ballard withdraw his rose because he is not of the ruling class? he angrily asks. But Carol is no stuffy aristocratic female. She challenges him: if he believes so strongly that the system is wrong what is he doing about it? *She* spends her holidays doing settlement work, she points out, and thus puts Vin in his place as an armchair liberal who prefers speeches to action. Despite this, Carol is smitten with him. Again the point is made that the younger generation in England is different from the older ruling class. Carol Beldon is her own woman—an unusual characteristic for a 1940s film.

The parish church unites all Englishmen under the roof of God, though in class-segregated seats. In front sit Lady Beldon and Carol, to the side the Minivers, in the back the stationmaster, surrounded by his fellow workmen. As the minister begins her sermon he is interrupted. Sadly he announces that Germany has invaded Poland and that England is now at war: "I will say merely this, that the prayer for peace still lives in our hearts, coupled now with the prayer for our beloved country. . . . Our forefathers for a thousand years fought for the freedom that we now enjoy and that we must now defend again." With that he dismisses the congregation. Can these people of England pull together as a single unit? Is their love for freedom and democracy stronger than their class system?

The rest of the film shows how the people unite. The workers are the first to rise to the defense of England: many join the army; others are in charge of local civil defense. And in this crisis the workers are suddenly giving orders to their betters. Lady Beldon again grouses about it but gives in. She obeys orders for a blackout and establishes an air raid shelter. The Minivers pitch right in, too. Vin joins the RAF. Clem is a member of a local watch patrol and joins the armada of small boats that rescues troops stranded at Dunkirk. Mrs. Miniver singlehandedly captures a wounded German flier.

The people live through the increasing air raids in the best stiff-upper-lip tradition. The Miniver home is bombed but the family carries on as if it were a mere inconvenience. The romantic angle is satisfied when Carol and Vin plan to marry. Lady Beldon announces to Mrs. Miniver her opposition to the marriage, and the audience naturally assumes it is because of their different stations in life. But Mrs. Miniver knows better. She gets Lady Beldon to admit that she too married during the first World War—at age sixteen. Her husband was killed just three weeks later, and she does not want Carol to go through the same agony she herself experienced. The lovers marry very simply, but everyone lives in fear that Vin will soon be killed.

The flower show must go on: It serves as a symbol of a united English democracy. Ballard's rose is the subject of much discussion in the village. Many of the common people are opposed to his entry—it is Lady Beldon's right, they argue. In a dramatic scene the decision of the judges is given to Lady Beldon to announce. She has again won first prize, even though Ballard's rose is clearly superior. But the spirit of democracy has overcome the matron who, after a moment of hesitation, reverses the decision and announces that first prize goes to Ballard, "our popular stationmaster." A spontaneous roar of approval erupts from the audience.

An air raid interrupts the flower show. Vin, who is at the

show with Carol and his mother, must be rushed back to his base. On their way home Carol and Mrs. Miniver are caught in an air raid on the village. The bombing and strafing are so intense that they must pull their car off the road. Carol is killed by a stray bullet.

The final scene takes place in the church. As the congregation files in it is apparent that several people are missing. The camera pans over the people and then slowly points upward revealing a huge hole in the roof. The minister begins his sermon: "We in this quiet corner of England have suffered the loss of friends." George West, a young choir-boy, killed. James Ballard, Stationmaster, dead just one hour after winning the rose competition. And, most tragically, Carol Beldon. "Why, in all conscience, should these be the ones to suffer?" he asks. "I shall tell you why! Because this is not only a war of soldiers in uniform. It is a war of the people—of all the people—and it must be fought not only on the battlefield but in the cities and in the villages, in the factories and on the farms, in the home and in the heart of every man, woman and child who loves freedom. . . . This is a people's war! It is our war! We are the fighters!" As the sermon concludes the camera moves from the minister to the hole in the church roof. With "Onward Christian Soldiers" playing on the sound track, the sky is suddenly filled with English fighter planes going off to battle. A united England will survive.

It was the right film at the right time. The public loved it, as did most of the critics. The *New Yorker* labeled it "stupendous." *Newsweek* brushed aside the charge that it was "contrived propaganda" and said it packed "more persuasive wallop than half a dozen propaganda films pitched to a heroic key." To *Time* the film represented "that almost impossible feat, a great war picture that photographs the inner meaning, instead of the outward realism of World War II." The *Catholic World* was so taken with the film that its reviewer wished "it had been some Catholic's privilege to have . . . directed *Mrs. Miniver*. Perhaps it was God's retort to anti-Semitism to have chosen William Wyler." Manny Farber of the *New Republic* cast a dissenting vote. He found the Minivers "prissy and fake." They behave, he wrote, "according to Will Hays and whoever wrote 'Little Lord Fauntleroy.'"[8]

From London the *Spectator* blasted the film as "well-meaning but unconsciously pro-fascist propaganda." The film offended its reviewer, Edgar Anstey, by showing the English as having no "inkling whatsoever" that war was coming in September 1939. *Mrs. Miniver*, he wrote, presented British war aims as a "defense of bourgeois privilege." He admitted, however, that the film settled down into a good war movie and correctly predicted it would be popular in Britain.[9]

Opinion within OWI was divided. Reviewer Marjorie Thorson found the film "so patronizing . . . it verges on insult." Poynter, however, praised it as a model. His instincts were correct. *Mrs. Miniver* was a sort of British *Since You Went Away.* Audiences accepted both pictures not in spite of their character's wealth and high status but because of it. A public that believed almost everybody was middle class eagerly embraced the myth that the characters played by Greer Garson and Claudette Colbert embodied their own situation transposed up a notch. Mrs. Miniver, despite her luxury, suffered grievously, responded heroically, and kept the common touch.[10]

The memory of *Mrs. Miniver* was fresh when another British extravaganza from Metro, *The White Cliffs of Dover*, hit Poynter's desk. OWI's lingering doubts about *Mrs. Miniver* had been augmented by two other MGM features. Producer Sidney Franklin, who made something of a wartime specialty of British subjects, supervised *Random Harvest* (late 1942), a love story which also starred Greer Garson, this time with Ronald Colman. The picture skirted the war, but BMP tried unsuccessfully to get the studio to show a more democratic Britain by sprinkling a few Labour members in the Parliament scene. OWI was even more distressed by *A Yank at Eton* (1942), branding it "poisonous from start to finish" for its story of a cocksure American (Mickey Rooney) who cuts a swath through England's most prestigious prep school. By 1943 the Motion Picture Bureau had had enough, and decided to take a stand.[11]

Alice Duer Miller's narrative poem, *The White Cliffs*, captured the plight of Britain and the island nation's tie with America. "I am American bred,/ I have seen much to hate here—much to forgive," she wrote. "But in a world where England is finished and dead,/ I do not wish to live." These sentiments created a sensation. More than 300,000 copies were sold in the United

Trying to resolve the dilemma of love and separation faced by millions of moviegoers, Ronald Reagan as stage manager of an armed forces entertainment troupe gets married to his sweetheart (Joan Leslie) in *This Is the Army*. They receive the benediction of the stage manager's beaming father, played by George Murphy, who also attained political stardom as U.S. senator from California. *(All photos in this section from MOMA)*

Despite half-hearted efforts by OWI to win a better break for blacks, racist imagery persisted in wartime movies, as exemplified by *This Is the Army*'s vision of Harlem (opposite page). The real "brown bomber," Joe Louis, salutes. In David O. Selznick's hymn to the wartime home, *Since You Went Away*, the ever true servant returns to help out her war-worker mistress for no pay. At right Fidelia (Hattie McDaniel) initiates thirteen-year-old Brig (Shirley Temple) in kitchen mysteries. The home front theme of young mother turned factory worker while her husband is overseas was played out by Ginger Rogers (below), who casts a jaundiced eye on a fellow worker's overtures toward her housemates in *Tender Comrade*.

Hollywood scrapped its negative view of the Soviet Union for glowing positive images, most notoriously *Mission to Moscow* (above). The American ambassador to Moscow, Joseph E. Davies (played by Walter Huston who was not a look-alike for the real Davies, inset), absorbs a lesson in geopolitics from an avuncular Joseph Stalin (Manart Kippen). Other Russian pictures, such as *The North Star* (below), offered a romantic view of an Americanized Soviet Union in an effort to build solidarity with our wartime ally.

The movies' image of the Chinese was almost as fictional as the depiction of the Russians, and matters were not helped by giving the leading role to Caucasians with doctored eyes—witness these freedom fighters from *Dragon Seed* (above), Walter Huston, and Katharine Hepburn. In one of OWI's favorite pictures, *Mrs. Miniver* (below), Greer Garson exemplifies the upper crust Englishwoman as democrat and war heroine. She graciously accepts a rose named in her honor by the local station master (Henry Travers), who knows his place.

The Japanese, bursting toward American troops in *Gung-Ho* (above), were deceitful, faceless hordes who took on the uncivilized attributes of their jungle fighting habitat. Hollywood almost never showed a good Japanese, but the movies distinguished between Nazis and good Germans. (Left), Tonder, a German lieutenant played by Peter Von Eyck, desperately seeks love from Molly Morden (Dorris Bowden), a young widow in an occupied Norwegian village in *The Moon Is Down*. By pretending to yield to his entreaties she lures him to his death—a metaphor for the indomitable resistance.

Alfred Hitchcock's *Lifeboat* (1944) stirred up a bitter controversy because the rescued German U-boat captain Willi (Walter Slezak), consulting a compass, impressed some viewers as a stronger figure than the boatload of bewildered democrats. They include Tallulah Bankhead and John Hodiak, who strike up a quick romance, William Bendix, and black actor Canada Lee in an ambiguous role. The picture looked toward the peace settlement with the question on everyone's mind: "What do you do with people [Germans] like that?"

Wilson (1944), the most expensive picture made up to that time, tried to prepare the public for internationalist postwar policies by invoking the memory of the martyred president. Darryl Zanuck poured lavish resources into such scenes as the reenactment of the 1912 Democratic national convention. But the effort to humanize Wilson (Alexander Knox), greeting World War I doughboys, reduced most of the politics to platitudes.

States, and actress Lynn Fontanne broadcast the poem over the NBC Blue Network; Jimmy Dorsey recorded a musical version which proved to be one of the most popular songs of 1941; and MGM turned the poem into a major motion picture starring Irene Dunne and Alan Marshall.[12]

The White Cliffs is the story of Susan Dunn, a young American girl who visits England just as World War I breaks out. She falls in love with a young English aristocrat, Sir John Ashwood, and marries him. They have a son but her husband is killed in the war. Sue and her son return to the United States after the war only to find it dominated by prohibition, gangsters, and political scandal. Sue flees to civilized England, determined to bring up her son in the aristocratic tradition of his father. But England is no paradise either—it is dominated by arrogance, a rigid class structure, and appeasement. When war comes to England in 1939 Lady Ashwood complains bitterly that once again young men will fight and die for worthless causes. Her son joins the military and, like his father, is killed in battle. In the end Lady Ashwood realizes that these sacrifices are necessary to build a better world.

The script arrived at BMP headquarters in March 1943. The staff hated it. World War II was presented as a simple repetition of World War I. The global character of the war was ignored, as were the United Nations. Unlike the symbolic democracy of *Mrs. Miniver,* the war was reduced "to the scale of a cricket match, the stakes the preservation of Ashwood Manor, its lord and retainers," said BMP reviewers. The English were a nation of snobs. The entire Ashwood family, Susan included, was "condescending and patronizing" to its servants and the working class. Where is the England of today? OWI asked. "We are shown nothing which would indicate a total mobilization of the English people for war [or] the great social change the war has already brought to England." Nor were the English the only problem. Americans appeared "snobbish, simple, and clumsy, or boorish." Susan's father was rude, crude, and an isolationist to boot. To OWI, Dunn was not representative of American attitudes and ideals. The agency suggested he be turned into a man like William Allen White.[13]

Nelson Poynter sent a long critical evaluation to Sidney Franklin and vice president Eddie Mannix. The major problem,

Poynter said, was that the script left the impression that the United States and Britain could only cooperate during a period of crisis. Could our common heritages be incorporated in the script "without bitching it up?" Mannix, however, was reluctant to make changes.[14]

Mellett also read the screenplay, but he did not want to fight this one. Most of the attitudes expressed in the film existed, and he was confident that the "common sense of American audiences" would draw positive feelings from the film. As in *So Proudly We Hail* and *Pittsburgh,* he thought Poynter had gone too far. He noted that if the studio took all of the OWI suggestions seriously the entire script would have to be rewritten. The result might be worse than the present script. Poynter objected to the young soldier's saying he is "dying for England." Poynter wanted him to deliver a death-bed sermonette on the concept of the United Nations and perhaps a salute or two to Chiang K'ai-shek or Stalin. But Mellett warned that if the screen writers attempted such a death-bed speech they might deliver "something pretty mawkish and unconvincing."[15]

Poynter backed off but the Hollywood office was not pleased with the film. Ulric Bell agreed with Poynter. He had established contact with two British representatives of the Ministry of Information, the British equivalent of OWI, and they agreed that the script was "just the sort of thing that shouldn't be done." Yet without support from Mellett there was little that Poynter or Bell could do. Poynter continued to work with the studio. Sidney Franklin admitted that he had been "indeed shocked" when he first read the OWI evaluation, but upon reflection admitted that many of the agency's criticisms were valid.[16]

Eventually MGM submitted some eighty pages of script changes to OWI. Following orders, Poynter told Franklin that the script would now be "of great value to Anglo-American friendship and understanding." But his staff did not agree with him. They judged the changes to be very minor. A few lines were inserted to indicate that England was changing, and an air of comedy was put in the film to lighten the impression of criticism. Egalitarianism was established by having John Dunn, the son of Susan, fall in love with and marry a tenant farmer's daughter. When the film was released in March 1944 BMP's overseas branch in Hollywood recommended against foreign distribution. In December 1944 the New York office ruled that *The White Cliffs of Dover* could play in France and Italy but was otherwise restricted to American audiences.[17]

American reviewers agreed with OWI's criticism. *Newsweek* found the film a questionable confirmation of Anglo-American solidarity: "The English you are asked to love and identify with ... are exclusively and belligerently aristocratic." James Agee likened watching the film to "drinking cup after cup of tepid orange pekoe at a rained-out garden party." *Time* thought the film would give "genuine admirers of good cinema and credible Englishmen the jimjams."[18]

The theme of England as a class-ridden society was perhaps most directly dealt with in the Darryl Zanuck production, *This Above All* (1942). Based on the novel by Eric Knight, the film was directed by Anatole Litvak. It starred Tyrone Power as a young, embittered, lower-class Englishman and Joan Fontaine as his upper-class lover. Philip Hartung of the *Commonweal* termed it "the most interesting movie that Hollywood had made about this war."[19]

The hero, Clive Briggs (Power), is a member of the British army who fought in France. He is rescued at Dunkirk, but deserts on his return to England because he feels the army is inefficient, unprepared, and run by upper-class snobs. He sees no reason to fight for a country that refuses to treat him as an equal. Enter Prue Hathaway (Fontaine), a member of a wealthy, aristocratic family. To the utter astonishment of her family she joins the WAF as a private. As in *Mrs. Miniver* the younger generation is rejecting the class structure of British society.

Clive and Prue immediately fall in love. Aided by a minister, she tries to persuade Clive that no matter what faults England has, life under Nazi Germany would be much worse. "Whatever happens," she says, "let us decide it, not the enemy." Clive agrees in the final reel. As the film ends, he says: "It's going to be a different world when this is over. But first we've got to win this war." He returns to his regiment, and one assumes that the war will not only defeat fascism but bring down the class structure.

Hollywood and OWI invoked similar sacred and sentimental symbols for both Britain and America to suggest identical interests between the two countries. As had happened with the American home front, these symbols were used to deny the permanence of gaping social cleavages in British life. The British could indeed unite against their common enemy, but that did not mean class cleavages would melt away as the democratic ethos wafted through the world. Fearing that any recognition of serious problems in British society would compromise American support, the Bureau of Motion Pictures sought a portrayal as false as Hollywood's great-house charades. Even with America's closest ally, OWI found it hard to take theater audiences into its confidence.

The problems OWI encountered with the depiction of Britain were minor, however, by comparison with those regarding China. The Chinese reality posed perhaps as great a propaganda challenge as did the Soviet Union, and the distortions wrought by the Bureau of Motion Pictures and Hollywood were nearly as serious as those of the pro-Soviet pictures. The wartime propaganda drive underscores historian Michael Hunt's point about U.S. perceptions of China throughout our history: "Americans with their unique historical experience and outlook are [likely] to ignore diversity in the world and instead reduce cultures radically different from our own to familiar, easily manageable terms."[20]

The wartime alliance between the United States and China was fraught with misunderstanding, frustration, and apprehension. The Japanese invaded China in 1937 and, overrunning much of the eastern part of the country, soon forced the Kuomintang (Nationalist) government of Generalissimo Chiang K'ai-shek to flee to Chungking in the south. Roosevelt increased his support for Chiang in the hope that he would counter Japanese domination of East Asia. FDR also gave Chiang equal billing with the other allies and proclaimed the U.S., Britain, Russia, and China to be the "four policemen" of the world. Washington poured large amounts of military aid into Chungking during the war and through its crusty military adviser in China, General "Vinegar Joe" Stilwell (who contemptuously referred to Chiang as "the peanut"), tried to reform—and at one point even take over—the Kuomintang army.[21]

But Roosevelt could not create through rhetoric and showmanship what the Kuomintang refused to build for itself. Chiang's government was mired in hopeless corruption and tragic brutality that alienated large segments of the Chinese population; the Kuomintang was anything but the enlightened democracy and efficient fighting force pictured in government and private propaganda. Chiang hoarded the supplies Washington sent and contrived excuse after excuse to avoid engaging the Japanese. For he believed that his real enemy was not the Japanese but Mao Ze-dong's Communists. Chiang called the Japanese a "disease of the skin" but the Communists a "disease of the heart." As the Kuomintang stagnated, Mao gathered support among the peasantry, built an efficient fighting machine, and indicated his willingness to lead a patriotic crusade against the Japanese. After the war the Communists would topple the Kuomintang in the world's first successful peasant revolution.

If these realities were ignored by official Washington, the average American was not even aware of them. In mid-1942 pollsters asked citizens to locate China—a pretty good-sized place—on a blank outline map of the world; 40 percent could not do so. China was a far-off land of mystery, teeming with millions of people who spoke a strange language, ate with sticks, and worshipped their ancestors. But as the polls indicated, Americans' ignorance of the real China did not keep them from carrying on a long distance love affair with the world's most populous nation. Since the nineteenth century, when that alluring land had first attracted both dedicated missionaries and unscrupulous fortune hunters (many in the vile opium trade), Americans had felt their country enjoyed a special, if deeply patronizing, relationship with China.[22]

Hollywood reinforced these contradictory impressions of the Chinese with its occasional forays into the mysterious East, highlighted by such epics as D. W. Griffith's *Broken Blossoms* (1919) and Thalberg's *The Good Earth* (1937). Movieland China was populated with evil mandarin villains like Fu Manchu, whose unintelligible spells baffled Westerners, and inhuman warlords who terrorized women and children; but it also embraced the simple, gentle peasants of Pearl Buck's vision, and the genial, wise Charlie Chan, a beloved detective who used Confucian logic to befuddle crooks. Whether benign or sinister, China consistently was pictured as backward, poverty-stricken, and unfamiliar with modern science and technology. China, it seemed, needed Western help to modernize and prosper.[23]

Such an interpretation was not acceptable to Washington's propagandists during the war. Chiang's China had to be on the road to modernity and democracy. Just as public and private propaganda mills spewed out an industrial, somewhat democratic Soviet Union, so too they were summoned to create "the new China." But their celluloid country bore tragically little resemblance to its namesake. Frank Capra's *Battle of China*, part of his "Why We Fight" indoctrination series for the army, put it blatantly: "The oldest and youngest of the world's great nations, together with the British Commonwealth, fight side by side in the struggle that is as old as China herself. The struggle of freedom against slavery, civilization against barbarism, good against evil." OWI's Bureau of Motion Pictures had much the same attitude, though it sought to clothe its views in the Hollywood idiom. The bureau believed that, although Americans had warm feelings for the Chinese, they little understood that she was "an important world power and ally" who had been fighting Axis aggression since 1933. The manual for the movie industry said pointedly: "China is a great nation, cultured and liberal, with whom, inevitably, we will be closely bound in the world that is to come."[24]

What OWI reviewers saw of Hollywood's treatment of this subject in 1942 resembled anything but the "new China." Instead a spate of "B" pictures, such as *Bombs Over Burma, Escape from Hong Kong,* and *A Yank on the Burma Road,* showed American heroes battling the Japanese with the Chinese either invisible or distinctly subordinate. The John Wayne vehicle *Flying Tigers* (1942) glorified General Claire Chennault's aerial exploits in flying supplies from Burma to Chungking over "the Hump"— Himalayan peaks that towered to 24,000 feet. Wayne, not the Chinese, engaged the Japanese. China became little more than a backdrop for American action. In *China Girl* (1943) the Chinese fought effectively only if led by an American. In view of Chiang's resistance to committing his forces to the war, Hollywood may have been closer to the truth than OWI knew, but of course for the wrong reasons.[25]

More to the propagandists' taste was Paramount's *China* (1943), which showed the happy conjunction of a cynical American who grew to understand the war and Chinese who evolved into the fighters Stilwell kept trying to shape in real life. Alan

Ladd plays Jones, a hard-bitten, cynical, apolitical American oil salesman who is making good profits living in China and selling oil to the Japanese occupiers. The film opens with Jones and his partner "Johnny," played by William Bendix, on their way to Shanghai with another delivery of oil for the Japanese. Jones drives like a mad-man, running masses of Chinese refugees off the road. He couldn't care less about the plight of the "new China." That is until he runs into Miss Grant (Loretta Young), who is escorting a group of women Chinese students to the interior. They are trying to escape advancing Japanese troops. Jones, naturally, is unconcerned about their peril and is furious when he learns that his partner allowed the girls and Miss Grant to ride in the back of his truck—the extra weight might keep him from reaching his destination.

Miss Grant spends several reels trying to convince Jones that he should join the fight for democracy in China. The Chinese guerrillas are "freedom fighters" working for the same goals as her American forefathers, and his. Jones is not moved. Miss Grant tells him about the great things Chiang K'ai-shek is doing for China. Jones tells her he has some pretty good friends in Tokyo. Political conversion seems impossible.

But Japanese brutality accomplishes what Miss Grant could not do. One of the girls, Tan Ying, leaves the group to visit the home of her parents. Johnny, to the disgust of Jones, has also adopted a small Chinese baby, which he had named "Donald Duck," and whom they decide to leave with Tan Ying's parents. When Jones and Grant visit the parents they discover the Japanese soldiers have been to the farm. Tan Ying's parents and "Donald Duck" were "butchered," and Tan Ying had been raped by three Japanese soldiers. Jones walks into the house just as the Japanese soldiers are leaving and is so incensed that he mows them down with a machine gun. Jones is converted to a freedom fighter.

He now fights as an equal alongside the Chinese guerrillas. While Jones is clearly a leader, OWI was able to convince Paramount that the Chinese should be more than just his followers. In the released film OWI was pleased to see that the Chinese freedom fighters were presented as "realistic and intelligent" fighters "who take the initiative and plan the action."[26]

But *China* was, after all, a vehicle for Alan Ladd, not for

Chinese freedom fighters. It is Jones who plans the final victory over the Japanese. After stealing some dynamite from the enemy, Jones plants the charges in the mountains directly above a pass through which the Japanese troops must pass. Jones then halts the Japanese convoy and taunts its general, who delights in telling him that Pearl Harbor has just been attacked and there is a "New Order" in the Far East. Jones counters that the "New Order" will fail because "millions of little guys all over the world have freedom in their blood." Just as he finishes his speech the dynamite explodes, killing all the Japanese, along with Jones who willingly gives his life for the "new China."

OWI loved it. The conversion of Jones showed "the fallacy of thinking that Americans ... can remain neutral." *China*, in OWI's opinion, was a positive statement "for our Chinese allies." But perhaps more realistically *PM* labeled it "a hodge-podge of propaganda, violence, romance and corn" with a large portion of the "stereotyped and the silly thrown in for good measure," while the *New York Journal of Commerce* resented the "injection of tawdry speeches ... as unnecessary and pathetically cheap." To Bosley Crowther it was just another "artificial romance with a topical theme."[27]

Despite the spate of war films with the new China as background, the most significant of all Chinese images remained for Americans the venerable Charlie Chan, whose activities took place on American soil. Hollywood produced 99 feature films between 1931 and 1945 that had some aspect of China as a major theme; 31 of these were Chan mysteries. During the war years six Chan films were produced, and the rigors of total war required that OWI subject the inscrutable detective to its own meticulous investigation.[28]

Charlie Chan in the Secret Service (Monogram, 1944), which starred Sidney Toler, was typical. The thin plot revolves around the mysterious murder of George Melton and the theft of his blueprint for a new powerful secret weapon. In familiar fashion, Chan, somewhat hindered by his meddlesome children, solves the murder, uncovers a German spy ring, and retrieves the valuable documents. To most observers, this was simply another harmless Chan mystery designed to satisfy the constant demands of his fans.

OWI, however, thought the characterization of Chan "would prove offensive to our Chinese allies." The film upset the propaganda agency for numerous reasons. It dragged the war into a conventional series and would "contribute nothing to American-Chinese relations," which was OWI's primary objective for every film with a China setting. In fact, OWI believed the film might even damage relations—Confucius and the Chinese use of "chop-sticks" were constant sources for gags. It was the image of the Chinese as presented through Chan and his children that most upset OWI. The propagandists feared that the portrait of the bland and inscrutable oriental who spoke in pidgin English would be taken as an insult by the Chinese. Further, although Chan was all-knowing, his children knew nothing. OWI worried that this characterization of Chan's children "might raise grave doubts on the part of the Chinese people as to the value of a Western upbringing."[29]

The propaganda agency recommended that the script be submitted to T. K. Chang, the Chinese consul in Los Angeles, who served as a script advisor on many films dealing with China. If Chang agreed with OWI's evaluation of the script, the reviewing section recommended that Ulric Bell urge Monogram "to abandon not only this film but the entire Chan series." This was certainly a harsh recommendation. Happily for Chan fans everywhere, Chang kept the matter in perspective. He told OWI that he found nothing offensive in the script or the series in general. Monogram could continue to make Chan films. However, OWI refused to recommend an export license, thus banning this Chan film from audiences in Europe and Asia.[30]

OWI continued to monitor the Chan series closely through the remaining war years. In a script review of *Charlie Chan in the Mystery Mansion* (Monogram, 1944) the agency took strong objection to the theme that blacks are frightened of the dark, especially in a haunted mansion. To OWI, Monogram's insistence on maintaining this image was reason enough to ban the film from export. But OWI also was furious that the local American police were shown as generally incompetent and "hopelessly stupid" when compared to Chan. OWI wanted every film to create the impression that in a democratic society the police were fair and efficient—always bringing in their man for a fair trial. The propaganda agency wanted the studio to revise the script to indicate that the police and Chan worked together as a team in capturing the crooks![31]

But while the image of blacks as fearful was gratuitous and expendable, the depiction of the police as bunglers was essential to Chan's broad comic appeal. Dorothy Jones, who wrote some of the OWI reviews on the Chan series, recognized this fact a decade after the war. In 1955 she praised the Chan series as an American tribute to China's wisdom and antiquity, conveniently forgetting that during the war she had recommended the series be cancelled. She was wrong in 1944 and accurate in 1955. The Chan series had always been popular in Asia, where audiences delighted in his superiority. The series also indicated a certain democratic quality—Americans were willing to laugh at themselves and their culture. The racism in Chan films was somewhat muted by the fact that everyone in the film—cops, government officials, judges, lawyers, and Chan's kids—were all inferior to Chan and fair game for jokes and insults.

In 1944 Hollywood issued two major films with a China setting. Instead of a "*Mrs. Miniver* of China" Nelson Poynter got Katharine Hepburn as a freedom fighter in *Dragon Seed* and Gregory Peck as a Catholic missionary in *The Keys of the Kingdom*. Both films were recrafted by OWI to reflect the propaganda agency's goal of presenting a unified, democratic China determined to drive fascist aggressors from their land so that a "new China" could be born.

OWI first saw the proposed script of Pearl Buck's *Dragon Seed* in September 1942. It was the story of a Chinese peasant family and their gradual exposure to the horrors of modern war. As the war engulfs them, the family of Ling Tan learns to fight for a free China. While OWI believed the subject matter was potentially beneficial, it objected to MGM's first script because it portrayed the Chinese as backward illiterates. In returning the script for rewriting, OWI asked MGM to see *Dragon Seed* as a "golden opportunity" to make a major contribution to the war effort. A revised script should try to develop a sense of equality between China and the West by showing the "deep-rooted democracy in China," and should stress that "American foreign policy has backed up the Chinese since the beginning of the Japanese war against them."

When MGM resubmitted the screenplay some ten months later the agency was delighted that the script had been "completely rewritten" and now promised to be "an inspiring presentation of the people of Fighting China." By the use of new dialogue and added scenes *Dragon Seed* would show that the people of China were willing to sacrifice their lives and property to drive the enemy from their land. *Dragon Seed* now showed the war in China as a "people's war."[32]

When OWI reviewed the final print of the film they glowed with pride. *Dragon Seed* "emerges as a document not only of the fighting Chinese people but, by implication, of people all over the world who have united to fight aggression." It was "highly recommended for distribution in liberated areas." To OWI the saga of Ling Tan and his wife, Jade, was a stirring war drama that would help explain the plight of China to American and world-wide audiences.[33]

The film opens with Ling Tan, played by Walter Huston, a simple, hard-working Chinese farmer who enjoys a comfortable life surrounded by his sons, their wives, and his grandchildren. One son has an unusual wife, Jade (Hepburn). Jade is a modern woman, a free-thinker, who wants to learn to read and write. She is a frequent embarrassment to her husband since she constantly challenges her station in life. One day in the local village she encounters a group of university students, representing the new China, who are trying to convince the local farmers that the war in the North is their war. The peasants ignore the students, but Jade immediately recognizes the issues and tries to spur the local people to resistance. Old Ling Tan is not convinced. When the Japanese soldiers first arrive in his village he tries to reason with them. He soon learns the true nature of Japanese aggression as the soldiers kill, rape, and loot.

Ling Tan's family is forced to take refuge in a local mission. The West again provides safety. Jade, who is pregnant, is forced to flee inland for safety. The ravages of war are now a part of the daily lives of all the Chinese. After Jade's baby is born she rejoins the family and becomes a freedom fighter. They kill many Japanese, but this small group of freedom fighters cannot win the war. In a stirring conclusion, Jade convinces Ling Tan and her fellow fighters that they must burn their homes and fields, and retreat inland to join the growing guerrilla forces. The men quickly see the virtues of Jade's arguments, torch their village and farms, and escape to the interior. To OWI *Dragon Seed* was a notable contribution to the war effort—a film that would show Americans that the Chinese understood what they were fighting for and that they were willing to die for freedom.

Critics outdid themselves in shredding *Dragon Seed*. James Agee thought it was an "unimaginably bad movie." He could not recall having seen another film "so full of wrong slants." The Japanese were played by Chinese while the Chinese were played by Caucasians "with their eyes painfully plastered in an Oriental oblique." Agee continued: "I shan't even try to say how awful and silly they looked—Miss Hepburn especially, in her shrewdly tailored, Peck-&-Peckish pajamas." The *Chicago Tribune* noted that "the garbled English, apparently intended to suggest the Chinese language, comes out of an international grab bag. Miss Hepburn talks like Katharine Hepburn. Mr. Huston employs the clipped Yankee accents of a Cal Coolidge." As Manny Farber pointed out, *Dragon Seed* failed to create either convincing Chinese or Japanese characters.[34]

Why was OWI so enthusiastic and the reviewers so critical? One reason is that OWI did not see Hepburn and Huston in ridiculous make-up. Instead, they heard professions of Chinese solidarity. They saw and heard film characters preach about a new China and a people's war. They assumed that this would convey the correct message—China was a democracy just like us. But *Dragon Seed* was not credible—neither the idyllic farms of the peasants, the buck-teeth of the evil Japanese, the various accents of the characters, nor the characters themselves. It is hard to imagine a less likely Chinese heroine than tall, high cheek-boned Katharine Hepburn. Her propaganda preachments were impossible to believe. Hollywood's attempt simultaneously to glamorize and democratize China was dismissed as so much movieland hokum.

The Keys of the Kingdom dealt with China in the early years of this century. Since the early part of the nineteenth century Catholic and Protestant missionaries had flocked to China determined to convert millions of Chinese to Christianity. In 1941 Twentieth Century-Fox purchased an action-packed best-seller that traced the life of an unorthodox Catholic missionary in China. A. J. Cronin's novel, *Keys of the Kingdom*, chronicles the career of Father Francis Chisholm, a young Scotsman who turns to the priesthood after a melodramatic courtship with his first cousin ended in failure. At college, in seminary, and as a young priest, Chisholm is considered a failure by everyone except kindly Bishop MacNabb who recognizes that Chisholm is blessed with true Christian character. MacNabb sends Chisholm to China where he encounters poverty, famine, war, corruption, banditry, and resistance to Christianity. But Chisholm conquers all with his simple, Christian approach to life.

Twentieth Century began working on a script in 1941 and submitted a first draft to the Breen office. The Production Code Administration warned the studio that the image of China and the Chinese government would probably provoke vigorous protests from Chiang's diplomats. The screenplay remained dormant for some eighteen months. In January 1943 the studio was ready to go forward with the film, but this time had to submit the story to OWI. The agency was appalled by what it read. The screenplay, by two top writers, Nunnally Johnson and Joseph Mankiewicz, presented China as a nation beset by civil war, torn apart by racial conflicts and superstitious beliefs, and overrun with ignorant, backward, and cowardly people. Even though the film was set in the early part of this century, OWI would not approve this depiction of China. A revised script submitted in January 1944 merely added a foreword stating that the film had nothing to do with present-day China. OWI found that unacceptable, and Ulric Bell refused to approve the script. Randolph Sailer, in the China section of OWI, admitted that the agency could not expect "films on China that will make all Chinese good, even if such a film could be imagined," but neither did the agency want a film that assumed China was still a backward nation. Such an image would not help America's commitment to build China into a recognized world power.[35]

The agency provided the studio with specific concepts for rewriting the script. For example, the agency told the studio that depicting a period of civil war in China in which both sides (Manchu and Republican) were pictured as bandits was counterproductive. In the script all soldiers were shown as ruthlessly pillaging and slaughtering their fellow countrymen. The war was a battle of war-lords, not a battle for a better China. It was immaterial to OWI that the script was faithful to the book written by Cronin, and perhaps to history. Why, OWI asked, was it necessary for a Republican officer to speak out bitterly about fighting and dying for the "ridiculous dream" of a Chinese Republic? Would it not be just as easy for the officer to say he was fighting for the creation of a republic, thereby suggesting that the people of China were trying to unite during this period of revolution? Chiding the company for not even attempting to show that the film took place in a period of transition from the Old China to the New China, OWI read the studio a lecture in current politics: "China is today taking her place as one of the four great United Nations of the World. She is contributing immeasurably toward the defeat of our Japanese enemy, and is destined to play an important role in the peace to come.... This emphasis on Chinese disunity and internal strife is particularly unfortunate today when it is important to acquaint audiences in all parts of the world with a new and unified China." T. K. Chang seconded OWI's assessment. The script, he said, would only create "misunderstanding and resentment in our relationship."[36]

In an attempt to eliminate the kinds of problems indicated by OWI, the studio began to work more closely with the agency and also hired several technical advisers. Wei Fan Hsueh was hired on Chang's recommendation as an adviser on Chinese affairs; a former missionary to China, Father Albert O'Hara, S. J., and Father Wilfrid Parsons, S. J., editor of *America*, were brought to Hollywood to advise on religious affairs. By April 1944 OWI could report tremendous progress in changing the film to present a more positive image of life in China. BMP representative William Cunningham toured the set at the invitation of the studio and saw the transformation at first hand. Three sets showed China's progress over the thirty years covered by the story. The first village consisted of "straw thatch shacks and is rather primitive but does not indicate squalor.... In the final one the houses are neat, little brick places with considerable feeling of civilization about them. I would say it would be a very favorable inland village." The Chinese lived like middle-class Americans in neat little brick homes. The inland village could have been located in Iowa.[37]

Cunningham was convinced that the overall impression of the script was no longer one of Chinese ignorance and superstition. Indeed Father O'Hara believed the revised script presented the Chinese in a more "favorable light than the actual conditions at the time would have required." The story content had been changed so that the Republican Army was shown as triumphant over decadent Manchu forces, "indicating the start of the great Chinese Republic of today." Cunningham finally was able to tell Twentieth Century-Fox that he was positive *Keys* "would meet with our approval."[38]

The film opens with a very old Father Chisholm. He is once again in trouble because of his odd behavior. During an investigation Chisholm's journal of his experiences in China is discovered. The camera zooms in on the first page of the journal: "How different the China of today is from the China to which I came so long ago." The narration explains that some thirty years ago, when the priest first came to China, the nation was struggling for self-respect. Today that same China is a unified nation fighting for independence against a common enemy. OWI's goal of a united nation was accomplished.

The film then uses a flashback to show Chisholm's experiences in China. The church to which he was sent was in a shambles. There were two "rice Christians," the Wangs, who offer to help Chisholm recruit converts for a fee. Chisholm refuses and the Wangs pelt him with mud and eggs. This represented a change from the original script, which called for all the Chinese in the village to pelt Chisholm with mud and eggs every time he left the village. Such an image would not illustrate Western/Eastern cooperation. So the script was changed to show the Wangs as individuals turning against Chisholm because he refused to buy their help.

Throughout the film the Chinese are shown respecting Chisholm and his methods. When the son of the local mandarin officials becomes ill with an infected arm, Chisholm is called in to administer Western medicine. The original script called for the boy to have a badly infected arm because the Chinese doctors had plastered him with mud and paper. No such impression is given in the film, and Chisholm with the help of nothing more than a medical dictionary cures the boy. The mandarin repays Chisholm by helping him secure land for a new mission, and making clear to his village that the priest is to be treated with kindness and respect.

Although a civil war is raging around the village, there is no longer any hint that the Republic is a "ridiculous dream." Instead the Republican forces are led by a brave young officer who cares for his people and his troops. His men do not rape or pillage. He cooperates with Chisholm to defeat the local warlord and thereby save the village for the Republic. The point the film makes time and again is that cooperation between the Western missionary and the people of China is possible and desirable. Just as the Chinese were fighting for democracy at the turn of the century, so today they are united with the Allies to drive out the Japanese.

Keys of the Kingdom, as released, was a very different film from that first proposed by the studio. But the OWI-approved image of China was as unrealistic as the film industry's previous "mysterious orient" view of China had been. *Keys of the Kingdom* updated the mythology of the special relationship, but China, though becoming modern, still was under America's tutelage. The wartime screen images of China reflected the Roosevelt administration's propaganda needs, which in turn were based on a blend of ignorance, apathy, and optimism about the real situation.

Hollywood and OWI were latecomers, however, to the hyping of the Kuomintang. As in the case of the facelift administered to the Soviet Union during the war, so too the Chinese government enjoyed influential salesmen throughout the media and the government. Indeed, Chiang's promoters operated from the 1920s into the 1960s, and they had a profound influence on American policy towards China, in contrast to the fleeting wartime romance with Stalin. Publisher Henry Luce, the son of Presbyterian missionaries in China, placed Chiang on the cover of *Time* on six occasions between 1939 and 1945—more than any other mortal. Time-Life's crack reporter, Theodore White, knew the truth about the Kuomintang but could not publish it in Luce's pages. A few "China hands," such as John Stewart Service and O. Edmund Clubb, sent prescient reports to Washington on Mao's revolution, but their expertise was ignored. For their perspicacity they were "Hurleyed out of China" by the U.S. ambassador, Patrick Hurley, who made common cause with Chiang. As the Communists moved inexorably toward their triumph in the late 1940s, the China lobby hounded the experts out of government and succeeded in locking America's China policy in an anti-communist stance until Nixon's stunning rapprochement with Peking.[39]

The intertwined approach of wartime policy and propaganda to both British imperialism and Chinese revolution was prophetic. Among the most important developments after World War II have been the collapse of the European empires, the rise of Third World nationalism, and the frequent attempts by the United States to channel those surging passions. Washington's inability to grasp the implications of anti-imperialism during the war left policymakers as well as the public unprepared for a postwar world that did not fit the models of either Henry Luce or Henry Wallace. The American approach to China, in both policy and propaganda, proved to be a prototype for Washington's policy toward Third World revolutions, and the obsession with the possible spread of Mao's Communist model helped draw the United States into its longest war—Vietnam.

Wartime film propaganda about China and Great Britain was not just a problem of myth versus reality or of misleading the public while the White House knew better. The issue includes those things but also something more. Propaganda is directly linked to policymakers' perceptions of the world, and to the policies they pursue. Just as Joseph Davies rewrote his own history, so Franklin Roosevelt and his aides constructed a fictitious China on which to base their policy. Policymakers and propagandists reduced the turbulent, alien diversity of China to "familiar, easily manageable terms," but these proved to be disastrous guides during World War II and the Cold War. The wartime collaboration of Hollywood and OWI did not create American misconceptions of China from scratch, but it extended them in important ways. The case of China illustrates as clearly as any the dangerous symbiosis of policy and propaganda.

IX.

The Beast in the Jungle

In Europe we felt that our enemies, horrible and deadly as they were, were still people. But out here [the Pacific] I soon gathered that the Japanese were looked upon as something subhuman or repulsive; the way some people feel about cockroaches or mice.

—Ernie Pyle

If America and its allies were the epitome of righteousness, the enemy embodied all evil. The enemy threatened all that America held dear. But how, specifically, to portray evil incarnate was the problem facing Hollywood and OWI. World War I offered two types of propaganda about the enemy that attracted the film makers once again—atrocity stories and hate pictures. OWI's Bureau of Motion Pictures disagreed sharply with such approaches, for it believed that the emotional release such tactics generated was subject to unpredictable collapse and eventual disillusionment. Moreover, such efforts did little to help the public understand the war issues. The propagandists thus struggled to get the movie makers to avoid hate pictures and to use the screen to explain the nature of the enemy. OWI found the studios more receptive to a nuanced treatment of the German enemy than of the Japanese; despite all the agency's lobbying, the Japanese were shown primarily as the beast in the jungle.

The depiction of the enemy raised two questions. Who was the enemy? and what was fascism? Neither question had a simple answer. Officially the Roosevelt administration considered the Axis governments, not their people, to be the enemy. As potential democrats, the people were redeemable. Although Allied policies such as unconditional surrender and civilian bombing targeted the people as well as their governments and armed forces, enemy governments were still the primary target.

OWI had high hopes for motion pictures, which (said BMP) could, "enlighten the people in concrete terms" about the enemy better than any other medium could. But the bureau gave Hollywood unclear messages on just who was a fascist and what fascism was. It was easier to say who and what they were not. The enemy was not just Hitler, Mussolini, Tojo or their ruling cliques. OWI feared that dissident elements might stage a coup, throw out the ruling clique, and then sue for peace; but the essential elements of fascism would still be in place. The propagandists demanded unconditional surrender, the precondition for a thorough house cleaning that would avert a repetition of the post-World War I experience. On the other hand, the enemy was not the entire German, Italian, or Japanese people, and the movies should not "inspire hatred" for the masses. The people, purged of their evil leaders and exercising their naturally democratic desires, would prevail. Tired of films that showed wise-cracking Yanks single-handedly whipping the enemy, OWI warned the studios not to underestimate the "cunning, tough, cruel" foe. He could be defeated—he was not a superman—but the magnitude of the task should not be underestimated.[1]

The closest the bureau came to a definition of fascism and fascists, in its manual for the motion picture industry, was to say that the "enemy is many people infected with a poisonous doctrine of hate, of might making right." Although such an attitude was certainly true of the Axis powers, it would characterize in varying degrees a large number of nation states. OWI offered several characteristics of fascists: They engaged in wars of aggression, denied their own citizens democratic government, curbed labor organizations, stirred up racial and religious hatreds, and pitted various classes against each other. So long as fascism continued to exist, the security of all Americans was imperiled. While most of these statements were accurate enough descriptions of the activities of fascist governments, they did little to isolate the specific characteristics that might define fascism. Many scholars would argue the very term *fascism* was a misnomer, applying to a specific European context, not the Axis as a whole. But the convenience of such a term for Germany,

Italy, and Japan, however vague and blunt, was as irresistible as the label of democracy for all the Allies.[2]

By insisting on fascism as the concept with which to explain the enemy, OWI tried to counter the prevailing tendency in American media to picture the Japanese in racial terms. "We are fighting a system not a race," the Bureau of Motion Pictures kept reminding the studios. The OWI manual advised them not to show the Japanese as "a little buck-toothed treacherous Jap." As liberals, OWI staff members deplored racism per se. Moreover, the agency wanted to avoid identifying the Japanese by race, since some American blacks and many colonial subjects tended to identify with the Japanese as fellow people of color who were throwing off white rule.[3]

Yet in a country still steeped in racist stereotypes, and dogged by a history of virulent anti-Japanese prejudice, the temptation to cast the Japanese in racial terms was overwhelming. In trying to soften racist imagery in the movies, OWI was fighting not only Hollywood's racism, but a pervasive national reflex. While Americans imagined they enjoyed a special relationship with the Chinese, antagonism characterized the encounters between Washington and Tokyo. Japan represented the "yellow peril," and anti-Japanese prejudice, which was especially virulent on the West Coast, culminated in severe restrictions on immigration to the United States. The Roosevelt administration's internment of Japanese-Americans on the Pacific Coast both reflected and legitimated this racism. "A Jap is a Jap," said Lieutenant General John L. De Witt, commander of the Western Defense Command, in justifying the roundup. De Witt's inelegant language expressed bluntly the widespread view that, while Germans and Italians might be treated as individuals, Japanese as a race possessed a herd instinct that led to fanatical loyalty to their emperor. Frank Capra's propaganda masterpiece *Know Your Enemy—Japan* (1945) compared the Japanese to "photographic prints off the same negative."[4]

Years of anti-Japanese propaganda in the United States, reinforced by Pearl Harbor and well-publicized accounts of what Tokyo's militarists had done to our Asian friends the Chinese, produced overwhelmingly negative images in American popular culture. In 1944 a poll showed that 13 percent of Americans wanted to kill all Japanese. In 1945 some 22 percent of the public expressed disappointment that more atomic bombs were not used on the Japanese. The ubiquitous term *Jap* in itself "helped inculcate the idea that the West was fighting a different species," contends historian Christopher Thorne. Popular songs carried such titles as "We're Gonna Have to Slap the Dirty Little Jap," "You're a Sap, Mister Jap," and "Mow the Japs Down." Hadley Cantril of Princeton University conducted a poll for OWI in which he asked Americans to choose from a list of words describing the Japanese; 73 percent selected treacherous, 62 percent sly, and 55 percent cruel.[5]

Journalism and popular literature reinforced these concepts. *Time,* apparently worried that its readers could not distinguish Japanese from Luce's beloved Chinese, published a how-to-do-it article, complete with photographs, on "How to Tell Your Friends From the Japs." Racial traits bore physical expressions, according to the magazine. Virtually all Japanese were short while Chinese were sometimes tall. Japanese "often dry up and grow lean as they age," but Chinese were often fat. Racial distinctions, moreover, produced different personality traits. Not surprisingly the Chinese exhibited positive, if somewhat childlike, qualities. "The Japanese are dogmatic and arrogant while the Chinese expression is kindly and placid," the piece continued. Japanese are "hesitant, nervous in conversation [and] laugh loudly at the wrong time." Japanese walked stiffly (the tramp of the conqueror, presumably); the Chinese had an easier gait. Even the bespectacled stereotype was brought in with the sage observation that "most Chinese avoid horn-rimmed spectacles." *Collier's* commemorated the first anniversary of Pearl Harbor with a cover showing a Japanese as a vampire bat, blood dripping from its teeth, about to drop its bombs on the naval yard.[6]

Eminent scholars buttressed such opinions, building interpretations of Japanese aggression on a racial foundation. Geoffrey Gorer, an influential English anthropologist, argued that the Japanese fixation with cleanliness, especially "drastic toilet training," resulted in the formation of "situational value systems" in which the Japanese had no absolute concept of right or wrong. When faced with an alien situation the Japanese had no established ritual or code of behavior to follow. Reacting to years of living in a highly regimented society, Japanese troops vented their frustration with an outburst of violence directed toward their enemies. (Gorer was one of the first to suggest that any attempt to remove the emperor would have disastrous consequences.) Other scholars weighed in with similarly harsh assessments. Margaret Mead described Japanese culture as "childish" and "pathological." Historian Frank Tannenbaum found twenty-eight points of comparison between the Japanese character and the American gangster. Anthropologist Weston La Barre believed the Japanese were "collectively ill." He found that it was almost impossible not to like the Chinese while the Japanese "were almost always fanatical, arrogant, and suspicious." They were, he wrote, "probably the most compulsive people in the world ethnological museum."[7]

These attitudes contrast sharply with those toward the Allies' other principal enemy, Germany. (Italy received little attention by comparison with its two chief allies.) Americans did not define their European—and white—adversaries in racial terms. Though most Americans found Nazism abhorrent, they still made distinctions between Nazis and good Germans. Europeans retained scope for individual action, even resistance to their totalitarian governments—a notion all but absent from ideas about the Japanese monolith. Although the Gestapo and the S.S. were reviled for their barbaric conduct, the regular German military establishment was still seen as consisting of honorable professional soldiers. There is a historical irony in these perceptions, for the knowledge of the Holocaust has now indelibly colored our view of Germany. Though documented in Britain and the United States by late 1942, the extermination of the Jews remained outside the cognizance of mainstream media. The fate of the Jews met largely with indifference in the Roosevelt and Churchill governments. In contrast, in view of the easy credence given reports of Japanese atrocities, it seems likely that rumors of a Japanese "final solution" would have received more serious attention.[8]

The Japanese harbored their own racist notions. The result was to create, on both sides, a concept of the Other—a race, or virtually a species, so alien as to constitute something with which coexistence was impossible. "The natural response to such a vision was an obsession with extermination on both sides—a war without mercy," writes historian John W. Dower. In war novels,

such as Norman Mailer's *The Naked and the Dead*, G.I.'s shoot prisoners and mutilate the bodies for souvenirs. Of the American
and British prisoners of war captured by Germany and Italy, 4
percent died; but 27 percent of American and British POWs
died at the hands of the Japanese. There were virtually two different wars in Europe and Asia. As Ernie Pyle wrote: "In Europe
we felt that our enemies, horrible and deadly as they were, were
still people. But out here [the Pacific] I soon gathered that the
Japanese were looked upon as something subhuman or repulsive; the way some people feel about cockroaches or mice."[9]

Americans fit the savage war in the Pacific into one of the
oldest archetypes of their popular culture—Indian warfare.
"Emotions forgotten since our most savage Indian wars were
reawakened by the ferocities of Japanese commanders," said Allan Nevins, one of the nation's most eminent historians. Government officials as well as creators of popular culture invoked
the analogy to which Nevins alluded. "The only good Jap is a
Jap who's been dead for six months," said Admiral William
(Bull) Halsey in 1944. "We were fighting no civilized, knightly
war," explained Harvard historian Samuel Eliot Morison, who
became a rear admiral for his service to naval history. "We were
back to primitive days of fighting Indians on the American
frontier; no holds barred and no quarter." Japanese tactics—
treachery, camouflage, deception   recalled the perceived bar-
barity of Indian methods.[10]

The geography of the war reinforced these attitudes. The
European war, both factually and cinematically, took place in
the midst of civilization, in cities and villages where the impress
of human order could be seen in churches, plazas, streets, and
homes. The enemy seemed knowable, the battles regularized.
The Pacific war, by contrast, took place in the wilderness, much
of it a particularly frightening wilderness: the jungle. There is
a long tradition in the West of identifying the wilderness with
the absence of civilization—indeed, as a place of evil, where the
hard-won norms of civilization give way to savagery. In civilized
warfare the rules are understood, but there are no rules in the
wilderness. Hence the apparent correlation of Japan's unscrupulous tactics with the physical environment—sneak attacks
(Pearl Harbor), deceit (negotiating in Washington even as the
task force steamed toward Hawaii), brutality (the Bataan death

march), and torture. Japanese soldiers camouflaged themselves so ingeniously that they seemed to take on the attributes of the jungle itself. This alien setting—dark, unbearably hot, impassable—sheltered the subhuman enemy. Both the environment and the racial edge to the Pacific war reinforced the sense of the conflict as outside normal human bounds.[11]

Hollywood readily absorbed the national imagery of the war with the Japanese. If Halsey and Morison summoned the analogy of Indian fighting from America's past, the movie industry's beloved westerns gave it ample practice in themes readily transferable to the Pacific war. The studios' first impulses after Pearl Harbor were to capitalize on the theme of Japanese treachery and brutality and to label them with racial epithets. By the time OWI's Bureau of Motion Pictures began functioning in mid-1942, Hollywood had rushed into release a number of pictures that embellished the stab-in-the-back thesis of *Little Tokyo, U.S.A.* In *A Prisoner of Japan* the enemy kills "for no apparent reason other than to satisfy their blood-lust," said OWI. *Menace of the Rising Sun* described Tokyo's diplomacy as a "filthy game of treachery" and the Japanese as "murderers." *Remember Pearl Harbor* and *Danger in the Pacific* repeated the theme of the "fiendish, diabolical" enemy. *Pacific Rendezvous* and *Manila Calling* embroidered the espionage theme. It was a rare film that did not employ such terms as *Japs, beasts, yellow monkeys, nips,* or *slant-eyed rats.*[12]

The Bureau of Motion Pictures recoiled from such portrayals, as it had from *Little Tokyo, U.S.A.* BMP decided to try to get the studios to shift from these clichés to the theme of fascism, not racism. OWI faced an almost impossible battle, however, in hacking a trail through the jungle of racist stereotypes.

Movies about Japan made little effort to develop a Japanese character or explain what Japan hoped to accomplish in the war. The Japanese remain nameless, faceless, and almost totally speechless. No attempt was made to show a Japanese soldier trapped by circumstances beyond his control, or a family man who longed for home, or an officer who despised the militarists even if he supported the military campaign. This stands in sharp contrast to the portrayal of the German soldiers, who were often shown as decent human beings distinct from the Nazis.

Hollywood could draw on Pearl Harbor and the heroic stand

that small bands of outnumbered American troops made in other Pacific outposts. The Japanese followed their attack on Pearl Harbor with a series of coordinated attacks against other American military outposts in the Pacific. In the Philippines, General Douglas MacArthur ordered a general retreat to Corregidor, an island in Manila Bay, and deep into the peninsula of Bataan. The Japanese struck MacArthur's forces on Corregidor December 29. Outnumbered, but not outfought, some 6,000 American and 45,000 Filipino troops fought fiercely and inflicted heavy casualties on the Japanese. Resistance ultimately collapsed, however, and Bataan surrendered on April 9, 1942, Corregidor on May 6. But the heroic stand of American troops fighting a strange new enemy in remote jungles made Americans realize the Japanese were not invincible.

These combat situations became a Hollywood staple. Paramount was the first studio to capitalize on the interest in these battles when it released *Wake Island* in August 1942. Starring Brian Donlevy, MacDonald Carey, William Bendix, and Robert Preston, the film was a box-office smash. With a screenplay by W. R. Burnett and Frank Butler, the film tried to recreate the facts surrounding the 377 Marines who resisted the Japanese on Wake Island. Directed by John Farrow, who chose the Salton Sea in the California desert to recreate Wake, the film had the full cooperation of the Marine Corps. It was, according to *Newsweek*, "Hollywood's first intelligent, honest, and completely successful attempt to dramatize the deeds of an American force on a fighting front." But in retrospect *Wake Island* is important chiefly for its announcing what soon became clichés of the Pacific war.[13]

The opening sequences establish Japanese perfidy by showing Tokyo's smiling diplomatic contingent, enroute to Washington to talk peace, being hosted by the Marines of Wake. The movie soon veers into the combat scenes which continue without end until the last Marine is killed. The men of Wake fight to the last man, which was seen as a heroic defense of freedom and democracy—not an indication that American troops were suicidal and fanatic.

Paramount had paid close attention to the OWI manual in preparing the script. For dramatic purposes the film developed antagonism between the Marines and a construction crew building a landing strip. The two groups bickered over which had the most important job. But when war came, that antagonism quickly evaporated as both construction men and combat troops put aside their differences and combined into a single fighting force. Men constantly volunteered for dangerous assignments. OWI praised Paramount for this skillful illustration of American teamwork. The studio removed one piece of dialogue that indicated the war was being fought to "destroy destruction." This was not an approved war aim, and the studio agreed to OWI's request to snip the offending statement from the release print.[14]

While the setting for *Wake Island* was not a jungle, the fighting took place on a remote island far from civilization. Trapped, without any hope of rescue, the men of Wake fought overwhelming odds against an enemy that showed no mercy. No Japanese character emerges in the film—the Japanese hordes attack without quarter. The Japanese are shown shooting the wounded and bayoneting defenseless men. Tokyo had tricked America into being asleep and now the Marines were paying the price. *Wake Island* showed audiences that war in the Pacific was going to be a tough, dirty war fought with few rules and even fewer heroes.

By 1945, however, *Wake Island* was causing embarrassment. With victory close at hand, the New York office of OWI Overseas was unwilling to export a film to Asia which showed an American defeat at the hands of the Japanese. *Wake Island* was a film for 1942. Three years later it seemed like ancient history. The battle scenes were unrealistic, as were the preachments in the trenches about fighting for democracy. As one combat veteran observed years after the war: "I remember those Hollywood films where people sat in their trenches and had ideological discussions about the beauties of democracy at home. Oh, bullshit! I remember those movies. They were stupid."[15] *Wake Island* was popular in 1942 because it fed the public's desire for anything about the war. The battle scenes had a sanitized quality that made war seem more like a big football game than a mortal encounter. Three years later, when audiences knew much more about the reality of war, *Wake Island* seemed like a naive period piece.

MGM brought out its version of a World War II Alamo when

it released *Bataan* in April 1943. Directed by Tay Garnett, with a screenplay by Robert Andrews, the film starred Robert Taylor and Lloyd Nolan. The film opens with the chaotic American retreat in full swing. Suddenly Japanese planes appear and attack a Red Cross ambulance and fire indiscriminately into the column of people. Women and children are killed, quickly establishing that the enemy does not fight by established rules of conduct. Something must be done to slow down the Japanese if the retreat is to be successful. A small group of men agree to remain behind to try to keep the Japanese from crossing a key bridge as long as possible. Alone deep in the jungle, a handful of Americans stand guard—a West Pointer, a working-class sergeant, an air force officer, a Latino, a black, a young sailor, and two Filipinos. At first this rag-tag collection squabbles over minor issues, but as the Japanese attack, they become bound together as one fighting unit determined to fight to the last man.

One by one they are killed by the enemy, who snipe unseen from nearby trees, capture men on patrol, and torture them to drive the remaining men crazy. The pilot, trying to go for help, is shot. Dying from his wounds, he crashes the plane into the bridge, delaying the Japanese advance. One of the Filipinos attempts to break through Japanese lines at night. The next morning he is found mutilated and swinging from a tree. The young sailor screams: "Dirty, dirty, dirty. . . . " Soon only three men are left. One is killed by a sniper, another stabbed in the back by a Japanese pretending to be dead. Finally the Japanese storm out of hiding. As they run directly into the screen, looking like a swarm of insects, Sergeant Dana (Taylor), the only remaining American, fires away at them with his machine gun, determined to take as many of them with him as he can. "Come and get it, suckers. We're still here—we'll always be here—come and get it."

As he dies a narrator tells the audience: "So fought the heroes of Bataan. Their sacrifice made possible our victories in the Coral Sea, at Midway, on New Guinea and Guadalcanal. Their spirit will lead us back to Bataan." Again the Americans went down to the last man, which was seen as an heroic defense of democracy and not a senseless sacrifice. As the sergeant told his men: "Maybe it don't seem to do much good to fight here but we figure the men who died here may have done more than anyone to save the world. It don't matter much where a man dies as long as he dies for freedom."

MGM began discussing the film with OWI soon after the Bureau of Motion Pictures opened its office in Hollywood. A complete script was submitted in September 1942, and OWI was pleased with the results of close collaboration. The enemy's strength was properly depicted. But most important to OWI was the democratic nature of the armed forces. "Superior officers are willing to take suggestions from men under them. . . . Thus, the army reflects the democratic way of life—which is one way of demonstrating the difference between our ideology and the Fascist doctrine," the agency noted. It also applauded the inclusion of a black private, played by Kenneth Spencer—an act of pure deception, for there were no integrated combat units then. Nor were the thirteen Americans professional soldiers—they were soda jerks, salesmen, farmers, and teachers before the war. The American soldier was the common man. *Bataan* illustrated that "this is a people's army, fighting a people's war," wrote OWI.[16]

Stressing Allied cooperation was also of prime concern to OWI. In the original screenplay the Filipino characters remained in the background like children, seen but rarely heard. The final film, after much OWI prodding, corrected that oversight. While neither of the two Filipinos played a major role, OWI was pleased that they displayed "an invincible determination to drive out the invader."[17]

The Japanese are faceless treacherous hordes. They kill civilians, torture wounded men, and are able to use the jungle to their advantage. They send a message to the Americans saying if they surrender they will be "treated fairly" and then kill the first person who stands up. OWI found these depictions of Japanese tactics to be accurate. The film makes no attempt to explain Japanese behavior or develop a Japanese character.[18]

Yet both Nelson Poynter and Ulric Bell were delighted with the film. Poynter said: "It's our idea of a wonderfully useful picture—a swell show with convincing, dramatic war interpretation." Bell informed the Office of Censorship that *Bataan* "makes an especially good contribution" with its handling of the allies and should be given an export license. Neither seemed concerned that *Bataan* had no interpretation of the enemy except that he was a guy with a gun trying to kill American troops—just what OWI had said it did not want. The propaganda agency was willing to overlook the image of the enemy in the film for the positive portrayal of American and Allied unity. For OWI this message was the most important theme of *Bataan*.[19]

Guadalcanal Diary, usually considered a better picture than *Wake Island*, was released in 1943 and embroidered the racial themes announced in the earlier movie. A Twentieth Century-Fox production, *Guadalcanal Diary* was based on Richard Tregaskis's best-selling book of the same name. Few people had heard of the tiny, sparsely populated island in the Solomons until American troops landed there in August of 1942. The fighting was fierce, and each side suffered heavy losses until the Japanese surrendered in February 1943.

The book was adapted for the screen by Lamar Trotti, whose other wartime credits ultimately included such major efforts as *The Ox-Bow Incident* (1943), *Wilson* (1944), and *A Bell for Adano* (1945). *Guadalcanal Diary* opens with a large convoy of ships somewhere in the Pacific on July 26, 1942, a lazy, boring Sunday as the men about to do battle try to relax. As the camera sweeps across the deck, the universal platoon again comes into view. William Bendix plays a taxi driver from Brooklyn who thinks of nothing but his beloved Dodgers (he might have deserted if he knew they would desert him for California); Anthony Quinn represents minority America as Soos Alvarez, who can think of nothing but his girlfriend; Lloyd Nolan is the tough veteran sergeant; Richard Conte is the captain who loves his men; and Richard Jaekel plays the young soldier facing his first battle.

The landing on Guadalcanal takes place without incident. The island appears to have been deserted. But as the men advance inland, one is suddenly killed by a sniper. A narrator tells the audience that men "are lurking" in the jungle. Bendix mistakenly attacks a tree limb and sheepishly explains: "I swore I could see his buck teeth." The Japanese troops have withdrawn into the interior of the island, and the Marines are in for a long tough battle. This strategy, praised when undertaken by American troops in *Bataan* and other movies, is presented as devious and unfair when done by the Japanese.

The rest of the film details the treachery of the Japanese.

The enemy are described as apes and monkeys who hide in trees and use unfair tactics to lure unsuspecting Americans to their death. When Nolan is asked how he feels about killing people, he replies: "Well, it's kill or be killed—besides they ain't people." As the men fight on, they discover the Japanese are dug into the mountains and holed up in caves, which will require close hand-to-hand fighting to drive them out. The narrator tells the audience: "He is a constant menace to our patrols. He must be driven out. . . . The men behind the machine guns are fanatics, some are chained to the weapons. One by one they must be blasted from the earth that hides them." And blasted they are. In a series of extremely bloody scenes, the Marines in hand-to-hand combat defeat the Japanese, but they take no pleasure in performing their duty. As Bendix explains: "I'm no hero, I'm just a guy. I'm out here because somebody had to come. I don't want no medals. I just want to get this thing over with and go back home. I'm just like everyone else and I don't like it."

Guadalcanal Diary scored lots of propaganda points, and posed few problems for OWI in the scripting stage. The most significant issue was the screenplay's use of a priest to tell the men they were fighting a righteous war. A righteous nation, he said, was "economically sound, politically sound, and spiritually unassailable." OWI pointed out that this was not only "bad theology" but also "bad political philosophy" because China, Greece, and Yugoslavia, among others, would scarcely qualify as righteous nations under this standard. Trotti and MGM solved the problem in typical fashion—the speech was written out.[20]

OWI reviewers praised the film as "the most realistic and outstanding picture" about the Pacific war they had seen. The enemy were "formidable" but not "supermen." American soldiers represented a "cross-section of the nation." The film was recommended for distribution overseas.[21]

As usual, the reviewers were divided. *Saturday Review* judged it enthralling, as did *Newsweek*. *The Commonweal* praised the lack of glorification of war in the film, which Philip Hartung found an "honest tribute" to the soldiers. *Time* argued, however, that "the picture never makes clear how desperately expendable the Marines felt on Guadalcanal. . . . There is hardly a moment when kill-or-be-killed becomes an electrocuting fact rather than an energetic re-enactment at second-hand. U.S. audiences ... want and need more than that, if they are to live in the same world with the men who fought on Guadalcanal." The point was valid. The film effectively uses newsreel footage in some of the battle scenes. These scenes stand in stark contrast to the Hollywood recreations which confuse war with locker room horseplay. *Guadalcanal Diary* gave movie audiences little feeling for the reality of the bloody battles that actually took place.[22]

None of the reviewers commented on the pervasive racism of *Guadalcanal Diary.* While OWI sometimes protested against a racial interpretation of the enemy, the agency made no mention of this fact in its communication with Twentieth Century. Perhaps it is only in retrospect that the racism is so apparent. Every Japanese move was portrayed as deceitful. For example, a Japanese soldier waltzes into the American camp and tells them he will take them to an isolated area where a large number of Japanese are waiting to surrender. The Americans go along with this "devious plot" and when the Japanese attack only one man escapes with his life. In reality, any American officer dumb enough to fall into such an obvious trap would have been, and should have been, courtmartialed. In *Guadalcanal Diary* the Japanese remain nameless, faceless enemies. No Japanese character has any significant speaking part in the film and the audience is given no opportunity to understand why the Japanese are fighting. They were "things" to be killed—driven from the earth, according to the film's narrator. The racism was not challenged because few people dissented from it in 1943.

Perhaps the strongest jungle motif during World War II, and one of the most vicious anti-Japanese films, was the Errol Flynn vehicle *Objective Burma* (1945). In this Warner Brothers production, Flynn leads a small group of paratroopers on a raid of a key Japanese radar station deep in the Burma jungle. As much as any film made during the war, *Objective Burma* asked film audiences to hate the Japanese.

The writers for the film were Alvah Bessie, Lester Cole, and Ranald MacDougall. Bessie, who had fought in Spain in the International Brigade, and who, with Cole, was soon to be a member of the Hollywood Ten, noted in his autobiography how the subject matter originated. Producer Jerry Wald called Bessie into his office and told him that he wanted to make a film about

American paratroopers fighting in Burma. When the writer discovered there were no American troops in Burma and called this to Wald's attention the producer was unconcerned: "So what? It's only a moving picture. So, look, put in some British liaison officers and stop worrying." Bessie had little choice but to follow orders.[23]

To add authenticity Warners used an introduction from General "Vinegar Joe" Stilwell. Known for his salty language, Stilwell had the indiscretion to say that we got a "hell of a licking" from the Japanese and it was "damn humiliating" to have to retreat from Burma. Stilwell's language was unacceptable to Joseph Breen. Breen's ruling touched off a furor. One movie fan wrote to Breen protesting his actions, wondering why the Hays office was so upset over the use of the word "hell" when she had heard the Japanese referred to on the screen again and again as "dirty yellow rats," "blasted monkeys," and the like. She assured Breen she was going to see *Objective Burma* and "I'll be waiting for that stifled vulgarity that would evidently shock the pants off some of our narrow-minded Carrie Nations." Breen very reluctantly gave the studio permission to use *hell* because it was an "exact quotation of the General's words." But under no circumstances would the studio be allowed to use "by God," which Breen branded "intrinsically objectionable."[24]

The plot of the film is rather simple. American paratroopers raid a Japanese radar station in Burma and are successful in "liquidating Japs so thoroughly that not one survives to shoot back, or even squirm." The plan called for the men to be picked up at an airfield and flown to safety, but the Japanese cut them off and the men have to abandon their plans. Now they have to walk 150 miles to safety through a jungle "slithering full of the enemy." The Americans face two enemies in the film—the Japanese and the jungle. Nelson (Flynn) and his men do not have the slightest idea of how to survive in the hostile jungle environment. For supplies they have to rely on prearranged air drops, which reveal their location to the enemy. By contrast it is implied that the Japanese are perfectly comfortable in the jungle.[25]

Accompanying the troops on their mission is Williams, a newspaper correspondent played by character actor Henry Hull. After being trapped in the jungle, Nelson decides to split his men into two groups to increase their chances of reaching safety. They agree to meet at a small village they believe to be friendly. However, the Japanese capture one group and kill everyone. When Nelson and his men arrive at the village they discover the bodies of their friends, many of them mutilated beyond recognition. When the correspondent sees what has happened he bursts out with the most vindictive film speech of the war: "I thought I'd seen or read about everything one man can do to another, from the torture chambers of the middle ages to the gang wars and lynchings of today. But this—this is different. This was done in cold blood by people who claim to be civilized. Civilized! They're degenerate, immoral idiots. Stinking little savages. Wipe them out, I say. Wipe them off the face of the earth. Wipe them off the face of the earth." Nelson says nothing. He has seen it all before. He quietly orders the bodies buried.

This scene was hotly debated at the studio. When Bessie and Cole saw the final shooting script they were shocked by the scene, which had been changed by MacDougall. They protested to Wald that the new scene was "very dangerous." In Bessie's version Nelson had answered the correspondent: "There's nothing especially Japanese about this. . . . You'll find it wherever you find fascists. There are even people who call themselves American who'd do it, too." But Wald cut Nelson's reply. Bessie thought that ruined the point of the scene. "You are falling into the enemy's trap. Wiping people off the face of the earth is a private idea—and policy—of fascists," he told Wald. Had it remained intact, Bessie's dialogue would have been a rare example in World War II films of identifying Japanese brutality with fascism, not with the Japanese people. Perhaps the reference to Americans scared off Wald; perhaps he believed, as did most people, that this type of brutality was inherently Japanese. Unfortunately, the OWI records on *Objective Burma* are missing and there is no evidence in the studio production file that the agency was aware of the debate over the speech, which could have been taken directly from its manual for Hollywood.[26]

The film, while occasionally exciting, reeked with hatred of the Japanese, but reviewers seemed not to notice. Manny Farber noted only that the newspaper correspondent "contributes too little to the movie to warrant the great trouble that was taken to put him in it." *Time* found the film "as good as they come" for a fictional war movie. In Great Britain the film touched off a furor, but only because Flynn, not British troops, was winning the war in Burma. *Objective Burma* called on audiences to hate all Japanese and made no attempt to distinguish between fascists and the Japanese, as Bessie and Cole had tried to do.[27]

Gung-Ho, a 1943 Universal release produced by Walter Wanger, repeated many of these same themes but stressed that the Japanese were intellectually inferior and therefore no match for American troops. *Gung-Ho* said that when Japanese troops were placed in an unusual situation they could not adopt new tactics because they are incapable of independent thinking. In contrast, when Americans are placed in unusual situations their individualism and common sense will pull them out. It was another version of the inferiority of the Japanese as a race.

The film opens at a Marine base in San Diego where a special unit is being trained to conduct secret raids on Japanese bases. The call goes out for volunteers, and each man is asked during an interview: "Why do you want to kill Japs?" Each has his reason. Says one: "My brother was killed at Pearl Harbor." Another: "I fought in Spain—we're still fighting fascism." And a third: "I don't like Japs." The men are anxious to get an opportunity for revenge.

Randolph Scott is in charge of training for the raiders. The Pacific war will be won by teamwork, he tells his men. They must work together, and in order to do so, they must each eliminate all prejudice from their system. Ironically *Gung-Ho* proceeded to be one of the most rabid "hate the Jap" films made in Hollywood—and the raiders are all white.

As the men embark on their mission—Minkin Island—Scott says they must kill every "Jap" on the island in less than twenty-four hours. As in *Guadalcanal Diary,* the landing on the island takes place without resistance. The men creep from the beach into the jungle. Nothing. No enemy soldiers in sight. Suddenly the camera moves from ground level with the American soldiers and points upward—the trees are teeming with "Japs"! Without warning they open fire, shooting the Marines in the back. The Marines quickly adapt to this unforeseen situation, blast hundreds of Japanese out of the trees, and are finally able to move on.

As the Americans advance through the jungle they encounter situations they had not prepared for, but each time the officers and the men adjust easily and defeat the enemy. When Scott finds that enemy planes are approaching he has an American flag painted on the top of a building that the Americans have captured, then orders a retreat. The Japanese fall into this trap and charge into the building. When the approaching Japanese planes see the flag, they immediately attack—killing their own troops. Had this trick been played by the Japanese, it would have been condemned. But as our trick, it was simply clever adaptiveness. The film is littered with references to "Japs" and "monkeys who live in trees." Several wounded Japanese fake death to try to kill unsuspecting Americans. Three Japanese pretend that they want to surrender. As soon as one of the Marines drops his guard the Japanese kill him. The message is clear that there are no rules. Scott announces that the Pacific War is "unorthodox" and the Marines are going to have to learn a few tricks of their own if they are going to survive.

The film ends with every Japanese killed—mission accomplished. As a submarine takes the men home, Scott delivers a final speech. They fought bravely, but what of the future? "Our course is clear. It is for us . . . to dedicate ourselves again, our hearts, our minds, our bodies to the task ahead. We must . . . make sure that the peace that follows this holocaust is a just and equitable and conclusive peace. And beyond that to make sure that the social order which we bequeath to our sons and daughters is truly based on the freedom for which these men died." A noble sentiment, but an improbable mouthful for a man who, with a small group of Marine raiders, had just killed hundreds of enemy troops.

These combat movies did not make up Japanese brutality out of whole cloth. Barbaric behavior was all too real, and all countries engaged in varying degrees of it. One would not expect an American propaganda agency or the country's movie makers to call attention to their side's horrors. When questionable Allied tactics were noticed at all, they were passed off as the generic horrors of war or justified as a response to Japanese brutality. German atrocities tended to be linked to the Nazis, not necessarily to an entire people. The importance of these Japanese images lies, rather, in the reason behind their use. In large measure because of racist assumptions, one country was singled out as almost uniquely savage in its actions, and in turn, the depiction of that behavior as single-minded reinforced the view that the Japanese were subhuman and hence somehow deserving of whatever barbarism might be visited on them.

Although the jungle theme was no longer applicable, this view of the Japanese continued as Hollywood focused on the nation's home islands. The dramatic bombing raid on Tokyo, led by Lieutenant Colonel James H. Doolittle on April 18, 1942, gave Americans a much needed morale boost. It was a natural for the screen. Doolittle and his men were to launch sixteen B-25 bombers from the aircraft carrier *Hornet*. Their objective was to score a surprise attack on the Japanese mainland and then escape to Chinese airfields. Unfortunately, the *Hornet* was sighted by the Japanese, and the Doolittle Raiders were forced to leave ahead of schedule. Though able to complete their mission, they ran out of fuel before reaching the safety of Chinese-controlled territory. Most of the planes crash landed in Japanese-controlled territory in China, and eight of the fliers were captured, tried for war crimes, and found guilty. The sentences of five of the eight were reduced to life in prison; the remaining three were executed on October 10, 1942. The American public was not informed of the executions until April 23, 1943, when President Roosevelt denounced the Japanese act as "inhuman and depraved."[28]

The Doolittle raid had all the elements necessary for a dramatic war picture. Captain Ted Lawson, one of the pilots who escaped, returned to America and wrote a best-selling account of his role. MGM snapped up movie rights to the book and assigned veteran screenwriter Dalton Trumbo to adapt the book to the screen. The result was *Thirty Seconds Over Tokyo*, directed by Mervyn Leroy and starring Spencer Tracy as Doolittle, Van Johnson as Lawson, and Phyllis Baxter as Lawson's wife. OWI saw the proposed script in November 1943 and was pleased that Trumbo hit so many of its suggested themes. Training and teamwork of American combat men were stressed. The film follows the real life situation closely with relatively few Hollywood dramatics. The Chinese ally was portrayed in a positive manner. By implication Japan was a difficult but not invincible enemy.[29]

The film centers on Lawson and his crew. After a successful raid on Tokyo, they run out of fuel and crash land in Japanese-occupied China, where Chinese resistance leaders rescue them. Lawson, who loses his legs from injuries sustained in the crash landing, lives to be reunited with his wife in Washington. Doolittle, who visits a depressed Lawson, remarks: "It would be some kind of deal for our kids if we could make sure this was the last war."

OWI was naturally concerned that *Thirty Seconds Over Tokyo* place the Chinese in the right context. Trumbo did. The film is littered with *Good Earth*-style smiling peasants who gladly risk their lives for the American crew. The competent Chinese doctors who perform the operation speak impeccable English. With understatement the image is clear—China is fighting fascist aggression in alliance with America. As he is about to leave, Lawson tells his hosts that America and China can fight side by side because "you're our kind of people." Indeed they were. OWI believed that the film showed "genuine cooperation and friendship" between the two allies and recommended the film "for special distribution in liberated areas."[30]

While OWI made no special note of it, *Thirty Seconds Over Tokyo* was remarkably free of racial slurs directed against the Japanese. Several good chances for rousing anti-Japanese speeches are passed over. At one point Lawson muses about the upcoming mission. He concedes he does not like the Japanese; but on the other hand, he does not hate them either. This was a rare confession by an American fighting man in films dealing with the Japanese. While OWI wanted this type of presentation, the real credit must go to Dalton Trumbo. He deplored racism in American films and kept *Thirty Seconds Over Tokyo* free of the usual "hate the Japs" material that dominated American war films.

The Purple Heart, released in 1944, also dealt with fliers downed in China after a raid on Japan. In this Darryl Zanuck production the fliers were not rescued by Chinese allies, but rather were captured by Chinese "puppets" who turned them over to the Japanese. *The Purple Heart* was the first Hollywood film to deal directly with the treatment of America POW's by the Japanese. The subject matter was explosive. The War Department had refused to approve any film dealing with the Japanese treatment of POW's after the Doolittle raid for fear that such movies would provoke reprisals. That ban was lifted in

1943 after the publication by the War Department of Japanese atrocities in the Philippines.

The film was directed by Lewis Milestone, fresh from *The North Star*. The film starred Dana Andrews as Captain Harvey Ross, Richard Conte as Lieutenant Angelo Canelli, Kevin O'Shea as Sergeant Jan Skvoznik, Farley Granger as Sergeant Howard Clinton, and Sam Levene as Lieutenant Wayne Greenbaum. The universal platoon was well represented in *The Purple Heart*. The main Japanese character, General Ito Mitsubi, was taken by the omnipresent Richard Loo. Playing on American fears that no Japanese was to be trusted, the film reveals that Mitsubi worked for some time on a fishing boat in Santa Barbara, where he charted the waters off the California coast.

The script was written by Zanuck and a group of staff writers at the studio. As this was the first film to treat the execution of American POW's, Zanuck realized that false drama and bravado were unnecessary. He set the tone for the film in a story conference with his staff in June 1943 when he stressed that the film "should be almost documentary in its honesty.... We don't want any business such as fliers chalking up the names of the victims, etc. No mock heroics." Zanuck demanded that the "woman spy stuff" be removed from an early draft and instructed the team of writers to be straightforward in their approach. Ironically, racism encouraged the ostensible understatement; he thought reality was dramatic enough because "everyone knows Japs are fanatics."[31]

The film opens as a prologue scrolls down the screen: "Out of the dark mists of the Orient have come no details of the actual fate of the heroic American aviators forced to earth in the bombing of Tokyo. Perhaps those details will never be known. The Japanese Government, in mingled hate and fear, announced only that some were executed. This picture, therefore, is the author's conception of what may well have happened, based on unofficial reports." The screen dissolves to a courtroom in Tokyo, dominated by a huge Japanese flag. Flashbacks inform the audience that the men crash-landed in China and were lured into the house of Yuen Chiu Ling. He promised the men protection, but it turned out that he was a Japanese puppet governor of Kunlin Province. Ling is at the trial with his son Moy Ling to testify against the fliers. The guilty verdict has already been determined. The purpose of the trial is to force a public confession from the men that their operation was carrier-based, not land-based. The Japanese high command fears the public will panic if the bombing raids originated on land—the assumption being that the Americans could then bomb Japan at will.

The trial begins in great secrecy. The judge is Toyama, head of the "dreaded Black Dragon Society." Counsel for the Americans is a Princeton-educated lawyer who refuses to take any action in defense of the men. The men refuse to tell the Japanese where they came from. A frustrated General Mitsubi resorts to terror and torture. Two of the men are driven mad, one returns with both hands amputated, others have limbs broken. Still they refuse to break. The Japanese prepare to show films of the destruction caused by the raid. As the lights are lowered a shot rings out. When the lights are turned on a horrified Japanese judge looks at Moy Ling, who has killed his father. He proudly tells the incredulous judge that his father had brought shame on the family by collaborating with the enemy and so he killed him. Moy Ling is arrested.

The Americans' refusal to reveal their point of origin constitutes a small victory over General Mitsubi. Having "lost face" the general has no choice—he commits suicide in the courtroom. The men spurn an offer of their lives in return for testimony. Captain Ross tells the court why: "It's true we Americans don't know very much about you Japanese, and never did—and now I realize you know even less about us. You can kill us—all of us, or part of us. But if you think that's going to put the fear of God into the United States of America and stop them from sending other fliers to bomb you, you're wrong—dead wrong. They'll blacken your skies and burn your cities to the ground and make you get down on your knees and beg for mercy. This is your war—you wanted it—you asked for it. And now you're going to get it—and it won't be finished until your dirty little empire is wiped off the face of the earth!"

When OWI read the script they were delighted by its portrayal of the captured American fliers and the presentation of Japanese fascism. One issue bothered the propagandists: the Chinese quisling was resented by the Chinese consul in Los Angeles. Ulric Bell asked Owen Lattimore, director of Pacific Operations for OWI in San Francisco, for his opinion. Bell and Lattimore thought the son, "who is representative of the new China, is a hero," and more than balanced out the Chinese traitor. The agency urged the studio to make it clear that the father is a traitor to the New China and that his son is not only a hero, "but more specifically a representative of the young Chinese who are fighting for freedom."[32]

In the revised script Moy Ling's role is accordingly strengthened. After killing his father Moy tells the judge: "This, at least excellency, is the truth . . . [turning to the fliers]. I am a soldier of China. My father has answered to his Honorable ancestors for your betrayal." But while OWI was happy with the speech, Breen objected strenuously to the "murder of revenge" committed by Moy Ling. Breen's code said all murderers must be punished, so the script was changed to have the Japanese arrest Moy Ling for murder.[33]

William Cunningham, the OWI representative who had been involved with the film from its inception, reviewed the final print. He was pleased that the role of the young Chinese patriot had been improved to "show his comradeship with the American flyers." He was especially pleased with the final scene where the men march off to their execution wearing broad smiles, which Cunningham believed would prove to world-wide audiences that "human beings can subordinate their own interests and their lives to the cause of freedom." *The Purple Heart* was "highly recommended for special distribution in liberated areas."[34]

In its final feature review OWI made no reference to the fact that all Japanese were shown as brutal and sadistic. The courtroom trial offered possibilities for at least one Japanese, perhaps the lawyer assigned to "defend" the fliers, to voice protest over the treatment of the men. This could have made the point that not all Japanese were evil. In films about Germany a character in situations like *The Purple Heart* was used to establish that not all Germans were fascists. Manny Farber titled his review "Hate for Sale." "I dislike it thoroughly," he wrote. Rather than attempting to enlighten the audience on the nature of the Japanese character, the film offered " . . . endless . . . Japanese brutality, the effect of which is to narrow and solidify hatred of a group of people into hatred of a whole people."[35]

When OWI gathered some viewer responses to *The Purple Heart* Farber's point was proven all too clearly. "I felt like piercing the eyes of the Japanese," said one viewer. Another was more specific: "Whoever has seen this film of torture of men by apes dressed as generals and admirals with decoration down to their knees, needs for psychological release a film showing these brave aviators throwing heavy caliber bombs on the capital of these inhuman creatures."[36] This was not the kind of audience education OWI hoped the movies would provide. *The Purple Heart* was only a step removed from *The Beast of the East* (1942), which was not far removed from the World War I production, *The Kaiser—The Beast of Berlin*. The agency had tried to soften racial propaganda in 1942. But by 1944 the emotional impact of the Japanese treatment of American POWs was being felt. The popular conception of the Japanese as inhuman beasts was too ingrained to counter, and too convenient a propaganda tool to abandon.

The only film that attempted, however unsuccessfully, to take up OWI's early challenge to examine the nature of the enemy, and the impetus behind what it indiscriminately called fascism, was RKO's *Behind the Rising Sun* (1943). This was the only major wartime picture set in Japan that attempted to portray the growth of Japanese militarism in the 1930s. The film was directed by Edward Dmytryk, who wanted "to prove that the Japanese government was bad because it was in the hands of the military," not because it was Japanese. The military, he believed, kept itself in power through war, and war took perfectly good young men and "hardened them to the point where there was no longer room in their minds for liberalism, consideration of the people, or any of the ideas which make possible a free government of the people." In long conversations with Nelson Poynter he became convinced that films which painted all members of a race as barbarians did little to explain the Japanese. *Behind the Rising Sun* was a rare film in that it at least started with the premise that the Japanese were like other humans, but distorted by militarism.[37]

A young Japanese, Taro Seki (Tom Neal), returns to Japan in 1936 full of idealistic dreams of using his engineering degree from Cornell University to help modernize Japan. He hopes to join an American engineering firm in Japan run by Clancy

O'Hara (Don Douglas), an American who is an old friend of the Seki family. But he discovers Japan has changed drastically in four years. His father, Ryo Seki (J. Carrol Naish), a wealthy Japanese publisher, urges his son to join the Army because he fears that otherwise Taro will be eliminated like the other liberals in Japan. He shows Taro a map of the world and predicts that Japan is destined to become the new leader. There was a time when we said Asia for the Asiatics, but now the time will come "when we will see who is master and who is slave," he says.

The Americanized Taro scoffs at his father's prophecy. He dresses like a college kid of the 1930s and speaks perfect English including American slang. He no longer observes Japanese customs, forgetting to bow to his father. His grandmother witnesses his odd behavior and begins to scream that Taro has turned into an American and forgotten that in Japan the family is everything. Taro wants to find his own job and not rely on his father. He is imbued with ideas of democracy and liberalism and wants to use his new degree to build, not destroy.

Taro takes a position with O'Hara's firm and falls in with Japan's international community. Sara Brayton (Gloria Holden) is an American journalist and O'Hara's girl friend. Lefty O'Doyle (Robert Ryan) is an American manager for a Japanese baseball team. The last member of the group is Boris Malakoff (George Givot), a gregarious Russian who is both a journalist and a spy. Under the influence of his American education and his foreign friends, Taro's rejection of his Japanese tradition continues. He falls in love with a beautiful young Japanese girl, Tama (Margo), who works for O'Hara as a secretary. Taro's family feels disgraced because Tama comes from a poor peasant family. Ryo Seki refuses to accept Tama and will not bless the coming marriage.

The war intrudes. Japan attacks China in an "undeclared war." Taro is drafted, and Sara rushes off to China to cover the war for her newspaper. Taro's first experiences in the war shock him. When he sees Japanese troops giving opium to the Chinese he protests to his superiors. But a fellow officer tells him to forget it—after all opium is cheaper than bullets and the Chinese people are not human beings anyway. Sara, who is in the same area as Taro, witnesses several Japanese acts of brutality, and begs Taro to do something to stop the killing and looting. But Taro's transformation has begun. He is cold toward Sara and tells her nothing can be done. The Chinese must be defeated. As they are talking the camera swings to Japanese troops who find a small baby in a second story apartment. The troops toss the baby out the window to troops below, who catch the baby on the end of a bayonet. (This action was not shown on the screen but was clearly implied by the action of the troops). The scene ends as the camera pans to a large poster: PROCLAMATION: ALL CHINESE WOMEN WILL WELCOME JAPANESE SOLDIERS INTO THEIR HOMES. Taro Seki is no longer a caring human being but a brutal killer and rapist. Japanese militarism has taken its toll.

Meanwhile his father has been named Japanese Minister of Propaganda. O'Hara, who is still friendly with Ryo Seki, arranges a big party to celebrate this appointment. Lefty, Sara, Boris, and Tama are all present. Tama has won over the elder Seki, who now approves of the marriage. Taro, who is now a major, is also present. Sara suggests to him that perhaps as entertainment he could bayonet a baby or two. Taro is insulted and begins to fight with O'Hara. Seki is shocked at his son's behavior. He tells O'Hara that he no longer believes Japan is on the right path and points to his son as an example of what the new Japan really stands for. The Japanese doctrine of racial superiority has made Taro into "nothing more than a savage." Ryo Seki warns O'Hara to leave Japan because war with America is coming.

O'Hara ignores Seki's warnings and is trapped in Japan by the attack on Pearl Harbor. O'Hara, Lefty, Sara, and Tama are arrested as spies and tortured, but the Japanese learn nothing. Taro returns to Tokyo to testify against them. They are found guilty and sentenced to death. They face execution, but the Doolittle raid hits Tokyo and in the confusion the prisoners escape. They are aided by Seki, who has arranged for them to escape Japan aboard a Portuguese steamer. Tama refuses to leave. She is determined to stay and work for a better Japan.

In a dramatic finale, Seki, who learns that his son has been killed in battle, commits a ritual suicide. He understands he has made a terrible mistake by supporting Japan's insane quest for world conquest. He explains: "I do not die for the Emperor, a little man on a white horse. I die for the hope that the people of Japan can redeem themselves before the civilized world. But if that is not to be—then the Japan I know must die with me for one can't build honor on dishonor. To whatever gods that are left in the world, destroy us as we have destroyed others. Destroy us before it is too late."

Behind the Rising Sun is an unusual movie. In Ryo Seki, and especially Tama, we see highly unusual characters—individuals who recognize Japan's methods and goals are wrong. Tama, however small her role in the film, announces that she will stay in Japan and fight for a better future. Yet the ending is at best ambiguous. Emmet Lavery, who did the screenplay, maintained that, in keeping with Dmytryk's goal, the conclusion was "a dramatic statement on the necessity for better understanding between the people of Japan and the people of America in a postwar world." He disagreed with critics at RKO who thought the picture called for the slaughter of the Japanese "to the last man, woman and child." Lavery's contention made sense if one emphasized the first part of Seki's farewell speech and believed, as the screenwriter apparently did, that the Japanese could redeem themselves if they were freed of the militarists. But if one thought, as most viewers probably did after the wartime barrage of racial propaganda, that the Japanese were incapable of national regeneration, Seki's concluding words were a powerful confirmation of the urge for extermination.[38]

When OWI saw the script they were disappointed. Several months of conferences with RKO resulted in dialogue being added stressing that it was the militarists who brought fascism to Japan. OWI maintained that the film did not make it clear that the racial theories of Japan were fascist theories. OWI's point confused the studio, which pointed out that Ryo Seki clearly condemned Japan's racial policies. But OWI wanted him to actually state in clear terms that Japan was a fascist state.[39]

The agency was more on target when it complained that Taro's transition from a young idealist to a sadistic killer happened without explanation. The movie seemed to confirm the popular belief that all Japanese were "unpredictable and that they will inevitably 'revert to type'—revert to the hysterical anti-Western ideology promulgated by the Japanese ruler caste." But Dmytryk held to his belief that the transformation had been explained through visual development and that no changes were necessary. One has to side with OWI on this point. The film offers no rationale, visual or otherwise, for Taro's sudden change. He is a Japanese Dr. Jekyll and Mr. Hyde—one moment a caring human being, the next a sadistic monster. OWI flatly refused an export license, calling the film "too openly propagandistic."[40]

Reviews were mixed, as usual. *Time* dismissed the film as "an 88 minute jag of ferocious anti-Japanese propaganda" with its "grueling patchwork of cinematrocities ... likely to make most cinemaddicts as mad at the film as at the Japanese." *Commonweal* praised the film for at least attempting to portray "some of its Japanese characters as sincere people not under the spell of the brutal war lords," but thought Seki's suicide undermined the point that could have been made. By the end of the film the audience had begun to feel sympathetic toward Seki. All of that was lost when the character reverted to stereotypical Japanese actions.[41]

In the final analysis the film failed to advance Dmytryk's thesis. *Behind the Rising Sun* did present two sympathetic characters. Ryo Seki is practically the only character in a war movie that could qualify as a "good Japanese." While he had supported the militarists, the experience of his son showed him the evils of militarism. The film would have countered racial images more effectively had the film ended with Ryo Seki determined to work for a new Japan. Instead, the only major Japanese character in a war movie to come to such a conclusion commits suicide. Tama, a poor peasant girl accused of treason, lives, but what chance does she have to change Japan? Yet while Dmytryk came up short he at least tried to penetrate the pervasive racial imagery and examine Japanese militarism. Sadly his ending, with its own tinges of Western stereotypes of Japanese behavior, compromised a notable and lonely effort.

Blood on the Sun, a United Artists release of 1945, purported to explain the origins of Japanese aggression by treating the Tanaka Memorial as Tokyo's master plan for world domination. The memorial, a document supposedly presented to the emperor in 1927 by Prime Minister and former War Minister Baron Tanaka, was actually discovered and published in China, and is considered by most scholars to be an artful forgery.[42] But that knowledge would not have deterred the studio. The memorial did, after all, sketch out a plan for Japanese domination first of China, then the Pacific, then the world. Screenwriter Lester Cole wove an astonishingly silly plot around its origins. Most of the movie is a tale of intrigue between a cocky, pugnacious newspaper reporter (played by James Cagney) and Japanese militarists for possession of the document. Cole includes one good Japanese, "the old prince," who indicates his lonely opposition to the memorial. His stand seems merely eccentric; the implication is that Japan embraced the blueprint for conquest wholeheartedly.

Betrayal From the East, an RKO release (1944), was similar fare. It featured an introduction by journalist Drew Pearson, who stated the film was a true story. The "true story" documented how all Japanese-Americans were spies for the Emperor. In this case Richard Loo repeats his role as a Japanese spy—this time masquerading as a language student from Stanford University. The War Relocation Authority protested the film, as they had *Little Tokyo, USA.* OWI's William Cunningham thought the film unfortunate but not worth a long fight with the studio and contented himself with getting the censor to deny it an export license.[43]

A clear trend emerged in OWI's reaction to movies dealing with the Japanese. It still believed the enemy should be portrayed in terms of fascism rather than racism, but had failed to convince Hollywood that the Japanese could be shown as something more than a "buck-toothed little Jap." Beginning with *Little Tokyo, USA* and *Air Force,* OWI had urged the industry to portray the Japanese government and military as fascist. But in order to do that films needed to develop some characters who were "anti-fascist." A resistance movement, an Army officer who might be appalled by gratuitous brutality, a POW who showed remorse, or a double-agent working for peace—any of these could have been the subjects for a film or an individual in a film. Instead, each film reinforced the theme of the Japanese as sub-human. Only in the flawed *Behind the Rising Sun* do the Japanese emerge as individuals. By 1944 OWI had all but given up. Finding it impossible to change the image of the Japanese, the agency was content to restrict the films to American audiences.

Hollywood's portrayal of the Japanese perpetuated a racist view of America's Asian enemies stretching back to the Philippine insurgency of the turn-of-the-century and forward to Vietnam. In this respect the film industry was no worse than other American media. But the movies, despite OWI's efforts, for the most part reinforced an interpretation of Japan that gave the Pacific war its particular savagery. So long as American media—and indeed many policy makers—continued to think of Asian enemies in racial terms, the American approach to Asian enemies would retain a particular and tragic virulence.

X.

Nazis, Good Germans, and G.I.'s

*In the end we will win. I hope we can rejoice in our victory, but humbly....
As for those beneath the wooden crosses we can only murmur, thanks,
pal, thanks.*

—Burgess Meredith as Ernie
Pyle in *The Story of
G. I. Joe*

Midway through *The Moon Is Down*, a Twentieth Century-Fox release of 1943, we encounter a remarkable scene. A Norwegian
coal-mining town has been under German occupation for four
months, and the nerves of a young German lieutenant, Tonder,
are beginning to fray. Desperate for people to talk to, he visits
a local bar, where he tries to engage a farmer in conversation
by sharing his experiences growing up on a farm in Germany.
The Norwegian meets every question with a stony one-word response and leaves the bar the moment he can. Growing progressively more agitated, Tonder fears the bartender has poisoned his beer and forces him to taste it first. Nothing is wrong
with the drink. Back at officers quarters, the lieutenant recounts
the hilarious dream he had last night—that Hitler is crazy! He
talks almost hysterically of flies conquering the fly paper. He
pleads: If the war were going badly, they would tell us, wouldn't
they? The ramrod straight captain answers by slapping the lieutenant to his senses.

278

Tonder bolts from his quarters and crunches down the snowy street to see a pretty young widow, Molly Morden, who sits reading the Bible by a dim light and a dying fire. Her husband, Alex, was shot by the German army recently for accidentally killing an officer. Tonder begs her to let him in, and she at last relents. "Can't we forget the war?" he says. "Can't we talk together like people? I'm only a man, not a conquering man." She tells him the Germans killed her husband. He says he is sorry. She softens a bit. "I've seen no kindness in a woman's eyes in so long," he says. They laugh. He reads a poem he says he has written for her, and then confesses that it is Heine's. He offers her favors, which she refuses. She tries to brush him off; you just want love tonight, she says. "I am lonely," he replies. "I only know that this minute I love you." She finally relents. She goes to her bedroom, takes a pair of shears from her sewing basket, hides them under her pillow, and softly calls him to her bed and his death. Fadeout.

The Moon Is Down is half a world away from the movies about Japan, not only geographically but also attitudinally. There are no scenes like this in wartime movies about the Japanese. In just these brief scenes we come to know the lieutenant as a flesh-and-blood character; no cold-blooded killer, he can't even stand being shunned by the locals in the bar. The German war machine has not corrupted him, and he doubts the Third Reich's vaunted invincibility. Virtually no Japanese has been shown to us in so sympathetic a fashion. Compare the younger Seki, who, despite the advantages of an American college education, reverted to racially based savagery. Seki knows only the power of a bayonet; the cultured German knows and exploits the power of Heine. Indeed, but for the uniform and the phony accent, he might be Rusty Marsh from Heartfield, Iowa.

The lieutenant is the softest of the German officers. The others are brutal, to be sure. Although they abide by the forms of legal procedure in holding a trial for Alex, the proceedings are cynical, the verdict fore-ordained. Colonel Lanser, played by Sir Cedric Hardwicke, is prepared to shoot five—fifty—five hundred men if necessary "to show who's master." But he knows the folly of occupying a country against the people's wishes, and he tries through favors to selected townspeople and appeals to the mayor to secure their cooperation instead of resorting to force. Hollywood, while showing instances of Nazi brutality, still presents a balanced picture of the German occupation of Norway. Contrast this with the manner in which it usually portrayed a Japanese occupation, that of China for example. The Japanese occupation forces turn at once to opium to keep the population quiet, and bayonet babies for sport. German brutality is real but rational; it serves the larger goal of conquest. The Japanese actions are little more than a mindless lapse into barbarism.

Lanser's tactics do not work: The Norwegian resistance intensifies. *The Moon Is Down* shows that, although the government had been delivered into the hands of the Nazis by Vidkum Quisling, whose name became an instant synonym for traitor, the people do not surrender. Molly exacts revenge for the killing of her husband. The townspeople sabotage the crucial coal mine, halting production for two months. They signal British RAF planes where to drop weapons, although it means one of the signal bearers, a grandmother, will be killed. Even mass executions cannot break the people's indomitable spirit.

Movies such as *The Moon Is Down* played a vital role for the Office of War Information's Bureau of Motion Pictures, for they explained the nature of the German enemy and also told film audiences that, though countries might be occupied, the people still were willing to fight and die for democracy. BMP worked closely with the studio in the production of the Norwegian story because of its controversial origins. Twentieth Century-Fox had paid John Steinbeck $300,000 for the rights to his enormously popular novel and play of the same name. But Steinbeck's original had gone even further in showing the human side of the German army. Colonel Lanser, in particular, had struck some critics as rather unmilitary for a Junker. Under pressure from OWI, screenwriter Nunnally Johnson (who had adapted *The Grapes of Wrath* for the screen) purged much of Lanser's defeatism. The propagandists also worried that Johnson's screenplay advanced the idea that "if ten particular German heads were lopped off, they'd be destroyed." This sounded too much like the notion that once you got rid of Hitler and his immediate circle, the Germans could be brought back into the fold of civilization. The bureau insisted the corruption went deeper, necessitating unconditional surrender. The studio's changes pleased OWI Overseas Branch officer Ulric Bell. Viewing the release print in February 1943, he praised the movie as "a bang-up presentation of several OWI themes." Reviewers for the most part agreed, and the film skirted the controversies of Steinbeck's original novel.[1]

Pictures dealing with the German occupation of Europe, buttressed by a few essays on life inside Germany, became important vehicles for depicting the nature of the German enemy. Combat pictures, which had been a natural for the Japanese phase of the war, were relatively rare. After all, American troops did not engage the Germans until a year after Pearl Harbor, and since an "A" picture could take a year or more to produce, battle films about the European war came late in the conflict. By the last year of the war, the public's obvious desire for escapist movies undercut interest in German battle movies. Thus films about the European war were distinct from those about the Pacific theater in several respects: in their choice of subject matter, the conclusions they drew about the enemy, American soldiers' experience of war, and their intimations of the world that beckoned after victory.

Hollywood's first inclination was to graft the Nazi threat onto mystery and cowboy pictures. For the most part they were quickly produced "B" features, and epitomized the spy hokum that bedeviled OWI's early efforts in the movie capital. In *Enemy Agents Meet Ellery Queen* (1942), Nazi spies hunt a Dutch diamond. Why this diamond will help win the war is unclear, but Queen naturally foils their plans. The picture ends with marines beating up the spies. In a plot worthy of postwar Bulwinkle satires, *Yukon Patrol* (1942) showed the Northwest Mounties thwarting Nazi efforts to obtain "compound X," a vital ingredient for their new secret weapon. The Nazis really got around. They penetrated the American West in *Phantom Plainsman,* but the cowboys outshot them and checked their sinister plot to buy up noble American steeds for the Third Reich. And if American troops could not rout the German army, U.S. reporters could at least land a punch for democracy. In *Berlin Correspondent* a typically brash newspaper reporter easily outwits the Gestapo. Early in the war the Germans could even be the butt of comedies, such as *To Be or Not to Be* and *The Devil with Hitler.*[2]

The Japanese, however, were evidently too repulsive to laugh at. There were no comparable pictures about the empire of the

Rising Sun, unless one counted the unintentionally farcical plots of Hollywood's early Japanese pictures. The Germans really were different from the Japanese, the movies seemed to say. In November 1942 the OWI's Bureau of Intelligence analysed portrayals of the enemy on the screen, and uncovered distinct differences in the way Hollywood treated the two Axis powers. German soldiers were generally shown as being efficient and obedient, but rarely "cruel and barbarous" like the Japanese. German officers were usually "gentlemen with whom it would be possible to treat as an equal;" by contrast the Japanese "can only be killed." Many Germans were disaffected from Nazism; in turn, qualities of fanaticism and arrogance were ascribed and restricted to Gestapo or SS officials. In short, there were Nazis, and there were also good Germans.[3]

The movies reflected similar patterns in American opinion. Many Americans found it hard to believe the worst about the Nazis—until the worst turned out to be the truth. They also doubted that Hitler really enjoyed popular support. An OWI survey in August 1942 revealed that 39 percent of respondents did not believe the German people were loyal to their government. Fifty-five percent of those polled favored postwar re-education for the German people, but nothing stronger. On the other hand, 46 percent favored the death penalty for Hitler and his lieutenants. As a group the Germans were not, therefore, cruel or sadistic. They were a people temporarily ruled by a brutal, aggressive regime. These distinctions in attitude were not extended to the Japanese.[4]

Germans were—well, more like Americans. They were European and many Americans had German ancestors. Their forms of religion, culture, and social organization were recognizable. Americans listened to Beethoven and Brahms as performed by the NBC Symphony every Sunday afternoon, they respected Goethe, Schiller, and Thomas Mann, and they lauded German science. But who in 1941 read a Japanese book, or went to a Japanese play, or contemplated a Japanese garden? If Germans were ruled by a maniacal or slightly comic dictator—Americans had not yet entirely decided how to think about Hitler—they also had a democratic past, however truncated it may have been. To most Americans the Japanese government represented an unrelieved militarism. Americans found Germany's

class system even more troubling than Britain's, for the bur-
nished helmets and brushcuts of the Kaiser and the Junkers were
still a vivid memory in many minds. But if Americans remained
suspicious of Prussian militarism and feared that it now appeared in the new guise of Nazism, they also admired the German sense of discipline and organization. Asked to choose the
words they most associated with Germans, Americans picked
two—"hard working," a highly positive trait, and "warlike," a
negative term but one uttered not without an undercurrent of
admiration. On the other hand the words associated with Japan—treacherous, sly, and cruel—were unambiguously condemnatory.[5]

Even the Nazi doctrine that in retrospect became the most
odious—anti-Semitism—did not seem to be an unalloyed evil
early in the war. A 1942 public opinion poll indicated that 40
percent of Americans believed Jews had too much power in the
United States. Eighteen percent agreed with Hitler's measures
against the Jews, to the extent that those measures were known
at that time. However perverted the Nazi idea of Aryan superiority, large numbers of Americans shared a measure of Anglo-
Saxon racism, and in fact anti-Semitism in the U.S. grew
perceptibly worse during the war. With shared prejudices it
somehow seemed easier to regard Germany as a temporary enemy, its people redeemable once the Nazis were overthrown.
The Germans were not, as the Japanese became, the Other.[6]

OWI thought Hollywood's tremendous resources were well
suited to bring home the nature of Nazi society. *Phantom Plainsman* and its ilk only obstructed the ideological understanding
the agency sought. The propaganda manual's ideas on the nature of the enemy applied to Germany even more pertinently
than they did to Japan. The Wehrmacht was formidable but
beatable. The exploitation of racial, religious, and class differences were well-honed Nazi tactics. By showing the regimenta-
tion of life in the Fatherland and the oppression in occupied
countries, the cinema could clarify the origins and corrosive
power of fascism. If the public understood Nazism they would
grasp the necessity of unconditional surrender. Although the
agency reiterated that the enemy was the German ruling elite,
not the people, it feared the public would focus too narrowly
on Hitler and his immediate helpmates as the sole problem.

OWI warned: "The German militarists will destroy Hitler, Goebbels, Goering, Ley, Ribbentrop, Himmler, and a few others;— then they will seek a negotiated peace." Unconditional surrender was imperative so that a thorough cleansing could be carried forth. "Hitler and Nazism are nothing but Prussian militarism in a new garb," the manual warned. OWI's understanding of the German reality was cloudy. Nazism was a qualitative step beyond innate Prussianism, and by equating the two OWI blurred that essential distinction. OWI's interpretation also tended to contradict its point that World War II was not just a bigger World War I. Nonetheless, the propagandists were groping, however fitfully, for ways to convey a monstrousness that most Americans still found impossible to fully countenance.[7]

One of the war's most powerful cinematic treatments of fascism was Lillian Hellman's *Watch on the Rhine*. Noting the play's successful run on Broadway in 1941, Warner Brothers, the leader in producing antifascist movies before the war, snapped up the film rights. Hellman's lover Dashiell Hammett was hired to do the screenplay while she hovered close by his typewriter and the sound stages. Set in Washington, D.C., in 1940, the picture traced the awakening of an elite American family to the reality of fascism.[8]

Fanny Farrelly (Lucile Watson) and her son, David (Donald Woods), eagerly await the arrival of Sara Farrelly Müller (Bette Davis), who has been living in Germany with her husband Kurt (Paul Lukas), and their three children. When the Müllers arrive in Washington they discover that the Farrellys have other house guests. Teck De Brancovis (George Coulouris) is a displaced Roumanian diplomat who longs to return to his native country. Broke and unemployed, he is anxious to sell his services to the Nazis. Marthe De Brancovis, his wife, is an old family friend of the Farrellys. A Washington socialite, she married into European nobility. But the marriage has gone sour, and Marthe is upset by Teck's pandering to the Nazis. She is also in love with David Farrelly and is determined not to return to Nazi-controlled Europe.

The Farrellys know very little about how Kurt and Sara have been living. They are shocked at their obvious poverty, and Kurt is forced to tell Mrs. Farrelly that he no longer works as an engineer but is an anti-fascist. With some humor he adds it is not a position that pays well. Why, we are all anti-fascist, she says. Yes, Sara rejoins, "but Kurt *works* at it." The Farrellys learn that Kurt is a leader of the resistance movement in Germany, where he is a hunted man. He intends to return to Germany with $20,000 he has raised for his organization.

Teck also discovers Kurt's secret. Teck regularly plays poker at the German Embassy, where the men around the card table provide a diverse image of Nazi Germany. Blecher is the Gestapo agent, an uneducated and "completely savage" man feared by everyone at the table. In sharp contrast is Philip von Ramme, a tall blond army officer from the nobility. He despises Blecher and calls him a butcher, but as a loyal German officer he does his duty for the state. The other poker players are parasites. Dr. Lauber is a German-American who publishes a pro-Nazi newspaper strictly for profit. He and Blecher hate each other but work together out of a convenience. Chandler, an American businessman, sells oil to the Nazis.

Teck's passport is Kurt, whom he is ready to betray to the Germans. Kurt must return to Germany immediately to try to bribe officials to release a newly imprisoned resistance leader. This news surprises David Farrelly, playing the naive American, who accepted the myth of Nazi superiority. Sara leaps in: "What wonderful work Fascists have done in convincing people they are men from legends. . . . We don't like to remember, do we, that they came in on the shoulders of some of the most powerful men in the world? . . . That makes us feel guilty and so we prefer to believe that they're mysterious men from the planets. Well, they aren't. They're smart and slick and cruel." Kurt interrupts: "Yes, but given men who know what they fight for, and will fight hard. . . . "

Kurt tells the Farrellys what he has been doing—fighting in Spain, bribing Nazi officials, raiding Gestapo headquarters, moving from one country to the next in search of safety and funds to continue the fight. He is always one step ahead of capture; Sara and the children live in constant danger. Sara supports him completely. The Farrellys are speechless.

Teck returns from the German Embassy, and tells Kurt that if he tells the Germans what he knows, Kurt will be picked up and killed before he can reach his destination. Kurt explodes: "You are wrong. I would get back. There are many men they would like besides me. I would be allowed to walk directly to them until they had all the names and all the addresses. Roumanians would pick me up before hand. . . . The Germans would not." Kurt is proud of being a German; his battle is with fascism and people like Teck.

Teck offers Kurt a deal—his silence for one month at a price of $10,000. Kurt refuses to give him a cent, but the Farrellys agree to Teck's terms. When the Farrellys leave the room to get the money, Kurt knocks Teck down, drags him onto the back lawn and kills him. Kurt acts sadly and reluctantly but this is his only choice. He explains to the Farrellys and to his children that his action was wrong. All killing is wrong, but Teck had given him no choice. The Farrellys agree to help Kurt escape and to help cover up the murder. They have been given a lesson on the nature of fascism. Fanny says: "Well, we've been shaken out of the magnolias."

The final scene takes place between Sara and her oldest son, Joshua. It has been months since Kurt departed for Germany. They have heard nothing from him. Joshua is preparing to return to Germany to take up his father's fight. At first the distraught Sara refuses to allow Joshua to go. But he quietly tells her that in five months he will have a birthday and will be a man. If no word has been heard from Kurt, he will go to continue the fight against fascism. Sara says simply: "When the time comes—when it comes I will do my best."

Watch on the Rhine was in production before OWI was officially in business, and the agency first saw it in October 1942. BMP reviewers saw great merit in the film's stress on Spain as the first arena in the battle between fascism and democracy. OWI also supported the portrayal of the enemy's multiple faces. The people's resistance to fascism also appealed to OWI. But the propagandists saw *Watch on the Rhine* as "two years out of date." America no longer needed to be awakened to the dangers of fascism, which OWI thought was the main point of the film. Nor did the agency like the underlying message of an "apathetic, complacent America." The Farrelly's wealth and "retinue of obsequious colored servants" troubled OWI, which wanted America to be seen as a land of common people who recognized, like Kurt, the need to resist fascism. The Farrellys' ignorance of events in Europe was also troubling.[9]

OWI's objections were hard to credit. The movie's anti-isolationist message was outdated, to be sure, by the time it reached the screen. But *Watch on the Rhine* still gave a chilling view of how fascism ruined lives; the movie blessed the nobility of resistance, and warned that it could happen here. Lukas, a Hungarian-born anti-fascist, acted his convictions and was rewarded with an Oscar and the New York Film Critics Award for best actor of 1943. The *New Yorker* judged that the film had "as much timeliness" as most recent films "and more sense than most of them." In retrospect, too, the message of *Watch on the Rhine* remains powerful with "its high-minded insistence that all men must be free, or those who are must bear the moral responsibility for those who are not wherever in the world they may be." But historian Geoffrey Perrett warned: "Only the despised isolationists caught sight of the other side of this sharp and flaming sword." However, that troubling underside to the anti-fascist vision of the internationalists could not be accommodated, in wartime propaganda.[10]

The heroism of the resistance was a popular theme of Hollywood and OWI. It suffused Warner Brothers' *Casablanca* (1943). The movie was based on an unpublished play, *Everybody Goes to Rick's*, by Murray Burnett and Joan Alison. Julius and Philip Epstein adapted it for the screen, and Howard Koch provided additional dialogue. The studio gave the project only a fighting chance to be a decent picture; instead, it emerged as a modern film classic, perhaps the favorite picture of World War II.

The film opens as a narrator explains that war-torn Europe has created thousands of refugees fleeing Nazi terror. It is December, 1941, just before the Japanese attack on Pearl Harbor. From Paris to Marseilles the refugees work their way to Casablanca, where a fortunate few with money, influence, or luck obtain visas. Casablanca is under the control of collaborationist Vichy France. Corruption is the norm; the local police captain, Louis Renault (Claude Rains), routinely extracts money or sexual favors in exchange for a visa. In the first scene police stop a man and ask him for his papers. He tries to run away and is shot. The police are conducting a roundup of refugees and liberals because a German courier has been murdered and two letters of transit are missing. Major Strasser (Conrad Veidt), who has come to Casablanca determined to capture Victor Laszlo, head of the Czechoslovakian resistance movement, orders Renault not to give Laszlo a visa no matter how big a bribe he is offered.

In Casablanca everybody goes to Rick's Cafe Américain. Rick (Humphrey Bogart) is a cold, cynical expatriate who shuns politics. He sticks his head out for no one and no cause. But behind this rough exterior is a man who used to care. He fought the fascists in Ethiopia and Spain, and his employees represent his true political commitment. The bartender is Russian, the head waiter, Carl, is a former professor of mathematics and astronomy at the University of Leipzig, and his girlfriend is French. Sam the piano player (Dooley Wilson), a close friend, is a black American.

While everyone comes to Rick's, not everyone is welcome. When a pompous German collaborator demands entry into the club's gambling room he is turned away, though he insists he is the second leading banker in Amsterdam. "That wouldn't impress Rick," Carl says shaking his head. "The leading banker in Amsterdam is now the pastry chef in our kitchen." Rick not only used to care, he still cares.

As the film progresses the major characters come to Rick's cafe. Ugarte (Peter Lorre) admits that he killed the couriers and just before he is arrested by the police gives the letters of transit to Rick. Major Strasser questions Rick on his background—even though the Germans have a complete dossier on him. Strasser warns Rick not to help Laszlo escape but Rick is cool and noncommittal. He tells Strasser: "Your business is politics. Mine is running a saloon."

At this point Laszlo (Paul Henreid) enters the cafe with his wife Ilsa Lund (Ingrid Bergman). Love and politics now become intertwined. Ilsa and Rick had an affair in Paris. They were going to run away together before the Germans arrived. But Ilsa stood Rick up at the train station and Rick escaped to Casablanca by himself. Here is the real reason for Rick's cynicism— broken love, not lack of political commitment. Strasser meets Laszlo and asks him for an official interview the following day.

In Renault's office Strasser offers Laszlo an exit visa if he will give the names of the leaders of the underground movement in several cities. Laszlo: "Even in Berlin?" Yes, Strasser wants the names of all the leaders. Laszlo refuses. But this con-

versation establishes that in every country the Nazis have conquered, and even in Germany itself, resistance movements are
active. The Nazis cannot crush the people and are even powerless to arrest Laszlo in Casablanca. Strasser can pressure Renault but the police captain refuses to make an arrest without
cause. This was a bit farfetched, but consistent with the image
the movies projected of the Germans: they played by the rules.

The next evening a conflict erupts at Rick's between a
French officer and a German officer. The Frenchman yells at a
woman for going with a German. The men start to argue and
Rick breaks it up. As the Frenchman leaves he mutters: "Sale
boche, un jour nous aurons notre revanche!" (Dirty German,
some day we'll have our revenge!) Renault, who along with
Strasser has overheard the conversation simply shrugs: "My dear
Major, we are trying to cooperate with your government. But
we cannot regulate the feelings of our people."

The tension continues between the French and the Germans. Several German soldiers, drinking too much and nostalgic for the Fatherland, start singing "Watch on the Rhine."
Everyone else remains sullen and silent. Laszlo tells Sam to play
"La Marseillaise." Sam hesitates, then looks to Rick, who gives
him an almost imperceptible nod of approval. Slowly the entire
cafe begins to sing louder and louder until the Germans are
isolated and humiliated. The scene was one of the most powerful and memorable in World War II films. The Germans might
be conquerors but they could not crush the people's desire for
freedom.

In the end, of course, Rick gives the letters of transit to
Laszlo and Ilsa. (We learn by flashback that before having the
affair with Rick Ilsa had been told her husband had been killed
in a Nazi concentration camp. She left Rick when she found her
husband was alive.) Rick rediscovers commitment and pushes a
reluctant Ilsa on the plane with her husband. When Strasser
detects the plot he rushes to the airport and confronts Rick and
Captain Renault. Strasser goes for his gun and Rick shoots him
in "self-defense." As the plane disappears in the fog, Rick and
Renault walk off arm-in-arm. "Louis," Rick says, "I think this is
the beginning of a beautiful friendship."[11]

Casablanca seemingly fulfilled OWI's idea of good propaganda. The film used understatement and emotion to establish

the point that the people—in Germany as well as in the occupied nations—continued to resist Nazi rule. The German officers were painted as evil, but there were plenty of good Germans. As for Rick, he had excellent anti-fascist credentials.

But OWI, while liking many things about the film, was upset over the role of Rick and the image of the French. He was too cynical for too long, according to one OWI evaluation. Neutrality had no place in the war against fascism. More troubling to OWI was the view of the French. America's messy relationship between Vichy France and DeGaulle's Free French government was a touchy problem for OWI. U.S. policy was hardly clear on this issue in late 1942 and early 1943 when *Casablanca* was playing. Robert Riskin, a leading Hollywood writer who ran the New York Office of OWI's Overseas Branch, found *Casablanca's* message troubling. He withheld it from shipment to North Africa "on the advice of several Frenchmen within our organization who feel that it is bound to create resentment.[12]

OWI-approved themes were addressed more explicitly in a series of films about Nazi-occupied countries. Occupation films contrasted idyllic prewar conditions with Nazi ruthlessness. Before the war the countries were peaceful, prosperous democracies. The wartime occupiers trample everything held dear and impose a brutal regime in which refusal to cooperate often means death. But the people cannot be conquered. Although some individuals collaborate (often the socially prominent members of the bourgeoisie), common citizens keep alive the torch of resistance.

Two of Hollywood's leading talents, director Jean Renoir and writer Dudley Nichols, sought to move beyond *The Moon Is Down* by examining the ideology of Nazism and the resistance in *This Land Is Mine* (RKO, 1943). The director recalled: "We were dissatisfied with films against Fascism we had seen, because they all seemed distortions which dealt only with the surface of evil ... we knew we had to deal in ideas." The ideas Nichols and Renoir explored were the nature of fascism, the convenience of collaboration, and the determination of the common man to fight for freedom.[13]

The setting for *This Land is Mine* is "somewhere in Europe." German troops move slowly into an unnamed town. There is no resistance. The camera moves to a declaration from the collaborationist mayor: "Our Schools, Courts, Police and Public Offices remain free. . . . Please cooperate by obeying all regulations and so help to keep our civilian life free." And it soon appears that most of the leaders in the community are also collaborating. George Lambert (George Sanders), superintendent of the railroad yard, is in full sympathy with German objectives. He and the head of the German occupation force, Major von Keller (Walter Slezak), make perhaps the only attempt in a World War II film to define fascism. After the first act of sabotage, Lambert and von Keller try to figure out who might have been responsible. Von Keller is distressed that this has happened and does not want to be forced into shooting hostages. He is also concerned about an underground publication—*Liberty*—and asks Lambert to help determine who is printing the paper.

> George (bitterly): You think they'll [the workers] tell me anything? No. I'm the man who gives orders around here—and they regard anyone who gives orders as an enemy.
>
> von Keller: I can remember the time when we had the same problem in Germany—during the Republic, under Capitalism. I fought in the streets for our Fuehrer, Lambert—I killed workers with my own hands. For my class it was either kill or be killed. But we won, and now we are brothers! Absolute obedience!

Lambert says he too fought the workers. But no leader emerged in his country (while a location is not identified in the film the assumption is that the action took place in France) and that is why the Germans have invaded. Von Keller admits they have invaded but not as the enemy of the managers—only as the enemy of the workers. Lambert agrees with the ideas of the new order. False democratic ideas have destroyed my country, he tells von Keller. While German workers were working 70 hour weeks we were having union strikes for a 40-hour week. Lambert realizes he must cooperate, but concludes: "I don't like the occupation." "Neither do I," replies von Keller.

Fascism as the union between business and government was rarely ever discussed in the popular media. *This Land Is Mine* made the connection between business and the state. The fascists were opposed to unions and 40-hour weeks. Given Hollywood's attitude toward unions and the support of Hays and

Breen for business, that little piece of dialogue could only have taken place during the war. The film put the rest of the middle class in the same boat with Lambert. The mayor, who rose from the working class, was now using his position to buy up large amounts of property. The local merchants were getting rich off the occupation by selling goods to the Germans for inflated prices that the people could not afford.

In *This Land Is Mine* it is the workers and intellectuals who do not collaborate. The intellectual leader is Professor Sorel (Philip Merivale), headmaster at the local school. When the Germans order him to censor his textbooks, he complies reluctantly, saying: "It's a very delicate surgical operation—to cut out the heart without killing the patient." Louise Martin, a teacher in the school (Maureen O'Hara), battles the Germans at every step. She despises collaborators and breaks off her engagement with Lambert when she discovers he is a collaborator. Her brother, Paul (Kent Smith), seemingly is also a collaborator. Louise is ashamed of him until she discovers that his actions are a cover for his active role in the resistance. "Now you're the brother I've always been so proud of," she tells him.

As the film progresses, Albert Lory (Charles Laughton), a cowardly school teacher, sees his mentor Sorel arrested. Lory loves Louise, but is afraid to tell her. He discovers that Paul is the saboteur but keeps silent. Then he is selected as a random hostage by von Keller. His arrest drives his mother to tell the Germans who the guilty party really is—one more act of co-operation with the enemy. The Germans release Lory, who is now thoroughly confused. His mother admits to him that she told George Lambert that Paul Martin was the leader of the resistance. Albert Lory, finally finding courage, rushes off to confront Lambert, who he now realizes is a collaborator. But Lambert, unable to live with his own guilt and the rejection by Louise, has committed suicide. The Germans arrest Lory for his murder.

The Germans are again shown using the legal procedure of a court trial. The judge and jury are from the town. Lory exposes the corruption of the entire town. Even before the war, Lory tells the jury, "our mayor was convinced that our enemy was not the Germans but a part of our own people." Lory is beginning to sway the jury and the packed courtroom. The German prosecutor demands an adjournment. The scene switches to Lory's cell, where von Keller comes to discuss the teacher's performance which is undermining his occupation. He tells Lory: "Of course we Germans could take over the courts, schools, town halls, the administration of the whole country— but we're not tyrants—we prefer not to do that. We prefer to collaborate." If Lory will cooperate, von Keller will make him a free man. Lory asks for a cigarette and the scene fades out as he considers the offer of collaboration.

The next morning Lory awakes to the sound of soldiers marching in the courtyard. Looking out his cell window he sees the Germans execute ten men, among them the gallant Sorel. Lory now understands that the Germans find the weakness in each individual and offer that person freedom, position, or money to cooperate. In the courtroom he summons new courage to expose German methods. The occupation is based on lies, he tells the jury. "It's very hard for people like you and me to understand what is evil and what is good," he continues. "It's easy for working people to know who the enemy is because the aim of this war and occupation is to make them slaves. . . . I see now that sabotage is the only weapon left to a defeated people—and so long as we have saboteurs the other free nations who are still fighting on the battlefields will know that we're not defeated."

The jury finds him not guilty. Lory is released but the Germans cannot allow him to go free—he has told the truth. The final scene takes place in his classroom. His students, who now see him as a hero, pay close attention as he reads the "Declaration of the Rights of Man." German troops enter the classroom and arrest him. As they take him away Louise Martin continues to read from the declaration.

This Land Is Mine identified workers and intellectuals as the strength of the nation and accused the middle class of being more concerned with protecting property and position that in maintaining a free society. The image of the Germans in the film was not unlike that in *The Moon Is Down*. Slezak's von Keller is not a brutal killer but a reluctant one. His goal is an orderly society based on cooperation between government and business. He even goes to Lory and offers him his freedom if he will stop telling the truth at the trial. For some reason he declines to stop the trial. Only after Lory refuses his offer is the teacher re-arrested. The Germans are again reluctant fascists—educated, sophisticated men simply doing their duty. The soldiers endure insults from Louise Martin and drink and joke with the townspeople. They are relatively civilized occupiers.

OWI loved it. "It think *This Land Is Mine* is superb—one of the most useful war films I have had the opportunity to read," Poynter wrote when he first read the script in October 1942. As usual he offered some suggestions. He asked Nichols to try to bring out the involvement of the United Nations to "make the point that the people of the conquered countries are not alone." Nichols added some dialogue in Lory's last speech. Poynter also wanted a more graphic depiction of the horrors of occupation. He also suggested to Nichols that the scene in the classroom was unnecessary.

> Would it be possible to end the picture with the vital and extremely effective speech of Albert in the classroom? He could, perhaps, leave the courtroom with Louise, carried along by the admiration and acclaim of all the townspeople present in the courtroom. It is possible that the townspeople might be so aroused by Albert's speech that they would be ready to defy the authorities in an uprising, but Albert might assure them that the time is not ripe for this action, that the fight for their freedom is going on all over the world and when the time comes they can rise up against the enemy.[14]

Nichols ignored Poynter's ending. The film already stretched the bounds of credulity by allowing Lory to orate against them in court and then return unfettered to his classroom. For the Germans to have allowed him to call for an uprising right under their noses was scarcely credible. The Germans more plausibly would have dragged him from the courtroom and shot him.

Most reviewers gave the picture high marks for its intentions but thought it made a rather static film. Manny Farber praised the film's treatment of the differences between Nazism and democracy but thought it read "more like a commendable textbook in civics than a movie." The film missed the tragedy and terror of life under Nazi occupation. Poynter's optimistic ending could only have exacerbated this problem. Philip Hartung echoed Farber's complaint. He applauded the presentation of the confusion of the middle class and the fascists' hatred of unions, but he thought an epic poem or stage play would have been a better vehicle for the material. These flaws seem more pronounced to critics distanced from the emotional milieu of World War II. Leo Braudy, arguing that *This Land Is Mine* is not one of Renoir's better pictures, points out that Laughton, for all his eloquence, remains "a man orating in a locked room."[15]

Hollywood and OWI had a commendable objective in offering a salute to the resistance movements. Members of the resistance were heroic, and it was important for Americans to know that, even when governments surrendered or collaborated, part of the population continued to fight. Yet these films underestimated the corrosive effects of the occupation, how it shattered the morale of the subject people, and posed agonizing dilemmas in one's daily life that could seldom be solved by pat formulae. The decision to join the resistance was not nearly so easy as Poynter's proposed ending suggested.

Few films were made about the French resistance, perhaps because of the public's suspicions about the collapse of this supposedly decadent nation, and the continuing ambiguities about relations with the Vichy government. MGM offered a typically upbeat interpretation with a generic resistance story, *The Cross of Lorraine* (1943). Although Peter Lorre plays a sadistic Gestapo officer who clearly loves his work, his concentration camp is rather sanitized, even for 1943 movies. He is balanced by some good Germans. Escape seems relatively easy, and the occupied French town rises up as one to aid the escapees. When the Nazis move into the town in force to punish the citizens, the townspeople march off to the hills to continue the struggle. Their joyous demeanor and the light glistening on the path suggests a passage to the promised land rather than a flight from terror.

Humphrey Bogart abandoned the laconic, ostensibly cynical pose of *Casablanca* for fervent commitment to the Free French in one of his lesser known pictures, *Passage to Marseilles* (Warners 1944). For being an antifascist newspaper editor, he was unjustly shipped to Devil's Island. But even that notorious penal colony could not extinguish his love for France. He masterminded an escape with several other prisoner-patriots, made his way to England on a tramp steamer, and then became a bombardier for the Free French flying sorties against Germany. On one night bombing raid he was mortally wounded.

Though a well-intentioned tribute to the French resistance, the picture contained a key scene with a troubling moral ambiguity. Passengers and crewmen on the tramp steamer shoot down a German plane that has tried to sink them. Then Bogart machine guns to death the three aviators who have climbed out on the wing of the plane, which is floating in the water, and wave their arms in the air trying to surrender. Warner Brothers felt his action was justified by the Germans' attack on the steamer. This scene offended OWI, which informed censor Rothacker of the objectionable encounter. The Legion of Decency also objected and placed the film in its category "B" ("objectionable") because "we were committing the same crime against humanity that we accuse the Germans and Japanese of." In this case the Legion had a point; such a scene was stock material to prove German or Japanese treachery. Warners did not want to give the Legion veto power over scenes, so it left Bogart's exploits intact for domestic release. To meet the objections of OWI and the Office of Censorship, however, it deleted the scene so the movie could get an export license.[16]

The Czech resistance, which enjoyed a stature in Hollywood similar to that of the Norwegian opposition, became the subject of two films based on the demise of Reinhard Heydrich, deputy chief of the Gestapo and an architect of the final solution. His murder in 1942 provoked Hitler to devastate the town of Lidice, which was immortalized in Edna St. Vincent Millay's poem "The Murder of Lidice." Lidice seemed the epitome of Nazi horror to a world still largely unbelieving about the death camps. One film was *Hitler's Madman*. But most attention centered on *Hangmen Also Die* (United Artists), the product of a collaboration between the German emigrés Fritz Lang and Berthold Brecht, with substantial help from screenwriter John Wexley who received full credit for the screenplay. Brecht had wanted to give the film the suggestive title "Trust the People," but the studio chose instead the name suggested by a secretary in a $100 prize contest. Despite some Hollywood touches that Brecht detested, *Hangmen Also Die* graphically depicted Nazi brutality and highlighted the two Czech guerrillas who tossed the grenade that left Heydrich mortally wounded. The film was equally significant for what it left out. Lang, who was Jewish, objected to scenes by Brecht, who was a Gentile, that showed Jews being mistreated or wearing the Star of David. Deemed too controversial, those scenes were eliminated—this in the year 1942![17]

If resistance pictures offered an obvious structure for films, the depiction of conditions inside Germany did not lend itself to clearcut approaches. Satire had been effective in Chaplin's *The Great Dictator* in 1940. Ernst Lubitsch asked audiences to laugh at the Nazis in *To Be or Not to Be*, a United Artists picture that starred Jack Benny and Carole Lombard. But by the time of its release, 1942, some critics were questioning whether we should "laugh at some broad anti-Nazi satire while we are weeping over the sad fate of stricken Poland."[18]

As Hollywood took a more serious look at Nazi reality, the industry focused on the obvious and sensational aspects of the regime. The deeper questions of what lay behind Nazism and its success, which were admittedly harder to show cinematically, received little analysis.

The prison camp, including the inevitable escape, fit Hollywood conventions. In 1943 MGM released the Fred Zimmerman production *The Seventh Cross*, starring Spencer Tracy as an escapee from a concentration camp. While no OWI records have been found, the film fits into the pattern of the people coming to recognize the inhuman nature of fascism. Based on a novel by Anna Segher, the setting is Germany, 1936. The place was Westoven, a concentration camp full of political prisoners who look like the familiar universal platoon—there are teachers, farmers, grocery clerks, musicians and George Heisler (Tracy), an anti-Nazi newspaper editor.

Seven men escape the horrors of the camp where prisoners live in fear for their lives. Heisler has been beaten and tortured many times. The narrator says Germany is a nation of "beasts" but that a few good Germans are still left. The seven discover there are all too few. Seven crosses are erected at Westoven to crucify the escapees, all of whom are easily captured but Heisler. The people of Germany, even children, make a game out of turning in the men. A crowd watches with great delight as one man is chased by the police across the rooftops of a series of buildings. He leaps to his death rather than submit to a return to the camp. The crowd seems disappointed.

Heisler somehow survives capture to make the major point of the film. He makes contact with the resistance, which helps him escape to Holland and freedom. Germany has been exposed as a sick nation, but there are still some Germans who are willing to risk certain death to help someone in trouble. These people are the future of Germany. *The Seventh Cross* was a prime example of this propaganda point, a favorite of OWI's. But the film was so slow and ponderous one wonders if anyone stayed awake long enough to catch the message. Tracy seemed to have been shot in slow motion, and the use of a narrator to explain every point reinforced the film's didacticism. As James Agee noted, MGM crucified the possibilities for a fine movie.

As sensational a movie subject as concentration camps was the Third Reich's program of forced breeding. RKO's Edward Golden filmed the major statement about this chilling aspect of Nazism with *Hitler's Children* (1943), based on Gregor Ziemer's *Education for Death,* an exposé of brainwashing, forced procreation, and sterilization. (Monogram seconded RKO with *Women in Bondage,* whose title indicated its sensational overtones.)

Combining sex and violence, *Hitler's Children* was difficult to film with the requisite seriousness and taste. OWI worried that such a film might backfire. Upon reading an early version of the screenplay, in May 1942, Poynter wondered: "Will the public feel defrauded ten years from now and claim they were bamboozled by such a picture?" Mellett's reading of the script made him worry that "it would probably arouse more skepticism on the part of the average audience than acceptance." Remembering how World War I atrocity stories had backfired, Mellett and Poynter did not want it to happen again. In 1942 they, like many Americans, had yet to grasp the ever-escalating horror of Nazism.[19]

Poynter conferred regularly with the studio, particularly screenwriter Emmet Lavery, and was pleased with the final product. OWI reviewers decided that *Hitler's Children* exposed a little-understood aspect of the Third Reich and that the role of good Germans indicated that "Germans basically are decent human beings who appreciate freedom." The film began in prewar Germany with Karl Bruner (Tim Holt), a young Nazi who blindly accepts everything the Fatherland tells him. His teachers remind him: "Germany was robbed in the Treaty of Versailles—robbed of land which has always been and always will be holy German soil." He is taught that since German expansion and war will need many babies, it is therefore the duty of all healthy young Germans to bear children. His girlfriend, Anna Miller (Bonita Granville), happens to be an American student living in Germany. She is of German heritage and is selected to be placed in a woman's maternity clinic where she is expected to have a child for the Fuehrer. Karl is horrified when she refuses to cooperate. But when she is scheduled to be sterilized for her defiance, Karl is shaken out of his Nazi stupor and realizes that fascism is wrong. He rescues Anna when S.S. guards begin a public lashing, and they are both tossed into prison. When he pretends to recant, the Germans stage a public trial, complete with a national radio broadcast of Karl's return to Nazism. But he tricks the Nazis when he announces over the radio: "Long live the enemies of the German Reich!" He and Anna are killed in a dramatic finale.[20]

Joseph Breen had watched *Hitler's Children* with apprehension but it contained enough circumlocutions that he approved it. There were limits to what he would tolerate, however, and this posed a severe constraint on what could be shown about Nazi Germany. Just as Breen tried to censor General Stilwell's salty language, so he was determined to channel the horrors of war within the confines of the production code. B. G. (Buddy) DeSylva, Paramount's executive producer, found how frustrating Breen's limits could be when he made *The Hitler Gang*, which he promised would tell the truth about Hitler and his henchmen. DeSylva strove for verisimilitude in some respects. He claimed the screenplay was "authenticated from every available source;" he wove documentary footage into the picture from some 300,000 feet of German material; and he hired look-alike actors to play roles familiar to the public, such as Robert Watson, who was kept very busy playing the Fuehrer during the war.[21]

The film reconstructed the rise of National Socialism from the end of World War I to the bloody purge of 1934. DeSylva appealed to both OWI and the Department of State for technical assistance. All parties agreed that the project would be a valuable contribution to the war effort, so much so that it produced a rare example of OWI and State working together on a project. Paramount, which normally refused to provide OWI with scripts, promised Mellett full cooperation.[22]

Breen's PCA was another story. When the screenplay reached Breen in August 1943, he declared the material "thoroughly and completely unacceptable." The offending script suggested that several of the Nazi leaders were homosexuals and that Hitler was impotent and had an unhealthy attraction to young girls. The script was also shot through with violence. Breen was disturbed that the script promised "an orgy of bestiality and brutality such as the civilized world has never witnessed." Blasphemy also upset him, especially a speech which read: "We need no God on a distant throne. Adolph Hitler is the Jesus Christ as well as the Holy Ghost of the Fatherland." The speech had to be removed even though it was an exact quote. All these things might be true about the Third Reich, but they were forbidden under the production code.

DeSylva, cheered by his blessing from OWI and State, was furious. He told Breen the Nazi leaders were a bunch of "degenerate gangsters," and in making this clear "he was making a very definite, worthwhile contribution to the cause of this nation in the hour of war." Breen was unmoved and repeatedly told DeSylva he would not approve the film if it contained these offensive scenes. DeSylva stormed out of the meeting, refusing to meet any of Breen's conditions. Neither OWI nor State was willing to interfere with the internal operations of the Hollywood film industry. Lacking support DeSylva finally informed Breen some five months after their confrontation that he would alter the material in question to fit the Hays office code. The producer agreed to insert several speeches in the film that would establish that Hitler's relationship with his sister and his niece was not sexual. Breen decided that *The Hitler Gang* was now safe for American audiences to see.[23]

Released in May 1944, *The Hitler Gang* was judged by OWI to be Hollywood's best treatment of Nazism. It exposed the "industrialists and German army leaders who gave Hitler their support" and contained a strong statement against a negotiated peace. The final scene, a montage of Allied armies on the march, promised ultimate victory. Less self-interested viewers were wary. DeSylva's notion that the Hitler gang were "degenerate gang-sters," augmented by titillating glimpses of usually forbidden subjects, might make the case that the Nazis were evil. But it could not explain the sweeping phenomenon of Nazism. Manny Farber noted that the film showed the Nazi leaders as "extra-simple, extra-naive." Paul Kennedy wrote in the *New York Times* that Hitler came across as "little more than a confused, con-temptible person." The film's mistake was to confuse evil with stupidity. If Hitler and his movement were as ignorant and in-competent as the movie said, how did they manage to enslave half of Europe? *The Hitler Gang* had no answer.[24]

The cooperation of PCA and OWI did not really help mat-ters. Although Breen bent the code somewhat to show the en-emy's evil ways during the war, his office still kept the industry in leading strings. Even as the Nazi crematoria worked full tilt and millions of Europeans daily felt the Third Reich's oppres-sion, Breen labored to delete the suggestion of a blood rela-tionship between Hitler and a young girl with whom he had an affair. (That still did not satisfy the Legion of Decency, which condemned *The Hitler Gang* as "unwholesome.")[25] Perhaps not wanting to precipitate a jurisdictional battle with Breen, OWI did little to help Paramount in its fight with the production code. The propagandists, after all, had cautioned against mak-ing battle scenes seem too awful. And if they had found Amer-ican morals "incredibly cheap" in a spoof like *Palm Beach Story*, they were not likely to take up the cudgels for greater freedom of expression on taboo sexual topics. Nor was OWI's interpre-tation of fascism much help in explaining Nazism. For, once all the Nazis' pernicious tactics were acknowledged, one was still left with the realization that in Germany and other countries Nazism enjoyed widespread popular support—a reality that was hard to square with OWI's invocation of "the people" and the resistance.

As the United States and Britain opened a second front in North Africa in late 1942, then in Italy in mid-1943, and finally in France in June 1944, Hollywood's treatment of the European war could move from pictures of occupation and resistance to movies showing direct combat with the Germans. These films represented a growing maturity in the movie capital's understanding of combat, and they showed marked differences with battle pictures from the Pacific.

One of the first attempts to illustrate combat between Americans and Germans was the Columbia film *Sahara* (1943), built around the fall of Tobruk in mid-1942. OWI played a key role in convincing Columbia that their original idea, for a film to be called "Trans-Sahara," would damage the war effort. "Trans-Sahara" was to take place on the Nazi railroad from the Mediterranean to Dakar and presumably would be crawling with spies and refugees. But Columbia, perhaps influenced by the OWI manual, which had just been distributed to the studios, wanted to do more. Columbia intended to show why France collapsed. Using Marshall Pétain and Pierre Laval as real characters, the film would illustrate how the Nazis undermined civilian and military morale. The film would illustrate the inherent "democratic spirit" of the French people and show "the great role that the Colonial peoples can take in defeating the Axis." Columbia asked OWI how such a film would fit into current relations with the French and, even more importantly, if it would be given an export license.[26]

Poynter told the studio to go ahead but sought Mellett's opinion. Mellett fired back a stinging reply, branding the script a bit of "bad fiction." Hollywood could make bad movies if it wanted to, he said, but the studios were not free to "invent their own answers to important questions." He had checked this out at the very top and "the subject is one to leave alone.... Certainly, an export license for it is out of the question."[27] Columbia recrafted its North African adventure into the much safer *Sahara.* It avoided the political considerations of dealing with Vichy France. Since the Roosevelt administration was trying at one and the same time to woo Vichy, negotiate with Admiral Darlan in North Africa, and flatter the Free French under General DeGaulle, "Trans-Sahara" entered sensitive ground. Columbia dropped it without protesting about government interference or censorship.

Sahara begins with an American tank, "Lulubelle," isolated, almost out of fuel, and attempting to reach the British lines. (How "Lulubelle" jumped the gun on the American landing in North Africa by six months Columbia did not bother to explain.) Surrounded by hostile German troops, "Lulubelle" sets out across the dangerous and forbidding desert. The tank is under the command of Sergeant Joe Gunn, played by Humphrey Bogart. As it proceeds it comes across a bombed-out Allied hospital, where they pick up a British doctor, several troops, and a Frenchman who was active in the resistance movement. They rumble on and run into Tambul, a Sudanese corporal, played by black actor Rex Ingram, and his Italian prisoner, Giuseppe. The tank population has become a microcosm of the Allies. Tambul tells Gunn about an oasis in the desert some sixty miles away, and the tank sets course for it. They are attacked by a German plane, but they manage to shoot it down and take the pilot prisoner. The Frenchman begs Gunn to let him kill the German, but unlike the Bogart character in *Passage to Marseilles* Gunn refuses. The Allies play by the rules.

Finally they reach the oasis, only to discover that the well is almost dry. Unfortunately, the Germans also know about the well, and a battalion of 500 men arrive to confront this small band of men. The Germans offer to let Gunn and his men go if they can have some water. Gunn refuses, and the men agree to fight to the last man as happened on Bataan and Corregidor. The battle begins, and one by one, the men are killed. The pilot tries to convince the Italian to escape with him so they can tell the German troops that the water is almost gone, that they are wasting lives fighting for a dry water hole. The Italian refuses and denounces fascism and Hitler. The enraged German kills him and escapes. But Gunn sees the Nazi and orders the Sudanese to stop him. With symbolism raging on the desert, the black tackles the blond and kills him with his own hands: so much for Aryan superiority. The Sudanese is shot trying to return to the safety of the oasis.

The Germans are dying of thirst. As they bombard the oasis, a shell scores a direct hit on the well and water comes bubbling to the top. As it does, the Germans surrender. They are not so tough. They do not fight to the last man; instead, they give up when they become too thirsty. The unity and determination of the Allies makes them seem stronger than the Germans.

OWI worked closely with screenwriters John Howard Lawson and Zoltan Korda to strengthen certain propaganda themes. At OWI's urging, they made the Sudanese an equal instead of "a sort of faithful Gunga Din." The Frenchman originally begged Gunn not to let the German capture him, leaving the impression he was afraid to die. The revised edition did "high justice to the Fighting French." *Sahara* affirmed the unity of the United Nations. Just as combat films dealing with American troops had an ethnically all-American platoon, *Sahara* had an international platoon. From a propaganda perspective, the image of the enemy was also correct. The Germans were tough but not unbeatable. The Italians were presented as despising fascism. *Sahara,* released in July 1943, was a timely confirmation of Allied policy toward Italy.[28]

The ultimate example of World War II combat films was a story of the Italian campaign, produced late in the war: *The Story of G. I. Joe.* This picture has a maturity and relentless realism that was possible only as the war neared its end. The mud; the seeming endlessness of war (you took one ridge only to find another beyond it); the randomness of death—these things could neither have been shown nor comprehended in feature films until late in the war. *The Story of G. I. Joe* is so far removed in its seriousness and candor from early battle films like *Wake Island* as to seem to be from a different war.

Directed by William Wellman, *The Story of G. I. Joe* was based on the reporting of Ernie Pyle, whose accounts of the common foot soldier earned him a Pulitzer Prize in journalism and the undying respect of the G.I. Pyle's stories of courage, tragedy, fear, and humor were matter-of-fact tributes to the infantrymen who bore the brunt of the war under the most miserable conditions. He went along with the troops, asked for little, and died as they died when a Japanese sniper killed him on Okinawa in 1945. *The Story of G. I. Joe,* which began as a salute to the common soldier, became also a tribute to the writer who understood them best.

Building on Pyle's material, Wellman achieved a remarkable degree of realism in a wartime entertainment film. He interwove scenes from the graphic documentary, *The Battle of San Pietro;* the fictional scenes are good enough that the fit between them and those from the documentary is almost seamless. A Lester Cowan production, the film featured Burgess Meredith as Pyle and Robert Mitchum in a strong performance as Captain Walker. Most of the cast were unknowns, and included 150 combat veterans who were assigned to the film for a six-week working leave. Wellman gave several of them speaking parts, and he forced all the actors to train with the vets. After their stint before the cameras, the G.I.s were shipped to the Pacific. Only a few returned.[29]

The Story of G. I. Joe follows a group of American infantrymen who fight their way toward Rome after the Allied landing on the Italian peninsula in September 1943. Mussolini had been deposed in favor of Marshall Pietro Badoglio, and the Italians left the war that month. But the Germans decided to turn Italy into a battleground and put up such a fierce resistance that Allied forces did not enter Rome until June 1944, and Milan until April 1945. Pyle goes along to record the G.I.'s experiences in this bloody campaign. For the most part the film avoids false heroics, pronouncements about beating the fascists, and sermons about winning the war for democracy. In one scene Pyle and the captain talk about writing and the war. Walker tells Pyle he writes too, but he writes home to parents, girlfriends, and wives about men who have been killed. They were scared kids who did not know what this was all about—just scared stiff. "If only we could create something good out of all this energy," he says. Pyle just looks at him. Nothing said. Nothing needed.

The relatively few battle scenes are stark and spare. As the men advance into a bombed out town, they run from street to street, building to building against an unseen enemy. Walker and the sergeant move into a bombed out church. The captain shouts "lousy kraut swine" in an attempt to flush the hidden enemy. It works, and one German is killed. "Funny place to be killing men in, isn't it," says the sergeant, and kneels to pray. Suddenly a German soldier fires from the bell tower, but Walker picks him off. Nothing is said. No histrionics about wiping savages off the face of the earth.

The film does not lose sight of the ordinary rhythms that pace army life. It rains constantly, and the relentless mud is almost as grim as the fight against the enemy. Light touches relieve the monotony. A soldier's concern for his puppy—a familiar, hokey touch in too many war pictures—comes off as a deft comment on the contrasting roles a soldier has to assume. A G.I. gets a record with the voice of his infant son; he wears it literally next to his heart; and in every town he searches frantically for a phonograph so that he can hear his son's first words.

This depiction of a father's separation from his family is more believable than any windy, sentimental dialogue.

The most serious lapse in the picture is the handling of the hotly controversial bombing of the Benedictine monastery, Monte Cassino, the cradle of western monasticism. Allied troops believed the Germans were holed up in the monastery high on a ridge, from which they trained a withering fire that halted the Allied advance. The high command hesitated to bomb the shrine because of a policy to spare religious and cultural monuments. But the G.I.'s are unequivocal. "I'm a Catholic and I say bomb it," avers one. "Think I want to die for a piece of stone?" When headquarters finally decides to bomb the monastery, the troops break into ecstatic cheers. The treatment of the incident beckons the audience to join in the applause. In reality, however, the Germans were not holed up in the monastery, and, ironically, pounding it to rubble simply created an ideal landscape where they could dig in. The foot soldier had to go in and slug it out anyway. In contrast to the film's propaganda, General Mark Clark in his memoirs concluded the bombing of the monastery was a military and propaganda mistake of the first order.[30]

Having finally dislodged the Germans from Monte Cassino, the Allies are again advancing toward Rome. As they rest by the side of the road, a pack train slowly moves by. The bodies of dead soldiers are slung over the backs of the mules. The men watch mutely until they see the corpse of the captain. They are devastated. Some gaze in uncomprehending silence and then plod on to the next battle. One soldier kneels beside his dead captain and murmurs how sorry he is, another holds his hand. Walker's closest buddy, overcome with emotions for which he has no words, bends over the dead man for an eternal moment and tenderly, somewhat furtively, strokes his face. Then he straightens up and digs his boots into the road to Rome.

Pyle says in a voice-over: "This is our war. We will carry it with us from one battleground to another. In the end we will win. I hope we can rejoice in our victory, but humbly. . . . As for those beneath the wooden crosses we can only murmur, thanks, pal, thanks."

Those flat, hopeful, wary words provided a fitting epitaph to a four-year cycle of combat pictures. They could not have been spoken in 1942, and they were still rare in 1945. No OWI records have been found for this film, but it seems unlikely that the propagandists would have approved of its non-ideological, often bleak, portrait of war. Throughout the war the uneasy collaboration of Hollywood and OWI had produced a fairly consistent interpretation of American soldiers—who they were, where they came from, and what they became. The capstone of that interpretation, *The Story of G. I. Joe* also stood somewhat outside that corpus.

The movies presented the military experience as an enactment of civic virtue and as an exercise in collective self-improvement. Military service became yet another variation on Hollywood's favorite theme: the success story. The war took average guys from every corner in the land—Flatbush, or Smith Center, Kansas, or El Centro, California—and gave them purpose, commitment, and courage. The war may shake a young man out of a period of personal drift (Rusty Marsh), or represent a higher calling (John in *Tender Comrade*), or offer a break from a pleasant but monotonous routine (Al Schmid in *Pride of the Marines*). The young men are characters of studied innocence who have to be taught the art of war; they are a far cry from the bloodthirsty savages of Japan or the coldly efficient killers of Germany. Some have moral qualms that have to be assuaged. Sergeant York had to find a way to rationalize killing at all; the new recruit in *Bombardier* had to find a justification for bombing innocent civilians. The men fight with an innate sense of the rules, and deviations from the code of war are justified by the enemy's routine crimes. (One of the few Allied fighters to swerve from the code, Bogart in *Passage to Marseilles,* is a French civilian.) Foxholes are miniature democracies: all races, creeds, and classes are welcomed on a basis of equality. The movies do not yet have a Sergeant Croft, the sadistic platoon leader in Norman Mailer's *The Naked and the Dead,* who kills Japs out of blood lust, drives his own men beyond endurance for no rational purpose, and is responsible for the needless death of the weak private he found contemptible.

The citizen soldiers and sailors are led by tough, heroic, yet sensitive men, most of them only recently out of civilian clothes. The troops respect, even revere their leaders. With the mourning of Captain Walker, *The Story of G. I. Joe* came as close as the movies dared to speaking of male love. The exalted ranks of generals are almost as divine as Lionel Barrymore's cloud-swathed heavenly staff room in *A Guy Named Joe*. Generals and admirals appear almost exclusively in remote cameos of command and decisiveness. There are no generals like Mailer's Cummings, who can deal with his ambivalent, part homoerotic, part competitive feelings towards his aide only by banishing him to a senseless and inevitably fatal reconnaissance. Nor do movie officers yet worry, like Mailer's general, whether the way they conduct a battle will generate another star. When *A Bell for Adano* tried to deal with Patton's much publicized shooting of a peasant's mule out of pique, the incident had to be converted into an instance of overzealous pursuit of a reasonable objective.

In the end the military experience culminated in upward mobility—a societal expression of personal fulfillment. Some men died, to be sure, but they and their loved ones understood why. They usually died as heroes, taking a clutch of enemy soldiers with them, not with the utter randomness and sheer impersonality of *The Story of G. I. Joe*. Some men like Al Schmid were badly wounded, but a welcoming society, and a woman's love, assured a relatively easy readjustment to civilian life. For the rest the postwar, though not without ominous possibilities, promised greater happiness and personal advancement than these young G.I.s had ever known. The depression was behind, they had new skills and self-confidence, and the G.I. Bill of Rights was society's way of paying them back. As the wounded men of *Pride of the Marines* debate postwar prospects in an immaculate San Diego veterans hospital, they expect their prewar fantasies to be realized. One is going to buy that store on the corner; another intends to use the G. I. Bill to become a lawyer and enter politics; they will all own a home of their own. A pessimist is shouted down. As the Jewish soldier says: If we just pull together, in peace as in war, we can make this thing work.

For many, though not all, it happened that way. For others the propaganda was a cheat. But for everyone, veterans and audiences alike, the war success stories were a deception. Few pictures besides *The Story of G. I. Joe* dared breathe what everyone knew but found hard to voice aloud—that death was random and success only partly related to one's desserts. Faced with some of the most profound of human experiences, Hollywood and OWI could only graft the prepackaged emotions of the success story onto the war.

We would win. We would be able to rejoice in victory, though not humbly. There would be anxious moments, notably the Battle of the Bulge. But if not at Monte Cassino then at least by the time the beachhead at Normandy was consolidated, the outcome was sure. It was only a question of how much time and how much blood. And when victory came, then what? What would we do with our victory? What would we do with our enemies, particularly Germany?

Hollywood and OWI did not think about those questions very much, other than to promise a world of international good fellowship, based on the premise of a resolute rejection of isolationism for collective security. But at least one major picture spoke to those issues in the European context. And since that question was inseparable from ideas about the nature of the enemy, the film addressed the strength of fascism too, and in a hotly debated way.

This picture was *Lifeboat,* an atypical Alfred Hitchcock picture released through Twentieth Century-Fox in early 1944. Some critics thought the picture showed the Nazi submarine captain as the strongest character, while the various representatives of America and England came off as weak and disunited. Dorothy Thompson, the prominent political columnist, gave the picture ten days to get out of town. Bosley Crowther could scarcely believe that Hollywood made a film "which sold out the democratic ideal and elevated the Nazi 'superman.'" The picture also had its defenders. Ironically, some people who criticized the movie industry for making unrealistic, formulaic pictures disliked *Lifeboat* because it did not reinforce their own unrealistic, formulaic notions of what wartime films should say.[31]

Lifeboat was based on a story written for Hollywood by John Steinbeck. Inspired in part by Eddie Rickenbacker's twenty-four day ordeal on a raft after being shot down, Steinbeck wrote about a cross section of survivors from a freighter torpedoed by a German U-boat. In "Lifeboat," as in *The Moon Is Down,* he explored the dilemmas of ordinary people caught in the grip

of circumstances beyond their power to shape or fully compre-
hend. In Steinbeck's "Lifeboat" all are victims, regardless of
rank or nationality.[32]

The survivors from the freighter include the crewman-
narrator Bud Abbott; Constance Porter, a congresswoman and
former actress (modeled on Clare Booth Luce); a wealthy factory owner; Albert Sheinkowitz, a Pole from Chicago; Joe, a
black steward; a nurse; and a woman with a baby. They detect
a blob in the fog, row over to him, and pull him aboard. It is a
crewman from the submarine that sank the freighter. He has
torn off his insignia so his rank cannot be detected. He is weak
and suffering from a broken arm. The group argues about what
to do and decides to keep the German aboard. Huddled together in the lifeboat, Steinbeck's people realize their common
plight as the dispossessed of war, even though one of their number is an enemy. The nurse helps set the German's broken arm.
The Pole explains that, while he still hates Germans, "once you
lay your hand on a man why you couldn't hate him the same
any more."[33]

Bud is the detached observer who senses how war corrupts
human judgment. The German probably had no idea what his
country had done in Poland. "They just tell the German people
what they want them to know and it's all good," Bud says. But
war's conformism and brutality are not limited to the enemy.
"Most people were kind of comfortable with war," he says, "because they didn't have to think any more. We were all good and
the enemy was all bad. And it made it kind of simple. When
they bombed us they were murderers and when we bombed
them, why we were winning for some good reason . . . etc." This
message, as pertinent as it was rare during the war, did not survive in the film version.

The major change from Steinbeck to Hitchcock was in the
character of the German. In the film the robust German is a
catalyst, but in the story he is rather passive and his death is
inadvertent. One night Bud allows the German to relieve him
at the tiller. As he suspects, the prisoner changes course and
heads them toward a German supply ship. Bud tells the others.
Scared and mad, they rush to the back of the boat. Albert weakly
strikes the German, who topples overboard. Joe jumps in to try
to save him but cannot. When the others ask Joe why he risked

his life for the German, he explains: "Hell, you fellows were a mob and I'm scared of mobs." Most of them are overcome with remorse, for they all feel they have had a role in a murder. Bud gets them to focus on the need to survive. Finally they are rescued by an American ship.

To alter the story for the screen Hitchcock turned to Jo Swerling, a top writer who did screenplays for such well known pictures as *Love Me Forever, The Whole Town's Talking, Pride of the Yankees,* and *It's a Wonderful Life.* Swerling and Hitchcock worked closely and it is hard to sort out their respective contributions. They sharpened the German's character and set the stage for controversy. The changes so angered Steinbeck that when he saw the movie he demanded that Twentieth Century remove his name from the credits. The studio, as always, refused.[34]

For Hitchcock, as for Melville, shipboard society affords a microcosm of the larger society. The film master retained Steinbeck's characters but changed the story to an explicit allegory of the origins and impending end of the war. Porter was changed to a globe-trotting correspondent, superbly realized by Tallulah Bankhead in her first screen role in eleven years. The director and the actress approached each other warily, but their relationship developed so amicably that he referred to her (affectionately) as "Baghead" and she reciprocated with "Bitchcock." As the film opens the correspondent, Constance Porter, is alone in the lifeboat. Gradually she is joined by seven other survivors—Kovac (John Hodiak), a leftist oiler from the ship; Rittenhouse (Henry Hull), an industrialist; Gus (William Bendix), another crewman; Joe (Canada Lee), the black steward; Stanley (Hume Cronyn), a British radio operator; a nurse; and a shell-shocked English mother with babe-in-arms. Then two grimy hands appear over the side of the boat, and another man clambers aboard. It is ... the submarine captain (Walter Slezak). Some survivors want to throw him back in the ocean, but they vote to keep him aboard as a P.O.W.[35]

They head for Bermuda but are blown off-course in a storm. The captain takes command and steers them toward a German supply ship. A surgeon in civilian life, he amputates Gus's gangrenous leg. He navigates effortlessly and possesses seemingly superhuman strength. Gus catches him using a secret compass, as well as drinking from a flask of water and swallowing vitamin tablets. Gus is washed overboard before he can warn the others. When they discover his secret sources of energy and inspiration, they rush the captain and, according to the script, "in an orgasm of murder," beat him, mutilate him, and throw him overboard to drown. Now they are truly sunk. The supply ship looms on the horizon; they are about to be taken prisoner and sent to a concentration camp. But wait! An Allied vessel blasts the supply ship out of the water. Rescue is at hand. Then a crewman from the supply ship swims to the lifeboat. After some discussion, the survivors decide to allow him in—and vow to keep him under close guard. Kovac's last line, an echo of earlier comments, lingers: "What are you going to do with people like that?"

For OWI reviewers this script presented more problems than any they had previously seen from Twentieth Century. The theme unwittingly became "the triumph of Nazism over democracy," they said. They feared that with slight editing the picture could be turned into a propaganda piece by the Nazis. Warren Pierce presented a long bill of particulars. First, the Americans and British came off as weak, disunited, and selfish. Porter, said Pierce, was "a selfish, predatory, amoral, international adventuress." Rittenhouse, "a 110 percent American," is willing to do business with the fascists and thinks a lot about beating the British to postwar markets in Spain and China. (He was also described as belonging to one of the sixty families who own America. OWI took offense at this reference to class divisions in America, even though it derived from Ferdinand Lundberg's book on America's sixty wealthiest families and the Senate antimonopoly hearings of 1938.) Kovac was better, but he seemed to cheat at cards. And "his love exploits recorded in the tattoo work on his chest" hardly made him OWI's type of guy. Gus, Joe, Stanley, and the nurse seemed not to know why we were at war. Second, the attempt to make Joe a rare sympathetic black character—he was the only person who did not join in the assault on the captain—was undercut in several ways: He was referred to initially as "Charcoal"; he was an adept, if reformed, pickpocket; he seemed surprised when offered a vote on the Nazi's fate and, unaccustomed to the franchise, turned it down; and he was quite deferential toward people in authority. When Steinbeck saw the film he was angered that instead of the dignified man in his script Joe had been changed to "a stock comedy Negro." Third, the Spanish Loyalists got a bum rap. When Kovac reveals he fought for them, Porter exclaims: "I thought so! Tovarich!" He asks her how much Franco is paying her to be his press agent. She retorts: "What are you trying to do, organize a Soviet on the boat?" Rittenhouse chimes in that a new Spain is coming. Kovac allowed these remarks to pass uncontested.[36]

Fourth, and most damaging, the captain came across as a virtual demigod, seeming to substantiate the Nazis' claims of a superior race. He was bright, strong, cool under pressure, not without charm, and even skilled at romantic advice. Yielding to his winning attributes, the rest of the survivors become in effect prisoners of their P.O.W. His death seemed unjustified, for in the face of the others' weakness, he could plausibly contend that his flask of water and stash of energy pills made it possible for him to save the rest.[37]

Many changes were made to satisfy OWI's objections in the revised final script, which the agency read in September 1943. The most important shift was to have Willi throw Gus overboard after the merchant seaman discovers the compass and pills. This gave a certain justification to the group's killing him. But, like OWI, Joe Breen still worried about the appearance of "mob action" and insisted that material be added to indicate some of them had pangs of remorse. Kovac became a stronger character, taking over command of the boat, with the consent of the rest, after Rittenhouse proves to be incompetent. The weakness of the democratic eight was traced to their supplies having have washed overboard. The offending references to the Spanish Civil War were removed, as was Rittenhouse's zeal for beating the British in the scramble for markets. Porter was toned down, but there was still Miss Bankhead to contend with. Like Mae West she could wriggle out of practically any corset a censor tried to lace.[38]

The OWI crew was guardedly optimistic, for Hitchcock promised to make further changes as he shot and cut the picture. What emerged was a minor Hollywood classic whose artistic merits tended to be submerged in wartime political controversy.

Miss Bankhead, as might be expected, dominated the movie. As *Lifeboat* opens we see the freighter's smokestack crumple under the waves, followed by Porter alone in the lifeboat. A glittering diamond bracelet dangles from her wrist as she pounds away on her typewriter. She has escaped with her mink coat, lap robe, luggage, and camera, which she uses to photograph the debris of the wreck. She has a real scoop, and that's the most important thing to this journalist-vixen.

But like the democracies, circumstances change her. She is attracted to Kovac (who else!). She tells him they have the same background—"back of the yards, Chicago." Then she got this, she says, indicating her lipstick, and made it to the Gold Coast. They kiss hotly. But Kovac doesn't give up his political principles that easily. That bracelet still makes him suspicious of her.

Hitchcock uses Porter's gradual divestment of her possessions as a motif to mark her progress from prima donna to a democratic spirit. For the British director this was perhaps symbolic of the Empire's sacrifice of its assets in order to survive. She loses the camera with all those great pictures overboard. The typewriter she's taken all over the world goes too. She is stripped of the tools of her trade and symbolically reduced to another bereft survivor. She loses her mink coat when the English woman, to whom she had lent it to warm her and her baby, drowns herself at night. Her suitcase goes overboard in a storm. When the starving band decides to try to fish for food but has no bait, Porter offers her bracelet with the mordant comment: "I can recommend the bait. I've bit on it myself." Just as they catch something, they sight the ship ... and pole, fish, and bracelet go into the sea. Porter bursts into laughter. She has given up material things, but she has gotten something priceless in return—life and freedom.

The picture's detractors ignored Porter's transformation and focused on Willi, well played by Slezak. OWI found Hitchcock's realization of the film better than the script. It still worried, however, that the Nazi's charm and command in crisis substantiated the Aryan myth. The BMP reviewers recommended against foreign distribution. Since postwar viewers sometimes reach similar conclusions about the film, this wartime interpretation was not implausible. Steinbeck considered the picture "dangerous" to the war effort and did not think it was right for the studio to continue its exhibition. Darryl Zanuck urged Hitchcock to make some cuts in the first part of the picture. He thought Willi remained the strong man for too long. Hitchcock found himself on the horns of a dilemma: To build suspense he had to develop the almost overpowering strength of the German, but in so doing he muddied his political allegory.[39]

Nevertheless, when the picture is considered as a whole, Hitchcock's allegory remains intact. Willi was, after all, a submarine captain, which should have given him a leg up in experience in running a boat. The captain is, however, an ersatz superman. Without his artificial advantages, he would not be able to row endlessly. The film effectively builds the myth of Willi's superiority, paralleling the Nazi buildup of the 1930s and early war years, and then demolishes the myth by demonstrating its artificial underpinnings.[40]

The aroused democrats finally emerge victorious. Though they are admittedly quarrelsome and vacillating for a time, they, like the Allies, were simply pushed too far. Morally outraged by the Nazi's killing of the helpless Gus—substitute any of the little countries Hitler swallowed up—they kill the captain, even though this means their chances of survival are thereby diminished. No remorse should have been necessary. In accordance with the rules of war, they had allowed him into their lifeboat. He had betrayed their trust. Only when solid evidence is uncovered do they act. As Zanuck said: "When they find the compass watch, they are idiots if they don't pounce upon him instead of talking. This is concrete evidence that even a child could understand." Acting as a symbolic society, they execute him in accordance with usually understood norms.[41]

There was, finally, the matter of the ending. Some critics thought the octet was still vacillating and placed its faith in a miracle. "When we killed the German, we killed our motor," the tycoon says. Joe says they still have a motor. The literal minded industrialist asks, who? Joe motions skyward. His response was not very practical, said Crowther in the *Times*. But what else was the sun-baked, dehydrated, starving group to do? Porter lashes out at Joe, Rittenhouse, and Kovac for not doing anything. She at least offers her diamond lure for the fishing party. But as producer Kenneth MacGowan said, they are saved by the only thing that ever rescues people adrift at sea—the chance appearance of another ship. Call it a miracle if you wish.[42]

What of the startling appearance of the young sailor from

the supply ship in the film's closing moments? "Figuratively the war was over," MacGowan explained. The people had come through to the "peace of rescue." Here was, quite literally, a second chance for democracy—a second chance to reconstruct the postwar world. The sailor expects to be killed. Rittenhouse has argued: "You can't treat them as human beings. You've got to exterminate them." But in contrast to Nazi ruthlessness, they decide to hold him as a prisoner. This decision also mitigates the killing-for-cause of Willi. Now the haunting question: "What are you going to do with people like that?" In one version the picture was to end with an eloquent, ambiguous shrug from Kovac. Instead in the ending that was chosen Stanley is thinking of Gus and the mother and her baby. Porter in closeup: "Well, maybe *they* can answer that." On that decidedly ambiguous note the film concludes, with the camera, echoing the first scene, picking up debris from the shipwreck.[43]

OWI was disturbed by the varying responses to what to do with the Germans. The film implied that "if there is an answer to the problem of what to do with the Germans after the war, the Americans don't know it," said BMP reviewers. But wasn't that the point? As *Time* pointed out: When *Lifeboat* ends, they are still debating, like the world, what to do with the German."[44]

In 1944 the Allies knew they wanted unconditional surrender and not much more. Even unconditional surrender was not so clear as the propaganda implied. The doctrine had enough latitude to embrace deals with the fascist collaborators Darlan and Badoglio. Would a similar bargain be struck with the Germans, despite OWI's insistence to the contrary? Would Germany be carved into five pastoral republics never again able to make war, as Secretary of the Treasury Morgenthau wished? Policy towards Japan was still murkier; keeping the emperor would have seemed an absurd twist of a Hollywood screenwriter's imagination. Soon America's most enigmatic ally, the Soviet Union, would overshadow everything else as a threat to steal the hard-won victory, and erstwhile enemies would be converted into bulwarks against the communist threat. As Americans began to debate the postwar world, Hollywood and OWI turned to the sainted figure of Woodrow Wilson as guide and mentor on how to win the peace.

XI.

Hollywood, 1945

As the war drew to a close, Americans found their situation to be analogous to that at the end of World War I. President Roosevelt tried to correct what he perceived to be the mistakes of his predecessor by insisting on unconditional surrender. This time the enemy would have no doubt he had been thoroughly defeated. There would be no room for legends to grow that a still resilient foe had been the victim of a "stab in the back" or of a "Carthaginian peace." The other piece of the analogy involved convincing Americans not to retreat into isolationism, which, in the popular interpretation OWI shared, had led to World War II. In this interpretation the United States had made a catastrophic mistake in rejecting Woodrow Wilson's League of Nations and its commitment to collective security. "What do you do with people like that?" The answer seemed to be that the victors should act as the four policemen of the world to ensure that "fascism," whether European or Oriental, would never threaten us again. In an almost providential way America had been given a second chance.[1]

OWI pushed this idea eagerly. Hollywood moguls were attracted to it. But making a gripping entertainment picture of an abstract concept—and a vague one at that—was hard. The major attempt to do so, Darryl Zanuck's *Wilson,* proved to be an expensive fiasco.

Several studios sized up the proposition. RKO's Edward Golden, who had produced *Hitler's Children,* considered making a film titled simply "Democracy," based on an outline by Emmet Lavery, his writer for the Nazi picture. Golden became enthusiastic about the project when, at a luncheon in the fall of 1942, he heard Nelson Poynter appeal to the producers to make big, serious pictures. Golden urged screenwriter Lavery to ransack the OWI manual for ideas. "Maybe my arm is fill of hop, maybe I am taking too much territory, but Emmett—no—it ["Democracy"] has it!" said the producer. Lavery's outline traced a young soldier who, disillusioned by the Versailles treaty, became a cynical college professor and trained a generation of uncommitted youth, only to regain his patriotism and sign up for another hitch in World War II. Poynter liked the idea and conferred with Golden and Lavery in an effort to enhance its propaganda value. For unknown reasons, perhaps fears that the subject might lack box office appeal, RKO did not follow through on the production.[2]

The risks entailed in dealing with such an overtly political subject furrowed the brows of Louis B. Mayer, E. J. Mannix, and other MGM brass as they considered making a $2 or $3 million picture titled "Versailles Tragedy" in 1943. They foresaw that any film on this subject that had even a trace of realism would offer up the unedifying spectacle of the Allies bickering and conniving. Moreover, the government might object to the picture and deny it an export license. The project's screenwriter, John Balderston, fresh from his brush with bad history in *Tennessee Johnson,* came up with an ingenious way to show why Versailles failed. It was not the fault of the quarreling Allies at all, but rather an incipient fascist conspiracy. He planned to show German and Japanese delegates already hatching their string of 1930s conquests in 1919, right under the noses of the Allied representatives! This stood history on its head even more than did *Tennessee Johnson*—Japan was allied with the U.S., Britain, and France in World War I, and Germany was not allowed to send a delegation to the peace talks. Asked for his opinion, Lowell Mellett tried to steer Balderston away from Versailles. The BMP chief suggested instead an allegory of *Pilgrim's Progress* with mankind as the pilgrim "struggling to achieve the Four Freedoms." In Mellett's mind the Four Freedoms evidently had a sacred status worthy of religious striving.[3]

In April 1944 the State Department brought an end to the efforts of these acolytes by branding the project as "extremely dangerous" to the prospects for "a permanent peace plan." This was, of course, the very opposite of the studio's expressed intentions. Though Balderston tried to keep the project alive, OWI was not inclined to buck the State Department on the subject of the peace negotiations. MGM dropped the feature. Mayer no doubt was relieved. He worried about political pictures and probably did not want to produce a film that, by elevating Wilson, would boost the political fortunes of Franklin Roosevelt, who cast himself as the man who intended to make good on giving collective security a second chance.[4]

With the demise of "Democracy" and "Versailles Tragedy," Darryl Zanuck was alone in the field. The Twentieth Century-Fox chief, who had produced film biographies of Disraeli, Alexander Graham Bell, and Abraham Lincoln, had become interested in Wilson before Pearl Harbor. He shelved the project while he spent time in the Army Signal Corps as a colonel. Upon his return to the studio in 1943 he found that his old interest in Wilson dovetailed nicely with a national revival of interest in the once-maligned president. Colonel Zanuck's war experience confirmed his internationalist politics and his desire to upgrade Hollywood's standards. An admirer of Wendell Willkie, who headed Twentieth Century's board of directors, Zanuck saw in Wilson "an early day Willkie" whose wisdom would "help clear the path toward lasting peace for the new generation." If the Wilson project was a success, the producer planned to make a film of Willkie's million-copy-seller *One World,* an account of the presidential nominee's globe-circling trip in 1942 and his admittedly misty blueprint for the peace. Zanuck may have hoped that a conflation of Wilson and Willkie would propel the latter toward the White House in 1944. The colonel was also convinced that the war had opened Americans to more serious screen topics. Movies still had to entertain—there would always be a market for "Betty Grable and Lana Turner and all that tit stuff," he said—but Twentieth Century had to make films that would "match the new climate of the times."[5]

The task of blending entertainment and seriousness fell to Lamar Trotti, a distinguished screenwriter and producer fresh from *The Ox-Bow Incident* and *Guadalcanal Diary.* Trotti worked closely with Ray Stannard Baker, whose adoring eight-volume biography of Wilson won the Pulitzer Prize in 1940. The resulting screenplay won enthusiastic praise from OWI reviewers, who singled it out for special distribution in liberated areas.

BMP suggestions focused on reinforcing the almost mystical bond between Wilson, the quintessential democrat, and the people. The Princeton president's tangle with the college eating clubs (referred to only briefly out of deference to the university's sensitivity) became a simple issue of populism versus privilege. When OWI said the powerful role of machine politicians would be "most discouraging" to other countries, Trotti revised the script to show principle crushing political dealmaking. Governor Wilson spurns Boss Smith's demand that he nominate him for the Senate. The florid politician bellows: "I elected you." Wilson rejoins icily, "Then you should have exercised better judgment in your choice," and dismisses him. The people did not lose faith in the president or his League. A professor is introduced to explain that various side issues precluded the people from having "a decent chance to express themselves" on the League. Thus Wilson and the people are as one from the time of his first election to the demise of the League at the hands of unscrupulous politicians.[6]

Zanuck poured his prodigious energy and plenty of money into the picture. "It was the *only* time I saw him on set," said the director, Henry King. The price tag—something over $5 million when a big publicity budget was included—made it the most expensive film produced to that time. For all his protestations about the need to make serious pictures, he still thought in the clichés of Hollywood's golden age. A serious point might be attempted, but it had to be sugarcoated in glamour, romance, and spectacle. He insisted that "if this isn't entertainment we're sunk." He dreaded praise from "the intellectuals and the well-meaning political commentators. . . . We made it for the regular mugs and bobby-sockers, and we don't want them getting the idea it's highbrow." Zanuck's ideas about how to combine entertainment and political seriousness were reminiscent of the industry's attempt to make *Prelude to War* appeal to the "chewing gum crowd" by promoting it as "the greatest gangster picture ever made." Privately he joked: "If this picture doesn't make it, I'm never going to make another one without Betty Grable."[7]

Woodrow Wilson did not possess much glamour, and Zanuck chose an obscure Canadian stage actor, Alexander Knox, for the role. The second Mrs. Wilson, played by Geraldine Fitzgerald, dazzled audiences with a stunning trousseau. But there were no romantic sparks in their White House courtship. The president's romantic overtures were not unlike his arch and convoluted diplomatic notes. And whenever she edged toward him, he backed against a pillar. Perhaps Hollywood thought showing a president in physical contact—even holding hands—with his betrothed transgressed the bounds of good taste. Lesser roles were assumed by Thomas Mitchell as Wilson's devoted secretary Joseph Tumulty, Charles Coburn as Professor Henry Holmes, and Vincent Price as Secretary of the Treasury McAdoo. Sir Cedric Hardwicke, who had recently oppressed the people of Norway as Colonel Lanser, was summoned to play the arch-villain, Senator Henry Cabot Lodge. Filmed in technicolor, *Wilson* boasted half a million dollars' worth of sets alone, with painstaking replicas of the House of Representatives chamber and rooms in the White House. To re-enact the Democratic convention of 1912, fifteen hundred extras packed the Los Angeles Shrine Auditorium for a fairly short, but visually magnificent, scene.[8]

This huge commitment of resources went for naught. Although willing to attempt a serious theme from which other producers skittered away, Zanuck did not have the nerve to give it the treatment it needed. He might have attempted a probing character study of his Aeschylean subject, or he might have genuinely delved into the political issues of the Wilson era. Yet each of these approaches posed serious problems. A character study would have revealed a man who, whatever his personal strengths, was also aloof, self-righteous, and stubborn to the point of destroying his own creation. An informed political study, no matter how enlightening, would also have shown a morass of unsolved and unsolvable issues, petty rancor and sheer vindictiveness on the part of the Allies, and Wilson's own questionable dealings at certain points. Neither picture was calculated to appeal to the box office or to the propaganda needs of 1944–45.

Instead, with OWI's enthusiastic backing, Zanuck set out to humanize Wilson. In turning the scholar-president into a regular Joe, however, Hollywood made him a bore. Sports and music were the two primary vehicles. Wilson cheers madly for the Princeton football team, offers fatherly advice to the players, and feels gloomy in defeat. He is an avid, if inept, golfer. As

governor he regularly sneaks away to Broadway to take in musicals—in this case a cameo appearance by the aging song-and-
dance man Eddie Foy. Almost any occasion is seized for the Wilson family to gather around the family grand and pound out a
period hit (bits of 87 songs larded the 150-minute feature, obviously inserted out of fear that the story would not carry itself).
The one moment of genuine pathos concerns the death of his
first wife. When not acting out his sentimentalized personal life,
Wilson is the efficient, righteous, all-seeing statesman, issuing
ex cathedra statements on all manner of affairs of state. Respectful Wilson quotations stand out as half-familiar maxims
but do little to explain him or his actions. Trotti's screenplay
made Wilson neither a believable family man nor a credible
political figure; the two sides of him never met.

Worse, the politics—the only reason for making the picture—got lost. Why we went to war with Germany was not clear,
except that the evil Germans did it to us. Wilson summons the
Kaiser's ambassador for a dressing down, but instead of providing us with understanding the scene offers vicarious joy at
the tongue-lashing of evil. Versailles was covered in a brief scene
in which the president bests Clemenceau in arguing about
whether France should take German territory. The League cov-
enant becomes practically the tablets of stone a divinely inspired Wilson brought back from Paris. The opposition of Senator Lodge and his cohort appears simply petty and vindictive.
There is no acknowledgment that Lodge and others might have
well-founded reasons for opposing the League; Wilson's refusal
to accept any compromise on the League appears to be strictly
noble. The president's national speaking tour rushes by through
a series of set pieces composed of Wilsonian phrases followed
by applause from adoring crowds. Then he is laid low by a
stroke. Clear in mind if broken in body, he hurls a last epithet
at Lodge, who can only watch in awe as the president shuffles
from the screen.

Wilson's initial reception was enthusiastic. Six thousand people gave the picture a rousing ovation at its premiere in New
York on August 1, 1944. Wendell Willkie and the Woodrow Wilson Foundation hosted a buffet supper for the movie and political stars, including Wilson's widow; Mrs. William Gibbs
McAdoo, the president's daughter; and James Cox, the Demo-

cratic standard-bearer in 1920. Arthur Sweetser, president of the Wilson Foundation, found the picture "infinitely better, more dignified and more eloquent than we had dared hope." *PM* greeted the picture with an eight-page spread under the headline: "*Wilson* Wartime Wisdom May Help Win for FDR." Since Willkie had been knocked out of the running for a second presidential bid by disastrous showings in the spring primaries, Roosevelt ironically stood to benefit most from *Wilson*.[9]

Film critic Manny Farber termed the picture "tedious and impotent" and its impossibly noble Wilson and America a "lie." These judgments stand up well in retrospect. Yet most reviews were favorable. *Life,* promoter of such pictures as *Mission to Moscow, North Star,* and *An American Romance,* crowned its wartime reviewing record by terming *Wilson* "one of the best pictures Hollywood ever made." Here truly was a film for the hour, thought OWI, which found it not only "vital to the psychological warfare of the United Nations" but endowed with "rare entertainment value."[10]

The "ordinary mugs and bobby-sockers" filed past the box office in respectable numbers. An estimated ten million people saw the picture by February 1945. With its huge budget, however, *Wilson* had to be a block buster, and it wasn't. Twentieth Century lost a significant, but indeterminate, amount on the movie. *Wilson* won five of the lesser Academy Awards, but the Oscar for best picture that Zanuck coveted eluded him until his 1947 release about anti-Semitism, *Gentleman's Agreement.* He stood by his film. Accepting the trophy in 1947, he said: "Many thanks but I should have won it for *Wilson*." Zanuck, meanwhile, turned next to *Laura,* starring Gene Tierney—not Betty Grable, the G.I.s' favorite pin-up, but close enough. He did not exercise his rights to film *One World.*[11]

Wilson was neither good entertainment nor good politics, and it brought to an unhappy end the wartime convergence of propaganda and popular culture. After some early skirmishes to establish the ground rules, the Office of War Information and Hollywood found their interests compatible in both style and content. The Bureau of Motion Pictures read 390 screenplays from September, 1943 to August, 1944 (the last period for which records have been found) and recorded changes to meet their objections in 71 percent of the cases. For the war years the agency reviewed 1,652 scripts before Truman abolished it effective Aug. 31, 1945. Even the *Motion Picture Herald* concluded that the OWI connection was highly valuable to the industry.[12]

BMP personnel, such as Nelson Poynter and Dorothy Jones, wished the studios had made more significant pictures on some themes, particularly the home front and collective security for the postwar era. Nonetheless they believed that OWI's liaison efforts in Hollywood helped democratize the movie industry by supporting more diverse political views, and that their experience offered a model for future cooperation between the government and mass media. OWI in Hollywood represents the most comprehensive and sustained government attempt to change the content of a mass medium in American history. Wartime censorship told the mass media what not to make known. OWI not only told Hollywood what should be excluded but what should, in fact, be included. The combination of government power with a cartel bore an uncomfortable resemblance, however, to foreign corporatist experiments. The wartime propaganda experience thus invites evaluation both for the messages generated by this unique liaison and for its implications for the control of popular culture.

Wilson suggests the problems inherent in the fusion of entertainment and propaganda. The movies did little to prepare Americans for dealing with their victory, which was, after all, the point of the war. The problem was not lack of movies. The pictures that might have been made—Golden's "Democracy," Balderston's "Versailles Tragedy," or Mellett's "Pilgrim's Progress"—would only have compounded *Wilson*'s shortcomings. Neither Hollywood nor OWI was prepared to go beyond a vaguely felt appeal for internationalism and collective security as an antidote to the mistake we made after World War I; theirs was an idea based on the simplistic notion that history repeats itself. The Roosevelt administration was not much clearer, for that matter, since FDR thought that too detailed a discussion of postwar plans would only endanger Allied unity. But the propagandists and the movie makers did little to give Americans a basis for judgment and discrimination in their new world of internationalism. The supposedly united, modern China of the movies soon slipped into civil war. The old European empires— one of the propaganda unmentionables—began to break up, setting the stage for an agonizing American conflict in Vietnam, and bloody revolutions in other parts of the Third World. The dream of an American-led era of collective security proved to be more ambiguous, costly, and divisive than anticipated. Above all, the Soviet Union and communism soon replaced the Axis and fascism as the embodiment of evil and the locus of complete peril. The war pictures also obscured the sometimes questionable tactics the U.S. and its allies used to fight the war. The symbolism of World War II movies, by excluding pertinent truths about their subjects and framing issues in misleading ways, was thus, as Robert Merton warned, "dangerously manipulative."

Wartime movies fused two powerful myths that had deep roots in American popular culture and political discourse. One was the division of the world into slave and free. They divided a world of total peril into forces of either ultimate evil or righteousness. Having assumed responsibility for freedom everywhere, expectations were raised that with complete victory the Allies would guarantee liberty globally. The Allies' own imperialism and denial of rights at home could barely be mentioned. The other myth was a newly universalized version of the idea of regeneration through war. Literary critic Richard Slotkin has shown that a dominant myth of nineteenth-century America, derived from the Indian wars, was that "the different races and classes that divided American society might restore their 'harmony,' through a sanctified and regenerative act of violence."[13]

In the OWI/Hollywood vision, the war produced unity. Labor and capital buried their differences for a greater cause; class, ethnic, and racial divisions evaporated in the foxholes and on the assembly line; even estranged family members were reconciled through the agency of war. These images, which conveyed more a hope than a reality, implicitly argued that war, however horrible, might be a tonic. No longer limited to America, the myth now extended worldwide. The wartime United Nations had harmonious political and social structures and fought for the same goals. If they remained unified, they might eradicate the environment of total endangerment. This might be the "American Century" or the "Century of the Common Man," but both relied on a vision of war as an extension of reform. Since World War II was widely perceived as "the good war," both na-

tionally and personally, the myths received added sanctifica-
tion.

Having defined the stakes in global terms, and promised
that war brought internal and international harmony, the wartime propaganda had coincidentally helped prepare America
for the Cold War. Many of the liberals and leftists who played
key roles in the creation of wartime movie propaganda deplored the Cold War, or at least its excesses. Yet in modernizing
some of America's oldest myths they forged tools which, given
the structure of the mass media and the changing international
climate, would prove adaptable to purposes antithetical to
theirs.

Hollywood, perhaps aptly, provided one of the first settings
for this new application of the wartime imagery. The movie industry, racked by declining profits and labor strife immediately
after the war, was forced onto the political defensive when the
House Un-American Activities Committee turned its guns on
the industry in earnest in 1947. A parade of witnesses, many of
them associated with Sam Wood's Motion Picture Alliance for
the Preservation of American Ideals, testified to the presence
of communists and fellow travelers in the movie colony. They
also condemned what they termed "communist propaganda" in
the movies, chiefly the salute-our-ally-Russia films of the war
years. They implied, but could not demonstrate, a causal link
between the presence of Reds in lotus land and red and pink
sentiments on the screen. The hearings demonstrated, rather,
the strict control the studio hierarchies exercised over film content.

The reigning moguls wielded their power decisively in the
Cold War climate. They withdrew their now embarrassing Russian films from circulation. Some pictures were not shown again
for two decades. Others, such as *North Star,* renamed *Armored
Attack* and fitted with new narration that tried to correct the
political slant, were earning profits from television within a decade. The studios atoned, profusely, for their Russian films with
some fifty anti-communist pictures in the late 1940s and early
50s. Some executives, such as Jack Warner, twisted and turned
and recanted before the committee and threw underlings—such
as Howard Koch, whom he had strong-armed into working on
Mission to Moscow—to the wolves to keep them away from his

sleigh. The industry was purged of those who would not recant and aid the inquisition. The most famous were the "Hollywood Ten," ten men (mostly writers) who were sent to jail for contempt of Congress when they refused to cooperate with HUAC's questioners. The industry did the rest on its own, running a blacklist that ruined many careers, forced some creative talent to flee to Europe, and trapped many in agonizing choices about personal and political loyalty. Since there was little communist propaganda to root out of films, naming names was chiefly an exercise in ritual humiliation and provided a means of reasserting control of the industry.

Ironically, even as these sordid proceedings escalated, the ground was beginning to shift beneath the feet of the once entrenched executive elite. Zanuck had been right, although he had not known how to capitalize on it in 1944. The war had made the public willing to accept the serious "big theme movies" of which he dreamed. Though some Hollywood decision makers, notably Louis B. Mayer, clung to the prewar formulas, many were increasingly receptive to subjects and approaches that in the 1930s would have been too controversial to consider. Movie critics of the late 1940s noticed an increasing trend to make pictures dealing with social problems, such as *The Lost Weekend* (1945) in which Ray Milland played an alcoholic; Zanuck's *Gentleman's Agreement* (1947), one of several pictures about anti-Semitism, in this case featuring the arch-WASP Gregory Peck who passes for Jewish; and *Pinky, Home of the Brave,* and *The Boy with Green Hair,* each of which explored, however tentatively, the personal tragedy of racism. While these passed the Production Code Administration relatively unscathed, the vigilant Joseph Breen sensed a seismic event. In 1950 he complained to Father Daniel Lord, the author of the code, that his job was growing increasingly difficult because many of the new men in Hollywood did not respect the code and were determined to destroy it.[14]

External forces accelerated the decline of the classic Hollywood. The television set in the living room displaced the corner movie house as the seat of visual popular culture. The Supreme Court decided in 1952 that film now came under the protection of the First Amendment, which spelled eventual doom for the network of state and municipal censorship boards.

The industry's own censorship apparatus had been dealt a body blow some years earlier, when in 1948 the high court ruled that the major firms' control from production through exhibition violated the antitrust laws. They were required to divorce their production and exhibition components, and thus lost their control of the American market. This development gave independent producers a much better chance to have their pictures shown; it also meant that film makers could thumb their noses at the Production Code Administration and still find houses in which to show their products. Otto Preminger's first independent production, *The Moon Is Blue* (1953), employed such hitherto unmentionable terms as "virgin" and "pregnant"; it was released without Breen's seal of approval "to test a principle," found ample play dates, and made money. Although the code was liberalized in 1956, and continued to exist until 1968, when it was replaced by today's rating system, producers increasingly evaded it, and its enforcers carved ever larger holes in it.

As the movies became less popular they became more free. Crucial to that growing freedom was the breakup of the old studio oligopoly and its replacement by a legion of independents. Hollywood had always claimed that it only gave the public what it wanted, and cited the movies' popularity as proof. But since the cartel controlled the range of choice, Hollywood was saying only that the public bought what it was given. The movies were popular culture in only a quantitative sense; they were not popularly determined. Hollywood gave the public what it (i. e., the major companies) wanted the public to have. During the war the government, through the Office of War Information, increased the control over messages that were allowable in the movies. The diversification of control from the 1950s onward has produced a diversity of viewpoints.[15]

Hollywood, 1945: politics, profits, and propaganda could reinforce each other to create symbols of a unified, harmonious society. But the new world ushered in by the war—a world of increasing diversity both nationally and internationally—doomed the old Hollywood and its message.

Notes

CHAPTER I.

1. Garth Jowett, *Film: The Democratic Art* (Boston, 1976), Vachel Lindsay, *The Art of the Moving Picture* (New York, 1916), p. 215.
2. Leo Rosten, *Hollywood: The Movie Colony, the Movie Makers* (New York, 1941), pp. 61–63; Mae D. Huettig, *Economic Control of the Motion Picture Industry* (Philadelphia, 1944). The eight consisted of the "Big Five"—Loew's Inc. (of which Metro-Goldwyn-Mayer was the production arm), Twentieth Century-Fox, Paramount, Warner Brothers, and Radio-Keith-Orpheum (RKO)—and the "Little Three"—Universal, Columbia, and United Artists.
3. Norman Zierold, *The Moguls* (New York, 1969), p. 254; Lary May, *Screening Out the Past: The Birth of Mass Culture and the Motion Picture Industry* (New York, 1980), p. 171.
4. Ibid., pp. 183–85.
5. Ibid., pp. 185.
6. Rosten, *Hollywood*, p. 35.
7. Ibid., p. 37.
8. Warner quoted in Patricia Erens, "Between Two Worlds: Jewish Images in American Films," in Randall M Miller, ed., *The Kaleidoscopic Lens: How Hollywood Views Ethnic Groups* (1980), p. 124; F. Scott Fitzgerald, *The Last Tycoon* (New York, 1941), p. 118; Robert Sklar, *Movie-Made America: A Cultural History of American Movies* (New York, 1975), p. 193.
9. Rosten, *Hollywood*, p. 16; Parker Tyler, "Hollywood as a Universal Church," *American Quarterly*, 2 (1950), 166.
10. Hortense Powdermaker, *Hollywood: The Dream Factory* (Boston, 1950); on Cohn see Bob Thomas, *King Cohn* (New York, 1967).

11. Rosten, *Hollywood,* pp. 80–90.

12. Otis Ferguson, "Hollywood Will Fool You If You Don't Watch Out (Didn't It?)," in Robert Wilson, ed., *The Film Criticism of Otis Ferguson* (Philadelphia, 1971), p. 429.

13. John Balderston to Lowell Mellett, Sept. 17, 1941, box 1431, Records of the Office of War Information, Record Group 208, Washington National Records Center, Suitland, Maryland (hereafter OWI Files).

14. Rosten, *Hollywood,* chap. 14; Larry Ceplair and Steven Englund, *The Inquisition in Hollywood: Politics in the Film Community, 1930–1960* (Berkeley, 1983), chap. 1.

15. Henry James Forman, *Our Movie-Made Children* (New York, 1933); John Clellon Holmes, "15¢ Before 6:00 P.M.: The Wonderful Movies of 'The Thirties,'" *Harper's* (Dec., 1965), 51.

16. Robert Coles, *The Moral Life of Children* (Boston, 1986), chap. 1. For an informed discussion of the issue of the movies' effects see Jowett, *Film: The Democratic Art,* chap. 11.

17. *Mutual Film Corporation v. Ohio,* 236 U.S. 230.

18. Will H. Hays, *The Memoirs of Will Hays* (New York, 1955), pp. 448–51.

19. Ibid., p. 450.

20. Wallis to Warner, Aug. 20, 1934, "Marie Antoinette" file, Warner Brothers Production Files, Doheny Library, University of Southern California, Los Angeles (hereafter USC).

21. Ralph Jester, "Hollywood and Pedagogy," *Journal of Educational Sociology* (November 1938), 137.

22. The production code is reprinted in Gerald Mast, *The Movies in our Midst: Documents in the Cultural History of Film in America* (Chicago, 1982), pp. 321–33. The authors' conclusions about the code's effects are based on their examination of the files for hundreds of movies from the Production Code Administration Records in the Margaret Herrick Library, Academy of Motion Picture Arts and Sciences, Beverly Hills, California (hereafter PCA Files, Academy Library).

23. Authors' interview with Philip Dunne, January 1985, Malibu, California; "Propaganda or History?" *Nation* (Sept. 20, 1941), 241.

CHAPTER II.

1. U.S. Senate, 77th Congress, 1st Sess., *Propaganda in Motion Pictures,* Hearing before a Subcommittee of the Committee on Interstate

Commerce, on S. Res. 152, Sept. 9–26, 1941, (Washington, D. C., 1941).

2. Willkie statement, ibid., pp. 18–22.

3. On the United States' path to war see Robert Divine, *The Reluctant Belligerent* (2nd ed., New York, 1979) and Wayne S. Cole, *Roosevelt and the Isolationists, 1932–1945* (Lincoln, Neb., 1983); on the Atlantic Charter see Theodore A. Wilson, *The First Summit: Roosevelt and Churchill at Argentia Bay* (Boston, 1969).

4. Wheeler to Hays, Jan. 13, 1941; Hays to Wheeler, Jan. 14, 1941; Hays to Roosevelt, Jan. 17, 1941, President's Personal File 1945, Franklin D. Roosevelt Library (hereafter FDRL), Hyde Park, N.Y.

5. Robert Sklar, *Movie-Made America* (New York, 1975). p. 245.

6. *Variety,* April 3, 1934, p. 13; Raymond Moley, *The Hays Office* (New York, 1945), p. 172.

7. *Variety* (April 3, 1934), 13.

8. Joseph Breen to Daniel Lord, S. J., Dec. 5, 1937, Daniel Lord Papers, Jesuit Missouri Province Archives, St. Louis, Mo.

9. *New York Times,* June 15, 1935; Robert E. Sherwood, *Idiot's Delight* (New York, 1936).

10. Geoffrey Shurlock memo on "Idiot's Delight," March 25, 1936, Joseph Breen to Frederick Herron, April 11, 1936, Herron to Breen, May 7, 1937, Herron to Breen, Jan. 7, 1937, Breen to Files, May 12, 1937, R. Caracciolo to Breen, June 8, 1937, Hunt Stromberg to Breen, June 23, 1937, Caracciolo to Breen, June 20, 1938, Breen to Mayer, Aug. 26, 1938, PCA Files, Academy Library; John Mason Brown, *The Worlds of Robert E. Sherwood: Mirror to His Times, 1896–1939* (New York, 1962), pp. 334–38.

11. *Newsweek* (Feb. 6, 1939), 24; *North American Review* (Sept. 1939), 174–75.

12. John Howard Lawson, *Film: The Creative Process* (New York, 1964), pp. 124–125.

13. Breen to Walter Wanger, Jan. 4, 1938, "Blockade," PCA Files, Academy Library; Larry S. Ceplair, "The Politics of Compromise in Hollywood: A Case Study," *Cineaste*(8), 2–7.

14. Winchell Taylor, "Secret Movie Censors," *The Nation* (July, 1938), 38–40.

15. Ibid., 39; Lawson, *Film: The Creative Process,* p. 125.

16. Joseph Breen to Walter Wanger, June 18, 1938, "Personal History," PCA Files, Academy Library; "Questionnaire #21," n.d., "Foreign Correspondent," O'Brian Files, box 186, Wisconsin State Historical Society (hereafter WSHS); Walter Wanger, "120,000 American Ambassadors," *Foreign Affairs* (Oct. 1939), 45–59.

17. Breen to Will Hays, June 21, 1938, "Personal History," PCA Files, Academy Library.

18. Breen to Wanger, June 21, 1938, *ibid.*

19. K. L. to Breen, n.d., "Confessions of a Nazi Spy," PCA Files, Academy Library; George Gyssling, German consul in Los Angeles to Breen, Nov. 23, 1938, *ibid.*

20. Luigi Luraschi to Breen, Dec. 10, 1938, *ibid.*

21. K. L. to Breen, n. d., *ibid.*

22. Breen to Jack Warner, Dec. 30, 1938; Breen to Hays, Dec. 30, 1938, ibid.

23. Ibid.

24. Ibid.

25. Eric J. Sandeen, "Confessions of a Nazi Spy," *American Studies* (April, 1979), 69–81; Larry Ceplair and Steven Englund, *Inquisition in Hollywood: Politics in the Film Community, 1930–1960* (Berkeley, 1979), pp. 308–310.

26. *The New Republic* (May 10, 1939), 20; *The Hollywood Reporter,* April 28, 1939; *Variety,* May 3, 1939.

27. See "Confessions of a Nazi Spy," PCA Files, Academy Library.

28. Breen to Hays, Mar. 18, 1940, ibid. Also see "The Legion Rides Again," *The New Republic* (Dec. 22, 1941), 801.

29. Tino Balio, *United Artists: The Company Built by the Stars* (Madison, Wis., 1979), p. 164.

30. Brooke Wilkinson to Breen, Mar. 3, 1939, "The Great Dictator," PCA Files, Academy Library.

31. Breen to Al Reeves, Sept. 6, 1940, ibid.

32. Ibid.

33. Breen to Francis Harmon, June 8, 1940, "Pastor Hall," PCA Files, Academy Library.

34. Ibid.

35. Breen to James Roosevelt, July 7, 1940, ibid.

36. *Variety,* July 21, 1940.

37. Richard W. Steele, *Propaganda in an Open Society: The Roosevelt Administration and the Media, 1933–1941* (Westport, Conn., 1985), pp. 157–58.

38. Ibid.

39. Breen to Louis B. Mayer, Sept. 15, 1939, "The Mortal Storm," PCA Files, Academy Library.

40. Geoffrey Shurlock to Guerney, Oct. 9, 1939, "Escape," ibid.

41. Breen to Hays, Mar. 4, 1941, "Man Hunt," ibid.

42. Otis Ferguson, *The New Republic* (June 23, 1941), 859.

43. *The Nation* (Mar. 15, 1941), 305. Mellett to FDR, Mar. 17, 1941, White House–1941 folder, Lowell Mellett Papers, Franklin D. Roosevelt Library, Hyde Park, New York (hereafter FDRL). Fritz Hippler, head of the cinema department of the Reich Ministry of Propaganda, stated that if Hollywood films carried the "ideals of a free nation" throughout the world then "American ideals must be light amusement." The Germans were upset over *Confessions of a Nazi Spy, The Mortal Storm, and the Great Dictator.* See *Variety,* March 12, 1941.

44. Studio pressbook for *Sergeant York,* summer 1941, in possession of Gaylord Marr, Kansas City, Mo.

45. Wallis to Jesse Lasky, Jan. 4, 1941, Robert Buckner to Wallis, June 4, 1940, Sergeant York file, Warner Brothers Production Files, USC.

46. Howard Koch, *As Time Goes By* (New York, 1979), p. 75.

47. Studio pressbook for Sergeant York.

48. Gerald Nye, "War Propaganda," *Vital Speeches,* (Sept. 15, 1941), 720–723.

49. Ibid.

50. Nye to Page Huffy, Sept. 4, 1941, Gerald Nye Papers, box 43, Herbert Hoover Library, West Branch, Iowa (hereafter as HHL).

51. *Time* (Sept. 22, 1941), 13; *Life* (Sept. 22, 1941), 21–25.

52. *Propaganda in Motion Pictures,* Hearings, 11, 17.

53. Lowell Mellett to Roosevelt, Aug. 27, 1941, Official File 73, FDRL.

54. Mark L. Chadwin, *The Warhawks: American Interventionists before Pearl Harbor* (New York, 1968), pp. 216–18, Nye to Henry Mooberry, American First Committee, Sept. 4, 1941, Nye Papers, box 43, HHL.

55. Steve Neal, *Willkie* (New York, 1983), pp. 216–18.

56. *Time* (Sept. 22, 1941) 13.

57. *Propaganda in Motion Pictures,* Hearings, 19–20.

58. Ibid.

59. Ibid., 338.

60. Ibid.

61. Ibid., 234; Cole, *Senator Gerald P. Nye and American Foreign Relations,* p. 192.

62. Margaret Frakes, "Why the Movie Investigation," *Christian Century,* 58 (1941), 1172–74.

63. *Propaganda in Motion Pictures,* Hearings, 100–104.

64. *PM,* Sept. 10, 1941; "Propaganda or History?" *Nation* (Sept. 20, 1941), 241; Norman Cousins, "Our Heroes," *Saturday Review* (Oct. 25, 1941), 10.

65. Walter Wanger, "120,000 American Ambassadors," *Foreign Affairs*, 18 (1939), 45–59.

CHAPTER III.

1. Harold Lasswell, *Propaganda Technique in the World War* (New York, 1927), pp. 14–15.
2. On the Creel Committee see Stephen Vaughn, *Holding Fast the Inner Lines: Democracy, Nationalism, and the Committee on Public Information* (Chapel Hill, N.C., 1980), and James R. Mock and Cedric Larson, *Words That Won the War: The Story of the Committee on Public Information, 1917–1919* (Princeton, 1939).
3. Richard Steele, "Preparing the Public for War: Efforts to Establish a National Propaganda Agency, 1940–1941," *American Historical Review*, 75 (1970), 1640–53; Louis DeJong, *The German Fifth Column in the Second World War* (Chicago, 1956); Charles J. Rolo, *Radio Goes to War* (New York, 1942).
4. Lenin quoted in Mira Liehm and Antonin J. Liehm, *The Most Important Art: Eastern European Film After 1945* (Berkeley, 1977), p. 1.
5. Michael Choukas, *Propaganda Comes of Age* (Washington, 1965), p. 37. On media frames see Todd Gitlin, *The Whole World Is Watching: Mass Media in the Making & Unmaking of the New Left* (Berkeley, 1980), pp. 6–7.
6. Allan M. Winkler, *The Politics of Propaganda: The Office of War Information, 1942–1945* (New Haven, 1978), p. 20.
7. Richard W. Steele, *Propaganda in an Open Society*, p. 74.
8. Bruce Catton, *The War Lords of Washington* (New York, 1948), pp. 184–85; Memorandum of Conversation between Lowell Mellett and Sidney Hyman, Aug. 8, 1949, Washington, D.C., box 3, Papers of the Franklin D. Roosevelt Memorial Foundation, FDRL.
9. Winkler, *Politics of Propaganda*, p. 25.
10. Steele, *Propaganda in an Open Society*, pp. 73–74.
11. Harold L. Ickes to Franklin D. Roosevelt, April 28, 1941, box 15, Lowell Mellett Papers, FDRL.
12. Mellett to FDR, May 5, 1941, box 15, Mellett Papers, FDRL.
13. Mellett to FDR, March 17, 1941, White House—1941 folder, Mellett Papers, FDRL.
14. Steele, *Propaganda in an Open Society*, p. 78.
15. Ibid., p. 94.
16. Richard Dunlop, *Donovan: America's Master Spy* (Chicago, 1982), pp. 284–90, 385–6.
17. Winkler, *Politics of Propaganda*, pp. 26–28.

18. Ibid., pp. 22–23. Archibald MacLeish says FDR was not in favor of establishing a propaganda agency and created OFF largely to sidetrack Eleanor Roosevelt's pressure for a large-scale propaganda agency. Bernard A. Drabeck and Helen E. Ellis, eds., *Archibald MacLeish: Reflections* (Amherst, Mass., 1986), p. 147.

19. Archibald MacLeish to Harry Hopkins, Oct. 27, 1941, box 324, Harry Hopkins Papers, FDRL; Winkler, *Politics of Propaganda*, p. 23.

20. *New York Herald Tribune*, Oct. 9, 1941. MacLeish understood the problem all too well. He said he took over OFF only because the president asked him to do it. "I suppose in times of peace, so-called, you could probably devote yourself to information, trying to help a self-governing people to govern themselves by seeing that they got the information they had to have," he recalled. "But in war you were always on the verge of propaganda and ... although some of the propaganda you could give your whole heart to, some you couldn't. I just detested it." (Drabeck and Ellis, eds., *Archibald MacLeish*, p. 155.)

21. *Variety*, Dec. 24, 1941.

22. Ibid., Jan. 21, 28, 1942.

23. M. E. Gilfond to Mellett, July 15, 1942, box 3, Mellett Papers, FDRL.

24. Koppes interview with Nelson Poynter, Jan. 8, 1974, St. Petersburg, Florida.

25. Harold Smith Diaries, March 7, April 10, June 6, 1942, Harold Smith Papers, FDRL; Bernard L. Gladieux to Sam Rosenman, March 24, 1942, box 5015, Office File, FDR Papers, FDRL; William J. Donovan to FDR, President's Secretary's File 166, FDRL.

26. Francis Biddle to FDR, April 22, 1942, Official File 5015, FDR Papers, FDRL; Steve Early to Harry Hopkins, box 213, Hopkins Papers, FDRL; Smith Diary, June 6, 1942, Smith Papers, FDRL; Winkler, *Politics of Propaganda*, 31–35. Indicative of the respect Davis commanded, Russell Crouse and 98 other luminaries in theater, literature, and journalism sent Roosevelt a letter endorsing the broadcaster as head of OWI. (Crouse to FDR, March 31, 1942, box 133, Hopkins Papers, FDRL.)

27. Executive Order 9182, Consolidating Certain War Information Functions Into an Office of War Information, June 13, 1942, *Federal Register*, 7 (June 16, 1942), 4468–69.

28. *Variety*, March 25, 1942.

29. Dorothy B. Jones to Nelson Poynter, "War Features Inventory as of Sept. 15, 1942," box 1435, OWI files.

30. Feature review, *Secret Agent of Japan*, April 1942, box 3518, OWI files; *Variety*, March 11, 1942.

31. Feature reviews, *A Prisoner of Japan*, July 22, 1942, box 3512, *Re-*

member Pearl Harbor, May 11, 1942, box 3516; *Danger in the Pacific,* July 12, 1942, box 3519; *Halfway to Shanghai,* June 29, 1942, box 3519, OWI files.

32. Gregory D. Black and Clayton R. Koppes, "OWI Goes to the Movies: The Bureau of Intelligence's Criticism of Hollywood, 1942–43," *Prologue,* 6 (1974), 44.

33. Ibid., 52.

34. Ibid., 54.

35. "War Features Inventory as of July 15, 1942," box 1435, OWI files.

36. *Weekly Variety,* May 6, 1942; Koppes interview with Poynter.

37. *Weekly Variety,* May 6, 1942.

38. Elmer Davis to Byron Price, Jan. 27, 1943, box 3, OWI files.

39. Poynter to Arch Mercey, June 13, 30, 1942, box 1557, OWI files.

40. Ibid.

41. Ibid.

42. Dorothy Jones, *The Portrayal of China and India on the American Screen, 1896–1955* (Cambridge, Mass., 1955), p. 83n64; *Variety,* June 17, 1942.

43. Henry A. Wallace, "The Price of Free World Victory: The Century of the Common Man," *Vital Speeches of the Day,* 7 (1942), 482–85; Henry Luce, "The American Century," *Life* (Feb. 17, 1941), 61–63; Norman Markowitz, *The Rise and Fall of the People's Century: Henry A. Wallace and American Liberalism* (New York, 1973), p. 50.

44. "Government Information Manual for the Motion Picture Industry," Summer 1942, box 15, OWI files. Revisions were made to keep the manual abreast of developments in the war, but this did not change the document's thrust. See the revisions dated April 29, 1943, and January 1944, box 15, OWI files.

45. Breen to Shurlock, Apr. 15, 1943, "Hitler's Madman," PCA Files, Academy Library.

46. Koppes interview with Poynter.

47. Ceplair and Englund, *The Inquisition in Hollywood,* pp. 177–83.

48. Script review, "For Whom the Bell Tolls," Oct. 14, 1942, OWI files.

49. Robert K. Merton with Marjorie Fiske and Alberta Curtis, *Mass Persuasion: The Social Psychology of a War Bond Drive* (New York, 1946), p. 186.

50. Feature review, *Little Tokyo, U.S.A.,* July 9, 1942, box 3518, OWI files.

51. Twentieth Century-Fox press release, June 19, 1942, "Little Tokyo, U.S.A." file, Academy Library.

52. Twentieth Century press release, June 16, 1942, ibid.

53. Final script, "Little Tokyo, U.S.A.," Twentieth Century-Fox collec-

tion, Theater Arts Library, University Research Library, University of California at Los Angeles.

54. Feature review, *Little Tokyo, U.S.A.,* box 3518, OWI files.

55. Ibid.; Poynter to Mellett, July 23, 1942; M. M. Tozier to Mellett, Aug. 26, 1942; Poynter to Mellett, Sept. 2, 1942, box 3518, OWI files; Elmer Davis to Norman Thomas, Sept. 23, 1942, box 1439, OWI files.

56. Poynter to Jason Joy, Sept. 2, 1942, box 3518, OWI files.

57. Two of the key arguments used by decision makers for the roundup were explicitly racial: (1) Caucasians could not distinguish among Japanese; (2) Japanese racial strains, and by assumption their concomitant loyalties, were undiluted by prolonged residence in the United States. On the first point an important legal opinion by three liberal lawyers supporting internment—Ben Cohen, Oscar Cox, and Joseph Rauh—stated: "Since the Occidental eye cannot readily distinguish one Japanese resident from another, effective surveillance of the movements of particular Japanese residents suspected of disloyalty is extremely difficult if not practically impossible." On the second point Colonel Karl Bendetsen, who as a lawyer in the provost marshal general's office played a key role in encouraging the program, averred: "In the war in which we are now engaged racial affinities are not severed by migration. The Japanese race is an enemy race and while many second and third generation Japanese born on United States soil, possessed of United States citizenship, have become 'Americanized,' the racial strains are undiluted." By contrast with this point of view, it should be noted that J. Edgar Hoover and the FBI thought the army simply lost its head in calling for the internment. See Peter Irons, *Justice at War: Story of the Japanese American Internment Cases* (New York, 1983), pp. 54–55, 59.

58. Mellett to Poynter, July 30, 1942, box 1439, OWI files.

59. See Larry Suid, ed., *Air Force* (Madison, 1983), which contains the shooting script.

60. Script review, "Air Force," Oct. 27, 1942, box 3515, OWI files.

61. "Fried Jap" is not in Nichols' script, so it presumably was added during shooting. The phrase is missing from some prints. Joseph Breen to Jack Warner, June 26, Oct. 9, Nov. 15, 1942, "Air Force A-59" file, Warner Brothers Production Files, Special Collections, Doheny Library, USC.

62. Script review, "Air Force," Oct. 27, 1942, box 3515, OWI files.

63. Mellett to Davis, May 31, 1943; Davis to Norman Thomas, May 31, 1943, box 3, OWI files; R. M. MacIver to Jack Warner, April 30, 1943; William Schaefer to R. M. MacIver, May 14, 1943, "Air Force" file, Warner Brothers Production Files, USC.

64. Davis to Mellett, Sept. 7, 1942; Mellett to Davis, Sept. 9, 1942, box 890, OWI files.

CHAPTER IV.

1. "'We Could Lose This War'—A Communique From the OWI," *Nation* (Aug. 17, 1942), 30.
2. Drabeck and Ellis, eds., *Archibald MacLeish: Reflections* (Amherst, Mass., 1986), p. 172.
3. Malcolm Cowley, "The End of the New Deal," *New Republic* (May 31, 1943), 732.
4. Geoffrey Perrett, *Days of Sadness, Years of Triumph: The American People, 1939–1945* (Madison, 1945), pp. 213–15.
5. Logs, BMP activities, Sept. 14, 1942, box 1556, OWI files.
6. Jack Temple Kirby, *Media-Made Dixie: The South in the American Imagination* (Baton Rouge, 1978), pp. 66–74.
7. Thomas Cripps, "Movies, Race, and World War II: *Tennessee Johnson* as an Anticipation of the Strategies of the Civil Rights Movement," *Prologue*, 14 (Summer 1982), 49, 54.
8. Office of Facts and Figures, Bureau of Intelligence, "Negroes in a Democracy at War," box 22, Philleo Nash Papers (Harry S. Truman Library, Independence, Mo.); Walter White, "The Right to Fight for Democracy," *Survey Graphic* (November 1942), 472. For a fuller discussion of these issues see Clayton R. Koppes and Gregory D. Black, "Blacks, Loyalty, and Motion-Picture Propaganda in World War II," *Journal of American History*, 73 (September 1986), 383–406.
9. Lena Horne and Richard Schickel, *Lena* (Garden City, 1965), p. 135; Cripps, "Movies, Race, and World War II," 58.
10. White to Mellett, Aug. 17, 1942, box 1431, OWI files.
11. Maurice Revnes to Mellett, Aug. 18, 1942, box 1433E, OWI files.
12. Poynter to White, Aug. 28, 1942, box 3510, OWI files.
13. Jones to Poynter, Aug. 6, 1942, box 3510; Poynter to Mellett, Sept. 24, 1942, box 3515, OWI files.
14. *PM,* Jan. 3, 1943.
15. Mellett to Louis B. Mayer, Nov. 25, 1942; feature review, *Tennessee Johnson,* Dec. 1, 1942, box 3510, OWI files.
16. Actors Cues press release, Dec. 7, 1942, box 3510, OWI files; White to Howard Dietz, Nov. 27, 1942; White to Edwin R. Embree, Feb. 13, 1943, box II A285, NAACP files, Library of Congress Manuscript Division, Washington, D.C.

17. Brian Henderson, ed., *Five Screenplays by Preston Sturges* (Berkeley, 1985), pp. 27–28; Dorothy B. Jones to Nelson Poynter, Nov. 6, 1942; feature review, *Palm Beach Story,* Nov. 4, 1942, box 6, Mellett Papers, FDRL. Breen to Luraschi, Nov. 17, 1941, "Palm Beach Story" file, PCA Files, Academy Library.

18. Same sources as n. 17.

19. Poynter to Mellett, note on Jones to Poynter, Nov. 6, 1942, box 6, Mellett Papers, FDRL.

20. Poynter to Charles Einfeld, Oct. 28, 1942, box 1438, OWI files.

21. Ibid.

22. Ibid.

23. BMP log, June 13, 1942, box 1556, OWI files.

24. Donald Ogden Stewart, *By a Stroke of Luck!* (New York, 1975), p. 262; feature review, *Keeper of the Flame,* Dec. 7, 1942, box 1435, OWI files.

25. Stewart, *By a Stroke of Luck,* p. 262.

26. Same sources as n. 24. A sidelight: Since the Production Code Administration decided that Mrs. Forrest was guilty of her husband's death, she too had to die; hence the good aim of her husband's secretary. The picture was saved from an infinite succession of deaths by the expedient of having the secretary accidentally run over by an innocent motorist. (Breen to Louis B. Mayer, Oct. 9, 1942, "Keeper of the Flame" file, PCA records, Academy Library). A further sidelight: When the film was released Will Hays queried Breen as to why the word *hell* was allowed. The PCA chief patiently explained that the word was all right when used as a descriptive term for the "Devil's den." (Breen to Hays, March 31, 1943).

27. Bergquist review, *Pittsburgh,* Poynter to Mellett, Dec. 2, 1942; Mellett to Poynter, Dec. 30, 1942, box 16, Mellett Papers, FDRL; *Hollywood Reporter,* Nov. 30, 1942; *Motion Picture Herald,* Dec. 5, 1942.

28. Script review, "So Proudly We Hail," Oct. 19, 1942, box 3511, OWI files.

29. Poynter to Mark Sandrich, Oct. 28, 1942, box 3511, OWI files.

30. Ibid.; John Houseman, *Front and Center* (New York, 1979), p. 112.

31. Final script, "So Proudly We Hail," Nov. 21, 1942, pp. 39–40, Paramount Collection, Margaret Herrick Library, Academy of Motion Picture Arts and Sciences, Beverly Hills, CA. It was not unusual for fairly substantial changes to be made in what was somewhat euphemistically called a "final" script.

32. "The Chaplain Speech—SO PROUDLY WE HAIL," Nov. 25, 1942, box 3511, OWI files.

33. "Re Janet's Speech," Nov. 25, 1942, box 3511, OWI files.

34. Sandrich to Poynter, Dec. 4, 1942, box 3511, OWI files.

35. Poynter to Sandrich and Allan Scott, June 22, 1943, box 3511, OWI files.

36. Manny Farber, "Love in the Foxholes," *New Republic* (Sept. 27, 1943). Joyce Baker notes that *So Proudly We Hail* was the only best-selling feature film to deal seriously with female soldiers but that it also reaffirmed conventional images of women's role in war. See her *Images of Women in Film: The War Years, 1941–1945* (Ann Arbor, 1980), p. 123.

37. Gilfond to Mellett, July 15, 1942, box 3, Mellett Papers, FDRL; *New York Times*, Sept. 24, 1942; Davis to Mellett, Sept. 7, 1942, box 890, OWI files.

38. Mellett to Davis, Sept. 9, 1942, box 890, OWI files.

39. Mellett to Poynter, Sept. 4, 1942; Poynter to Mellett, Sept. 15, 1942, box 1438, OWI files.

40. *Motion Picture Herald*, June 13, 1942; Poynter to Mellett, Oct. 29, 1942, box 1438, OWI files.

41. Davis press release, Sept. 11, 1942, box 3510, OWI files.

42. Bell to Riskin, Dec. 9, 1942, box 3510, OWI files.

43. Poynter to Mellett, Oct. 21, 1942, box 1438, OWI files.

44. Mellett address, "Wartime Motion Pictures," Nov. 12, 1942, box 1, Charles Hultan Papers, Harry S. Truman Library, Independence, Mo.; *New York Times*, Nov. 13, 1942; minutes, OWI board meeting, Oct. 31, 1942, box 41, OWI files.

45. *Motion Picture Herald*, Nov. 21, 1942; *Hollywood Reporter*, Nov. 13, 1942.

46. Mellett to various studios, Dec. 9, 1942, box 1443, OWI files.

47. *Variety*, Dec. 23, 1942; *New York Times*, Dec. 19, 1942; Harry Warner to Mellett, Dec. 16, 1942, box 1443, OWI files.

48. Bell to Robert Riskin, Dec. 22, 1942, box 3510, OWI files.

49. Excerpts from Elmer Davis press conference, Dec. 23, 1942, box 1442; Poynter statement to Hollywood media, Dec. 21, 1942, box 1443; statement on Mellett's New York meeting, box 1438, OWI files; *Hollywood Reporter*, Dec. 18–21, 24, 1942; *Variety*, Dec. 24, 1942.

50. *New York Times*, Dec. 24, 1942.

51. Minutes, Board of War Information meeting, Dec. 26, 1942, box 41; Jean C. Herrick to Gardner Cowles, Dec. 19, 22, 1942; Walter Wanger to Cowles, Dec. 8, 1942, box 12a, OWI files.

52. William Goetz to Cowles, Dec. 22, 1942, box 12a, OWI files.

53. Mellett to Poynter, Dec. 24, 1942, box 16, Mellett Papers, FDRL.

54. Mellett to Poynter, Dec. 30, 1942, box 16, Mellett Papers, FDRL.

55. Ibid.

CHAPTER V.

1. On Hollywood and the military see Suid, *Guts and Glory.*
2. Jerry Wald to Jack Warner, April 14, 1942; Wald to Hal Wallis, May 28, 1942, "Action in the North Atlantic File," Warner Brothers Production File, USC.
3. Winkler, *Politics of Propaganda*, p. 49.
4. Script review, "Torpedoed," June 20, 1942; script review, "Action in the North Atlantic," box 3505, OWI files. The screenplay afforded a beautiful example of the absurdities in which moviemakers sometimes found themselves because of the code. Since the code specified that cruelty to animals was not permissible, Joseph Breen insisted that the killing of a kitten be suggested but not shown. Showing human deaths was acceptable, of course. (Breen to Jack Warner, Aug. 11, 1942, "Action in the North Atlantic" file, PCA files, Academy Library).
5. Poynter to Mellett, May 18, 1943, "Action in the North Atlantic" file, Warner Brothers Production Files, USC; Norman Kagan, *The War Film* (New York, 1974), p. 60.
6. *Time* (June 7, 1943), 92.
7. *Hollywood Reporter,* Oct. 6, 1942.
8. Poynter to Mellett, Oct. 6, 1942, Oct. 20, 1942, box 1438, OWI files.
9. Davis to Secretaries of War and Navy, Dec. 3, 1942, box 1, OWI files.
10. Mellett to Maj. Gen. Alexander D. Surles, Jan. 5, 1943, OWI file, J. L. Warner Collection, USC.
11. *Motion Picture Herald*, March 20, 1943.
12. Mellett to Poynter, May 22, 1943, box 16, Mellett Papers, FDRL.
13. Transcript of Surles telephone conversation, March 26, 1943, Records of the Office of the Secretary of War, Bureau of Public Relations, box 1, Director's Conversations, Record Group 107, Modern Military Branch, National Archives, Washington, D.C. (hereafter Army PR files). On Capra see his *Frank Capra: The Name Above the Title* (New York, 1971).
14. Mellett to FDR, Nov. 3, 1942, President's Official File 73, FDRL.
15. Mellett to Davis, March 26, 1943, box 15, OWI files.
16. Surles telephone conversations with Gardner Cowles and Robert Patterson, March 19, 1943, box 1, Army PR files.
17. Mellett to Henry L. Stimson, May 12, 1943, box 8, Mellett Papers, FDRL; Memorandum, Program Committee of Theatres Division of War Activities Committee, box 3, OWI files.

18. John J. McCloy to Mellett, April 20, 1943; Mellett to McCloy, April 24, 1943, box 8, Mellett Papers, FDRL; Surles telephone conversation with F. H. Osborn, April 8, 1943, box 1, Army PR files.
19. Surles telephone conversation with Francis Harmon, May 5, 1943, box 1, Army PR files.
20. New York Board of Review, Office of Censorship, "Supplement to Circular of September 8, 1942, on Basic Information Prohibited in Film Form," Sept. 9, 1942, file 023, Film Censorship Regulations, Office of Censorship Records, National Archives.
21. *Motion Picture Herald,* Dec. 12, 1942; *Hollywood Reporter,* Feb. 17, 1943.
22. Poynter to Mellett, Dec. 16, 1942, box 1438, OWI files.
23. Bell to Riskin, Dec. 31, 1942, box 3510, OWI files.
24. Davis to Byron Price, Jan. 16, 1943, box 3, OWI files.
25. Price to Davis, Jan. 23, 1942, box 3, OWI files.
26. Bell to Riskin, March 31, 1943, box 3510, OWI files.
27. Bell to Riskin, Aug. 25, 1943, box 3515, OWI files.
28. Bell to William Gordon, March 24, 1943; Bell to Watterson Rothacker, April 6, 1943, box 15, OWI files.
29. Manny Farber, "Method in Its Badness," *New Republic* (Aug. 9, 1943), 190; *Time* (Sept. 20, 1943), 94, 96; preview comment cards, Fox Riverside Theater, Riverside, Calif., March 20, 22, 1943, box 3515, OWI files.
30. Bell to Riskin, Dec. 10, 1942, box 3; feature review, *Lucky Jordan,* Nov. 17, 1942, box 1435, OWI files.
31. Bell to Riskin, March 31, 1943, box 3510; Milton S. Eisenhower to Bell, Dec. 31, 1943, box 3, OWI files.
32. Bell to Riskin, March 31, 1943, box 3515, OWI files.
33. Poynter to Mellett, May 17, 1943, box 16, Mellett Papers, FDRL; Poynter to Bell, Feb. 13, 1943, box 1438, OWI files.
34. Same sources as note 33.
35. Poynter to Mellett, May 17, 1943, box 16, Mellett Papers, FDRL.
36. Poynter to Mellett, June 26, 1943, box 16, Mellett Papers, FDRL; Bell to Riskin, April 3, 1943, box 15, OWI files.
37. Poynter to Mellett, June 26, 1943, box 16, Mellett Papers, FDRL.
38. Sydney Weinberg, "What to Tell America: The Writers' Quarrel in the Office of War Information," *Journal of American History,* 55 (1968), 73–89.
39. Ibid., 86.
40. Winkler, *Politics of Propaganda,* 65.
41. Surles telephone conversation with Osborn, April 8, 1943, box 1, Army PR files.

42. U.S. Congress, House Subcommittee of the Committee on Appropriations, *National War Agencies Appropriation Bill for 1944*, 78th Cong., 1st Sess., Part 1, 704–20, 936–37, 985–86, 1046–49; Houseman, *Front and Center*, p. 85.

43. *Congressional Record*, 78th Cong. 1st Sess., vol. 89, part 5, 5983, 5985, 5990, 6021, 6103, 6133; Winkler, *Politics of Propaganda*, 70; Perrett, *Days of Sadness, Years of Triumph*, chap. 21.

44. *Congressional Record*, 78th Cong., 1st Sess., vol. 89, part 5, 6407, 6410; Houseman, *Front and Center*, p. 126; Koppes interview with Poynter.

45. *Motion Picture Herald* (March 6, 1943), 7–8.

46. Ibid. OWI's suggestions were scarcely as sinister as Quigley represented them to be. The Bureau of Motion Pictures had objected to *Random Harvest's* depiction of the House of Commons as populated only by members in striped pants and stiff collars and speaking in the "haughtiest Oxford manner." The bureau feared such a portrayal would be ridiculed in the United Kingdom, since the membership of the House was much more diverse. BMP suggested redoing the brief scene "with less immaculate clothing and more of the good healthy Yorkshire or Lancashire accent in evidence." (Unsigned BMP memo, Dec. 10, 1942, attached to feature review, *Random Harvest*, Oct. 5, 1942, box 3517, OWI files.)

47. Winkler, *Politics of Propaganda*, pp. 70–71; *Motion Picture Herald* (July 3, 1943), 9.

48. *Motion Picture Herald* (July 10, 1943), 20, (July 24, 1943), 19.

49. Bell to Robert Riskin, Nov. 1, 1943, box 3, OWI files.

50. Koppes interview with Dorothy B. Jones, Beverly Hills, Calif., Dec. 6, 1974.

51. *Motion Picture Herald*, Aug. 14, 1943.

52. Ibid.; Bell to Louis Lober, Dec. 15, 1943, box 3509, OWI files.

53. *Motion Picture Herald*, Aug. 14, 1943.

54. Riskin to Bell, Oct. 22, 1943, box 3510; Riskin to Edward Barrett, Aug. 12, 1944, box 19, OWI files; *Motion Picture Herald*, Aug. 7, 1943.

55. John Houseman, "Hollywood Faces the Fifties," *Harper's* (April 1950), reprinted in Houseman, *Entertainers and the Entertained: Essays on theater, film and television* (New York, 1986), p. 219.

CHAPTER VI.

1. "Government Information Manual for the Motion Picture Industry," summer 1942, box 15, OWI files; Perrett, *Days of Sadness, Years of Triumph*, p. 399.

2. "Government Information Manual," summer 1942, box 15, OWI files.

3. Luigi Luraschi to Preston Sturges, Oct. 16, 1942, box 10; Luraschi to Sturges, Oct. 28, 1942, box 40, Preston Sturges Papers, Special Collections, University Research Library, University of California, Los Angeles; "The Children's Army: Enlisting Every Boy and Girl in the War Effort," fact sheet no. 12, n.d., box 1517, OWI files.

4. Cinematicus, "Politics in Hollywood," *Nation* (June 16, 1944), 847–48; Ceplair and Englund, *The Inquisition in Hollywood,* 209–11.

5. OWI information manuals, summer 1942; April 29, 1943; Jan. 6, 1944, box 15, OWI files.

6. Ibid.

7. OWI information manual, Jan. 6, 1944, box 15, OWI files.

8. *Time* (Oct. 16, 1944), 94; *Theatre Arts* 28 (1944), 669. Gilfond wrote Vidor at least eight times during the production. He also promised to free Spencer Tracy from any war-related obligations if Vidor wanted him. See Gilfond to Vidor, Feb. 10, 1943, "An American Romance" file, MGM Collection, Special Collections, Doheny Library, USC, and Gilfond-Vidor correspondence, King Vidor Papers, Special Collections, Doheny Library, USC.

9. Elizabeth Wilson, "An American Romance," *Liberty* (Nov. 11, 1944), 35; King Vidor, *A Tree Is a Tree* (New York, 1953), 253.

10. Cunningham to Revnes, Feb. 17, 1944, box 3525, *OWI* files.

11. "America" script, King Vidor Papers, USC.

12. Script review, "America," Nov. 5, 1942, box 3525, OWI files.

13. Ibid.

14. Ibid.; Anne Wormser, "Notes on the story of Steve Dangos," n.d., "An American Romance" file, MGM Collection, USC.

15. A. van Der Zee to Vidor, Aug. 21, 1943; Vidor to van Der Zee, Sept. 7, 1942, "An American Romance" file, MGM Collection, USC.

16. Script review, "America," Nov. 5, 1942, box 3525, OWI files. But when the International Typographical Union struck Poynter's *St. Petersburg Times* in 1947 his reaction was much different. Poynter refused to bargain with the union and threatened to hire "scabs" to break the strike. He hired Thurman Arnold to negotiate for the paper, but Arnold resigned in frustration saying Poynter was the "best educated eleven year old boy I ever saw." (clipping file, box H3-8, Nelson Poynter Memorial Library, University of South Florida, St. Petersburg).

17. Poynter to Mellett, Nov. 12, 1942, box 3525, OWI files.

18. Gordon Kahn revisions, n.d., box 2, Vidor Papers, USC.

19. Vidor note on Kahn to Vidor, Jan. 12, 1943; notes on conferences about cuts and retakes after previews, box 2, Vidor Papers, USC; feature review, *America,* Feb. 17, 1944, box 3525, OWI files.

20. The *New York Times*, Sept. 23, 1944.

21. *Newsweek* (July 10, 1944), 85.

22. Bell to Selznick, Sept. 28, 1943; Cunningham to Selznick, July 21, 1944; feature review, *Since You Went Away,* July 20, 1944, box 3525, OWI files.

23. *Newsweek* (July 10, 1944), 85; *Life* (July 24, 1944), 53; Agee, *Agee on Film*, 106.

24. *Theatre Arts* 28 (1944), 543; *Commonweal* 40 (1944), 374–75.

25. Ralph B. Levering, *American Opinion and the Russian Alliance, 1939–1945* (Chapel Hill, N.C., 1976), 128; George Stigler, *Trends in Employment in Service Industries* (Princeton, N.J., 1956), p. 94.

26. Feature review, *Happy Land*, Nov. 1, 1943, box 1434, OWI files.

27. Script review, "Happy Land," March 17, 1943, box 1434, OWI files.

28. Agee, *Agee on Film*, 63.

29. Bell to Gordon, Dec. 30, 1943; Gene Kern to Gordon, Jan. 3, 1944, box 3515, OWI files.

30. Bernard F. Dick, *The Star-Spangled Screen: The American World War II Film* (Lexington, Ky., 1985), 220.

31. Feature review, Dec. 28, 1943, box 3515, OWI files.

32. *New Republic* (June 26, 1944), 850.

33. Agee, *Agee on Film*, 91; comment cards from preview audiences in Pasadena, Dec. 14, 1943, and Glendale, Dec. 16, 1942, RKO files, RKO headquarters, Los Angeles.

34. Long Range to Arnold Picker, April 7, 1945, box 3515, OWI files.

35. Henderson, ed., *Five Screenplays by Preston Sturges*, 685–87. *Hail the Conquering Hero* was Sturges's last for Paramount. He had faced mounting difficulties with Paramount head Y. Frank Freeman. At one point during the filming of *Miracle of Morgan's Creek* Sturges became so infuriated at Freeman's second guessing that he spent an entire day composing replies to a Freeman memo. In one draft Sturges exploded that he was tired of "being checked, cross-checked, tabulated, reported upon and as closely watched as a paroled convict." How long did one have to work at Paramount to be considered a valued employee? he demanded. Sturges did not send any of the drafts but instead with some difficulty arranged a dinner appointment with Freeman. (See drafts of Sturges letters, Nov. 5, 1942, box 40, Sturges Papers, UCLA.) It was a telling commentary on the Hollywood studio system that Freeman and Sturges were never fully able to patch up their differences, even though Sturges ranked second only to Cecil B. DeMille in the Paramount director-producer hierarchy in the early 1940s. After leaving Paramount Sturges embarked on an ill-fated venture with, of all people, Howard Hughes. His career never recovered.

36. Sturges to Edgar G. Erb, Feb. 17, 1945, box 40, Preston Sturges Papers, UCLA.

37. Agee, *Agee on Film,* 344–45; Richard Corliss, *Talking Pictures: Screenwriters in the American Cinema* (New York, 1974), 52–53; Henderson, ed., *Five Screenplays of Preston Sturges,* 17–29.

38. Sturges to Mrs. George F. Kaufman, April 4, 1944, box 40, Sturges papers, UCLA.

39. Dorothy B. Jones, "The Hollywood War Film: 1942–1944," *Hollywood Quarterly,* 1 (1945), 1–14.

40. Script review, "Home Front," Dec. 21, 1943; Bell note on conference with producer and writers, Dec. 23, 1943; Cunningham to Maurice Revnes, Feb. 17, 1944, box 3517, OWI files.

41. Script review, "One Destiny," April 27, 1943; memo on "One Destiny," March 24, 1943, box 1434; Warren Pierce to Mercey, June 17, 1943, box 3513, OWI files.

42. Script review, "Night Shift," Jan. 12, 1943; Poynter to Jack Warner, Feb. 26, 1943, box 3524, OWI files.

43. See various treatments and screenplays, as well as sketch outline by A. I. Bezzerides, Aug. 3, 1943, and Alvah Bessie to Arnold Albert, Feb. 26, 1945, "Night Shift" file, Warner Brothers Production Files, USC.

44. Perrett, *Days of Sadness, Years of Triumph,* 347–48.

45. Bell to Rothacker, Nov. 12, 1943; feature review, *Where Are Your Children?* Nov. 8, 1943; "Cuts Required for 'Where Are Your Children'" [Dec. 1, 1943], box 3530; script reviews, "The Dangerous Age," March 30, 1944, "Youth Runs Wild," box 3515, OWI files.

46. Perrett, *Days of Sadness, Years of Triumph,* 348.

47. Dalton Trumbo, "Minorities and the Screen," in *Writers' Congress: The Proceedings of the Conference Held in October 1943 under the Sponsorship of the Hollywood Writers' Mobilization and the University of California* (Berkeley, 1944), 497. For a more detailed analysis of blacks and wartime motion pictures see Clayton R. Koppes and Gregory D. Black, "Blacks, Loyalty, and Motion-Picture Propaganda in World War II," *Journal of American History,* 73 (1986), 383–406.

48. Script review, "Battle Hymn," Aug. 20, 1942, box 3527, OWI files.

49. Feature review, *The Ox-Bow Incident,* box 3526, OWI files.

50. Daniel Leab, *From Sambo to Superspade: The Black Experience in Motion Pictures* (Boston, 1975), 126.

51. Script review, "Lifeboat," July 31, 1943, box 3518, OWI files.

52. Agee, *Agee on Film,* 108.

53. *This Is the Army* final script, Warner Brothers Production Files, USC.

54. Feature review, *Cabin in the Sky,* Jan. 14, 1943; Ferdinand Kuhn to Bell, Feb. 17, 1943, box 3525, OWI files.

55. Feature review, *Stormy Weather,* May 5, 1943, box 3518, OWI files;

Walter White to Edwin R. Embree, Feb. 13, 1943, box II A285, National Association for the Advancement of Colored People files, Manuscript Division, Library of Congress, Washington, D.C. (hereafter LC).

56. Responses to Koppes and Black, "Blacks, Propaganda, and the Irony of American Democracy in World War II," paper read at annual meeting, Great Lakes American Studies Association, Oct. 13, 1984, Kent State University, Kent, Ohio; Lena Horne and Richard Schickel, *Lena* (Garden City, NY, 1965), 135.

57. Farber, "Great White Way," *New Republic* (July 5, 1943), 20; White to Virginius Dabney, April 8, 1940, box II A281, NAACP files, LC; Writers' War Board, *How Writers Perpetuate Stereotypes: A Digest of Data* (New York, 1945).

CHAPTER VII.

1. *Hollywood Reporter,* April 29, 1943.

2. David Culbert, ed., *Mission to Moscow* (Madison, Wis., 1980), p. 34. Culbert's valuable book includes, in addition to his introduction, the screenplay and various documents on the film's production and the public reponse to it.

3. Ceplair and Englund, *The Inquisition in Hollywood.*

4. *Red Square* file, PCA files, Academy Library; Levering, *American Opinion and the Russian Alliance,* chap. 2.

5. *Ninotchka* file, PCA Files, Academy Library.

6. Churchill quoted in Levering, *American Opinion and the Russian Alliance,* p. 40. See Levering, chap. 3, for a more general discussion of the shift in attitudes toward the U.S.S.R.

7. "Joseph E(dward) Davies," *Current Biography, 1942* (New York, 1942), pp. 177–78.

8. Beatrice Farnsworth, *William C. Bullitt and the Soviet Union* (Bloomington, Indiana, 1967), chaps. 5–6.

9. Joseph E. Davies, *Mission to Moscow* (New York, 1941), p. xi; George F. Kennan, *Memoirs, 1925–1950* (Boston, 1963), pp. 85–6.

10. Culbert, ed., *Mission to Moscow,* pp. 13–15.

11. Koch, *As Time Goes By,* 100–102; Koch statement on his political beliefs, n.d., ca. 1964, box 3, Howard Koch Papers, Wisconsin State Historical Society, Madison. Davies' sum paled by comparison with the $200,000 Wendell Willkie received for *One World* (1943) from Twentieth Century-Fox, of which he was chairman of the board.

12. *Film Daily,* Nov. 13, 1942; Koch, *As Time Goes By,* p. 111; Culbert, ed., *Mission to Moscow,* p. 254.

13. Culbert, ed., *Mission to Moscow,* p. 18–20.

14. Koch, *As Time Goes By*, 99; Culbert, ed., *Mission to Moscow*, 20–22.
15. Culbert, ed., *Mission to Moscow*, p. 25.
16. Ibid.
17. OWI Bureau of Intelligence poll, Dec. 1942, *Mission to Moscow* files, Warner Brothers Production Files, USC; OWI Bureau of Intelligence, "The American Public Views Our Russian Ally," June 10, 1943, box 6, Philleo Nash Papers, Harry S. Truman Library, Independence, Mo.
18. Davies, *Mission to Moscow*, pp. 201–2, 270–80, esp. 275. Soviet experts almost universally dismiss the treason charges, viewing the purges as a facet of Stalin's consolidation of personal power. See, for instance, Stephen F. Cohen, *Bukharin* (New York, 1973), chap. 10.
19. Nelson Poynter to Bob Buckner, Dec. 3, 1942, box 16, Mellett Papers, FDRL.
20. Activities logs, Jan. 5 and 13, 1943, box 1556, OWI files.
21. Culbert, ed., *Mission to Moscow*, p. 57.
22. *Time* (Dec. 29, 1941), 23.
23. The screenplay called for a scene in which, just after sentences are pronounced, Trotsky plots with von Ribbentrop, who is visiting Oslo. The scene concludes with Heinrich Sahm, the German minister to Norway, introducing von Ribbentrop to Quisling. Thus Trotsky is identified as a part of international fifth column activities. This absurd scene, to which Poynter strongly objected, was omitted from the release print.
24. Koch wanted a more understated ending, which, if still painfully obvious, would have recalled the plowshare imagery of his proposed opening scene. The members of a peasant family who are too old or too young for combat begin to reassemble the pathetic remnants of their war-devastated household. They dig out a bag of seeds buried in the foundation. The boy takes a hand plow and in a gesture of exuberant defiance presses its edge into the soil and begins plowing toward the camera. Koch explained: "Larger and larger grow plow and furrow, against an immense span of sky, and the clean earth surges in a cleft wave over the broken land, burying in its wake a steel helmet, the iron fragments of shells and a broken cannon wheel." With the plow silhouetted against a brightening sky, the chorus proclaims peace and good will. Koch was overruled by Davies and Buckner. The writer was also "extremely upset" that the motif of a sword transformed into a plow was eliminated from the opening. Buckner felt Koch was behaving in "a very highly opinionated way." He urged Jack Warner to simply tell him "you are doing it your way." Buckner, the new producer, added a revealing aside about rank and power in Hollywood: "I know it is not your policy to have writers override the decisions of those above them." (Buckner to J. L. Warner, Feb. 11,

1943, *Mission to Moscow* file, Warner Brothers Production Files, USC; Koch, *As Time Goes By,* 128–9; Culbert, ed., *Mission to Moscow,* p. 241.)

25. Davies to Koch, Aug. 31, 1945, box 2; Davies to Koch, Oct. 1, 1947, box 3, Koch Papers, Wisconsin State Historical Society.

26. Feature review, *Mission to Moscow,* April 29, 1943, box 3523, OWI files.

27. Ulric Bell to Robert Sherwood, April 29, 1943, box 3523, OWI files; Poynter to Davies, May 8, 1943, box 16, Mellett Papers, FDRL.

28. Same sources as n. 27.

29. Joseph I. Breen to J. L. Warner, Dec. 23, 1942, *Mission to Moscow* file, Warner Brothers Production Files, USC.

30. Harry Bridges to Jack Warner, July 1, 1943; William Randolph Hearst to Warner, April 30, 1943; Warner to Hearst, May 21, 1943; War Advisory Council of American Legion Los Angeles County Council to Warner, May 12, 1943, *Mission to Moscow* files, Warner Brothers Production Files, USC; Eugene Lyons to Herbert Hoover, May 18, 1943, Lyons file, Herbert Hoover Papers, Hoover Library, West Branch, Iowa.

31. *New York Times,* April 30, 1943; *Hollywood Reporter,* May 3, 1943.

32. *New Republic* (May 10, 1943), 636.

33. *Nation* (May 22, 1943), 749.

34. *New York Times,* May 9, 1943; William L. O'Neill, *A Better World: The Great Schism: Stalinism and American Intellectuals* (New York, 1982), 75–78. Arthur Upham Pope answered Dewey and LaFollette (unconvincingly) in *Soviet Russia Today* (June 1943), 8–9.

35. *New York Times,* May 9, 1943.

36. Lillian Hellman, *An Unfinished Woman* (Boston, 1969), pp. 121–25.

37. Ibid., 125; Lillian Hellman, *The North Star* (New York, 1943).

38. Bernard Dick, *Hellman in Hollywood* (Rutherford, N.J., 1982), pp. 104–5.

39. V. Bazykin to Mellett, Jan. 19, 1943, box 1432; BMP internal memo, Jan. 2, 1943, box 3515, OWI files.

40. Script review, "North Star," May 12, 1943, box 1434, OWI files.

41. Dick, *Hellman in Hollywood,* p. 101.

42. *Motion Picture Herald,* Oct. 23, 1943.

43. Agee, *Agee on Film,* p. 57.

44. Hellman, *An Unfinished Woman,* p. 125; Culbert, ed., *Mission to Moscow,* pp. 37–8; *New York Times,* Aug. 27, 1944. Peter Kenez has noted the condescension toward the masses that underlay Soviet propaganda efforts. (Peter Kenez, *The Birth of the Propaganda State,* p. 6.)

45. Script review, "Russia," Dec. 28, 1942, box 3517, OWI files; *Newsweek* (Feb. 21, 1944), 88.

46. Feature review, *Girl from Leningrad,* Sept. 21, 1943, box 3524, OWI files. (The picture's title was changed before it was released.)

47. Ibid.

48. Dick, *The Star-Spangled Screen,* pp. 211–13.

49. Script review, "Boy From Stalingrad," Jan. 5, 1943, box 3524, OWI files.

50. *Nation* (May 12, 1945), 554; *New Yorker* (May 26, 1945), 38; *Newsweek* (May 28, 1945), 112–13.

51. Gene Kern to Richard Sokolove, Jan. 28, 1944, Aug. 19, 1944, box 3514; feature review, March 15, 1945, box 3524, OWI files.

52. Paul Willen, "Who 'Collaborated' With Russia?" *Antioch Review,* 14 (1954), 259–83.

53. *Life* (March 29, 1943), 13, 15, 20, 29, 36, 50, 63–64, 91.

54. *Life,* (Nov. 1, 1943), 118–22; feature review, "North Star," May 12, 1943, box 1434, OWI files.

55. The Hollywood Ten got their name when they were cited for contempt of Congress in 1947, and received jail terms, for having declined to answer questions about their political affiliations before the House Committee on Un-American Activities. The Ten were producer-director Howard Biberman, director Edward Dmytryk, producer-writer Adrian Scott, and screenwriters Alvah Bessie, Lester Cole, Ring Lardner, Jr., John Howard Lawson, Albert Maltz, Samuel Ornitz, and Dalton Trumbo. All were blacklisted, although Dmytryk changed his mind in 1951, naming names, and was able to go back to work.

56. On the influence of Communists in films, Ceplair and Englund conclude "Whatever the historical era . . . the Hollywood screenwriter *never* had final say over what appeared on the screen. That was *always* the province of the front office." (Ceplair and Englund, *The Inquisition in Hollywood,* p. 300). Dorothy Jones found no Communist influence in pictures. (Dorothy B. Jones, "Communism and the Movies: A Study of Film Content," in John Cogley, *Report on Blacklisting, I., The Movies* [New York, 1956], pp. 196–304.) Efforts to detect Communist influence consequently evolve into obsessions with minutiae—a phrase here, a term there—or a label, such as "fascist," which though a favorite of Communists, was widely used by liberals as well and hence proves nothing about Communists. See, for instance, Bernard Dick's contention that "the giveaway is 'fascist.'" (Dick, *The Star Spangled Screen,* p. 161).

CHAPTER VIII.

1. *Motion Picture Herald,* Feb. 15, 1943.

2. OWI logs, June 13, 1942, box 1556, OWI files.

3. OWI manual for the motion picture industry, "The Issues," n.d., ca. fall 1942, box 1517, OWI files.

4. Ibid.

5. David Reynolds, *The Creation of the Anglo-American Alliance 1937–1941: A Study in Competitive Co-operation* (Chapel Hill, N.C., 1982), pp. 23–25; Koppes and Black, "Blacks, Loyalty, and Motion-Picture Propaganda in World War II," 387; Christopher Thorne, *The Issue of War: States, Societies, and the Far Eastern Conflict of 1941–1945* (New York, 1985), 178–84.

6. Mellett to Sam Goldwyn, Aug. 20, 1942; Goldwyn to Mellett, Aug. 22, 1942, box 1433b; Script Review, "Kim," Aug. 4, 1942, box 1438; Leo Rosten to Mellett, June 23, 1942, box 888; Mellett to Victor Saville, Sept. 23, 1942, box 3527, OWI Files.

7. "The Issues," n.d., box 1555, OWI Files.

8. *New Yorker* (June 6, 1942), 76; *Newsweek* (June 15, 1942), 63; *Time* (June 29, 1942), 72; *Catholic World* (Sept. 1942), 726; *New Republic* (June 15, 1942), 830.

9. *Spectator,* July 17, 1942, box 3524, OWI files.

10. Feature Review, "Mrs. Miniver," ibid.

11. "Weekly Summary," Jan. 14, 1943, box 15, OWI Files.

12. K.R.M. Short, "The White Cliffs of Dover: Promoting the Ango-American Alliance in World War II," *Historical Journal of Film, Radio and Television* (1982), 6.

13. Script Review, "The White Cliffs of Dover," Mar. 1, 1943, box 1556, OWI Files.

14. Poynter to Mannix, Mar. 12, 1943, ibid; Poynter to Mellett, Mar. 12, 1943, box 16, Mellett Papers, FDRL.

15. Mellett to Poynter, Mar. 22, 1943, ibid.

16. Poynter to Sidney Franklin, May 6, 1943; Franklin to Poynter, May 10, 1943; Ferdinand Kuhn, Jr., to Bell, Mar. 24, 1943, box 3529, OWI Files.

17. Feature Review, "The White Cliffs of Dover," Mar. 10, 1944, ibid.

18. *Newsweek* (May 29, 1944), 70; *Nation* (May 27, 1942), 634; *Time* (May 29, 1944), 94.

19. *Commonweal* (June 5, 1942), 160.

20. Michael Hunt, *The Making of a Special Relationship: The United States and China to 1914* (New York, 1983), pp. 312–13.

21. For a good overview of U.S.-Chinese relations in World War II see Michael Schaller, *The United States and China in the Twentieth Century* (New York, 1979), chap. 4.

22. Hunt, *Making of a Special Relationship,* p. 299.

23. Jones, *The Portrayal of China and India on the American Screen, 1895–1955,* pp. 15–21.

24. "Government Information Manual for the Motion Picture Industry," Summer 1942, box 15, OWI Files.
25. Feature Review, "Bombs over Burma," June 5, 1942, box 3530; "Weekly Summary," Oct. 15, 1942, box 15, OWI Files.
26. Feature Review, "China," box 3530, ibid.
27. *PM*, April 23, 1943; *New York Journal of Commerce*, April 22, 1943; *New York Times*, April 22, 1943.
28. Jones, *The Portrayal of China and India on the American Screen, 1895–1955*, pp. 111–129.
29. William Cunningham to Monogram Studio, Aug. 30, 1943, box 3529, OWI Files.
30. Script Review, "Charlie Chan in the Secret Service," July 29, 1943, ibid.
31. Script Review, "Charlie Chan in the Mystery Mansion," Aug. 19, 1944, ibid.
32. Script Review, "Dragon Seed," Sept. 10, 1942 and Sept. 15, 1942, box 3525, OWI Files.
33. Feature Review, "Dragon Seed," July 3, 1944, ibid.
34. *Nation* (Aug. 5, 1944), 165; *Time* (July 24, 1944); *Chicago Tribune*, Sept 25, 1944; *New Republic* (Aug. 7, 1944), 161.
35. Script Review, "Keys of the Kingdom," Jan. 19, 1944; Randolph Sailer to William Cunningham, April 19, 1944, box 3518, OWI Files.
36. Ibid.
37. Cunningham to Sailor, April 13, 1944, ibid.
38. Ibid.
39. Schaller, *The United States and China in the Twentieth Century*, chap. 5.

CHAPTER IX.

1. "The Manual for the Motion Picture Industry," April 27, 1943, box 15, OWI Files.
2. Ibid.
3. Ibid.
4. John Dower, *War Without Mercy: Race and Power in the Pacific War* (New York, 1986), pp. 80–81; William J. Blakefield, "A War Within: The Making of *Know Your Enemy—Japan*," *Sight and Sound* (Spring, 1983), 128–133.
5. Dower, *War Without Mercy*, pp. 53–54; 79; "The Nature of the Enemy," Aug. 13, 1942, box 4, Philleo Nash Papers, HSTL.

6. Sheila K. Johnson, *American Attitudes Toward Japan, 1941–1945* (Washington, D. C., 1975), pp. 8–9; *Collier's*, (Dec. 8, 1942).

7. Dower, *War Without Mercy*, chap. 6.

8. Johnson, *American Attitudes Toward Japan, 1941–1945*, pp. 8–9.

9. Dower, *War Without Mercy*, pp. 11, 78.

10. Richard Slotkin, *The Fatal Environment: The Myth of the Frontier in the Age of Industrialization, 1800–1890* (New York, 1985), p. 61; Dower, *War Without Mercy*, pp. 53–54.

11. Ibid.

12. "The Enemy in the Movies," Nov. 25, 1942, box 4, Nash Papers, HSTL.

13. *Newsweek* (Aug. 31, 1942), 260.

14. Feature Review, "Wake Island," Aug. 6, 1942, box 3511, OWI Files.

15. Joseph Handler to Louis Lober, Jan. 17, 1945, ibid; Studs Terkel, *The Good War: An Oral History of World War Two* (New York, 1984), pp. 95–98.

16. Script Review, "Bataan Patrol," Oct. 2, 1942, box 3511, OWI Files.

17. Ibid.

18. Feature Review, "Bataan," Apr. 1, 1943, ibid.

19. Poynter to Maurice Revnes, Apr. 2, 1943; Bell to Rothacher, Mar. 19, 1943; Bell to William Chernin, Mar. 25, 1943, ibid.

20. William Pierce to Jason Joy, Apr. 9, 1943; Feature Review, "Guadalcanal Diary," Oct. 25, 1943, box 3518, ibid.

21. Ibid.

22. *The Saturday Review of Literature* (Nov. 6, 1943), 30; *Commonweal* (Nov. 12, 1943), 97–98; *Newsweek* (Nov. 8, 1943), 84; *Time* (Nov. 15, 1943), 94.

23. I. C. Jarvie, "Fanning the Flames; anti-American reaction to Operation Burma (1945)," *Historical Journal of Film, Radio, and Television* (1981), 121.

24. Susan Seidman to Hays, "Objective Burma," Feb. 1, 1945; Breen to Seidman, Feb. 6, 1945; Breen to Warner, Dec. 21, 1944, PCA Files, Academy Library.

25. *Time* (Feb. 26, 1945), 92.

26. Bessie to Wald, "Objective Burma," Warner Brothers Production File, USC; Dick, *The Star-Spangled Screen*, p. 227.

27. *New Republic* (Mar. 5, 1945), 335; *Time* (Feb. 26, 1945), 92.

28. Dower, *War Without Mercy*, 48–50.

29. Script review, "Thirty Seconds Over Tokyo," Nov. 11, 1943, box 3517, OWI Files.

30. Feature review, "Thirty Seconds Over Tokyo," Sept. 12, 1944, ibid.

31. "The Purple Heart," June 29, 1943, Twentieth Century-Fox, Story Conference Files, Doheny Library, USC.

32. Bell to Lattimore, Oct. 19, 1943; Pierce to Joy, Oct. 21, 1943; Lattimore to Pierce, Nov. 10, 1943; Pierce to Joy, Dec. 16, 1943 box 3518, OWI Files. We would like to thank John Roston of McGill University for providing us with several OWI documents on *The Purple Heart.*

33. Breen to Joy, Oct. 14, 1943, "The Purple Heart," PCA Files, Academy Library.

34. Feature review, "The Purple Heart," Feb. 21, 1944, box 3518, OWI Files.

35. *New Republic* (Mar. 27, 1944), 407–410.

36. "Reactions to "The Purple Heart," April, 1945, box 19, OWI Files.

37. Edward Dmytryk, "The Director's Point of View," in *The Writer's Congress: The Proceedings of the Conference Held in October 1943 Under the Sponsorship of the Hollywood Writers' Mobilization and the University of California* (Berkeley, 1944), 44–45.

38. Emmet Lavery to William Knowles, Sept. 27, 1942; Lavery to Perry Leiber, Apr. 9, 1943, "Behind the Rising Sun," Production Files, RKO Archives, Los Angeles, California.

39. Feature Review, "Behind the Rising Sun," July 8, 1943, box 3522, OWI Files.

40. William Cunningham to Louis Lober, Feb. 7, 1944, ibid; John Roston, "The Influence of the Office of War Information on the Portrayal of Japanese-Americans in the U. S. Films of World War II, 1942–1945," (M. A. thesis, McGill University, 1983), 88–90.

41. *Time* (Aug. 9, 1943), 94; *Commonweal* (Sept. 3, 1943), 491–492.

42. Dower, *War Without Mercy,* p. 22.

43. Script Review, "Betrayal From the East," June 30, 1944, Stanton Griffis to Frederick, Aug. 11, 1944; Cunningham to Little, Sept. 11, 1944, box 3522, OWI Files.

CHAPTER X.

1. Warren Pierce to Joy, Dec. 2, 1942; Bell to Robert Riskin, Feb. 23, 1943, box 3521, OWI Files.

2. "The Nature of the Enemy," Aug. 13, 1942, box 4, Nash Papers, HSTL; Gregory D. Black and Clayton R. Koppes, "OWI Goes to the Movies": The Bureau of Intelligence's Criticism of Hollywood, 1942–43," *Prologue* (Spring, 1974), 44.

3. Ibid.

4. "The Nature of the Enemy," Aug. 13, 1942, box 4, Nash Papers, HSTL.

5. Ibid.

6. Richard Steele, "The Greatest Gangster Movie Ever Filmed: *Prelude to War*," *Prologue* (Winter, 1979), 228.

7. "Manual for the Motion Picture Industry," Summer, 1942, box 15, OWI Files.

8. Dick, *Hellman in Hollywood*, pp. 81–86.

9. Feature Review, "Watch on the Rhine," Oct. 26, 1942, box 3523, OWI Files. The film was released in August 1943.

10. *New Yorker* (Aug. 28, 1943), 50; Perrett, *Days of Sadness, Years of Triumph*, p. 125.

11. The influence of Breen and the PCA may have been instrumental in the ending of the film. The entire relationship between Rick and Ilsa had to be constructed carefully to avoid Breen's wrath about an "illicit sex affair." Ilsa had the affair with Rick only because she was convinced her husband was dead. The minute she discovered he was not she rushed back to her husband. There was no way Rick and Ilsa could have left Casablanca together with Laszlo still alive. Had they gotten on the plane together Breen may have insisted that it crash. The studio was aware of these issues and constructed the story to avoid censorship problems. See "Casablanca," PCA Files, Academy Library, and Warner Brothers Collection, USC.

12. Robert Riskin to Bell, Jan. 8, 1943, box 3510, OWI Files.

13. Dudley Nichols, "The Writer and the Film," *Theatre Arts* (Oct. 1943), 595.

14. Poynter to Nichols, Oct. 7, 1942, box 3515, OWI Files.

15. Leo Braudy, *Jean Renoir: The World of His Films* (Garden City, N.Y., 1972), p. 139.

16. Bell to Rothacker, Jan. 24, 1944, *Passage to Marseilles* file, OWI files.

17. Otto Friedrich, *City of Nets: A Portrait of Hollywood in the 1940's* (New York, 1986), pp. 126–29.

18. *Commonweal* (Mar. 13, 1942), 513.

19. Mellett to Poynter, July 20, 1942, box 3518, OWI Files.

20. Poynter to Mellett, July 14, 1942, *ibid.*

21. Breen Memo for Files, Sept. 8, 1943, "Hitler's Gang," PCA Files, Academy Library.

22. Robert Denton to Mellett, June 28, 1943, box 1433, OWI Files.

23. Breen to Luraschi, Aug. 9, 1943; Breen to Luraschi, Sept. 1, 1943; T. A. Lynch to Breen, Feb 16, 1944; Breen to Hays, July 6, 1944; "Hitler's Gang," PCA Files, Academy Library.

24. *New Republic* (May 29, 1944), 739; *New York Times*, May 8, 1944.

25. Breen to Carl Milliken, July 12, 1944, "Hitler's Gang," PCA Files, Academy Library. The written evaluations from the Legion of Decency are in the file.

26. D. A. Doran to Poynter, Aug. 25, 1942, "Sahara," box 1438, OWI Files.

27. Mellett to Poynter, Sept. 1, 1942, *ibid.*

28. Feature Review, "Sahara," July 8, 1943, *ibid.*

29. Frank T. Thompson, *William A. Wellman* (Metuchen, N.J., 1983), p. 214; William A. Wellman, *A Short Time for Insanity* (New York, 1974), pp. 90–94.

30. Louis Snyder, *The War: A Concise History, 1939–1945* (New York, 1968), pp. 427–28.

31. Bosley Crowther, "Adrift in 'Lifeboat,'" *New York Times,* Jan. 23, 1944; David Lardner, "Another Country Heard From," *New Yorker,* Feb. 5, 1944, p. 65.

32. Jackson Benson, *The True Adventures of John Steinbeck, Writer* (New York, 1984), p. 511; "Lifeboat," Revised original screenplay by John Steinbeck, Mar. 26, 1943, Twentieth Century-Fox Collection, Theater Arts Library, UCLA.

33. Ibid.

34. Francois Truffaut with Helen G. Scott, *Hitchcock* (New York, 1983), p. 154; Kantor treatment for "Lifeboat," Mar. 8, 1943, Kenneth MacGowan Papers, Special Collections, University Research Library, UCLA; Elaine Steinbeck and Robert Wallstein, eds., *Steinbeck: A Life in Letters* (New York, 1975), p. 267.

35. Jo Swerling treatment, "Lifeboat," April 30, 1943; temporary script, June 17, 1943; final script, July 27, 1943, Twentieth Century-Fox Collection, UCLA; "Hitchcock's Hand Steers 'Lifeboat' Through Film's Troubled Sea," *Newsweek* (Jan. 17, 1944), 68.

36. Script reviews, "Lifeboat," July 31, Sept. 11, Oct. 8, 1943; Warren Pierce to Eugene O'Neil, Aug. 2, 1943, box 3518, OWI Files; Steinbeck to Twentieth Century-Fox Film Corp., Jan. 10, 1944, in Steinbeck and Wallstein, eds., *Steinbeck: A Life in Letters,* p. 266.

37. Script reviews, "Lifeboat," July 31, Sept. 8, Oct. 8, 1943, box 3518, OWI Files.

38. Breen to Jason Joy, Aug. 4, 1943, "Lifeboat," PCA Files, Academy Library.

39. Feature review, "Lifeboat," Dec. 21, 1943, box 3518, OWI Files; Steinbeck and Wallstein, eds., *Steinbeck: A Life in Letters,* p. 267; Zanuck to MacGowan, Hitchcock, and Swerling, Aug. 19, 1943, MacGowan Papers, UCLA.

40. Zanuck to MacGowan, Hitchcock, and Swerling, Aug. 19, 1943, MacGowan Papers, UCLA.

41. Ibid.

42. Bosley Crowther, "Adrift in 'Lifeboat,'" *New York Times,* Jan. 23, 1944; Kenneth MacGowan, "The Producer Explains," *New York Times,* Jan. 23, 1944.

43. Ibid.

44. Script Review, "Lifeboat," Oct. 8, 1943, Box 3518, OWI Files; *Time* (Jan. 31, 1943), 94.

CHAPTER XI.

1. "The Issues," n.d., box 1517, RG 208, OWI Files; Robert A. Divine, *Second Chance: The Triumph of Internationalism in America During World War II* (New York, 1971), ch. 5.

2. Edward Golden to Emmet Lavery, Oct. 20, 1942, box 3518, RG 208, OWI Files.

3. John Balderston to Mayer, et al., Jan. 8, 1943; Mellett to Balderston, Jan. 19, 1943, ibid.

4. Script Review, "Versailles Tragedy," April 5, 1944, ibid.

5. Leonard Mosley, *Zanuck: The Rise and Fall of Hollywood's Last Tycoon* (Boston, 1984) p. 201; Thomas J. Knock, "History With Lightning: The Forgotten Film *Wilson*," *American Quarterly* (Fall, 1976), 525; Leonard J. Leff and Jerold Simmons, "Wilson: Hollywood Propaganda for World Peace," *Historical Journal of Film, Radio and Television* 3 (1983), 16–17.

6. Script Review, "Wilson," Sept. 19, 1943, box 3518, RG 208, OWI Files; Knock, "History With Lightning," *American Quarterly,* 526, 536; Mosley, *Zanuck,* p. 201.

7. Knock, "History With Lightning," *American Quarterly* (Fall, 1976), 525–530; Mosley, *Zanuck,* pp. 200–205; Divine, *Second Chance,* pp. 169–170.

8. Ibid.

9. Knock, "History With Lightning," *American Quarterly* (Fall, 1976), 536; *PM,* Aug. 2, Aug. 3, 1944.

10. *New Republic* (Aug. 14, 1944), 187; *Life* (Aug. 7, 1944).

11. Knock, "History With Lightning," *American Quarterly* (Fall, 1976), 542.

12. "Report of Activities, 1942–1945," Sept. 18, 1945, box 65, OWI files.

13. Slotkin, *The Fatal Environment,* pp. 32, 60.

14. Breen to Lord, Aug 9, 1950, Lord Papers, Jesuit Missouri Province Archives, St. Louis, Mo.

15. On the implications of corporate control of mass culture see Charles A. Beard and Mary A. Beard, *America in Midpassage,* vol. 2,

(New York, 1939), pp. 585, 592–95, 620, and Jackson Lears, "Truth, Power, Consequences," *Nation* (Sept. 13, 1986), 220–24. Poynter believed OWI's work in Hollywood helped democratize the industry. See his draft of an unpublished article on the wartime experience, n.d., box H4, Poynter Papers, Poynter Memorial Library, University of South Florida, St. Petersburg.

Bibliographical Essay

The basic sources for this book are archival materials and the films themselves. We have attempted to provide sufficient information in the text (film name, studio, date of release, and additional data for key pictures) to identify the more important pictures. We have screened the films discussed in a variety of settings. Many are available at the Library of Congress Motion Picture Division in Washington, D.C. Some are available on video cassette while some must be rented. Occasionally we caught a film on television, but because they are often cut for commercial station showing, this is an unreliable method. Hollywood films often exist in differing versions, and it is sometimes hard to determine which edition one is seeing. In a few instances we have been forced to rely on final shooting scripts.

Archival sources are indispensable to film history, but are too little used. Essential for this study were the records of the Office of War Information, housed in Record Group 208 at the Washington National Records Center in Suitland, Maryland. Of these massive records the files of the Bureau of Motion Pictures for both the Domestic and Overseas branches are particularly rich, containing reviews of screenplays and release prints, internal and external correspondence, and periodic reports. (Some of these materials have been reorganized since the authors used them; our citations refer to the location of documents when we did our research.) The Franklin D. Roosevelt Library in Hyde Park, New York, also contains important materials related to OWI and its predecessor agencies in the papers of Lowell Mellett, Harold Smith, Samuel Rosenman, and

Franklin Roosevelt. The National Archives in Washington, D.C., has useful data in the files of the Office of Censorship, Record Group 216, and the files of the Public Relations Branch of the U.S. Army, Record Group 44.

The increasing availability of studio records heralds a breakthrough in film history. We found the Warner Brothers Production Files in Special Collections, Doheny Library, University of Southern California, Los Angeles, to be especially useful. These records include screenplays in many versions, internal and external correspondence, and a host of other material. The Twentieth Century-Fox collection in the Theater Arts Library, University Research Library, University of California at Los Angeles, includes some manuscript material with its screenplays. The personal papers of film personalities are less available than they should be, but collections we found of value include the following at Special Collections, University Research Library, UCLA: Preston Sturges, King Vidor, and Kenneth MacGowan. The Wisconsin Center for Film and Theater Research at the Wisconsin State Historical Society, Madison, holds the Walter Wanger Papers, as well as additional Warner Brothers material. RKO records are available through the corporate office in Los Angeles, and MGM legal records through the company's legal division in Culver City.

One of the most important manuscript collections to be opened for research in film history is the Production Code Administration collection at the Margaret Herrick Library of the Academy of Motion Picture Arts and Sciences in Beverly Hills. These files document the extensive influence the organization had on film content, which may be followed through internal reports, correspondence, and Joseph Breen's communication with Will Hays.

We consulted a variety of other archival collections, which vary in their usefulness. They include the following personal papers: Nelson Poynter, Nelson Poynter Memorial Library, University of South Florida, St. Petersburg; Archibald MacLeish, Joseph E. Davies, and Elmer Davis, Library of Congress Manuscript Division, Washington, D.C.; Philleo Nash and Charles Hultan, Harry S. Truman Library, Independence, Mo.; Will Hays, Indiana State Library, Indianapolis; Gerald Nye and Herbert Hoover, Herbert Hoover Library, West Branch, Iowa; and Daniel Lord, S. J., Jesuit Missouri Province Archives, St. Louis. Of use on specific topics were the files of the National Association for the Advancement of Colored People, Library of Congress Manuscript Division, and the Archives of the Archdiocese of Los Angeles, San Fernando, Calif.

The only principals in OWI's liaison with Hollywood who were still living when our research began—they are since deceased—graciously consented to be interviewed: Nelson Poynter and Dorothy Jones.

Screenplays, in addition to those in previously cited collections, are available in the Louis B. Mayer Library of the American Film Institute, Los Angeles. For published scripts see John Gassner and Dudley Nichols, eds., *Twenty Best Film Plays* (New York, 1945), Gassner and Nichols, eds., *Best Film Plays, 1943–44* (New York, 1945), Brian Henderson, ed., *Five Screenplays of Preston Sturges* (Berkeley, 1985), David Culbert, ed., *Mission to Moscow* (Madison, 1980), and Larry Suid, ed., *Air Force* (Madison, 1983).

We profited from reading film reviews from the war period, especially those of James Agee, Manny Farber, and Bosley Crowther. Agee's reviews are collected in James Agee, *Agee on Film: Reviews and Comment* (Boston, 1958).

Since the footnotes indicate the secondary sources that were of use in specific cases, we will confine ourselves here to works that were of constant reference. For aspects of Hollywood history we found excellent material in Robert Sklar, *Movie-Made America: A Cultural History of the Movies* (New York, 1975), Garth Jowett, *Film: The Democratic Art: A Social History of American Film* (Boston, 1976), Lary May, *Screening out the Past* (Chicago, 1980), Leo Rosten, *Hollywood: The Movie Colony, the Movie Makers* (New York, 1941), Larry Ceplair and Steven Englund, *The Inquisition in Hollywood: Politics in the Film Community, 1930–1960* (Berkeley, 1980), Daniel J. Leab, *From Sambo to Superspade: The Black Experience in Motion Pictures* (Boston, 1975), and Thomas Cripps, *Slow Fade to Black: The Negro in American Film, 1900–1942* (New York, 1977). The best introduction to World War II films is Bernard Dick, *The Star-Spangled Screen: The American World War II Film* (Lexington, Ky., 1985), an interesting if often idiosyncratic reading of the subject which disdains archival research. On World

War II pictures see also Lawrence Suid, *Guts and Glory: Great American War Movies* (Reading, Mass., 1978), Colin Shindler, *Hollywood Goes to War: Film and American Society, 1939–1952* (London, 1979), and Dorothy B. Jones, "The Hollywood War Film: 1942–1944," *Hollywood Quarterly*, 1 (1945), 1–19. The present book extends and revises the authors' earlier assessments of OWI and wartime Hollywood. See Clayton R. Koppes and Gregory D. Black, "What to Show the World: The Office of War Information and Hollywood, 1942–1945," *Journal of American History*, 64 (1977), 87–105, and Gregory D. Black and Clayton R. Koppes, "OWI Goes to the Movies: The Bureau of Intelligence's Criticism of Hollywood, 1942–1943," *Prologue*, 6 (1974), 42–57.

For detailed studies of particular films see Thomas J. Nock, "History With Lightning: The Forgotten Film *Wilson,*" *American Quarterly*, 28 (1976), 525–43; Leonard J. Leff and Jerold Simmons, "*Wilson:* Hollywood Propaganda for World Peace," *Historical Journal of Film, Radio, and Television*, 3 (1983), 3–18; Gregory D. Black, "*Keys of the Kingdom:* Entertainment or Propaganda?" *South Atlantic Quarterly*, 75 (1976), 434–46; K.R.M. Short, "'The White Cliffs of Dover': Promoting the Anglo-American Alliance in World War II," *Historical Journal of Film, Radio, and Television*, 2 (1982), 3–23; Theodore Kornweibel, Jr., "Humphrey Bogart's *Sahara:* Propaganda, Cinema and the American Character in World War II," *American Studies*, 22 (1981), 5–19; and I. C. Jarvie, "Fanning the Flames: Anti-American Reaction to *Operation Burma* (1945)," *Historical Journal of Film, Radio, and Television*, 1 (1981), 117–37.

The basic source on OWI is Allan Winkler, *The Politics of Propaganda: The Office of War Information, 1942–1945* (New Haven, 1978). On prewar propaganda efforts and the formation of OWI see Richard Steele, *Propaganda in an Open Society: The Roosevelt Administration and the Media, 1933–1941* (Westport, Conn., 1985). Two older works on propaganda are still important: Robert K. Merton with Marjorie Fiske and Alberta Curtis, *Mass Persuasion: The Social Psychology of a War Bond Drive* (New York, 1946) and Harold Lasswell, *Propaganda Technique in the World War* (New York, 1927). Provocative is Jacques Ellul, *Propaganda* (New York, 1973).

Hollywood memoirs need to be used with caution but we

found the following to be helpful: Donald Ogden Stewart, *By a Stroke of Luck!* (New York, 1975); Philip Dunne, *Take Two: A Life in Movies and Politics* (New York, 1980); Howard Koch, *As Time Goes By: Memoirs of a Writer* (New York, 1979); and John Houseman, *Front and Center* (New York, 1979).

Index

Made in the USA
San Bernardino, CA
17 September 2019